AF790756

INTERNATIONAL AND NATIONAL PERSPECTIVES ON CHILD AND FAMILY LAW

INTERNATIONAL AND NATIONAL PERSPECTIVES ON CHILD AND FAMILY LAW

Essays in Honour of Nigel Lowe

Edited by
Gillian Douglas
Mervyn Murch
Victoria Stephens

intersentia
Cambridge – Antwerp – Portland

Intersentia Ltd
Sheraton House | Castle Park
Cambridge | CB3 0AX | United Kingdom
Tel.: +44 1223 370 170 | Fax: +44 1223 370 169
Email: mail@intersentia.co.uk
www.intersentia.com | www.intersentia.co.uk

Distribution for the UK and Ireland:
NBN International
Airport Business Centre, 10 Thornbury Road
Plymouth, PL6 7PP
United Kingdom
Tel.: +44 1752 202 301 | Fax: +44 1752 202 331
Email: orders@nbninternational.com

Distribution for Europe and all other countries:
Intersentia Publishing nv
Groenstraat 31
2640 Mortsel
Belgium
Tel.: +32 3 680 15 50 | Fax: +32 3 658 71 21
Email: mail@intersentia.be

Distribution for the USA and Canada:
International Specialized Book Services
920 NE 58th Ave. Suite 300
Portland, OR 97213
USA
Tel.: +1 800 944 6190 (toll free) | Fax: +1 503 280 8832
Email: info@isbs.com

International and National Perspectives on Child and Family Law. Essays in Honour of Nigel Lowe
© The editors and contributors severally 2018

The editors and contributors have asserted the right under the Copyright, Designs and Patents Act 1988, to be identified as authors of this work.

No part of this book may be reproduced, stored in a retrieval system, or transmitted, in any form, or by any means, without prior written permission from Intersentia, or as expressly permitted by law or under the terms agreed with the appropriate reprographic rights organisation. Enquiries concerning reproduction which may not be covered by the above should be addressed to Intersentia at the address above.

Images on cover © DavidCC – jbdodane – Hans Verburg / Alamy Stock Photo

ISBN 978-1-78068-641-7
D/2018/7849/23
NUR 820

British Library Cataloguing in Publication Data. A catalogue record for this book is available from the British Library.

FOREWORD

I can think of no-one in academic family law who is more deserving of a *Festschrift* than Nigel Lowe. What is a *Festschrift*? Literally it is a 'celebration writing' but more usually defined as 'a collection of essays or learned writings contributed by a number of people to honour an eminent scholar, especially a colleague'. Nigel is certainly worthy of the title 'eminent scholar'. The range of his contributions to scholarship in family law is quite extraordinary.

He is, first and foremost, a proper lawyer. He loves analysing decided cases at length and in real depth. This was apparent early on in his ground-breaking book with Richard White on *Wards of Court* and continues to be on show with every new issue of *Clarke Hall and Morrison on Children* to which he contributes. That he has agreed to take on the burden of its general editorship is tribute to his amazing resilience and energy. His work has always been of real value to legal practitioners as well as to academics, and he obviously enjoys working collaboratively with them.

But he was also an early pioneer of inter-disciplinary studies in family law, in particular in partnership with Mervyn Murch, with whom he conducted a number of studies on adoption funded by the Department of Health and the Economic and Social Research Council. Once again, he obviously enjoyed working collaboratively with a number of socio-legal scholars as well as with practitioners.

As if that were not enough, he then branched out into international collaboration, providing us with invaluable data on the practical working of the Hague Convention on the Civil Aspects of International Child Abduction, and working with both the Council of Europe and the European Commission on the various European instruments dealing with family law. No-one working in family law these days can afford to ignore its international aspects – such is the movement of people and families around the world but especially within the European Union. As we write, we are all wondering what reciprocal arrangements can and will be negotiated to provide for continued mutual recognition and enforcement of family court orders within Europe: unlike commercial lawyers, we cannot solve the problem with a simple choice of law and choice of forum clause.

This book is a rich and varied collection of contributions from academics, practitioners and judges, taking up each of the three themes which have dominated Nigel's work – the evolution of UK family law as it attempts to keep up with evolving patterns of family life, inter-disciplinary collaboration in socio-legal research, and the ever-increasing scope of international family law and practice – and always with a strong emphasis on children rather than adults. Nigel has always been much more interested in the law relating to children than the law relating to adults, which tells us a lot about him as a person.

The affection in which Nigel is held by so many colleagues and friends is apparent in this volume – as was the affection in which he was held by all his students in Sheffield, Bristol and Cardiff apparent to anyone who visited there and saw him with them. Another term for a *Festschrift* is a *Liber Amicorum* – literally, a book of friends. This, Nigel, is your book of friends – a book written by your friends for their friend. We all hope that you enjoy it.

Brenda Hale

ACKNOWLEDGEMENTS

We are enormously grateful to all our contributors for making this book a reality. To Nigel's wife, Brenda Sufrin, for managing to keep the secret, to Ann-Christin Maak-Scherpe for her enthusiastic support in publishing this volume and of course, to Nigel Lowe for being such an inspiration.

CONTENTS

LIST OF CASES

AUSTRALIA

CANADA

COURT OF JUSTICE OF THE EUROPEAN UNION

ENGLAND AND WALES

EUROPEAN COURT OF HUMAN RIGHTS

FRANCE

NEW ZEALAND

UNITED STATES OF AMERICA

OTHER JURISDICTIONS

LIST OF CONTRIBUTORS

Rebecca Bailey-Harris
Barrister and Mediator, 1 Hare Court, Temple, London, United Kingdom

Ruth Ballantyne
Professional Practice Fellow, Faculty of Law, University of Otago, Dunedin, New Zealand

Trevor Buck
Emeritus Professor of Socio-Legal Studies, School of Law, De Montfort University, United Kingdom

Julie Doughty
Lecturer in Law, School of Law and Politics, Cardiff University, United Kingdom

Gillian Douglas
Executive Dean and Professor of Law, The Dickson Poon School of Law, King's College London, United Kingdom

John Eekelaar
Emeritus Fellow, Pembroke College, University of Oxford, United Kingdom and Fellow of the British Academy

Ann Laquer Estin
Aliber Family Chair in Law, College of Law, University of Iowa, United States of America

Claire Fenton-Glynn
Lecturer in Law, Jesus College, University of Cambridge, United Kingdom

Frédérique Ferrand
Professor of Law, Faculty of Law, Jean Moulin Lyon 3 University, France and Faculty of Law, University of Augsburg, Germany

Marilyn Freeman
Principal Research Fellow, Law School, University of Westminster, United Kingdom

Stephen Gilmore
Professor of Family Law, The Dickson Poon School of Law, King's College London, United Kingdom

Cristina González Beilfuss
Professor of Private International Law, Faculty of Law, University of Barcelona, Spain

The Rt Hon Baroness Brenda Hale DBE
President of the Supreme Court of the United Kingdom and Visitor, Girton College, University of Cambridge, United Kingdom

Mark Henaghan
Dean and Professor of Law, Faculty of Law, University of Otago, Dunedin, New Zealand

Jonathan Herring
Vice Dean and Professor of Law, Exeter College, University of Oxford, United Kingdom and DM Wolfe-Clarendon Fellow in Law

David Hodson OBE
Co-Founding Partner of The International Family Law Group LLP, London, United Kingdom and Visiting Professor, University of Law, United Kingdom

Kathryn Hollingsworth
Professor of Law, Newcastle Law School, Newcastle University, United Kingdom

Maarit Jänterä-Jareborg
Professor of Law, Faculty of Law, Uppsala University, Sweden

Ruth Lamont
Senior Lecturer in Family and Child Law, School of Law, University of Manchester, United Kingdom

Dieter Martiny
Emeritus Professor, Faculty of Law, Europa-Universität Viadrina, Frankfurt (Oder), Germany

Judith Masson
Professor of Socio-Legal Studies, Law School, University of Bristol, United Kingdom

The Rt Hon Sir James Munby
President of the Family Division of the High Court of England and Wales, United Kingdom

Mervyn Murch CBE
Emeritus Professor, School of Law and Politics, Cardiff University, United Kingdom

Jens M. Scherpe
Reader in Comparative Law and Director of Cambridge Family Law, Gonville and Caius College, University of Cambridge, United Kingdom

Rhona Schuz
Professor of Law, Sha'arei Mishpat Law School, Israel and Adjunct Professor, Faculty of Law, Bar Ilan University, Israel

Leanne Smith
Senior Lecturer, School of Law and Politics, Cardiff University, United Kingdom

Helen Stalford
Professor of Law, School of Law and Social Justice, University of Liverpool, United Kingdom

Victoria Stephens
Freelance Researcher based in Lyon, France

Nicola Taylor
Director, Children's Issues Centre, University of Otago, Dunedin, New Zealand

The Rt Hon Sir Mathew Thorpe
Former Lord Justice of Appeal of England and Wales, Vice-President of the Family Division of the High Court and inaugural Head of International Family Law, United Kingdom

Velina Todorova
Associate Professor, Law Faculty, Plovdiv University, Bulgaria

Richard White
Honorary Visiting Professor of Child Law, School of Law and Politics, Cardiff University, United Kingdom and Tribunal Judge

INTRODUCTION

Nigel Vaughan Lowe: An Appreciation

Gillian Douglas, Mervyn Murch and Victoria Stephens

As a young lad Nigel used to collect train numbers. That was in the 1960s in the last days of British Rail steam engines. With other boys he would travel all over the country in search of some rare engine – perhaps a GWR Castle, a LMS Coronation or an elusive 'Black Five'. So determined was he that he would sometimes trespass on the railway and creep into some smoky old engine shed to find that much-sought-after missing number to complete his list. Occasionally he was caught and chased away but he would return when the coast was clear. Who would have thought such a minor juvenile delinquent would turn into the distinguished academic investigator that we all know and admire today?

But pause a moment and reflect. What are the characteristics revealed in the escapades of the young adolescent all those years ago? Three things stand out which mark his work today: first, a certain obsessive love of numbers; secondly, an unwavering determination to pursue his goals; and thirdly, a love of travelling, particularly by train. Let us explain …

Nigel began his career in the Law at the University of Sheffield (1966–1969), studying, inter alia, with Mary Hayes (now Professor Emeritus), who taught him Family Law. He was awarded a Duke of Edinburgh Entrance Scholarship and called to the Bar by the Inner Temple in 1972, but he began his academic career, slightly unusually for those days, by taking a post as a Research Associate at the University of Birmingham's Institute of Judicial Administration from 1969–1971. There, he worked with Professor Gordon Borrie on a major book, *The Law of Contempt* (1st edn. 1973). That period of focused concentration on exploring a complex, and at times very technical, legal subject gave him valuable experience on which to build his future independent research and scholarship: he has never been afraid to tackle difficult and large legal questions; he has always been a master of the 'black letter law'; and he has always seen the policy and practice implications of legal developments.

Nigel took up his first Lectureship at the University of Sheffield in 1972, before moving, with his wife, Brenda Sufrin (now Professor Emeritus), to the University of Bristol in 1974, where both were awarded Lectureships. There,

Nigel developed a distinctive Family Law course, which – highly unusually for the time – devoted as much time to the study of the law relating to parents and children as it did to marriage and adult relationships. His interest in child law led to his first major monograph in the subject, with child law practitioner, Richard White. Nigel and Richard noted that, from the late 1970s on, public child law was being significantly shaped by the increasing resort to a rather ancient jurisdiction – that of wardship – by local authorities seeking to protect children, through bypassing the statutory procedures laid down to govern cases of abuse and neglect. Together, they produced the first ever book devoted to the subject of wardship, *Wards of Court* (1st edn. 1979; 2nd edn. 1986). It has been described judicially by the President of the Family Division as 'a book of high authority' and remains the essential reference point in the field.

Nigel was made a Reader in Law at Bristol in 1984, and his academic reputation as a leading figure in family and child law was cemented during his time there by a very fruitful and important interdisciplinary collaboration with Mervyn Murch (now Professor Emeritus at Cardiff University). Although a law graduate, Mervyn had, through his training and practice as a probation officer, moved into what was known at that time as the academic field of 'social administration' and had conducted some of the first socio-legal empirical family research. Together with a team of distinguished researchers, including Joan Hunt (now Honorary Professor at Cardiff University), they carried out a series of studies into aspects of adoption law and practice, funded by the Department of Health and the Economic and Social Research Council (ESRC), published in a number of books and reports, including *Pathways to Adoption* (1991) and *Freeing the Child For Adoption* (1993). Nigel's interest in the care system and adoption law led naturally to his chairing (1984–1990) the British Agencies for Adoption and Fostering (BAAF) Legal Group, which brought together practitioners and academics from all disciplines working in the field, to share ideas and develop understanding in order to improve practice and policy. Its work, under Nigel's chairmanship, helped inform members of the judiciary and legal practitioners as to the importance of the research evidence on child abuse and on the experiences of children in care and long-term placement, in determining legal outcomes in the care system.

The enactment of the Children Act 1989, based on the government's review of child care law, and the work of the Law Commission (and in particular the work of Brenda Hoggett (now Baroness Hale of Richmond) as the lead Commissioner on the project), fundamentally reformed both private and public child law. It marked the recognition of Nigel's long-standing insight into the importance of child law for the study and practice of family law. As one of the leading academic commentators on the subject and someone who had always made sure to keep in close contact with the practice world through advice, consultancy and training, Nigel was appointed to a team of academics and practitioners (which included Richard White) tasked with the job of introducing the judiciary and the magistracy throughout England and Wales to the new concepts and processes that the legislation introduced. The experience gave him great insight into the concerns of those who had to implement the law and he has always been acutely aware of the need to take account of the practical realities when proposing legal reforms. He and Richard, with Paul Carr, brought their academic and practical expertise to bear in writing *The Children Act in Practice* (1st edn. 1990; 4th edn. 2008), an immensely useful and rigorous manual for practitioners.

Nigel was appointed Professor of Law at Cardiff University in 1991 and began to develop a new strand to his research – international child law, particularly regarding international child abduction. With his experience of empirical research, he saw the importance of gaining hard data on how the Hague Abduction Convention[1] was working, in order to inform discussion on the difficulties and challenges of applying one international instrument across different jurisdictions, with different understandings of welfare and parental rights, to produce the best outcomes for children – including the deterrence of abduction as a 'self-help remedy' for families in crisis. With funding from the Nuffield Foundation and ICMEC and NCMEC (International and National Centres for Missing and Exploited Children, USA), Nigel's links with practitioners and the judiciary were now further developed into close working relationships with key officials at the Hague Conference on Private International Law and the Council of Europe, as well as in many national governments, leading to inter and multi-national cooperation to produce the data and discuss their implications. In forging these relationships, Nigel, together with his researchers, including Victoria Stephens, undertook a heroic amount of international travel, including a trip Nigel made to New Zealand – for a week – and to Mexico – for four days, to gather data. All those escapades on British Rail in his youth have stood him in good stead for the rigours of international air travel.

The fruits of this work were published in a number of reports by the Hague Conference, from 2001 to 2011, with another recently completed. They constitute a unique record of how the Abduction Convention has been implemented and how that implementation has changed – and how it has been influenced by the findings themselves. Alongside these reports, Nigel and his researchers, Sarah Armstrong, Emily Atkinson, Katarina Horosova, Anest Mathias and Samantha Patterson also published several other important studies, including reports specifically focused on individual countries to provide their governments with

---

1 Please note that in this work, references to the different paragraphs of Art. 13 of the Hague Abduction Convention follow the Convention text, viz: Art. 13(a) or 13(b) or, in relation to the child's objection to return, Art. 13, as appropriate. However, where the Hague Conference *Draft Guide to Good Practice On Article 13(1)(b) of the Hague Convention of 25 October 1980 on the Civil Aspects of International Child Abduction Part V - Article 13(1)(b)* (HCCH, 2017) has been cited, we refer to the numbering used therein, viz: Art. 13(1)(b), Art. 13(2) etc.

tailor-made data on their own practice and implementation of the Convention provisions. These findings and Nigel's analysis of the law have influenced the handling of cases brought under the Convention in both England and Wales and internationally, and have been frequently cited in court, including by Baroness Hale in *Re M and Another (Children)* [2007] UKHL 55, by Sir Peter Singer in *Re A (A Child) (Custody); HA v MB* [2007] EWHC 2016 (Fam), where he acknowledged Nigel's assistance in researching the European jurisprudence, and in the US Supreme Court by Chief Justice Roberts in *Chafin v Chafin*, No. 11-1347, 568 US ___ (2013).

He has brought his expertise on child abduction law to bear through his co-authorship (with Mark Everall and Michael Nicholls) of *International Movement of Children – Law, Practice and Procedure* (1st edn. 2004; 2nd edn. 2016). Sir Mathew Thorpe, former Lord Justice of Appeal and former Head of International Justice, has described this work as a 'monumental title' and has said of it,

> Every lawyer will have a favourite law book to which he always refers for comfort as well as guidance. For me that has always been the *International Movement of Children*. On all my travels it is always in my case. I have yearned for the second edition and now at last it has come ... no family lawyer can afford to be without this title.

Her Honour Diana Bryant AO, former Chief Justice of the Family Court of Australia, in providing the Foreword to the new edition, refers to it as 'a bible, especially for those practising in the United Kingdom' and a 'repository of all the relevant information in relation to the international movement of children'.

Nigel's clear expertise and grasp of the issues involved in transnational legal practice led to numerous invitations and opportunities to broaden his commentary and advice on aspects of international family and child law. He worked with the Council of Europe on two projects including an evaluative overview of the Council's legal instruments across the field of family law (2006), was a member of the Panel of Experts appointed by the European Commission to advise on proposals to reform the revised Brussels II Regulation, and is a founder member of the Organising Committee of the Commission on European Family Law, a multi-national group of academics who have worked under the leadership of Professor Katharina Boele-Woelki to develop harmonising principles of family law. In that capacity, he is a co-author of numerous studies, including on the law regarding property relations between spouses, divorce and maintenance between former spouses, and parental responsibilities. He is also a long-standing member of the Executive Council, and past Vice President of the International Society of Family Law. He convened the World Conference of the Society at Cardiff in 1994 on the theme of 'Families Across Frontiers' (the conference proceedings were published under that title in 1996), and received the Society's Exceptional Service Award in 2014 for his long-term commitment to advancing knowledge and understanding of family law.

Somehow, alongside all this (not to mention his teaching and his roles as Deputy Head then Head of Cardiff Law School between 2006–2013) Nigel has also found time to continue to inform and advise practitioners in England and Wales about legal developments, through extensive lecturing and speaking, including regular contributions to events at Cumberland Lodge, and his long-term membership of the President of the Family Division's International Family Law Committee. And he has played a vital role in keeping the profession updated through his co-editorship of the *Family Law Reports*, General Editorship of *Clarke Hall and Morrison on Children* and Consultant Editorship of *International Family Law*. He has also co-authored the five most recent editions of *Bromley's Family Law* (including two with its original author, the late Professor Peter Bromley), the first major textbook written on Family Law, first published in 1957 and now in its 11th edition.

Nigel is now Emeritus Professor of Law at Cardiff University and a Fellow of the Centre for Social Policy, Dartington. He was awarded an LLD by Cardiff University for his contribution to research in 2008, and received the accolade of being made an Honorary Queen's Counsel in 2017. Despite his being diagnosed with lymphoma in 2004 and undergoing a bone marrow transfer, his unfailing optimism, energy and determination have meant that he has continued to play an important active role in developing understanding of family and child law, both domestically and internationally, throughout his career and still today. The many chapters in this book honouring him are testament to both the respect and the affection in which he is held by his peers, from academia to the Supreme Court. As editors of this volume, we have been delighted to bring together so many leading scholars, judges and practitioners to celebrate Nigel's contribution to the field of family and child law and to honour him as our most valued friend and colleague.

PART I

FAMILY AND CHILD LAW IN ENGLAND AND WALES

THE SUPREME COURT AND FAMILY LAW

Stephen Gilmore

1. INTRODUCTION

It is a great privilege and pleasure to contribute to this *Festschrift* celebrating Nigel Lowe's career as an eminent family law scholar. When one thinks of Nigel's distinctive contributions, the mind immediately alights upon the niche he has carved for himself as a pre-eminent scholar on international child law. Unpicking the complexity of the relevant international Conventions, their attendant case law and processes, and providing academic critical commentary thereon requires meticulous analysis and attention to detail – qualities which Nigel's work has always displayed. I first encountered Nigel's thorough accounts of domestic family and child law in *Bromley's Family Law*[1] when I was a student; and the first edition of his co-authored detailed commentary on the Children Act 1989, *Children Act in Practice*,[2] when I was a very junior lecturer. I say this not

1 Now in its 11th edition: see N. Lowe and G. Douglas, *Bromley's Family Law*, Oxford University Press, Oxford 2015.

2 Then White, Carr and Lowe, *Children Act in Practice*, Butterworths, London 1995, now in its 4th edition.

to make Nigel feel old, but to observe that his works were the places students and lecturers alike went for authoritative, detailed and thorough accounts of the law (and, of course, they still do). Each page packed with real mastery of the subject, the law was clearly explained and situated historically, the footnotes a veritable paper trail of Law Commission Reports and other pre-Parliamentary material, various Parliamentary reports, and accounts of Bills as they proceeded to law. Nigel's desire for a detailed understanding was evident also in his accounts of case law, in both the breadth and depth in which it was explored. An example is Nigel's tribute essay to PM Bromley,[3] which appeared not long after I had begun my academic career and which I (and no doubt many others) found useful in understanding the House of Lords' development, and interpretation, of the 'welfare principle'. It was this contribution which largely prompted an invitation to contribute his account of the landmark case *J v C*[4] to *Landmark Cases in Family Law*,[5] which was the first time I had the privilege of working with Nigel.

And so it is, with these reflections on Nigel's accounts of leading cases, and his focus on issues such as international child abduction, which is increasingly requiring the deliberations of our Supreme Court, that I am led to my choice of subject-matter for this chapter. In what follows I shall seek to provide an overview account of the family law cases heard by the UK Supreme Court since its inception in 2009. Space precludes more than short references to the main features of the cases. However, I shall provide a breakdown of the subject-matter, as well as data on the composition of Justices' panels, the delivery of lead judgments and dissents, and will offer some brief reflections.

2. FAMILY LAW CASES HEARD BY THE SUPREME COURT

The subject-matter of each decided UK Supreme Court case was examined and a judgement made by the author as to whether it would be viewed as a case of interest to family lawyers because of its impact upon family relationships and family resources/property. In the great majority of cases, categorisation was straightforward, the subject-matter falling squarely within the remit of the 'family court judge'. Cases on appeal from all UK jurisdictions were included, although those from Scotland and Northern Ireland constituted a very small number.

---

3 N. Lowe, 'The House of Lords and the Welfare Principle' in C. Bridge (ed.), *Family Law Towards the Millennium – Essays for PM Bromley*, Butterworths, London 1997, p. 125.

4 *J v C* [1970] AC 668 (HL).

5 N. Lowe, '*J v C*: Placing the Child's Welfare Centre Stage' in S. Gilmore, J. Herring and R. Probert (eds.), *Landmark Cases in Family Law*, Hart Publishing, Oxford 2011, pp. 27–45.

The analysis yielded 35 family law cases, ranging temporally from the decision in *GB v RJB and GLB (In Re B (A Child))* [2009] UKSC 5, delivered on 19 November 2009, to *Birch v Birch* [2017] UKSC 53, delivered on 26 July 2017. The cases and the panels of judges which heard them are set out in the Appendix to the chapter. Broken down by their year of citation, the numbers of cases in each year were as follows: 2009 (3); 2010 (3); 2011 (5); 2012 (3); 2013 (7); 2014 (2); 2015 (6); 2016 (3); 2017 (3). The Court thus currently hears on average between three and four family law cases a year.

Of the 35 cases, 23 addressed 'child law issues' and 12, 'adult family law issues'. Thus, almost twice as many 'child issues' cases have been heard by the Supreme Court as 'adult issues' cases.

2.1. CHILD LAW ISSUES

The 23 child law cases divided almost equally into three broad categories: international disputes; domestic child protection/welfare; and matters ancillary to substantive family law, such as evidence and procedure.

2.1.1. International Child Disputes

A perhaps surprisingly high number of six cases were concerned with one topic: international child abduction. In *E (Children)*[6] the Court clarified that, despite *dicta* in the ECtHR decision of *Neulinger and Shuruk v Switzerland*,[7] a full-blown child welfare inquiry is not required by Article 8 of the European Convention on Human Rights in proceedings under the Hague Convention on the Civil Aspects of Child Abduction 1980 (the Hague Convention 1980), provided decision-making is not arbitrary or mechanical. The Court felt the need to reiterate this view in *S (A Child)*[8] after the ECtHR repeated its view in *X v Latvia*.[9] In *Re S* the Court also clarified that a parent's subjective perception and anxieties, insofar as they would destabilise parenting, rendering the child's situation intolerable, are relevant to the defence in Article 13(b) of the Hague Convention 1980. The parent's anxieties need be neither reasonable nor realistic.

Three cases addressed the meaning of 'habitual residence', again perhaps a high number addressing just one concept. In *A (Children) (AP)*[10] the Court clarified that habitual residence is a matter of fact requiring a search for the child's integration into his or her social and family environment, and accordingly

6 *E (Children)* [2011] UKSC 27.
7 *Neulinger and Shuruk v Switzerland*, Application no. 41615/07, [2011] 1 FLR 122.
8 *In re S (A Child)* [2012] UKSC 10.
9 *X v Latvia*, Application no. 27853/09, ECtHR, 26 November 2013.
10 *In re A (Children) (AP)* [2013] UKSC 60.

there is no jurisdiction under Article 8 of the Brussels II Revised Regulation[11] to make orders relating to parental responsibility in respect of a child who has never been in the jurisdiction. Applying this approach, the Court held in *KL (A Child)*[12] that a child brought to England from Texas had acquired habitual residence here despite the Texan court order under which he had been brought being successfully appealed a year later; and in *LC (Children); LC (Children) (No. 2)*[13] it held that an adolescent's state of mind is relevant to the question of integration. Another case, *K (A Child) (Northern Ireland)*[14] held that 'rights of custody' in Article 3 of the Hague Convention 1980 include inchoate rights. The child's mother had wrongfully removed him from the grandparents' primary, officially recognised, de facto care in Lithuania and the Court was bound to return the child.

2.1.2. Domestic Child Protection/Welfare Issues

Seven cases focused on child protection or welfare issues in domestic law. *GB v RJB and GLB (In Re B (A Child))*[15] reaffirmed the central message in *Re G (Children) (Residence: Same Sex Partner)*[16] that when assessing the child's welfare under section 1(1) of the Children Act 1989, parenthood only assumes significance as a contributor to the child's welfare and that it is wrong to talk of a right to, or presumption in favour of, a parent–child relationship. The threshold for making orders in care proceedings exercised the Court's judgement on several occasions. In *S-B (Children)*[17] the Court held that the standard of proof for identifying a perpetrator of harm to a child is the balance of probabilities and not a heightened standard with reference to the gravity of the issue. In *J (Children)*,[18] confirming an *obiter dictum* in *S-B*, the Court held that consignment of a person to a pool of possible perpetrators of harm to a child is not of itself a sufficient foundation for an inference of likely harm within the meaning of section 31 of the Children Act 1989, although it may be relevant in combination with other facts. This was further endorsed in *EV (A child) (Scotland) and EV (A Child) (Scotland) (No. 2)*,[19] which provided guidance on the threshold test in section 84(5)(c)(ii) of the Children (Scotland) Act 2007 for making a permanence order, which is in similar

11 Council Regulation (EC) No. 2201/2003.
12 *In re KL (A Child)* [2013] UKSC 75.
13 *In re LC (Children); In re LC (Children) (No. 2)* [2014] UKSC 1.
14 *In re K (A Child) (Northern Ireland)* [2014] UKSC 29.
15 *GB v RJB and GLB (In Re B (A Child))* [2009] UKSC 5.
16 *Re G (Children) (Residence: Same Sex Partner)* [2006] 1 WLR 2305.
17 *S-B (Children)* [2009] UKSC 17.
18 *J (Children)* [2013] UKSC 9.
19 *In re EV (A child) (Scotland) and In re EV (A Child) (Scotland) (No. 2)* [2017] UKSC 15.

terms to section 31(2) of the Children Act 1989. In *B (A Child)*[20] the Court upheld a High Court decision to make a care order with a view to adoption of a child outside her family where the threshold of likely significant harm was barely crossed on the basis of future risk of emotional harm. The Court held, contrary to a statement in *J (Children)*, that Article 8 of the ECHR is not engaged at the threshold stage, only when making an order, and adoption must be 'necessary' as required by Article 8, in the sense of 'nothing else will do'. An appellate court can interfere if the lower court's decision was 'wrong'.

Two decisions considered the role of the United Nations Convention on the Rights of the Child (UNCRC) in interpreting Article 8 of the ECHR. *ZH (Tanzania) v Secretary of State for the Home Department*[21] considered the weight to be given to the best interests of children affected by a decision whether to remove a parent from the UK, holding that they must be a primary consideration in any proportionality assessment under Article 8 of the ECHR. In *R (SG) v Secretary of State for Work and Pensions*[22] the Court held that the alleged discriminatory impact of the Benefit Cap (Housing Benefit) Regulations 2012 on lone parents, and thus women, is lawful, and that the best interests of children as a primary consideration under Article 3 of the UNCRC are not material to interpretation of rights under Article 8 of the ECHR in this discrimination context.

2.1.3. *Jurisdiction, Evidence, Procedure and Costs*

A third category of 10 cases was concerned with matters ancillary to substantive family law, such as matters of jurisdiction, evidence, procedure or the costs of proceedings. Two cases addressed costs, both in the context of care proceedings. In *T (Children)*[23] the Court found that a local authority had no liability to pay the costs of interveners in respect of a fact-finding hearing at which they were exonerated of any abuse of a child. Thus there is no exception to the general practice of not awarding costs in care proceedings in the absence of reprehensible behaviour or an unreasonable stance. In *S (A Child)*[24] the Court held that this general practice applies equally to appellate proceedings concerning children.

Several cases have dealt with evidential matters, and it is noteworthy that these too have all been in public law proceedings. In *L and B (Children)* the Court held that a judge who had announced her decision orally on fact-finding in care proceedings could subsequently change her decision prior to the order being drawn up and perfected, as no judge should be required to decide a child's

20 *In re B (A Child)* [2013] UKSC 33.
21 *ZH (Tanzania) v Secretary of State for the Home Department* [2011] UKSC 4.
22 *R (on the application of SG) v Secretary of State for Work and Pensions* [2015] UKSC 16.
23 *T (Children)* [2012] UKSC 36.
24 *S (A Child)* [2015] UKSC 20.

future on a false basis. In *Re W (Children)*[25] the Court removed a presumption that a child will only exceptionally give evidence in family proceedings, holding that whether a child gives evidence must be the product of balancing, on the facts, the advantages to determination of the truth, against damage to the welfare of the child. In *A (A child)*[26] the Court considered whether a local authority should be ordered to disclose, in proceedings concerning a child, A, information in a social work file, which would reveal the identity of a person, X, alleging sexual abuse by A's father when she was a child. Interference with X's privacy rights was justified by the need for a fair trial and protection of the rights to respect for family life of A and her family.

Four appeals were heard relating to jurisdiction, all of which have an international context. In *B (A Child)*[27] the Court considered whether a child, who had recently been taken to Pakistan, was habitually resident in England so as to permit determination of applications under section 8 of the Children Act 1989. The Court found as a matter of fact that, at the material date of issue of the applications, the child had not sufficiently disengaged from this jurisdiction as to lose habitual residence in England. In *D (A Child)*[28] the Court concluded it had no jurisdiction to hear an appeal against an order to enforce a custody order in proceedings governed by the Brussels IIA Regulation;[29] and in *Re I (A Child)*,[30] held that Article 12.3 of the Regulation applied to a child who was lawfully resident outside the European Union, thus conferring jurisdiction to hear a contact dispute. In *J (A Child)*[31] the Court examined the scope of jurisdiction conferred by Article 11 of the 1996 Hague Convention on Jurisdiction, Applicable Law, Recognition, Enforcement and Co-operation in respect of Parental Responsibility and Measures for the Protection of Children, where a child is present but not habitually resident in the jurisdiction.

2.2. ADULT FAMILY LAW ISSUES

Of the 12 'adult family law' cases, a clear majority of eight were concerned with financial or property disputes, two with marriage, one with domestic violence, and another with inheritance.

---

25 *Re W (Children)* [2010] UKSC 12.
26 *In re A (A child)* [2012] UKSC 60.
27 *In re B (A Child)* [2016] UKSC 4.
28 *In re D (A Child)* [2016] UKSC 34.
29 Council Regulation (EC) No. 2201/2003.
30 *Re I (A Child)* [2009] UKSC 10.
31 *In re J (A Child)* [2015] UKSC 70.

2.2.1. *Financial and Property Disputes*

The Court heard an important case on the role of agreements in financial orders cases in *Radmacher (formerly Granatino) v Granatino*.[32] It provided guidance on the weight to be given to a pre-nuptial agreement, and introduced a general principle that:

> a court should give effect to a nuptial agreement that is freely entered into by each party with a full appreciation of its implications unless, in the circumstances prevailing, it would not be fair to hold the parties to their agreement.

In *Agbaje v Akinnoye-Agbaje*[33] the Court considered the proper approach to applications under the Matrimonial and Family Proceedings Act 1984 for financial provision in cases of a foreign divorce.

As with the child law issues, several cases were concerned with evidence and/or procedure. Two cases considered the duty of full and frank disclosure in the context of consent orders in financial orders proceedings. In *Sharland v Sharland*[34] a consent order procured by fraud was set aside for lack of full and frank disclosure; and in *Gohil v Gohil*[35] the Court held that a recital in a consent order which provides that a party believes that the other has not provided full and frank disclosure of financial circumstances but is compromising the claim to achieve finality, is of no legal effect. *Wyatt v Vince*[36] held that an ex-spouse's application for financial orders, made many years after separation and divorce, could only be struck out under rule 4.4 of the Family Procedure Rules if it had no reasonable grounds because it is not legally recognisable, not simply because it is perceived as having no real prospects of success. In *Birch v Birch*[37] the Court held that jurisdiction exists to hear a spouse's application to be freed from an undertaking to release her ex-husband from mortgage covenants with respect to the matrimonial home.

Not surprisingly, the family home also featured in other cases. In *Prest v Petrodel Resources Ltd*[38] residential properties held by a husband's company were found to be held on resulting trust for him and thus were property to which he was entitled either in possession or reversion, within the meaning of section 24 of the Matrimonial Causes Act 1973. However, the Court confirmed that the piercing of the corporate veil to obtain access to a spouse's company's property

---

32 *Radmacher (formerly Granatino) v Granatino* [2010] UKSC 42.
33 *Agbaje v Akinnoye-Agbaje* [2010] UKSC 13.
34 *Sharland v Sharland* [2015] UKSC 60.
35 *Gohil v Gohil* [2015] UKSC 61.
36 *Wyatt v Vince* [2015] UKSC 14.
37 *Birch v Birch* [2017] UKSC 53.
38 *Prest v Petrodel Resources Ltd* [2013] UKSC 34.

is possible in only limited circumstances, e.g., when it is used to frustrate or evade the law, and not by reference to some broader principle in matrimonial proceedings by virtue of section 24 of the Matrimonial Causes Act 1973. *Jones v Kernott*[39] considered the correct approach to calculating beneficial interests in property, holding that a common intention is to be inferred from the parties' conduct where possible, but if not, a court may impute an intention that each is entitled to a share which the court considers fair having regard to their whole course of dealing.

2.2.2. *Other Adult Family Law Cases on Marriage, Domestic Violence and Inheritance*

Two cases were connected with the subject of marriage. In *R (Hodkin) v Registrar General of Births, Deaths and Marriages*[40] the Court held that Scientology is a religion and a church of the Church of Scientology is a recordable 'place of meeting for religious worship'. In *R (Quila); R (Bibi) v Secretary of State for the Home Department*[41] the Court held that Paragraph 277 of the Immigration Rules, banning entry for settlement of foreign spouses unless both spouses are 21 or over, infringed the claimants' rights to respect for family life under Article 8 of the ECHR. *Yemshaw v London Borough of Hounslow*[42] considered the meaning of 'violence' in section 177(1) of the Housing Act 1996, holding that it is not confined to physical violence and includes 'threatening or intimidating behaviour and any other form of abuse which, directly or indirectly, may give rise to the risk of harm.' Finally, in *Ilott v The Blue Cross*[43] the Court provided guidance on interpretation of an adult child's claim under the Inheritance (Provision for Family and Dependants) Act 1975.

3. COMPOSITION OF PANELS OF JUSTICES IN CASES

A total of 19 Justices, indeed all except one of the Justices sworn in to date, have sat in at least one of the 35 family law cases. The only Justice not to sit in a family law case is Lord Saville of Newdigate, who retired early in the history of the Court, in 2010. Except in two cases, every case was heard by a panel of Justices of different composition. The exceptions are the cases of *Gohil* and *Sharland*, which were effectively heard together by the same panel of seven Justices, and the first

39 *Jones v Kernott* [2011] UKSC 53.
40 *R (Hodkin) v Registrar General of Births, Deaths and Marriages* [2013] UKSC 77.
41 *R (Quila); R (Bibi) v Secretary of State for the Home Department* [2011] UKSC 45.
42 *Yemshaw v London Borough of Hounslow* [2011] UKSC 3.
43 *Ilott v The Blue Cross and others* [2017] UKSC 17.

two family law cases which the Supreme Court heard in 2009, *I (A Child)* and *Re B (A Child)* which were heard by the same panel of five Justices.[44]

The vast majority of cases (28) were heard by a panel of five Justices, which is the norm. The Supreme Court publishes criteria to be used when considering whether more than five Justices should sit. The types of case which might warrant a larger bench are as follows:

> If the Court is being asked to depart, or may decide to depart from a previous decision.
>
> A case of high constitutional importance.
>
> A case of great public importance.
>
> A case where a conflict between decisions in the House of Lords, Judicial Committee of the Privy Council and/or the Supreme Court has to be reconciled.
>
> A case raising an important point in relation to the European Convention on Human Rights.

One case, *Radmacher v Granatino*,[45] was heard by a panel of nine Justices. No doubt this was seen as a case of high public importance, in its potential impact on the financial consequences of divorce, and one in which there was also potential for a decision which might conflict with a then recent Privy Council decision, *MacLeod v MacLeod*.[46]

There were six family law cases heard by a panel of seven Justices. These included the jointly heard cases of *Gohil* and *Sharland*,[47] where, in addition to a criterion in the list above, the hearing of two cases jointly with similar but slightly different issues might have justified a broader panel. The other cases were *Ilott v The Blue Cross*,[48] the first case on the Inheritance (Provision for Family and Dependants) Act 1975 to come before the highest court level; two cases of great public importance on the threshold for state intervention in family life to protect children, *S-B (Children)*[49] and *J (Children)*;[50] and *Prest v Petrodel*,[51] in which company law principles and the court's jurisdiction to make financial orders on divorce were in tension.

On one level, the facts above paint a picture of considerable variety in the make-up of panels hearing family law cases. However, a further picture emerges from an analysis of how frequently Justices sit in family law cases, the occasions

---

44 Lord Hope, Lady Hale, Lord Collins, Lord Kerr, and Lord Clarke.
45 [2010] UKSC 42.
46 *MacLeod v MacLeod* [2008] UKPC 64, [2010] 1 AC 298.
47 [2015] UKSC 60; and [2015] UKSC 61.
48 [2017] UKSC 17.
49 [2009] UKSC 17.
50 [2013] UKSC 9.
51 [2013] UKSC 34.

on which each delivers the leading judgment, and on which they dissent. The data are summarised in Table 1 below in order of frequency of sitting:

Table 1. Number of Cases, Lead Judgments and Dissents by Justice

Justice	Cases Heard	Lead Judgment	Dissent
Hale	34	18 (two jointly)	3
Wilson	25	9 (one jointly)	1
Kerr	19	1	1
Clarke	16	0	1
Neuberger	11	0	0
Hughes	10	1	1
Reed	9	2	0
Hope	8	0	0
Sumption	8	1	0
Brown	6	0	1
Collins	6	1	0
Hodge	6	0	0
Toulson	6	1	0
Mance	6	0	0
Walker	6	1 (jointly)	0
Carnwath	5	0	0
Phillips	5	2	0
Dyson	1	0	0

Source: Compiled by the author.

Lady Hale has sat in all but one of the family law cases heard by the Supreme Court, *R (Hodkin) v Registrar General of Births, Deaths and Marriages*.[52] She delivered the lead judgment in over half of the cases (18). Of the 23 cases on children issues, Lady Hale delivered the lead judgment in 15; that is approximately two thirds of such cases. One case in which she did not deliver the lead judgment was *B (A Child)*,[53] in which she dissented, the lead judgment in that case being provided by Lord Wilson. The other child law cases in which Lady Hale did not deliver the lead judgment were: a Scottish child protection case, *EV (A child) (Scotland) and EV (A Child) (Scotland) (No. 2)*,[54] in which, unsurprisingly, judgment was given by a Scottish Justice, Lord Reed; *T (Children)*,[55] the case on

52 [2013] UKSC 77.
53 [2013] UKSC 33.
54 [2017] UKSC 15.
55 [2012] UKSC 36.

costs, which was addressed by Lord Phillips; and three other cases in which Lord Wilson delivered the lead judgment (discussed below). Of the 12 'adult family law' cases heard by the Court, Lady Hale has delivered lead judgments in three: *Jones v Kernott*;[56] *Yemshaw v London Borough of Hounslow*;[57] and *Sharland v Sharland*.[58]

Lord Wilson has sat in 25 family law cases and has delivered the lead judgment in nine. His lead judgments have been largely on international issues in children law[59] and on matters of financial orders, particularly their procedural aspects.[60] Lord Wilson also delivered the lead judgment in *R (Quila); R (Bibi) v Secretary of State for the Home Department*[61] on spousal immigration.

Some Justices (Lord Clarke and Lord Neuberger) have sat in a significant number of cases (16 and 11 respectively), whilst never delivering a lead judgment, although there are occasions on which they have delivered detailed supplementary majority judgments.[62] Similarly, Lord Kerr has sat in a significant number of cases (19), yet has only delivered the lead judgment in one.

The delivery of lead judgments by members of the Court other than the main family law specialists, Lady Hale and Lord Wilson, is relatively infrequent. Lord Phillips has sat in relatively few family law cases (five), yet has delivered the lead judgment in two. However, it is perhaps not surprising, when the Court was sitting as a bench of nine in *Radmacher v Granatino* and Lady Hale found herself dissenting, that Lord Phillips, as President of the Court, should have taken the lead judgment in that case. That Lord Phillips, a former Master of the Rolls and Lord Chief Justice, should also have delivered the lead judgment in *Re T (Children)*, on costs, with policy issues surrounding access to justice, is similarly not surprising. Lord Kerr delivered the Court's opinion in *GB v RJB and GLB (In Re B (A Child))*.[63] Since this involved a clarification and reinforcement of principles in *Re G (Children) (Residence: Same Sex Partner)*,[64] in which Lady Hale delivered the lead speech, it may have been thought more appropriate for that endorsement to be delivered by another Justice. Lord Toulson delivered the judgment in *R (Hodkin)*[65] in which, as we have noted, Lady Hale did not sit.

---

56 [2011] UKSC 53.
57 [2011] UKSC 3.
58 [2015] UKSC 60.
59 *E (Children)* [2011] UKSC 27, *In re S (A Child)* [2012] UKSC 10, *In re LC (Children); In re LC (Children) (No. 2)* [2014] UKSC 1, and *In re B (A Child)* [2016] UKSC 4. As noted above, he also delivered judgment in *In re B (A Child)* [2013] UKSC 33.
60 *Wyatt v Vince* [2015] UKSC 14, *Gohil v Gohil* [2015] UKSC 61, and *Birch v Birch* [2017] UKSC 53.
61 [2011] UKSC 45.
62 For example, *In re B (A Child)* [2013] UKSC 33.
63 [2009] UKSC 5.
64 [2006] 1 WLR 2305.
65 [2013] UKSC 77.

Quite often the Justices sitting together with a family law specialist seem chosen for their (additional) relevant expertise. It is hardly surprising, for example, that Lord Reed (an ad hoc judge of the European Court of Human Rights) should deliver the lead judgment in the judicial review case *R (SG)*[66] involving complex human (and children's) rights issues, and that, as one of the Scottish Justices, he should have delivered the lead judgment in *EV*,[67] a case on appeal from Scotland. Lord Walker's joint delivery, with Lady Hale, of the lead judgment in *Jones v Kernott*[68] is also unsurprising given his Lordship's Chancery background. Lord Hughes, a former Family Division judge, delivered the Court's judgment in *Ilott v The Blue Cross*,[69] and Lord Sumption's relevant expertise in the Chancery Division was drawn upon in his lead judgment in *Prest v Petrodel Resources Ltd.*[70]

The data in Table 1 also show that there have been relatively few dissents: dissents by eight Justices in only six cases out of 35. There has thus been unanimous agreement as to the outcome in 83 per cent of cases. Of course, in some cases one or two judges have offered alternative reasons for reaching the majority outcome, but the overall level of agreement is strikingly high.

4. SUMMARY AND CONCLUDING THOUGHTS

Of the 35 family law cases heard by the Supreme Court, almost two thirds are concerned with children, within which international disputes are the dominant substantive subject-matter. Amongst adult family law issues, financial and property disputes dominate. Jurisdictional, evidential and procedural issues also figure prominently across the whole of the cases heard.

There is a high level of diversity of Justices in the overall composition of panels hearing cases, together with the inclusion of relevant expertise where possible. One is struck, however, by the high incidence of lead judgments delivered by the family law specialists, the high level of unanimity in the cases, and the high frequency with which a small number of the other Justices sit. While there are distinct advantages in bringing to bear family law expertise on family law issues, there are also potential dangers that the same judges' reasoning is employed in so many cases. Lead judgments may on their face represent entirely plausible positions and admit easily of agreement by other non-specialist Justices, but they may also become less convincing if counter-positions are fully explored. The role of academics and counsel in highlighting counter-arguments, and of the other

---

66 [2015] UKSC 16.
67 [2017] UKSC 15.
68 [2011] UKSC 53.
69 [2017] UKSC 17.
70 [2013] UKSC 34.

non-specialist Justices in being alert to them, are crucial safeguards in ensuring balanced reasoning, if lead judgments in specialist areas are to be dominated by a small number of Justices. An example is provided by *S-B* and *J (Children)* in which Lady Hale, who delivered both lead judgments, was left effectively 'defending' in *J (Children)* her *obiter* comments in *S-B* on possible perpetrators. Lord Brown had agreed with Lady Hale's judgment in *S-B* but, after retirement, having heard the counter-arguments, argued in Parliament against the reasoning in *J (Children)*.[71] There may also be subtle longer-term biases if the same styles of reasoning are employed time and again. There is some evidence, for example, that those Justices who were formerly Law Commissioners are more likely to draw upon Law Commission Reports in their judgments than Justices who were not.[72] Drawing on Law Commission Reports, even those written when the Justice was himself or herself the relevant Law Commissioner, may be useful, but there is at least a risk that that emphasis may readily be favoured, and even perhaps at the expense of other potential sources or arguments.[73] From the analysis carried out for this chapter, the evidence that there are at least some dissenting judgments and the willingness of Justices sometimes to offer alternative majority reasoning or supplementary judgments, may reassure that the dangers mentioned above are unlikely to surface in many cases. Nevertheless, we should remain alert to them.

APPENDIX OF CASES

CASE	PANEL
GB v RJB and GLB (In Re B (A Child)) [2009] UKSC 5	Hope, Hale, Collins, Kerr, Clarke
I (A Child) [2009] UKSC 10	Hope, Hale, Collins, Kerr, Clarke
S-B (Children) [2009] UKSC 17	Hope, Rodger, Hale, Brown, Collins, Kerr, Clarke
Re W (Children) [2010] UKSC 12	Walker, Hale, Brown Mance, Kerr
Agbaje v Akinnoye-Agbaje [2010] UKSC 13	Phillips, Rodger, Hale, Collins, Kerr
Radmacher (formerly Granatino) v Granatino (Appellant) [2010] UKSC 42	Phillips, Hope, Rodger, Walker, Hale, Brown, Mance, Collins, Kerr

(continued)

71 House of Lords *Hansard*, 21 October 2013, Column GC324, available at <http://www.publications.parliament.uk/pa/ld201314/ldhansrd/text/131021-gc0001.htm#13102123000197>.

72 J. Lee, 'The Etiquette of Law Reform' in M. Dyson, J. Lee and S. Wilson Stark (eds.), *Fifty Years of the Law Commissions: The Dynamics of Law Reform*, Hart Publishing, Oxford 2016, 274–296.

73 See, for example, *Re G (Children) (Residence: Same Sex Partner)* [2006] 1 WLR 2305 (HL) in which the Law Commission's view of the paramountcy principle in section 1(1) Children Act 1989 was drawn on heavily in interpreting it, yet the requirements of Article 8 of the ECHR were not.

(continued)

CASE	PANEL
Yemshaw v London Borough of Hounslow [2011] UKSC 3	Hope, Rodger, Walker, Hale, Brown
ZH (Tanzania) v Secretary of State for the Home Department [2011] UKSC 4	Hope, Hale, Brown, Mance, Kerr
E (Children) [2011] UKSC 27	Hope, Walker, Hale, Kerr, Wilson
R (Quila); R (Bibi) v Secretary of State for the Home Dept [2011] UKSC 45	Phillips, Hale, Brown, Clarke, Wilson
Jones v Kernott [2011] UKSC 53	Walker, Hale, Collins, Kerr, Wilson
S (A Child) [2012] UKSC 10	Phillips, Hale, Mance, Kerr, Wilson
T (Children) [2012] UKSC 36	Phillips, Hale, Mance, Dyson, Carnwath
A (A child) [2012] UKSC 60	Neuberger, Hale, Clarke, Wilson, Reed
L and B (Children) [2013] UKSC 8	Neuberger, Hale, Kerr, Wilson, Sumption
J (Children) [2013] UKSC 9	Hope, Hale, Clarke, Wilson, Sumption, Reed, Carnwath
B (A Child) [2013] UKSC 33	Neuberger, Hale, Kerr, Clarke, Wilson
Prest v Petrodel Resources Ltd [2013] UKSC 34	Neuberger, Walker, Hale, Mance, Clarke, Wilson, Sumption
A (Children) (AP) [2013] UKSC 60	Hale, Wilson, Reed, Hughes, Toulson
KL (A Child) [2013] UKSC 75	Neuberger, Hale, Wilson Hughes, Hodge
R (Hodkin) v Registrar General of Births, Deaths and Marriages [2013] UKSC 77	Neuberger, Clarke, Wilson, Reed, Toulson
K (A Child) (Northern Ireland) [2014] UKSC 29	Hale, Kerr, Clarke, Wilson, Hughes
LC (Children); LC (Children) (No. 2) [2014] UKSC 1	Hale, Wilson, Sumption, Toulson, Hodge
Wyatt v Vince [2015] UKSC 14	Hale, Clarke, Wilson, Hughes, Hodge
R (SG) v Secretary of State for Work and Pensions [2015] UKSC 16	Hale, Kerr, Reed, Carnwath, Hughes
J (A Child) [2015] UKSC 70	Hale, Wilson, Reed, Hughes, Toulson
S (A Child) [2015] UKSC 20	Hale, Kerr, Wilson, Hughes, Toulson
Sharland v Sharland [2015] UKSC 60	Neuberger, Hale, Clarke, Wilson, Sumption, Reed, Hodge
Gohil v Gohil [2015] UKSC 61	Neuberger, Hale, Clarke, Wilson, Sumption, Reed, Hodge
B (A Child) [2016] UKSC 4	Hale, Clarke, Wilson, Sumption, Toulson
N (Children) [2016] UKSC 15	Neuberger, Hale, Kerr, Wilson, Carnwath
D (A Child) [2016] UKSC 34	Neuberger, Hale, Clarke, Wilson, Hughes
EV (A child) (Scotland) and EV (A Child) (Scotland) (No. 2) [2017] UKSC 15	Hale, Kerr, Wilson, Reed, Hodge
Ilott v The Blue Cross [2017] UKSC 17	Neuberger, Hale, Kerr, Clarke, Wilson, Sumption, Hughes
Birch v Birch [2017] UKSC 53	Hale, Kerr, Wilson, Carnwath, Hughes

THE DEVELOPMENT OF PARENT–CHILD RELATIONSHIPS IN FAMILY LAW: THE CASCADE OF CHANGE

Leanne SMITH

1. INTRODUCTION

This chapter presents reflections on the rapidity of recent changes to the law related to parent–child relationships following a number of years of writing on changes in the law related to parenthood. The title of the chapter has been borrowed from Sachs LJ who, in the 1970 case of *Hewer v Bryant*, evocatively referred to 'a cascade of legislation' responsible for changing the nature of the law related to children in the twentieth century.[1] Many of the changes he was alluding to featured heavily in my undergraduate modules on family law. This was in no small part because I was privileged to be taught by Professor Nigel Lowe. I have two vivid memories of the experience. One is the image of him leaning intensely over the table and barking 'authority?!' in response to almost any student comment (an exercise in scholarly rigour that I sorely needed but,

1 *Hewer v Bryant* [1970] 1 QB 357, 371. The quote is highlighted in S. CRETNEY, *Family Law in the Twentieth Century: A History*, Oxford University Press, Oxford 2005, p. 527.

in truth, have yet to master).[2] The other is of a moment in a large lecture theatre, in which he related the facts and summarised the judgment from the case of *C v C*.[3] Sitting in the front row, I signalled my disapproval of Glidewell LJ's assertion of the innate superiority of heterosexual parenting arrangements. Perhaps I did this less quietly than I ought to have done because I attracted sufficient attention to elicit a response. A brief exchange concluded with Nigel commenting that this might be an interesting area for research. He must bear some responsibility for the fact that, not long afterwards, I commenced a PhD on the topic of lesbian parenting and the law.

As my doctorate approached its end, the law moved on apace. In the years following its completion I wrote on the parenthood provisions of the Human Fertilisation and Embryology Act 2008, as well as on common law developments connected with calls to recognise multiple parenting arrangements involving lesbian women and known sperm donors.[4] In reflecting on all this for the purposes of the present piece, my thoughts turned to broader questions about the direction of and drivers behind developments in the law related to parent–child relationships. Against the backdrop of these questions, this chapter outlines what I consider to be a convergence of trends visible in two bodies of often distinct work: work concerning the shifting balance of power within parent–child relationships on the one hand, and work on changes to the structure of legal parenthood on the other.

This chapter begins by reviewing how the ascendance of child welfare transformed the qualitative nature of the parent–child relationship during the twentieth century, displacing adult-centred laws in favour of child-centred ones. In doing this it will draw heavily and unashamedly on the excellent work of scholars such as Lowe and Cretney. It proceeds to trace the next stage in the development of the law on parent–child relationships, illustrating that the cascade of change has continued unabated. In doing so, however, it argues that two axes of change are visible in the progression of the law. First, the locus of change has shifted such that the dominant story told by more recent reforms

---

2 This is an indictment of my own learning capacities, rather than Nigel Lowe's teaching! In fact, he patiently and tirelessly continued to point out gaps and errors in the authorities I provided to our family law undergraduates well into my lectureship at Cardiff University. My lectures are no doubt much the worse for his retirement.

3 *C v C (a minor) (custody: appeal)* [1991] FLR 223 (CA). It will be recalled that, although it was held in the case that a mother's lesbian relationship does not necessarily render her unfit to care for her child, Glidewell LJ nonetheless stressed that he regarded it as 'axiomatic that the ideal environment for the upbringing of a child is the home of loving, caring and sensible parents, her father and her mother'.

4 L. Smith, 'Clashing Symbols? Reconciling Support for Fathers and Fatherless Families after the Human Fertilisation and Embryology Act 2008' (2010) 22 *Child and Family Law Quarterly* 46; L. Smith, 'Tangling the Web of Legal Parenthood: Legal Responses to the use of Known Donors in Lesbian Parenting Arrangements' (2013) 33 *Legal Studies* 355.

is of changes to the structure, rather than the consequences, of parent–child relationships. Secondly, in a striking change of direction from the preoccupation with the position and wellbeing of children throughout the twentieth century, the issues of the day increasingly reflect preoccupation with the status and position of *adults* vis-à-vis children.

2. THE TWENTIETH-CENTURY STORY: THE RISE OF THE CHILD'S BEST INTERESTS IN THE CONTEXT OF PARENT–CHILD RELATIONSHIPS

A wide body of work is indicative of the scale and significance of changes to the law affecting children in the latter half of the twentieth century. Freeman has noted that children barely figured at all in what was considered to be 'family law' a century ago.[5] By the end of the twentieth century, however, the law relating to children and their position within the family had 'become enormous in volume and exceedingly complex in nature'.[6] There had been, as Lowe and Murch noted at the turn of the twenty-first century, a 'great shift in English law'.[7] This shift was achieved over some time, and entailed a plethora of both legislative and common law developments. Chronicling the developments in detail is a task that has been admirably accomplished by several scholars.[8] Some of the developments they have charted are rehearsed briefly here to lay the foundations for discussion of how the cascade of change in parent–child relationships has developed over time.

2.1. LEGISLATIVE DEVELOPMENTS

It is impossible to make sense of the shift in the legal position of the child over the course of the twentieth century without considering it as a fundamental reconfiguration of the nature of the relationship between children and their parents. In the nineteenth century the social expectation was of 'dutiful children willingly obeying their parents'.[9] This was reflected in the law, with fathers being

5 M. Freeman, 'Fifty Years of Family Law: an Opinionated Review' in G. Douglas and N. Lowe (eds.), *The Continuing Evolution of Family Law*, Family Law, Bristol 2009, p. 147.

6 S. Cretney, above n. 1, p. 527.

7 N. Lowe and M. Murch, 'Children's Participation in the Family Justice System: Translating Principles into Practice' (2001) 13 *Child and Family Law Quarterly* 137–158, 137.

8 S. Cretney, above n. 1; N. Lowe, 'The Meaning and Allocation of Parental Responsibility: a Common Lawyers' Perspective' (1997) 11 *International Journal of Law, Policy and the Family* 192; G. Douglas and N. Lowe, *Bromley's Family Law*, 11th edn., Oxford University Press, Oxford 2015.

9 S. Cretney, above n. 1, p. 525.

invested with full authority and rights to determine matters related to their offspring. As illustrated to infamous effect in the case of *Re Agar-Ellis*,[10] this had the effect of eclipsing any claim over the life of her child that a mother might wish to make, and rendered irrelevant the wishes of children themselves.

The notion that the best interests of children were a matter worthy of consideration in legal proceedings that affected them had attracted some attention by the end of the nineteenth century.[11] However, it seems generally to be accepted that it was not until the Guardianship of Infants Act 1925 that significant statutory inroads were made into the absolute authority and rights of fathers.[12] The Act made child welfare the first and paramount consideration in proceedings concerning the custody or upbringing of children.[13] It did not, however, represent a moment of epiphany and revolution in the legal stance towards children. Rather, it was one chapter in the overarching narrative of concern for and campaigning against the many social and political inequalities faced by women.

That the objective of the 1925 Act was to promote equality between the sexes in the area of parenthood is evident from its preamble.[14] Cretney has observed that the Act in fact fell far short of even its own rhetoric in terms of its substantive impact on the relative position of men and women vis-à-vis their children – those who thought it would bring to an end years of campaigning for equal rights for fathers and mothers 'were deceived'.[15] In fact it was not until the Guardianship Act of 1973 that full equality was achieved in the respective position of mothers and fathers.[16] For present purposes, what is interesting is that the first major legislative commitment to child welfare was not about children per se.

10 *Re Agar-Ellis (No. 2)* (1883) 24 Ch D 317.

11 See G. Douglas and N. Lowe, above n. 8, pp. 312–313 for specific examples of nineteenth-century legislation and case law reflecting concern with the child's position.

12 Lowe notes that the first significant common law inroad was made in the generally overlooked House of Lords case of *Ward v Laverty* [1925] AC 101, in which much was made of the paramountcy of children's welfare in resolving disputes concerning their upbringing. N. Lowe, 'The House of Lords and the Welfare Principle' in C. Bridge (ed.), *Family Law Towards the Millennium – Essays for PM Bromley*, Butterworths, London 1997, p. 132.

13 Section 1.

14 The preamble stated that the principle of equality between the sexes, as embodied in the Sex Disqualification (Removal) Act 1919 and other legislation, should obtain with respect to the guardianship of infants and the rights conferred thereby. Writing extensively about the history of the Act, Cretney has argued that the inclusion of such a preamble was 'unusual' at that time. S. Cretney, 'What Will the Women Want Next? The Struggle for Power in the Family 1925–1975' (1996) 112 *Law Quarterly Review* 110–137, 124.

15 S. Cretney, above n. 1, p. 570.

16 The motivation for this Act was more widespread and unequivocal support for creating parity between the sexes in the area of parenthood. This is nicely illustrated by the titles of preceding reports by both Labour ('*Discrimination against Women*') and the Conservatives ('*Fair Shares for the Fair Sex*'). See discussion in S. Cretney, above n. 1, p. 574.

Rather it was expedient and instrumental; its purpose was to enable judges to chart a principled path through the competing claims of mothers and fathers and avoid a stalemate being reached in the case of conflict between two parents who now stood on an equal footing.[17] Nonetheless, with its nod to the potential importance of the child's best interests, it arguably laid the foundations for the dominant plotline of family law change in the following decades.

Within almost exactly the same timeframe as the near 50-year gap between the guardianship Acts, a parallel but separate set of legislative developments was running with a view to addressing the damaging consequences of the law related to illegitimacy. This issue is more often understood as concerning the status of the child than the promotion of child welfare. But the growing influence of child welfare on lawyers and policy-makers was very much in evidence here, just as it was in the development of legislation concerning parents' authority.[18]

Marriage was once the only foundation on which recognition of a parental relationship could be based. Children born outside of marriage were legally designated *filius nullius*, or 'the child of no-one'.[19] While all parental authority was invested in the child's father, recognition of the father in the first place was dependent on his marriage to the child's mother. The consequences of this were significant, with the law unfavourably differentiating the rights and status of illegitimate from those of legitimate children in a range of areas.[20] The first legislative move to address the problem came with the Legitimacy Act 1926, which simply provided for the legitimation of some children born illegitimate through the subsequent marriage of their parents.

The 1926 Act had a long inception. Cretney's account of its history indicates that much of the impetus for it was derived from concerns about the interests of children, but that those concerns were intermingled with, and often struggled to prevail over, less child-focused ones. Contemporary commentary on an earlier (unsuccessful) Bill in 1920 described broad support for 'the complete disappearance of the argument that the hardship to the mother and injustice to the child are necessary pillars of moral society', and advocated an approach in which 'it is the parents who are illegitimate and not the child'.[21] In other words,

---

17 Cretney notes that then Lord Chancellor, Lord Birkenhead, was specifically advised of the risk of the inevitable deadlock that equal rights for mothers and fathers would generate whenever there was a conflict. See S. Cretney, above n. 1, p. 569.

18 A full discussion of the development of the law on legitimacy can be found in S. Cretney, above n. 1, chapter 15.

19 See S. Cretney, above n. 1, p. 546 and C. Barton and G. Douglas, *Law and Parenthood*, Butterworths, London 1995, p. 51.

20 Particular problems arose from rules precluding illegitimate children from inheriting property or receiving maintenance.

21 S. Cretney, above n. 1, p. 546, quoting from *The Times*, 8 May 1920.

there was a growing consensus that it was inappropriate to allow the welfare of children to be sacrificed for the purposes of preserving the social morality associated with the marital family. However, Cretney goes on to quote 1924 Home Office legal advice on the need for legitimacy legislation. The advice noted the argument that 'the welfare of the child should be paramount in this matter', but simultaneously revealed the problematic conflation of child welfare with other issues:[22]

> [I]t is urged (1) that it is in the interest of the children generally to preserve family life, and that the interest of children generally is more important than the interest of a comparatively few bastard children ... (3) The fact that such a child[23] may become legitimated will remove a deterrent against adulterous intercourse ... be prejudicial to family life, increase divorce, and make it more difficult for a wife to restrain an erring husband.

Children's interests here are co-opted into supporting the case for sustaining the prevailing sexual morality and family norms of the time.[24] Ultimately, those advocating a focus on children's interests rather than parents' behaviour were unable to defeat the purveyors of this logic. Children of adulterous liaisons were excluded from the very modest remit of the 1926 Act.

Arguments about improving the position of children later gained more traction and exerted more genuine influence in efforts to mitigate the harsh consequences of illegitimacy. In 1959, those seeking to reduce the number of children affected by illegitimacy fought, and this time won, a hard battle to make possible the legitimation of more children, including those conceived through adulterous liaisons.[25] Efforts to erode the consequences of illegitimacy in the interests of removing hardship for children also found success with the introduction of the Family Law Act 1969.[26] By the time almost all remaining disadvantages of illegitimacy were removed, via the Family Law Reform Act 1987,[27] there was strong support for the central importance of children's interests, as revealed by the remit of the Law Commission consultation that preceded the Act. The consultation was explicitly and exclusively committed

---

22 Sir E. Blackwell, Home Office Note, PRO HO45/4655/12259, cited by S. Cretney, above n. 1, pp. 548–549.

23 The phrasing here is a reference to children born following an adulterous liaison.

24 The idea that the meaning of child welfare can be expediently adapted to suit particular values and agendas is not new. See J. Eekelaar, 'Beyond the Welfare Principle' (2002) 14 *Child and Family Law Quarterly* 327. Lowe and Douglas memorably describe the principle of child welfare as having 'chameleon properties' to convey its potential to serve different purposes, G. Douglas and N. Lowe, above n. 8, p. 431.

25 Legitimacy Act 1959, later replaced by the Legitimacy Act 1976.

26 This Act specifically improved the succession rights of illegitimate children.

27 This Act also removed the term 'illegitimacy' from the legal lexicon.

to rectifying problems arising from legal discrimination against children. The commitment was underscored by the Commission's refusal to make concurrent recommendations that would promote the position of fathers.[28]

At this point it is easy to understand why, in 1970, Sachs LJ described the volume of twentieth-century legislation addressing the position of children as 'a cascade'.[29] The best interests of children were not promoted explicitly through the Acts concerned with legitimacy, as they were in the shifts to parental authority achieved by the 1925 and 1973 Acts, but they did exert a strong motivational force in this area. Combined, the two streams of legislative development tell the story of the steady ascension of the interests of children, prompting the gradual demise of adult-centred laws governing parent–child relationships.

2.2. THE CASE OF *J v C*

The intertwining of the child's best interests with changes to the legal significance of parenthood in different situations continued through the common law, and was notably consolidated in the House of Lords case of *J v C*.[30] Outlining the importance of the case as a symbolic and substantive 'landmark' in family law, Lowe notes that it: 'signalled the change from a parent/status-dominated law to a child-welfare dominated one, thereby laying the foundation of our current child law.'[31]

What is interesting, for present purposes, is that in addition to unequivocally 'placing the child's welfare centre stage' the case prepared the way for the next chapter in the development of parent–child relationships.

The case concerned a long-running dispute between the parents and foster carers of a then 11-year-old boy. By arrangement with the boy's parents, later backed up through a care order, the English foster carers had looked after him for most of his life, while the parents lived abroad and had no direct contact with him. Following the foster parents' indication that they wished to adopt the boy, he was made a ward of court. The parents lost an application for care and control to the foster parents, and went on to lose their appeal against that decision. The question in the House of Lords concerned the reach of section 1 of the Guardianship of Infants Act 1925. As noted above, that section introduced the principle that the child's welfare was to be the first and paramount consideration in disputes concerning a child's upbringing. This case raised the question of

---

28 S. Cretney, above n. 1, pp. 563–564.

29 Above, n. 1.

30 *J v C* [1970] AC 668.

31 N. Lowe, '*J v C*: Placing the Child's Welfare Centre Stage' in S. Gilmore, J. Herring and R. Probert (eds.), *Landmark Cases in Family Law*, Hart Publishing, Oxford 2011, pp. 27–45, p. 44.

whether that principle ought to pertain in the case of disputes between parents on the one hand and third parties on the other, in the same way that it did in disputes between the parents themselves. Controversially, the House of Lords answered that question in the affirmative.

Lowe observes that the Law Lords' reasoning was critical. Their interpretation of the 1925 Act's welfare provision in such a way as to allow the welfare of the child to take precedence over all other factors 'firmly put the child's welfare centre stage', and heralded the start of an era in which family law has been 'welfare-dominated'.[32] Thereafter, the interests and entitlements of any parent have, at least in theory, been secondary to the interests of the child in this type of case. The longevity of the decision was ensured when its approach was effectively enshrined in today's paramountcy principle through section 1 of the Children Act 1989.

J v C demonstrates the astonishing scale of the impact of child welfare as a normative principle on the nature of parent–child relationships in law over the twentieth century. It would be difficult to overestimate the diminution of the status of parents in the face of the ascension of child welfare. Child welfare first propelled the dramatic shift from the absolute power of fathers to power sharing between the father and mother. It later precipitated an equally dramatic subversion of the status of both parents to the extent that they could be entirely displaced should that be in the child's best interests. The next section will explore how *J v C* paved the way for a new chapter in the development of parent–child relationships.

3. THE NEXT CHAPTER: FROM BEST INTERESTS TO NEW RELATIONSHIPS

Dramatic as the impact of *J v C* was, the temptation to see it as the finale in the story of the changing nature of parent–child relationships should be avoided. The decision continues to hold sway in contemporary jurisprudence; as Lowe notes, the points of law it established have survived the dramatic changes to family law occasioned by both the Children Act 1989 and the Human Rights Act 1998.[33] Nevertheless, the pace of legal change related to parent–child relationships has, I suggest, hardly slowed through the early years of the twenty-first century. At this point I wish to explore the ways in which my own work on the reshaping of parent–child relationships following assisted reproduction dovetails with the work that has been discussed above. For it is in relation to this topic that it is possible to discern the unfolding of a new chapter in the story of the changing

---

32 N. Lowe, above n. 31, p. 31.
33 N. Lowe, above n. 31, pp. 36–39.

nature of parent–child relationships in law. Though the aim is in part to trace the continuity evident in the sustained momentum of the evolution of parent–child law, I also want to suggest that change can be discerned along two axes. First, in relation to the *effect* of the changing law, recently, the change has been more about the structure of parent–child relationships than about their qualitative consequences. Secondly, there is a notable shift in the *motivations* behind change in the sense that recent developments are being steered by concerns about adult parenting practices, rather than by concerns to further elevate child welfare.

3.1. FROM QUALITATIVE TO STRUCTURAL REFORMS

The alterations to parent–child relationships discussed thus far concerned, for the most part, the legal consequences of those relationships. In that sense they were qualitative changes; they had an impact on the nature of the parent–child relationships in law, but they did not affect the structural configuration of those relationships. This is clearly true of the adjustments to parental authority effected via the guardianship Acts and by the common law, as exemplified by *J v C*. It is less obviously true of the changes to the laws on legitimacy outlined above. Given the status of children as *filius nullius* in law, one might well argue that the project to remove the consequences of illegitimacy brought about recognition of a parental relationship that did not previously exist – in other words, a structural change in the law related to parenthood. At least by the turn of the nineteenth century, however, the law was cognisant of the relationships between parents and their illegitimate children. The mother was by that time recognised as a holder of parental authority[34] and some legislation, such as the Bastardy Law Amendment Act 1872, implicitly recognised the fathers of illegitimate children too.[35] The problem by this stage was that law prevented specific, albeit very significant, legal consequences from attaching to a person's status as mother or father to an illegitimate child. As such, it is submitted that twentieth-century endeavours to reform the law related to illegitimacy were mostly concerned with the meaning and content of parent–child relationships in law. By contrast, the most noteworthy recent developments are characterised by adjustments to the very structure of the parental relationships that law recognises.

The first significant example of a newly structured version of legal parenthood occurred with the Family Law Reform Act 1987, which was closely followed by the Human Fertilisation and Embryology Act 1990. These Acts made provision for adults conceiving with the help of donated gametes to be recognised as parents

34 See *Barnardo v McHugh* [1891] AC 388.

35 This Act reformed the law for mothers to bring affiliation proceedings against the fathers of illegitimate children with respect to paying maintenance. See S. Cretney, above n. 1, pp. 530–532.

notwithstanding the absence of a blood-tie. The latter Act in particular has been described as 'a bold innovation' on the basis that it 'went further than any other legislation in demoting the significance of the blood tie and of the marriage bond' for the purposes of recognising parents.[36] As was the case with earlier legislative changes to parental authority and the meaning of illegitimacy, this legal innovation was reached only at the end of a long journey, following many efforts to resist it.[37] Moreover, some of the concerns that provided the impetus for these reforms were remarkably similar to those that drove the reform of the laws on illegitimacy. For example, concern was expressed about the capacity of children born following donor insemination to inherit property, given the lack of a formal legal relationship with their non-genetic fathers.[38]

The innovations introduced by the Human Fertilisation and Embryology Act 2008 were bolder still. In providing a framework for the recognition of two parents of the same sex, the 2008 Act not only continued the demotion of genetic ties, but also demolished the role of heterosexuality as part of the fundamental architecture of legal parenthood. Many would contest the significance of this change and assert that the 2008 Act actually replicated and entrenched heteronormative understandings of parenthood. This charge is made in reference to the continuation of a dyadic parenting model under the Act. The accommodation of new types of parent came only at the expense of the exclusion of others, so a child of two female parents can have no father, for example. In that sense, as Diduck notes,

> It seems to me that the new legal status parent does not overcome either the biological or proper nuclear family privilege that attaches to the concept of legal parenthood ... lesbian parenthood is acquired on the basis that mimics rather than overcomes traditional norms and biology.[39]

McCandless and Sheldon have also written at length on 'the tenacity of the sexual family form' as revealed in the continuation of the two-parent model through the 2008 Act.[40]

---

36 C. Barton and G. Douglas, *Law and Parenthood*, Butterworths, London 1995, p. 66.

37 The need for change to the law was considered, and firmly rejected, by a specially appointed committee chaired by the Earl of Feversham as early as 1958. See the *Report of the Departmental Committee on Human Artificial Insemination* (1960), Cmnd 1105. The issue was sufficiently contentious that even after a further committee – 'The Warnock Committee' – reported the clear need for legislation in 1984, it took another six years for the 1990 Act to pass through Parliament. See *Report of the Committee of Enquiry into Human Fertilisation and Embryology* (1984), Cmnd 9314.

38 See the Warnock Report, ibid.

39 A. Diduck, 'If Only We Can Find the Appropriate Terms to Use the Issue Will Be Solved: Law, Identity and Parenthood' (2007) 19 *Child and Family Law Quarterly* 1–23.

40 J. McCandless and S. Sheldon, 'The Human Fertilisation and Embryology Act (2008) and the Tenacity of the Sexual Family Form' (2010) 73 *Modern Law Review* 175–207.

Such arguments are not at all without merit and it is not my contention that the opportunity to rethink the foundations of legal parenthood has been fully grasped to optimal effect. Nonetheless, legal parenthood has in recent years been stretched and structurally altered in ways that are no less radical for being limited. In fact, as I have noted elsewhere,[41] the structural changes to the recognition of legal parents have outpaced changes to the legal recognition of different types of adult partnership structure. Recognition of same-sex adoptive parents preceded any debate on the introduction of the Civil Partnership Act 2004, and the provisions of the 2008 Act facilitated the ascription of parenthood to a same-sex couple long before the Marriage (Same Sex Couples) Act 2013 appeared on the horizon.[42]

Since the 2008 Act, a series of cases have occurred concerning the recognition of different adults involved in multiple parenting arrangements that are not fully captured by the Act's parenthood provisions. These cases are to some extent a vindication of arguments about the inherent conservatism of the 2008 Act's reform of the laws on parenthood, as they expose extant gaps in our framework for recognising parents in unconventional situations. That said, the cases have pushed towards further diversification in the parent–child relationships recognised through law. Their significance becomes clearer in relation to the second axis of change that I wish to discuss – namely, that reforms are increasingly adult-centred.

3.2. THE MOTIVATIONS BEHIND RECENT REFORM: IS CHILD WELFARE STILL CENTRE-STAGE?

As a matter of formal law, the answer to the question posed in the subtitle is, of course, yes. There has been no change in the position that the child's welfare is paramount in decisions concerning her upbringing. What has changed, I suggest, is the extent to which adult-centred, rather than child-centred, concerns have driven reform of the law concerned with parents and children.

The Human Fertilisation and Embryology (HFE) Acts do not appear to have been driven primarily, or even substantially, by concerns for the welfare of children. It is undoubtedly the case that a multiplicity of issues provided the impetus for each of them, including the necessity of addressing the practical consequences of changes in the science and technology of reproduction. Child welfare did feature in the debates preceding both Acts, and within the

---

41 L. Smith, 'Tangling the Web of Legal Parenthood: Legal Responses to the use of Known Donors in Lesbian Parenting Arrangements' (2013) 33 *Legal Studies* 355–381.

42 Similarly, it might be argued that the law evolved to accommodate unmarried parents, who are now treated on the same terms as married parents for most purposes, long before embracing cohabiting relationships, which are still very different from marriage in legal terms.

Acts themselves. The 1990 Act included a 'welfare provision' in the form of section 13(5). The provision set out that clinics should not provide women with assisted reproductive services unless they had considered 'the welfare of any child who might be born as a result of the treatment (including the need of that child for a father)'. This ostensible concern with child welfare should not be taken at face value. As Barton and Douglas noted, 'the extent to which this concern was based on prejudice against women as parents, as compared with evidence about the adequacy of upbringing in lone-parent families, may be open to question'.[43] Section 13(5) was as much about adding the ballast of conservative stability to legislation addressing technology's potential facilitation of fatherless families as it was about child welfare per se. The provision is reminiscent of how the understanding of child welfare was previously moulded to an altogether more adult-centred agenda: shoring up prevailing notions of public morality in response to the earliest efforts to reform the law on illegitimacy.

An amended version of the section 13(5) welfare provision was retained by the HFE Act 2008 – this one jettisoning reference to the need for a father in favour of a reference to the need for supportive parenting.[44] Resistance to this amendment as good as hijacked the debates during the Bill's passage through Parliament, and yet child welfare concerns cannot be said to have shaped the final Act.[45] For one thing, much of the opposition to amending the welfare provision represented 'displaced discomfort with the amendments relating to same-sex parenting, and an attempt legally to fetter same-sex parenting "through the back door"'.[46] So some of the wrangling over child welfare concerns was disingenuous and represented a further example of the concept of child welfare being appropriated to serve adult agendas.[47] In any event the effort to assert the importance of the need for a father as an integral part of child welfare was unsuccessful. The Government stuck steadfastly to its objective of using the 2008 Act 'to better recognise the wider range of people who seek and receive assisted reproductive treatment in the early 21st Century'.[48] The Act's parenthood provisions were a

---

43 C. Barton and G. Douglas, above n. 36, p. 64.

44 The amendment is effected by sections 14(1)–(2) Human Fertilisation and Embryology Act 2008.

45 L. Smith, 'Clashing Symbols? Reconciling Support for Fathers and Fatherless Families after the Human Fertilisation and Embryology Act 2008' (2010) 22 *Child and Family Law Quarterly* 46.

46 L. Smith, ibid., p. 51.

47 It should be acknowledged that there are reasons to be more sympathetic to some who resisted the amendment to section 13(5). As I have noted previously, the amendment was very much in tension with a series of policy developments – brought about by the same Government – that sought to promote the significance of fathers being actively involved in the lives of children. L. Smith, above n. 45, pp. 53–57.

48 Department of Health, *Review of the Human Fertilisation and Embryology Act*, (2006) Cm 6989, Norwich, TSO, para. 2.67.

direct result of the pursuit of an equality agenda related to adult relationship practices. I am not suggesting here that there is something inherently wrong with this; there are good arguments for saying that child welfare should not be used to restrict or control reproductive decisions.[49] My purpose is rather to highlight, as a matter of interest, evidence of shifts back towards adult-centred concerns in the most significant legal developments affecting parent–child relationships.

Surprisingly, and somewhat ironically, the influence of adult-focused concerns is also evident in a series of cases concerning multiple parenting arrangements that arguably have their roots in the principles established by *J v C* in 1970. A succession of cases have arisen involving disputes between lesbian couples and the known sperm donors of their children. In each case some level of involvement between the known donors and the children had been planned but conflict arose after a level of involvement was sought that the lesbian couple was not comfortable with. The disputes have arisen under the Children Act 1989 and as such the welfare of the child has been the paramount consideration in resolving them. These 'known donor' cases can be viewed as descendants of *J v C* insofar as they each called upon the courts to resolve a dispute about the child's upbringing between two legal parents and a person who was not a legal parent. However, the cases presented a novel twist on the persistent and 'troubling problem'[50] of how to resolve disputes between parents and third parties in that they involved legal parents and third parties who were asserting their own claims to be treated *as parents*.

As Lowe has noted, the courts have had repeatedly to wrestle with the 'inherent difficulty of how best to reflect the importance of parenthood without undermining the general application of the paramountcy test as established by *J v C*'.[51] This is reflected in a striking lack of consistency in the courts' approach to known donor cases. Some of the decisions demonstrate a struggle on the part of the judges to overcome the magnetic pull of 'natural' parents. So, for example, in *Re D* Black LJ was 'considerably influenced by the reality that B is D's father' even though she saw him as 'a parent of a very different sort'.[52] In *T v T* little distinction was drawn between the position of the known donor father and a father in a conventional heterosexual parenting arrangement.[53] And in *A v B and C*, Thorpe LJ rejected as 'demeaning' the notion that the known

49 See, for example, E. Jackson, 'Conception and the Irrelevance of the Welfare Principle' (2002) 65 *Modern Law Review* 176.

50 N. Lowe, above n. 31, p. 40.

51 Ibid.

52 *Re D (Contact and parental responsibility: Lesbian mothers and known father)* [2006] 1 FCR 556, pp. 582–583.

53 *T v T (shared residence)* [2011] 1 FCR 267. For a detailed discussion of this decision see L. Smith, '*T v T (Shared Residence)* [2010] EWCA Civ 1366' (2011) 33 *Journal of Social Welfare and Family Law* 175.

donor father should be considered only as a 'secondary parent'.[54] In other respects the decisions follow closely in the path of *J v C*, with the judges underplaying the de jure position of the known donor/father as the legal parent and focusing instead on the de facto need for the lesbian non-parent to be prioritised in the interests of the child. Thus Hedley J deemed an award of parental responsibility to the father in *Re B* to be 'wholly inconsistent' with the reality that the nuclear family comprised the child and the lesbian couple.[55] Similarly, in *R v E and F* the father's application for shared residence and parental responsibility was unsuccessful.[56] The judge asserted that the father was not as significant to the child as the lesbian couple were, a reality recognised through a joint residence order in the couple's favour.

The uneven rhetoric of the decisions is reflected in a dramatically different range of outcomes. In some instances the outcomes were creative – for example, conferring parental responsibility 'stripped of practical effect',[57] and structuring contact arrangements so as to differentiate the roles of 'primary and secondary parents'.[58] In others, conventional orders were made, most notably *T v T* where the known donor father was awarded shared residence and a timetable of contact that would be typical for a father in a separated heterosexual couple scenario.

Each of the known donor decisions was, of course, made with due regard to the paramountcy of the particular children's welfare. But a shared characteristic of the cases is that they concern the needs of the adults involved to clarify the terms and remit of the relationships resulting from their own choices about family type and parenting models. In that sense it is submitted that multiple parenting arrangements constitute the new and challenging territory on which the ongoing significance of child welfare, as defined in *J v C*, is being fought out. There is a deep irony here. The *J v C* principle that parental rights should give way to the best interests of the child, even vis-à-vis third parties, initially highlighted and consolidated a significant shift from parent-focused to child-focused law. Yet the very same principle has provided the basis for a new body of case law to emerge in which adults seek to overcome the inflexibilities of the statutory framework for recognising new types of parent and give some legal shape to their innovative designs for parenthood.[59] Not only, it seems, have we

54 *A v B and C* [2012] EWCA Civ 285.

55 *Re B (role of biological father)* [2008] 1 FLR 1015, 1022.

56 *R v E and F (female parents: known father)* [2010] 2 FLR 383.

57 *Re D*, above n. 52, p. 582. The father was prohibited from seeking any involvement with the child's education or medical care without prior written permission from the lesbian couple.

58 *Re P and L (minors)* [2011] EWHC 3431 (Fam), para. 3.

59 Again, the intention is not to suggest that this is a negative development. The persuasiveness of the idea that child welfare should always trump adult concerns has been challenged by a number of authors. See for example, H. Reece, 'The Paramountcy Principle: Consensus or Construct?' (1996) 49 *Current Legal Problems* 267; J. Herring, 'The Human Rights Act and the Welfare Principle in Family Law – conflicting or complementary?' (1999) 11 *Child and Family Law Quarterly* 223–235.

come full circle, returning to a situation in which the status of parents drives much of the development in parent–child law, but the particular trajectory that the rise of child welfare took in the twentieth century has facilitated that journey.

4. CONCLUSION

One of the main objectives of this chapter has been to illustrate that the 'great shift in family law', occasioned by changes to the parent–child relationship and noted by several commentators at the end of the last century, was not a completed project. Changes to the parent–child relationship have continued to effect substantial changes to the landscape of family law. The changes have arguably reached much further than those writing several decades ago could ever have contemplated. The foundational concept of legal parenthood has been stretched and altered in fundamental ways to accommodate diverse family structures. And it has been particularly interesting to note that we appear to have been more ready to use the law to respond to significant changes to parent–child relationship practices than to use it to respond to significant change in adult partnership practices. True, reform of the law on adult relationships has sometimes followed reform of the law on parenthood, i.e. in relation to the embracing of same-sex family relationships. Yet it is intriguing that the parent–child relationship should have functioned as a galvanising force for diversification of relationship recognition in law generally.

Why this might be so is open to conjecture, and there is perhaps a separate piece to be written exploring the meaning of a legal culture of experimentalism in relation to parenthood and relative conservatism in relation to adult partnership. What does seem true is that many of the more noteworthy changes to the law on parent–child relationships in recent years have had adult-centred concerns at their heart; the promotion of the interests of children has somewhat waned as a motivating force. An attempt to forecast the likelihood of a further shift in the balance between the interests of children and parents is probably premature but it seems likely that the parent–child relationship itself will continue to function as a fulcrum of family law.

COMMITMENT-BASED PARENTING: PARENTAL RESPONSIBILITY IN ENGLISH LAW

Gillian DOUGLAS

1. INTRODUCTION

I had the privilege of teaching Family Law at the University of Bristol with Nigel from the late 1970s. Nigel's Family Law course was rather different from others at that time, since he was absolutely clear that the law relating to the parent–child relationship should form a significant part of the syllabus rather than being confined, as was then common, to a few weeks of study at the end of the course. He rightly identified that the shift in family relationships away from marriage rendered the concept and content of legal parenthood of increasing importance and he was determined to reflect this approach in his teaching. I have had the enormous benefit of Nigel's example, advice and wisdom, to draw on for the rest of my academic career, as a colleague (first at Bristol and later, at Cardiff University), collaborator (on empirical projects, as co-editors – initially with Stephen Cretney – of the case reports in the journal *Family Law*, and as co-authors of *Bromley's Family Law*), and friend.

In this chapter,[1] drawing on Nigel's original insight regarding the centrality of the parent–child relationship, I examine developments in the law in England and Wales governing the grant to, and exercise by, fathers,[2] of parental responsibility. I seek to show that in determining this issue, the law has increasingly come to equate personal 'commitment' – by which is meant the emotional dedication[3] that the father shows towards the child – with the child's best interests, confusing parental inclination with children's welfare. I illustrate this thesis through a focus on two key areas: the automatic grant of parental responsibility to unmarried fathers who are recorded on the birth register; and the allocation of caring time between separated parents in shared parenting arrangements.

2. PARENTAL RESPONSIBILITY

In English law, while all married or civilly partnered parents have parental responsibility[4] automatically from the child's birth,[5] in the case of unmarried parents, only the legal mother holds parental responsibility and the father[6] has to take steps to acquire it to share with her. In the wake of greater social acceptance of birth outside marriage, when the Law Commission came to review the law relating to illegitimacy in the 1980s, they noted 'increasing recognition by the courts of the importance of the natural father's role in relation to the welfare of the illegitimate child.'[7] They recommended that such fathers should be enabled to obtain full parental authority[8] by court order, where this was in the child's best interests.[9]

They subsequently considered that, if the parents were in agreement that the father should have parental responsibility, it was an unnecessary expense and formality to require them to obtain a court order,[10] so in 1989, provision was made for the father to acquire parental responsibility by means of a registered

1 I would like to acknowledge the generosity of the Leverhulme Trust in funding the research on which this chapter is based, through the grant of a Major Research Fellowship.

2 Predominantly. Non-resident mothers in child arrangements disputes should be treated the same as non-resident fathers: see below.

3 I discuss the meaning of 'commitment' more fully in G. Douglas, *Obligation and Commitment in Family Law*, Hart Publishing, Oxford 2018, Ch. 1.

4 Children Act 1989, s. 3.

5 Children Act 1989, s. 2.

6 Or second female parent under the Human Fertilisation and Embryology Act 2008 ss. 43–46.

7 Law Commission, Law Com No. 118, *Family Law: Illegitimacy* HC 98 (1982) para. 7.20.

8 They had been able to seek physical custody or access since 1959, based on the child's best interests.

9 Law Com No. 118, para. 7.27. The recommendation was enacted in the Family Law Reform Act 1987, s. 4.

10 Law Commission, Law Com No. 172, *Family Law: Review of Child Law: Guardianship and Custody* HC 594 (1988) para. 2.18.

agreement with the birth mother.[11] Given that no provision was made for a 'welfare' enquiry into the suitability of the father to share parental responsibility with the mother before the agreement was registered, the purpose was clearly to facilitate the acquisition of parental standing for the father. The process was also perhaps envisaged as a way of 'nudging' unmarried fathers to take greater interest in their children by providing them with an easier way of acquiring parental rights than having to take court proceedings.[12]

2.1. PARENTAL RESPONSIBILITY ORDERS

The ability to seek parental responsibility by order remains in the law,[13] to cover cases where, for whatever reason, the parents are not in agreement. Such cases usually arise where unmarried parents have separated (or have never lived together). As noted, the Law Commission regarded parental responsibility orders as suitable so long as they would be in the child's best interests and it has certainly been held that the court's paramount consideration in making an order is the child's welfare.[14] But the extent to which welfare has determined the court's decisions in practice may be queried.

It has been held that there are three material factors for the court to consider as part of the overall welfare test when deciding whether to make an order: the degree of commitment which the father has shown towards the child; the degree of attachment that exists between the father and child; and the father's reasons for seeking the order.[15] The necessary degree of commitment and attachment appears to be easily met: courts have granted parental responsibility to a father who was not allowed to have actual *contact* with the child, and to another where the child was likely to be adopted.[16] But as Ryder LJ put it in *Re M (Parental Responsibility Order)*:

> Where a concerned though absent father has established a degree of commitment to his child, there is a degree of attachment between them and his reasons for applying for parental responsibility are neither demonstrably improper nor wrong, then prima facie, it would be in the interests of the child for a parental responsibility order to be made

[11] Children Act 1989, s. 4(1)(b). Unmarried female 'second parents' may obtain parental responsibility in equivalent ways to fathers under s. 4ZA.

[12] Law Com No. 172, para. 2.20.

[13] Children Act 1989, s. 4(1)(c).

[14] *Re M (Parental Responsibility Order)* [2013] EWCA Civ 969 [2014] 1 FLR 339 at [15].

[15] *Re H (Minors) (Local Authority: Parental Rights) (No. 3)* [1991] Fam 151, 158.

[16] *Re H (A Minor) (Contact and Parental Responsibility)* [1993] 1 FLR 484, CA; *Re H (Minors) (Local Authority: Parental Rights) (No. 3)* [1991] Fam 151, CA.

> and the court will need cogent evidence that the child's welfare would be adversely affected before considering otherwise.[17]

So the courts have effectively regarded demonstration of 'a degree of commitment' as sufficient to help raise a presumption that granting the father parental responsibility *will* be in the child's best interests. Only where the father's behaviour raises concerns, such as by inflicting violence, or he lacks mental capacity, or he is seeking to interfere with and control the mother's life with the child, is his application likely to be refused.[18] In the words of Ward LJ, a parental responsibility order is a means of 'conferring upon a committed father the status of parenthood for which nature has already ordained that he must bear responsibility.'[19] He reiterated in a later case, 'it is important that, wherever possible, the law should confer on a concerned father that stamp of approval'.[20] While Black J subsequently warned that 'parental responsibility is not a reward for the father for his commitment to and involvement with [the child]',[21] such decisions seem to have more to do with fulfilling the wish of the father to have full legal recognition, than with meeting the welfare needs of the child.

2.2. PARENTAL RESPONSIBILITY BY REGISTRATION

Yet, however easy it might have been to make an agreement, or to obtain an order, neither facility was in practice extensively used. In 1996, the last year the statistics for parental responsibility agreements were published, only 3,590 agreements were registered, and 5,587 orders made, compared with 232,516 births outside marriage – so representing 1.5 per cent and 2.4 per cent respectively of the total.[22] Ros Pickford found that this small proportion was not due to lack of interest on the part of parents; rather, they did not know that the father lacked legal rights, or did not feel the need to secure his legal position.[23]

---

17 *Re M (Parental Responsibility Order)* [2013] EWCA Civ 969 [2014] 1 FLR 339 at [15].

18 See e.g. *Re H (Parental Responsibility)* [1998] 1 FLR 855, CA; *M v M (Parental Responsibility)* [1999] 2 FLR 737; *Re M (Parental Responsibility Order)* [2013] EWCA Civ 969 [2014] 1 FLR 339.

19 *Re S (Parental Responsibility)* [1995] 2 FLR 648, CA at 657.

20 *Re C and V (Contact and Parental Responsibility)* [1998] 1 FLR 392, CA. For criticism of this and other cases taking this approach, see H. Reece, 'The Degradation of Parental Responsibility' in R. Probert, S. Gilmore and J. Herring (eds.), *Responsible Parents and Parental Responsibility*, Hart Publishing, Oxford 2009; P. Harris and R. George, 'Parental responsibility and shared residence orders: parliamentary intentions and judicial interpretations' (2010) 22 *Child and Family Law Quarterly (CFLQ)* 151.

21 In *Re M (handicapped child: parental responsibility)* [2001] 3 FCR 454, 479b.

22 Office of National Statistics (ONS), *Birth Summary Tables, England and Wales 2016* (2017) [online] <http://www.ons.gov.uk/peoplepopulationandcommunity/birthsdeathsandmarriages/livebirths/datasets/birthsummarytables> from Table 1.

23 R. Pickford, *Fathers, Marriage and the Law*, Joseph Rowntree Foundation, 1999.

But the Lord Chancellor's Department was concerned by this low figure and argued in 1998 that

> Parental responsibility may be important to people as a symbol of the legal status of parenthood, and it may be a particular source of grievance for some unmarried fathers that they may be forced to support their children financially, whether or not they have acquired parental responsibility under the Children Act.
>
> ...
>
> Discrimination between married and unmarried fathers in respect of parental responsibility is increasingly seen as unacceptable, in view of the large numbers of children who are now born to unmarried parents, many of whom are likely to be in stable relationships. It is clearly impossible to assume that most unmarried fathers are irresponsible or uninterested in their children, and do not deserve a legal role as parents.[24]

The law was therefore further amended to provide that registration on the child's birth certificate would automatically confer parental responsibility on the father.[25] Julie Wallbank has drawn attention to the government's wish (or hope) that joint registration would help to embed 'the values of responsibility' in parenting from the child's birth.[26] Sally Sheldon, too, has noted that while the government's motivation seemed in part to assuage the claims of fathers' groups (protesting strongly at that time about child support law) that they were discriminated against in family law, it also sought to

> foster men's commitment to their families ... Granting automatic [parental responsibility] to unmarried fathers is seen as a way of fostering an assumption of paternal duty to provide for the child's emotional and moral developments as well as their financial needs.[27]

The change in the law was not made retrospective when it came into force in 2003, but only 5.3 per cent of all births in England and Wales in 2015 were registered without the father's name.[28] Researchers have found that sole

---

24 Lord Chancellor's Department, Consultation Paper: *Procedures for the Determination of Paternity and on The Law on Parental Responsibility for Unmarried Fathers* (1998) [online] <http://webarchive.nationalarchives.gov.uk/+/http:/www.dca.gov.uk/consult/general/patfr.htm>, Summary, and Part II, para. 51.

25 Adoption and Children Act 2002, s. 111.

26 J. Wallbank, '"Bodies in the Shadows": joint birth registration, parental responsibility and social class' (2009) 21 *CFLQ* 267, 275.

27 S. Sheldon, 'Unmarried Fathers and Parental Responsibility: A Case for Reform?' (2001) 9(2) *Feminist Legal Studies* 93, 107–108.

28 ONS, *Births by Parents' Characteristics England and Wales 2015* [online] <http://www.ons.gov.uk/peoplepopulationandcommunity/birthsdeathsandmarriages/livebirths/bulletins/birthsbyparentscharacteristicsinenglandandwales/2015> Fig. 3.

registration is largely connected with poverty, social exclusion, the young age of the mother, the breakdown or failure of the parental relationship and unplanned pregnancy[29] – none of which suggest that giving the father automatic parental responsibility had the registration been done jointly would have had much positive impact on the welfare of the child. The reform was really about fathers, not children. It was intended to be a symbolic recognition – Ward LJ's 'stamp of approval'[30] – of (some) fathers' *wish*, their personal commitment, to play a role in their children's lives, a recognition reinforced by the second development to be discussed here – shared parenting after separation.

3. SHARED PARENTING AFTER SEPARATION

It has been well documented, particularly by Richard Collier,[31] that a powerful fathers' lobby has sought to challenge what it perceives as bias in the family courts resulting in the general allocation of primary care of children, after parental separation, to mothers (although the claim of bias is not supported by empirical evidence).[32] Despite the fact that the large majority of children still live with their mothers after separation, reflecting the status quo of how they were cared for before the break-up of the parents' relationship,[33] fathers have dictated the terms of a continuing debate over shared parenting, and shifted it from an earlier focus on the award of 'contact',[34] towards a demand for more equal allocation of caring time between both parents. In so doing, they have pointed to their emotional dedication and commitment to their children as one of the justifications for their continuing 'involvement' in their lives.

---

[29] J. Graham et al., *Sole and joint birth registration: Exploring the circumstances, choices and motivations of unmarried parents*, Department for Work and Pensions, Research Report 463, London 2007. They also found that sole registration was the deliberate choice of some lesbian parents.

[30] *Re S (Parental Responsibility)* [1995] 2 FLR 648, CA at 657.

[31] See R. Collier, '"The Outlaw Fathers Fight Back": Fathers' Rights Groups, Fathers 4 Justice and the Politics of Family Law Reform – Reflections on the UK Experience' in R. Collier and S. Sheldon (eds.), *Fathers' Rights Activism and Law Reform in Comparative Perspective*, Hart Publishing, Oxford 2006.

[32] J. Hunt and A. Macleod, *Outcomes of Applications to Court for Contact Orders after Parental Separation or Divorce*, Ministry of Justice, London 2008; M. Harding and A. Newnham, *How do County Courts Share the Care of Children Between Parents?* Nuffield Foundation, 2015.

[33] ONS, *Families and Households 2015* (2015) p. 8. See also, D. Norgrove (Chair), *Family Justice Review Interim Report* (2011) para. 5.33.

[34] Section 8(1) of the Children Act 1989 defined a contact order as one 'requiring the person with whom a child lives, or is to live, to allow the child to visit or stay with the person named in the order, or for that person and the child otherwise to have contact with each other'. 'Contact' has now been absorbed into a 'child arrangements order' – see below n. 40.

3.1. ENFORCING THE RIGHT TO CONTACT

Initially, the focus of the pressure for reform was on the working of the courts in dealing with contact between the non-resident parent and the child.[35] Fathers complained in particular that they were not able to play a full part in their children's lives and that mothers were able to frustrate contact because orders were inadequately enforced via fines and threats (but very rarely the imposition) of committal to prison for contempt of court.[36] At the start of the millennium an expert sub-committee (CASC)[37] recommended a two-stage approach to 'making contact work', beginning with an essentially non-punitive, educational response in which the non-cooperative resident parent would be directed to attend an information meeting, or a parenting programme or required to seek psychiatric advice. If these proved ineffective, the court would be empowered to impose an order with a penal sanction, such as community service or probation with conditions of treatment or regular attendance at parenting classes. Fines or imprisonment should be measures of truly last resort.[38]

Proposals largely reflecting these recommendations[39] were subsequently enacted in the Children and Adoption Act 2006.[40] This introduced first, a power to make an 'activity direction' while the court is considering what final order to make,[41] and to attach an 'activity condition' to a final order;[42] and secondly, new enforcement powers. Both reforms were intended to promote the exercise of contact. Activity directions/conditions empower the court to require a parent to 'take part in an activity that would, in the court's opinion, help to

---

35 It has been estimated that only around 10% of parents litigate over post-separation contact disputes: A. Blackwell and F. Dawe, *Non-resident parent contact*, Department of Constitutional Affairs, London 2003.

36 The shorthand term, the 'implacably hostile mother' was used in such cases: see e.g. *Re O (Contact: Imposition of Conditions)* [1995] 2 FLR 124, CA; *Re J (A Minor) (Contact)* [1994] 1 FLR 729, CA; *A v N (Committal: Refusal of Contact)* [1997] 1 FLR 533, CA.

37 The Children Act Sub-Committee (CASC), *Making Contact Work: A report to the Lord Chancellor on the facilitation of arrangements for contact between children and their non-residential parents and the enforcement of court orders for contact* (2002).

38 The Children Act Sub-Committee (CASC), *Making Contact Work: a Consultation Paper from the Children Act Sub-Committee of the Lord Chancellor's Advisory Board on Family Law (CASC) on the facilitation and enforcement of contact* (2001) Ch. 14, para. 14.53.

39 Department for Constitutional Affairs (DCA) et al., *Parental Separation: Children's Needs and Parents' Responsibilities*, (2004) Cm 6273; DCA et al., *Parental Separation: Children's Needs and Parents' Responsibilities: Next Steps*, (2005) Cm 6452.

40 As amended by the Children and Families Act 2014. As a result, the provisions outlined here apply generally to what are now known as 'child arrangements orders' and are not limited to contact.

41 Children Act 1989, s. 11A inserted by the 2006 Act (amended by the Children and Families Act 2014).

42 Children Act 1989, s. 11C.

establish, maintain or improve the involvement in the life of the child concerned' of that parent.[43] The activities envisaged include programmes such as anger management, counselling, and information and advice sessions, including the 'separated parents' information programme' (SPIP or PIP) which:

> helps you understand how to put your children first while you are separating, even though you may be in dispute with your child's other parent. The course helps parents learn the fundamental principles of how to manage conflict and difficulties.[44]

The existing enforcement measures of fines and imprisonment were supplemented by providing that a parent in breach of an order may be required to do unpaid work in the community, or pay compensation for loss incurred as a result of her or his breach.[45]

There are no national statistics available to indicate the number of directions or conditions made, or indeed the use of the general enforcement powers attached to a finding of contempt of court after breach of an order. The Family Justice Review,[46] which reported in 2011, found from unpublished court data that in 2010, there were nearly 1,000 applications for enforcement orders in respect of contact orders (e.g. for unpaid work to be undertaken) but only 55 orders were made. Over the same period, there were 13 applications for financial compensation, with only four orders made. Liz Trinder et al. found from a review of CAFCASS data that only 31 enforcement orders were made from 1,383 applications for enforcement in 2011–12.[47] Given that enforcement measures were always intended to be a last resort, the courts appear to have been following the CASC recommendations, and the researchers found that one year after the date of application, only nine per cent of cases had returned to court while a further 10 per cent remained open. They considered that this might indicate success, but lacked the information to know how cases that had not returned to court were faring.[48]

---

43 Children Act 1989, s. 11A(3).

44 https://www.cafcass.gov.uk/grown-ups/separated-parents-information-programme-(spip).aspx. Failure to comply with a direction is not punishable, but is taken into account when deciding on the final order; a condition *is* enforceable since it forms part of the final order itself.

45 Children and Adoption Act 2006 ss. 4, 5, inserting ss. 11J–11P into the Children Act 1989.

46 D. Norgrove (Chair), *Family Justice Review Interim Report* (2011) para. 5.35. Published statistics count the number of children covered by different orders, rather than the number of orders made. In 2010, 92,130 children were the subjects of contact orders: Ministry of Justice, *Judicial and Court Statistics 2010* (2011), Table 2.4.

47 L. Trinder et al., *Enforcing contact orders: problem-solving or punishment?* Exeter Law School, Exeter 2013, p. 2.

48 At p. 4.

Research evaluating the initial working of SPIPs found that after a slow start (and once charges for attendance were scrapped), the number of parents being referred began to increase. The researchers found that parents were generally supportive of the programmes and were positive about their purpose and focus. However, in terms of effectiveness in promoting contact, they found a positive impact on contact rates of only about eight percentage points, seemingly through converting cases where there had been 'no contact' into some, but not frequent, contact. The programmes did not seem to have any impact on parental relationship quality, and attendance did not seem to reduce resort to court.[49] It is difficult to assess the overall effectiveness of such measures, and they do not address the cases where the non-resident parent fails to exercise contact because he or she lacks the 'commitment' to do so, as distinct from those where he or she is prevented by the primary carer from doing so. Yet researchers have reported that, from the perspective of many mothers, the unreliability of the non-resident parent in keeping to contact arrangements is the real problem regarding lack of post-separation contact between the non-resident parent and child.[50]

3.2. VIEW THAT CONTINUING INVOLVEMENT IS FOR THE CHILD'S WELFARE

Fathers' groups also sought the introduction of a statutory presumption or requirement that parenting should be shared (equally) post-separation, or at least that the 'involvement' of both parents is to the child's benefit.[51] It is interesting to recall that there was something of a precedent for the latter in the Family Law Act 1996, which had included a requirement that in any proceedings for a divorce, the court was to have particular regard to:

> the general principle that, in the absence of evidence to the contrary, the welfare of the child will be best served by ... his having regular contact with those who have parental responsibility for him and with other members of his family.[52]

---

49 L. Trinder et al., *Building bridges? An evaluation of the costs and effectiveness of the Separated Parents Information Programme (PIP)* (2011); L. Smith and L. Trinder, 'Mind the gap: parent education programmes and the family justice system' (2012) 24 *CFLQ* 428.

50 V. Peacey and J. Hunt, *I'm not Saying it was Easy ... contact problems in separated families*, Gingerbread, London 2009, pp. 68–70.

51 For a full discussion of the background, and a powerful critique of the reform, see F. Kaganas, 'A presumption that "involvement" of both parents is best: deciphering law's messages' (2013) 25 *CFLQ* 270 and see CASC, *Making Contact Work: A Report to the Lord Chancellor on the facilitation of arrangements for contact between children and their non-resident parents and the enforcement of court orders for contact*, Lord Chancellor's Department, London 2002. Appendix 3.

52 Family Law Act 1996, s. 11(4).

It can be seen that this would not have amounted to a *presumption* but was expressed as simply a 'principle' to be taken into account. There was so much controversy surrounding the substantive divorce reform in the Act that very little attention was paid to this provision, and it was never implemented, so we cannot know how the courts would have addressed it.[53]

The idea of a statutory presumption was at first rejected by government on the basis that arrangements for children should reflect their individual needs and circumstances, and that the principle of shared parenting was already enshrined in the law through the fact that parental responsibility is shared (in most cases) by both parents anyway.[54] Nonetheless, the House of Commons Constitutional Affairs Committee, while rejecting the insertion of a presumption, did recommend a statutory requirement for courts to have regard 'to the importance of sustaining a relationship between the children and a non-residential parent'.[55]

This formulation of the principle demonstrates how fathers' groups had successfully framed their demands as claims not only for equal treatment with mothers but also as promoting the welfare of children – fathers' involvement is 'important', and in children's best interests. Accepting this view, the Family Justice Review panel in 2011 initially favoured 'a general statement of intent' being inserted into the Children Act 1989, which 'would reflect the case law on contact, reinforcing the importance of the child continuing to have a meaningful relationship with both parents, alongside the need to protect the child from harm.'[56] However, they rowed back from the position in their Final Report, having been convinced by the same argument that had been accepted by the Labour Government that any such amendment to the law would simply distract from the principle that the welfare of the child is paramount, pure and simple.[57]

3.3. A STATUTORY PRESUMPTION

Notwithstanding this considered view by an independent review team, the Coalition Government which inherited its work rejected the conclusion and

---

53 The divorce reform itself was abandoned, and the provisions repealed by the Children and Families Act 2014.

54 DCA et al., *Parental Separation: Children's Needs and Parents' Responsibilities*, (2004) Cm 6273, paras. 42, 43.

55 House of Commons Constitutional Affairs Committee, *Family Justice: the operation of the family courts: Fourth Report of Session 2004–05*, HC 116 Vol 1, (2005) para. 47.

56 D. Norgrove (Chair) *Family Justice Review Interim Report* (2011) paras. 5.77–5.78.

57 D. Norgrove (Chair), *Family Justice Review Final Report* (2011) para. 4.40. They were particularly influenced by evidence of the experience in Australia, which had introduced a complex presumption in 2006: paras. 4.35–4.36 and references cited therein.

consulted on how best to formulate a legislative statement 'of the importance of children having an ongoing relationship with both their parents after family separation, where that is safe, and in the child's best interests.'[58] It stated the mischief the provision was intended to tackle as follows:

> [I]n too many cases one parent is left in a position where it is very hard to retain a strong and influential relationship with his or her child. This can result in children losing contact completely with one parent (usually the father), often with a lasting impact on their lives. The Government firmly believes that parents who are able and willing to play a positive role in their child's care should have the opportunity to do so.[59]

The emphasis here was, as with the reforms to enforcement of contact orders, squarely on the non-resident parent being prevented (impliedly by the resident parent) from retaining (thus implying that there was such a relationship in the first place) a strong relationship with the child. This was linked to 'lasting impact' (implicitly detrimental) on the child's whole life.

The legislative provision eventually passed states:

> 1. Welfare of the child
>
> …
>
> (2A) A court … is as respects each parent … to presume, unless the contrary is shown, that involvement of that parent in the life of the child concerned will further the child's welfare.
>
> (2B) … 'involvement' means involvement of some kind, either direct or indirect, but not any particular division of a child's time.
>
> …
>
> (6) In subsection (2A) 'parent' means parent of the child concerned; and, for the purposes of that subsection, a parent of the child concerned–
> (a) is within this paragraph if that parent can be involved in the child's life in a way that does not put the child at risk of suffering harm; and
> (b) is to be treated as being within paragraph (a) unless there is some evidence before the court in the particular proceedings to suggest that involvement of that parent in the child's life would put the child at risk of suffering harm whatever the form of the involvement.[60]

58 Ministry of Justice/Department for Education, *The Government Response to the Family Justice Review: A system with children and families at its heart*, (2012) Cm 8273, para. 61.

59 Department for Education, *Co-operative Parenting Following Family Separation: Proposed Legislation on the Involvement of Both Parents in a Child's Life*' (2012) para. 3.2.

60 Children Act 1989, s. 1(2A) inserted by s. 11 of the Children and Families Act 2014.

Although the object of the reform is easy to state, the amendments are less straightforward to summarise, requiring a flow chart and five examples, covering half a dozen pages, of how the law is expected to work, in the official Explanatory Notes to the Act.[61] It should be borne in mind that parents may use, indeed, seem to be expected to use, this provision as guidance to shape their own arrangements without going to court.[62]

As is well known, similarly complex legislation enacted in Australia led to major problems, in particular an assumption on the part of both professionals and parents that parental 'involvement' means the amount of time spent with the child, and a down-grading of domestic violence concerns.[63] The language in the text in England and Wales is deliberately different to try to minimise such effects, but the President of the Family Division considered it necessary to amend the wording of the relevant Practice Direction to ensure that courts did not make the same mistake of minimising the risk of violence when deciding on child arrangements orders.[64] Leaving aside the domestic violence context, there is no clear evidence to suggest that the provision has had much impact at all, just as had been predicted.[65] After all, the true purpose of the legislation was not to alter the principles on which the courts had been operating for many years, but, as the parliamentary committee scrutinising the Draft Bill pointed out,

> to tackle *a perception of bias within the Courts that we have previously concluded has no basis in fact*, and in the hope of influencing parents to agree to make provision for shared parenting rather than risk entering the court process. (emphasis added)[66]

4. CONCLUSION

What the reform did reflect, however, was the general trend towards regarding personal commitment as the basis and rationale for the legal recognition

---

61 As noted by N. Lowe and G. Douglas, *Bromley's Family Law*, 11th edn., Oxford University Press, Oxford 2015, p. 433. The Explanatory Notes are available [online] at <http://www.legislation.gov.uk/ukpga/2014/6/pdfs/ukpgaen_20140006_en.pdf>, pp. 112–116.

62 Department for Education, *Cooperative parenting following family separation: proposed legislation on the involvement of parents in a child's life: Summary of consultation responses and the Government's response* (2012) pp. 4–5.

63 Norgrove, *Final Report*, paras. 4.35–4.38. See also the evidence presented by Prof H. Rhoades to the Review at Annex G.

64 See *Practice Direction 12J – Child Arrangements & Contact Orders: Domestic Violence And Harm* (2017). The revisions were prompted by lobbying from domestic violence charities including WAFE, through their report, *Nineteen Child Homicides*, WAFE, 2016.

65 See F. Kaganas, 'A presumption that "involvement" of both parents is best: deciphering law's messages' (2013) 25 *CFLQ* 270, 281–282.

66 HC Justice Committee, *Pre-legislative scrutiny of the Children and Families Bill: Fourth Report of Session 2012–13* HC 739, Vol 1 (2012) para. 153.

of family ties. Thus, in granting parental responsibility to unmarried fathers, there was a desire to encourage men to 'commit' to their children and to nudge them toward doing so by giving them rights (even if labelled as 'parental responsibility') as well as the liability of child support. This process has been achieved through gradually reducing what is expected of fathers before they are 'rewarded' with parental authority. That reduction has been driven by a seeming lack of concern amongst unmarried parents to take *active* steps to secure parental standing for fathers. Now, therefore, unmarried fathers have parental responsibility simply by virtue of their name appearing on the birth certificate. This is based on an assumption that all fathers must be treated alike regardless of their commitment *to the mother*, so long as they are prepared to have their biological link to the child made public. Their possibly minimal degree of personal commitment *to the child* suffices for and justifies their being given the 'stamp of approval' of full parental responsibility.

Even in the determination of the arrangements for post-separation parenting, where the child's welfare remains the paramount consideration, the focus of legal reform has been on accommodating the wishes of non-resident parents – generally fathers – to assert their relationship with the child and to recognise their 'commitment' to that child. Lack of involvement by fathers with their children has been ascribed to mothers' reluctance to facilitate contact, rather than to lack of interest on the part of some fathers. All this has resulted in a framing of fathers' claims as appeals to welfare as well as to rights and to equating a parent's commitment to and interest in his child with the child's best interests.

Placing the emphasis on the parent's emotional and personal commitment as the justification for the ascription of legal rights and authority in respect of a child might work well (assuming that there are no safety concerns for either the primary carer or the child) if the parent shows the requisite degree of interest in and commitment to the child, so that a 'meaningful' relationship between them can indeed develop or be maintained. But it does little to foster such a relationship where the parent lacks the commitment in the first place, or develops new family ties that supersede an earlier bond. And generally equating parental commitment with the best interests of the child ultimately serves only to prioritise parents' *rights* over the true interests and *welfare* of their children.

RIGHTS CHILDREN SHOULD NOT HAVE

John Eekelaar

Much discussion of children's rights focuses on the need to protect children's rights better, and in many cases to increase them. Nigel Lowe's work has contributed significantly to this, especially in the international arena, and a sustained case for doing this has recently been made by Michael Freeman.[1] I have long asserted how important it is to see children as right-holders.[2] But what rights should they have? It was fashionable in some quarters in the 1970s to hold that children should have the same rights as adults,[3] but today that would be regarded as an extreme position. Children need protection (itself a right) and treating children as if they had the same abilities as adults would weaken that. Nevertheless, many might still say that, provided a child had sufficient competence, he or she should indeed have the same rights as adults. Competence, not some arbitrary line (attainment of majority), should be the key.

But I want to consider some occasions when children do not, and perhaps should not, have the same rights as adults, even if otherwise competent. Take a straightforward example. A child cannot own land, and therefore cannot take

1 M. Freeman, *A 'Magna Carta' for Children: Rethinking Children's Rights*, Cambridge University Press, Cambridge 2018.

2 Most recently in J. Eekelaar, *Family Law and Personal Life*, 2nd edn., Oxford University Press, Oxford 2017, ch. 2.

3 R. Farson, *Birthrights*, Macmillan, London 1974; J. Holt, *Escape from Childhood: The Needs and Rights of Children*, E.P. Dutton, Boston 1974; H. Cohen, *Equal Rights for Children*, Rowman & Littlefield, Totowa, NJ 1980.

out a mortgage in the UK, whereas an adult can, provided he or she satisfies certain (mainly financial) conditions. But what if, exceptionally, a 17 year-old were to satisfy all those conditions, and possess as much financial understanding as most adults have? Should such a child have the same rights to the mortgage as an adult? If not, why not? Would this extend to a right to receive pornographic material?

1. WHAT DOES IT MEAN TO HAVE A RIGHT?

Part of the problem in addressing such issues is obscurity over what it means to 'have a right'. Neil MacCormick famously propounded a version of the interest theory in these terms:

> to ascribe to all members of a class *C* a right to treatment *T* is to presuppose that *T* is in all normal circumstances a good for every member of C, and that *T* is a good which it would be wrong to withhold from any member of *C*.[4]

What was essential for MacCormick was that there should be no ulterior purpose in ascribing the good: the good of the beneficiaries should be an end in itself. MacCormick also thought that the right preceded any duty to protect or respect it, writing: 'It certainly does not seem to me in any way objectionable to say that it is *because* children have a right to care and nurture that parents have the duty to care for them.'[5] However, the right rested on a 'presupposition' or 'supposition' (MacCormick uses both terms) by those conferring the right of what was good for the beneficiaries. In order to avoid the charge of moral paternalism, MacCormick allows the potential beneficiaries (but not children) to waive such rights 'if there is some good reason to leave it to the choice of individuals whether to have or not have what is, or is from the legislator's point of view believed to be, good for them'.[6] But he was clear that this was ancillary to and not intrinsic to the nature of the right.

On this view, therefore, children could indeed have different rights from adults if those creating the rights, who would be adults, presupposed that the protection or advancement of certain interests of adults was good for those adults, but would not be good for children; or, conversely that the protection of certain interests would be good for children, but not for adults. The discussion would solely be about what people felt was 'good' for adults and children, so

4 N. MacCormick, *Legal Right and Social Democracy: Essays in Legal and Political Philosophy*, Clarendon Press, Oxford 1982, p. 161.
5 Ibid., p. 162.
6 Ibid., p. 166.

that discussions about the rights of *anyone* would be reduced to nothing more than discussions about what people felt was good for other people. To be sure, such discussions could be inclusive of everyone involved, and there could even be a duty to hear their point of view (as is the case for children under Article 12 of the UN Convention on the Rights of the Child). But in the end we could just take a vote on what people thought was good for children in various contexts, which might be different from what we thought was good for adults, and that would be the kernel of any right conferred.

There is another view. This does indeed focus on the interests of potential right-holders. However, it sees the right as intrinsic to the respect owed to those persons' perceptions of what constitutes their interests. It involves more than just listening to what they say (though it certainly involves it) and then deciding what we thought was good for them. It lies, first, in recognising that people, or groups of people, define their interests in certain ways; second, in weighing them against any competing claims; and, third, if thought to be of sufficient weight, in accepting or creating a duty to (to put it crudely) do something about realising those interests so defined.[7] It can be seen that this is in essence a 'claim' theory, and a description of the process of coming to hold people have rights, and not a guide for identifying what those rights actually are. On this view choice is not ancillary but central to rights. Recognising in this way people's choices to live their lives in the way they value could be said to be a necessary element in respecting their humanity. Of course this does not imply that people have a right to anything they want, or that they have no duties to others.

This makes the matter of children's rights more difficult. First, there is the obvious point about competence. Respecting the way people define their interests makes no sense if they are unable to define them, or lack capacity to understand how to realise them. But much of this can be overcome by *imputing* a viewpoint, as one might do for someone who is unconscious or otherwise similarly incapacitated. Hence we can say that people nevertheless have rights which they would be very likely to claim if they did not have those limitations, for example, rights to a safe environment, health care, education and personal development. If you could not impute them, then they would not have them. You may say that this simply collapses into the interest theory, and in practice it may indeed lead to similar results. But there is a difference: the decision-maker does have to try to adopt the perspective of someone in the potential right-holder's position, which must be fully contextualised. In the case of children, it may also be necessary to reach a temporary or bridging solution which holds back from a definitive result while placing the child in a position where the child can develop experience and in time reach a definitive result. But in all these cases children

[7] This position is outlined in J. Eekelaar, above n. 2, ch. 2.

are not treated differently from adults because they are children, but because their capacities may be different. Adults who lack capacity are treated in the same way.

But what if a child *is* deemed competent, so no question of imputation arises, and is denied a right in circumstances in which the same claim made by an adult would be accepted as a right, for example, if a fully competent child chooses to work in a hazardous environment which we allow adults to choose to do and the degree of risk is the same? Not to allow that for a child for reasons we would not apply to an adult would be to deny the child a right just because the child is a child. But that might not be such a bad thing. It could be justified in terms of preventing child exploitation; or if the degree of risk is actually different (e.g. if an injury, should it occur, would be worse for a child). This is not the only occasion when children appear not to have the same rights as adults, even if they have the same capacity as adults. Here are some examples.

2. DRIVING, DRINKING, SMOKING AND VOTING

Except in some cases of disability, a person may not obtain a driving licence in the UK before their 17th birthday. Yet it is not inconceivable that many people under 17 are as competent to drive as many adults, perhaps more so. But the higher risk of accidents (endangering both themselves and others) among younger drivers *as a class* is well established and, while it might be possible, with extensive training, vetting, and testing, to confine licences for younger children to those who would be at low risk, this is simply not practicable. So we withhold a right we would allow to adults.

Eighteen is the minimum age at which people can buy alcohol or tobacco products, although it is not necessarily illegal for people under this age to drink alcohol or to smoke. These measures are directed more at the interests of children themselves than those of third parties, and could be seen as supporting the interest theory of rights. But the theory stumbles because, despite similar (if not quite as severe) risks, we allow adults to weigh up the benefits and risks of their consumption. Yet we wish to reduce the opportunities for children to do this even though there must be many people under 18 who are as competent as many adults to make this assessment. Indeed the minimum age for purchase of tobacco products was raised from 16 to 18 only from 1 October 2007.[8] So again we curtail a right in the case of children which we allow for adults. Perhaps the strongest justification lies in attempting to find a way to enhance the health of the future population.

[8] Children and Young Persons (Sale of Tobacco etc.) Order 2007.

The voting age was reduced from 18 to 16 in the Scottish referendum, but a similar reduction for the EU referendum was rejected, perhaps unfortunately for the 'remainers'. Here the interests of the potential right-holders and those granting the rights are thoroughly mixed up. It is possible that numbers of under 18s or even under 16s see it as in their interests to be able to vote, but presumably the case against it is that, as a class, they lack the requisite knowledge and the risks to the community are too great (although it would not be the voters, but the people they vote for who would do the damage). Or perhaps it is felt that young children are very likely to follow their parents' views, so extending the franchise in this way would give voting advantage to large families. This is actually quite a difficult issue about the nature of democracy and citizenship, and has been much discussed in recent years.[9] Michael Freeman takes the radical route, arguing that there should be no age restriction at all, on the ground that children are just as competent to make the necessary judgements as most adults are, and very young children just wouldn't bother (or be able) to vote.[10]

The competence argument can be slightly complicated here. Competence is not just a question of knowledge (or cognition), but also experience.[11] Normally one expects immigrants to reside for some period of time in a country before acquiring voting rights, not because of lack of competence in the cognitive sense, but to demonstrate some degree of commitment to the community, and acquire a greater 'feel' for the issues. Of course children are usually already settled in their community, and could be involved in civic activities, but given the normal circumstances of family life, are more dependent directly on and committed to their families than independent adults and may be less directly affected by the issues. If this were the reason, withholding the vote from them would not be to treat them very differently from the adult population.

3. MARRYING, MAKING A WILL AND HAVING SEXUAL RELATIONS

It has generally been considered to have been an *enhancement* of children's rights when very low marriage ages, especially for girls, have been removed. But this could in some cases be perceived as a *removal* of rights. We tend to sympathise

9 See J. Tonge and A. Mycock, 'Citizenship and Political Engagement Among Young People: The Workings and Findings of the Youth Citizenship Commission' (2010) 63 *Parliamentary Affairs* 182.

10 M. Freeman, 'The Human Rights of Children' (2010) 63 *Current Legal Problems* 1, 43. See also M. Freeman, above n. 1.

11 M. Freeman, 'Why it remains important to take children's rights seriously' (2007) 15 *International Journal of Children's Rights* 5.

with Juliet, who is not yet 14 when her forbidden romance with Romeo starts. Her father says he thinks she should wait two more years before marrying, to be told by Paris: 'Younger than she are happy mothers made', to which he wryly answers: 'And too soon marr'd are those so early made'.[12]

The Convention on the Elimination of All Forms of Discrimination Against Women (CEDAW) provides (Article 16.2) that 'The betrothal and the marriage of a child shall have no legal effect, and all necessary action, including legislation, shall be taken to specify a minimum age for marriage'. In General Recommendation 21 in 1994 the CEDAW Committee regarded 18 as the earliest age that marriage should be permitted. The Committee (paragraph 36) gave both competence and welfare grounds for its position, saying:

> When men and women marry, they assume important responsibilities. Consequently, marriage should not be permitted before they have attained full maturity and capacity to act. According to the World Health Organization, when minors, particularly girls, marry and have children, their health can be adversely affected and their education is impeded. As a result their economic autonomy is restricted.

The capacity requirement applies to adults too: marriages can be annulled for lack of (mental) capacity. But the 'economic autonomy' of adult women is frequently restricted by marriage, and they are not thereby denied it. Nor (perhaps sadly) is 'maturity' required for adults. But maturity in this case surely implies a significant degree of independence from the immediate family and understanding the responsibilities of the marital relationship. It is possible that some children under 18, or even 16, possess this, but fixing a minimum age obviates the need to assess individual circumstances, and gives necessary protection to children as a class, even if it removes rights from some otherwise competent children. The English Law Commission gave a similar reason for suggesting that the age of testamentary capacity in England, which they considered should be lowered from 18 to 16, should not be subject to exceptions if a child under 16 has sufficient capacity.[13]

In the UK the age of consent to sexual intercourse, both hetero- and homosexual is 16; in California it is 18, and in Germany, 14. The complications arise in regard to the age difference between the two parties. In England, anyone, whether over or under 18, who engages in sexual activity with someone under 16, commits an offence.[14] It seems that the 15 year-old commits no offence,

---

12 *Romeo and Juliet*, Act 1, scene 2. Shakespeare, as so often, capturing the essence of our problem.

13 Law Commission, *Making a will*, Consultation Paper 231 (July 2017), paras. 8.23 and 8.44. Testamentary capacity is attained at 12 in Scotland: Age of Legal Capacity (Scotland) Act 1991, s. 2.

14 Sexual Offences Act 2003, ss. 9–13.

unless both of them are under 16. But if both of them are 16 or 17 year-olds, there is no offence. Furthermore, a person who is in a position of trust commits an offence to engage in sexual activity with someone under 18. The person under 18 commits no offence.[15] Children over 16 therefore have no right to sexual activity with someone under 16, but in this they are in no different position than adults. Although it seems that a child under 16 commits no offence, it would be hard to say they have a right to the activity, given that it involves their partner in criminal liability. Children under 16 certainly have no right to sexual activity with one another. The expression 'sexual activity' is not restricted to penetrative sex, and it is not obvious that children of this age are necessarily incapable of understanding it, or that it is necessarily likely to be more harmful to them because they are children.

A justification given for this is that 'to a limited extent law can play some legitimate role in enforcing social norms to the benefit of vulnerable groups and can also operate as a "protective umbrella" facilitating interventions by state agencies in particular cases'.[16] Can treating children differently from adults in this respect be justified, like the prohibition on marriage, by reference to a need for maturity, or is this a right which 'competent' children should have? If it is, I perhaps need hardly add that, as in all cases of rights, it is not always desirable or responsible to exercise one's rights, and in fact it can be irresponsible sometimes to do so.

4. WHERE TO LIVE

Do children have a right to leave their home and go and live with someone of their choosing? Clearly adults can do this, at least in theory. The whole issue is tied up with a broader question: do children have a duty to obey their parents (including living where the parents say they should)?

A parent will usually have 'parental responsibility' regarding their child, and this includes the responsibility to accommodate, care for and bring up the child. But does this impose on the child reciprocal duties? Although the French Civil Code states that a 'child, at any age, owes honour and respect to his father and mother', and 'may not, without the permission of the father and mother, leave the family home',[17] it is hard to believe that in English law a child is *legally* obliged

15 Ibid., ss. 16–24.

16 M. Waites, *The Age of Consent*, Palgrave Macmillan, London 2005, p. 225.

17 Code Civil, Arts. 371 and 371.3. Article 31 of the African Charter on the Rights and Welfare of the Child asserts that children have responsibilities 'towards their families and societies, to respect their parents, superiors and elders, to promote and strengthen African cultural values in their relations with other members of their communities'. It is hard to see this as anything other than aspirational.

to comply with their parents' directions in this way. The parents' rights to look after their child are held against third parties (which may include the state), not against the child. Morally, no doubt, a child should usually do as a parent directs, but it is extending legalism too far to hold that a child has a legal duty to eat their breakfast, tidy their room, or even return home in good time. The parent has to exercise moral authority. Failure to exercise it successfully could lead to social intervention. But that concerns the rights and duties of the state authorities, not of the child.

Does this therefore mean that children have a right to disobey their parents and leave home (assuming that the parents are behaving properly) as an adult might? The answer I think is no, even if fully competent on these matters, at least in England and Wales, but one reaches it in a roundabout way. Suppose a child *were* to leave home, where would he or she go? A local authority in England 'may provide accommodation' for someone under 16 if a parent who is willing and able to provide it does not object,[18] but only if it thinks this is necessary in order to 'safeguard or promote' the child's welfare.[19] If the parents object, the authority will not be able to care for the child unless it resorts to specific statutory powers, for example, if it fears the child is at risk of significant harm. If the child is over 16, the authority may care for the child even though the parents object, but only if the child agrees.[20] So in that case the child may find care and accommodation, but that will depend on the decision of the local authority. If the authority concludes that it should not provide such resources (perhaps because the parental resources are satisfactory and there is no compelling reason why the child should not accept them), it is simply withholding resources from the child, not enforcing the child's duties towards the parents. In that event one would expect that the child would return to its parents for care. But suppose the child does not want to do that: he or she sleeps rough, or threatens to take up with undesirable companions. Then the authority must decide how to use its resources regarding the child. The child could be taken into police protection;[21] the authority might seek an Emergency Protection Order,[22] and perhaps eventually a care order.[23] If any of these things happened the child would fall under certain duties to co-operate with the authorities, so the ultimate result might be that the child returns home.

Suppose the child finds someone else to live with: maybe a grandparent. If the parents wish to 'recover' the child from the grandparent, the matter should

---

18 Children Act 1989, s. 20(7).

19 Ibid., s. 20(4).

20 Ibid., s. 2(11).

21 Ibid., s. 46(1): this is limited to 72 hours.

22 Ibid., s. 44.

23 Ibid., s. 31 (on the grounds that the child 'is suffering, or is likely to suffer, significant harm' and the child is 'beyond parental control').

(and in England, would) be dealt with through the application of the welfare principle, not on the basis of the child's duties to the parents. It would be like any contested case over where the child should live, where the child has formed a view about the matter. Whether the child's view about where he or she wants to live should conclude the matter is part of the decision about how the welfare test should be applied. But the final decision is for the court.

The upshot of all this is that a child, even if competent, does not have a right to decide where to live, as, at least in theory, an adult does. Any attempt by the child to exercise such a right could trigger an array of procedures which give various authorities the power to make the decision. While it is certainly not because of a straightforward duty the child owes to the parents, at the same time it demonstrates that the child does not have the same rights to choose where to live as an adult. Perhaps this is a good thing.

5. EDUCATION AND RELIGION

It is widely accepted that children have a right to education.[24] For children lacking in competence, this can be supported either on the interest theory or through imputed intention. It is difficult for young people to possess the maturity to assess their educational needs. However, in some circumstances a child might be thought competent enough to decide whether to receive education, or a particular aspect of it. Yet they may not be free to do this.

In some jurisdictions authorities can take enforcement measures directly against a resisting child, though in England the measures are primarily directed against the parents, bringing indirect pressure on the child. In either case the competent child is denied rights a competent adult has. A resisting child's duty to receive education is primarily owed, however, to the state, not to the parents. A competent adult certainly has no duty to receive education, and certainly not to undergo instruction of a kind that another person dictates. So here children are denied rights adults have, simply because they are children. This could be justified on the basis of the child's interests, but perhaps even more compellingly, on the basis of the public interest as a whole.

As regards religion the position may be different if the child's right to freedom of 'thought, conscience and religion' asserted by the UN Convention on the Rights of the Child (UNCRC) were to be held to give a child a right to resist the parents' choice of the nature of the education, which the European Convention protects. For example, may a child resist instruction in a religion

[24] See for example Articles 28 and 29 of the UN Convention on the Rights of the Child.

which its parents desire? Neither the UN nor the European Convention proclaims any clear right of a child to pursue a religion (or non-religion), or religious (or non-religious) education against the wishes of his or her parents. Some countries, such as the Netherlands, have considered that children have such a right,[25] and the Committee on the Rights of the Child has recommended that the UK should allow children to withdraw from religious *worship* at school 'independently', that is, without requiring authorisation by the child's parents.[26] That seems right: the parent's authority in these matters should rest on example and persuasion, not legal power. However, if the child has a duty to receive religious education or attend worship at school, it would be owed to the state rather than the parents. How far this coincides with the parents' wishes is a matter between the state and the parents.

6. HEALTH

It has understandably been in the area of medical decision-making that the most anxiety has arisen regarding the role of children's views. It is possible that English law does indeed allow a child the right 'to make his own decision when he reaches a sufficient understanding and intelligence to be capable of making up his own mind on the matter requiring decision',[27] but this view is contested.[28] Nevertheless, English courts tend to find that children who might otherwise be considered mature enough to consent to being given medical treatment, but who have declined life-saving medical treatment, usually for religious reasons, have been so affected by their situation as to lack sufficient understanding to make it.

But would an adult be treated in the same way? Probably not. In such cases it seems that a child who might otherwise be considered competent is being treated differently from an adult who has the same competence, and is therefore denied rights which an adult would have. The justification for this might be that, while it

25 See U. Kilkelly, 'The Child's Right to Religious Freedom in International Law' in M.A. Fineman and K. Worthington (eds.), *What is Right for Children?*, Ashgate, Farnham 2009, pp. 243–268.

26 Committee on the Rights of the Child, *Concluding observations on the fifth periodic report of the United Kingdom of Great Britain and Northern Ireland* (June 2016), para. 35.

27 *Gillick v West Norfolk and Wisbech Area Health Authority* [1986] AC 112, 186.

28 It is argued that Lord Fraser, in *Gillick* restricted the child's autonomy under the best interests principle. The contrary view sees Lord Fraser's qualification simply as recognising that doctors must always act only in the best interests of their patients, so are not bound to provide treatment that even a competent person wants if they think it medically undesirable. But that does not allow them to force treatment on a competent patient against their will: see J. Herring, R. Probert and S. Gilmore, *Great Debates in Family Law*, Palgrave Macmillan, London 2012, pp. 62–68.

is true that everyone is influenced by people around them (and in that sense 'pure' autonomy is impossible), family members (especially parents) exercise a unique influence on children during childhood and this renders suspect an apparently autonomous decision by a child which severely damages the child. The effect of family dynamics on children's psychology can be complex. This would be one of those limited occasions when a decision about a child's interests overrides the normal application of the concept of individual rights, and therefore denies the child a right in circumstances where an adult would have a right.[29]

7. CONCLUSION

There could be a real benefit in regarding the occasions I have mentioned where the wishes of competent children are overridden as examples of *withholding* rights from them rather than as *implementing* a right to a welfare decision. That is because this perception draws attention to the seriousness of doing this. One is not *just* doing what one thinks is best for the child, as one would in the case of a non-competent child. One is deliberately treating an individual who is otherwise in all respects in the same condition as other individuals in a different way from those others simply because of age. This can be justified, but standards of justification must be demanding, and the decision must always be taken with great care and thorough investigation of the circumstances.

There is a final point. Can one not say that children, of whatever capacity, *always* have a right to have decisions taken about them grounded in a judgement about their welfare, or best interests, as indeed is stated in Article 3 of the UNCRC? My answer is: yes, as a member of the class covered by that article (and indeed by section 1 of the Children Act 1989) they do have a right that in reaching the decision 'the best interests of the child shall be a primary consideration'. But in making the decision, in some cases it may be necessary to withhold certain specific rights from some children.

29 S. Gilmore and J. Herring, '"No" is the hardest word: consent and children's autonomy' (2011) 23 *Child and Family Law Quarterly* 3.

EMPIRICAL RESEARCH ON ADOPTION OF CHILDREN FROM CARE

Julie Doughty

1. INTRODUCTION

Adoption of children is unarguably one of the 'great debates' in family law,[1] an adoption order having been described by Stephen Cretney as 'irrevocable',

[1] J. Herring, R. Probert and S. Gilmore, *Great Debates in Family Law*, Palgrave Macmillan, Basingstoke 2012, pp. 117–144.

'dramatic' and 'different in kind from other legal processes'.[2] This debate cannot avoid questions of social policy and conceptions of family identity. It has also maintained a high political profile in England and Wales in recent years.[3] Accordingly, there has been a stream of socio-legal research into adoption systems.

Nigel Lowe and Mervyn Murch led a team based at Cardiff University and their studies make up a substantial proportion of, and a significant contribution to, the body of research that has built up in the past 20 years. They drew on records and the voices of families and professionals who were directly involved and affected. This chapter will review these studies and place them in the context of recent and ongoing research questions. The timeline will first be set out, followed by a section each on five reports by the Lowe and Murch team between 1988 and 2002. Comprehensive legislative reform took place 15 years ago, in no small part contributed to by findings from these studies. Policy and judicial interpretation have undergone continual changes and scrutiny; yet messages from these earlier investigations can still be cited as meaningful today.

2. A BRIEF HISTORY OF ADOPTION LAW AND POLICY

Family law about children is traditionally divided between private (involving family members in dispute) and public (where the state intervenes to protect children). The Children Act 1989, coming into effect in October 1991, reformed and consolidated private and public family law about children in England and Wales, applying the welfare principle, that the child's welfare was the court's paramount consideration in coming to decisions about their upbringing. However, adoption law (which crosses the private/public boundary) was omitted and was still, in the 1990s, governed by the Adoption Act 1976, which had been drafted when adoption was still based on what Lowe described as a 'gift/donation model'.[4] This had been an era when adoption in the UK was still regarded as a private solution to address the social problems of illegitimacy and infertility, and to normalise the child's status within a family.[5] The 1976 Act had, to some extent, been influenced by research that inspired a shift toward a more paternalistic and

2 S. Cretney, *Family Law in the Twentieth Century*, Oxford University Press, Oxford 2005, pp. 597–598.

3 D. Kirton, '"Kinship by design" in England: reconfiguring adoption from Blair to the coalition' (2013) 18 *Child & Family Social Work* 97–106. (Although England and Wales are still a single jurisdiction, adoption policy was devolved to Wales in 2007.)

4 N. Lowe, 'The changing face of adoption – the gift/donation model versus the contract/services model' (1997) 9(4) *Child and Family Law Quarterly* 371.

5 S. Sales, *Adoption, Family and the Paradox of Origins*, Palgrave Macmillan, Basingstoke 2012.

interventionist approach to removing children from disadvantaged backgrounds and which highlighted the benefits and positive outcomes of adoption compared to reunification or foster care.[6] In particular, Rowe and Lambert's *Children Who Wait* revealed evidence of many children drifting in state care.[7] By the late 1970s, practice was adapting to meet the needs of children who needed permanent homes, but the law did not meet the more complex developing demands of families where adoption might be contested, where post-adoption contact might be possible, and where adoptive families might need some support.[8]

Separately to the Children Act reforms, a government inter-departmental review was established in 1989. This included a brief research review by June Thoburn.[9] A White Paper followed, *Adoption: the Future*,[10] and a programme of research that aimed to build an evidence base, made available in 10 publications, four of which were authored by members of the Lowe and Murch team. These are described in the next section.

There was a hiatus following the White Paper, but, galvanised by the revelation of the extent of institutional child abuse in residential care that emerged in the late 1990s, a special report on adoption was prepared for and approved by the recently elected Prime Minister, Tony Blair, in 1999.[11] This identified three key problems: decisions about permanence were not sufficiently clear or timely; once made, plans were not delivered quickly enough; and a lack of post-adoption services. Another White Paper followed,[12] and wholesale legal reform introduced by the Adoption and Children Act 2002. The main aims of the Act were: to align adoption law with the welfare principle in the Children Act 1989; to improve adoption services; to widen the pool and diversity of potential adopters; to introduce a new procedure for separate placement and adoption orders; and to provide for an alternative type of permanent placement – special guardianship. The Act also introduced a simpler mechanism to replace step-parent adoption, and provision for independent reviewing officers to improve the care planning process. Although not raised in the White Paper, the Act also addressed the ongoing debate about contact, by introducing duties on agencies

6 L.F. Harding, *Perspectives in Child Care Policy*, Pearson, Harlow 1997, pp. 47–49.

7 J. Rowe and J. Lambert, *Children who Wait*, Association of British Adoption Agencies, London 1973.

8 R. Parker, *Adoption Now: Messages from Research*, Department of Health/Wiley, London 1999, p. 5.

9 Department of Health and Welsh Office, *Review of Adoption Law: Report to Ministers of An Interdepartmental Working Party*, HMSO, London 1992, pp. 115–125.

10 Department of Health; Welsh Office; Home Office; Lord Chancellor's Department, *Adoption: the Future*, (1993) Cm 2288.

11 *The Prime Minister's Review of Adoption: A performance and innovation report*, Cabinet Office, 2000.

12 Department of Health, *Adoption: A New Approach*, (2000) Cm 5017.

and the court to consider this within their welfare analysis. There were varying views on how far the new provisions reflected concepts of open adoption.[13] The Act was not fully implemented until December 2005, once sets of regulations and guidance had been agreed.

The Act had been subject to considerable consultation and debate, and law and practice became clearer and more consistent for families and practitioners. Although adoption became a more transparent and efficient process, the number of children being adopted remained relatively low, identified as a major failing for children in care by Martin Narey in a dramatic report written for *The Times* newspaper in 2011.[14] The government responded with new proposals to not only speed up adoption but to increase the numbers of children adopted.[15] Legislation in 2014 (applicable only to England) promoted early placement through a 'fostering to adopt' scheme; strengthened post-adoption support for adoptive families; and gave central government new powers to intervene in provision of local services.[16] In 2017, the welfare checklist in the 2002 Act was amended in response to developing case law which raised possibilities of children being moved back from adoptive placements after a late challenge.[17]

In his contribution to a book on family law in the UK and the USA published in 2000, Lowe gives an overview of the history of adoption law, concluding with some questions about its future in the twenty-first century.[18] At that time, adoption figures in England and Wales were relatively low, described as plummeting from 25,000 per year in 1968, to fewer than 5,000 in 1999. The current figure is also about 5,000 per year, having dropped between 2004 and 2011 to just over 3,000 and risen by 2013.[19]

In 2016, picking up some themes from the essay published 16 years earlier, Lowe wrote on the balance between children and birth parents' interests, how that was being drawn by the courts, and whether the concept of adoption needed

---

13 For example, Cullen was more optimistic about the prospect of consensual contact arrangements being reached under the Act than Bridge and Swindells: D. Cullen, 'Adoption – a (fairly) new approach' (2005) 17(4) *Child and Family Law Quarterly* 475; C. Bridge and H. Swindells, *Adoption: the Modern Law*, 1st edn., Jordans, Bristol 2003, pp. 232–235.

14 M. Narey, 'The Narey Report: A Blueprint for the Nation's Lost Children', *The Times*, 5 July 2011. Narey had worked in senior positions in the prison service and subsequently for children's charity Barnardos.

15 Department for Education, *An Action Plan for Adoption: Tackling Delay*, 2012.

16 Children and Families Act 2014, Part 1.

17 Section 9 Children and Social Work Act 2017. See A. McFarlane, 'Nothing else will do' Keynote address to the FLBA Conference, 22.10.2016.

18 N. Lowe, 'English Adoption Law – Past, Present and Future' in S. Katz, J. Eekelaar and M. McLean (eds.), *Cross Currents*, Oxford University Press, Oxford 2000, pp. 307–338.

19 In the year ending 31 March 2016, 4,690 children in England and 340 in Wales were adopted from care.

reappraisal.[20] He analysed the impact of recent judicial decision-making, and the new phenomenon of the relatively high numbers of children now being adopted in England whose parents are nationals of eastern European states. Not only is the child in these cases therefore losing contact with extended family members but also losing their national heritage and citizenship, a situation that has raised further political controversy.

3. THE LOWE AND MURCH RESEARCH FOR THE DEPARTMENT OF HEALTH

In the 1990s, children's services and adoption came within the responsibilities of the Department of Health at central government level and of local authorities at local level. The Department of Health commissioned a research programme for the adoption law review being undertaken between 1989 and 1992 and which led to the White Paper issued in 1993.[21] The programme comprised a total of 10 studies, which were synthesised in *Adoption Now: Messages from Research* in 1999, including four by the Lowe and Murch team, where they are described as the Pathways to Adoption study; the freeing study; the support study; and the Thomas and Beckford study. It should be noted that the latter was primarily the work of those two members of the team, Caroline Thomas and Verna Beckford. A fifth study, on adoption and long-term fostering was undertaken in 2000.

3.1. THE PATHWAYS TO ADOPTION STUDY[22]

The objectives of this study were to survey court data and investigate the views of social workers and lawyers in order to build an evidence base on achieving successful adoption. The court record survey (in five local authority areas) provided information on patterns of adoption between 1986 and 1988. The sample size was 650 cases. There were interviews with 52 social workers who wrote the adoption reports and 24 solicitors who had acted in the cases. The project was completed in 1991.

---

20 N. Lowe, 'Will Adoption Do? Reflections on the Law and Practice in Public Law Adoptions in England and Wales' in J. Eekelaar (ed.), *Family Law in Britain and America in the New Century – Essays in Honour of Sanford N. Katz*, Brill-Nijhoff, Leiden 2016, pp. 161–176.

21 Department of Health, *Review of Adoption Law: Report to Ministers of An Interdepartmental Working Group* 1992; Department of Health; Welsh Office; Home Office; Lord Chancellor's Department, *Adoption: the Future*, (1993) Cm 2288.

22 M. Murch, N. Lowe, M. Borkowski, R. Copner and K. Griew, *Pathways to Adoption*, HMSO, London 1993.

3.1.1. *Headlines from the Research*

The study focused on avoidable delay, which raised serious concerns, although the exact reasons for adoption taking so long could not be pinpointed. The interviews suggested a lack of expertise amongst generic child care social workers and the low priority they had to give adoption work because of pressure of their child protection caseloads. There was an average interval of five and a half months between approval of the adoption by the local authority panel and the court application being filed. If the children were freed for adoption, there was an additional average seven and a half months delay, before the adoption application was made. Generally, this added delay was seen by practitioners as outweighing the advantage of freeing.[23] The authors concluded that the system was too elaborate a process and too fragmented in operation. Recommendations by the researchers included imposing a timetable and limiting the number of courts that dealt with adoption (thereby encouraging more specialism and efficiency). One problem was the relatively high proportion of step-parent adoptions, which clogged the system. The authors recommended provision for some sort of three-way parental responsibility arrangement as an alternative to the cumbersome and inappropriate process of adoption as the only mechanism available to remarried parents. Interestingly, the authors also suggested that processes could be improved by regionalising adoption services. Concerns from a rights perspective were also indicated, in that the authors were surprised that adoption applications were almost always successful (even if drawn out) and that courts had no duty to consider making alternative orders such as a section 8 Children Act 1989 residence order.

3.1.2. *Developments*

Specialist 'adoption centre' courts were designated after the Prime Minister's review, and court timetables have been completely reimagined since the Family Justice Review recommended a 26-week time-limit on care proceedings in 2011, brought into effect in 2014, because placement orders are normally sought alongside the final care order.[24] The step-parent adoption problem was addressed by provisions in the 2002 Act allowing parental responsibility to be more simply acquired.[25] Many years later, regionalisation of adoption services took place in Wales in 2014 and, even more belatedly, is now taking place in England. The Welsh reorganisation into a National Adoption Service largely resulted from an

23 Discussed at section 3.2 below.

24 See Judith Masson, 'Pathways to Adoption: From Long and Winding Road to Obstacle Course?' in this volume.

25 Now section 4A Children Act 1989.

inquiry in 2010.[26] In England, 'adoption scorecards' and performance targets were introduced following the 2012 *Action Plan*, and Regional Adoption Boards, in 2015.

The grounds for dispensing with birth parents' consent were reformed by the 2002 Act so that consent could be dispensed with if the welfare of the child required it, to replace the previous, awkward, provisions about 'unreasonably withholding' consent. This was bolstered by the welfare checklist requiring the agency and the court to consider the effect on the child throughout his or her lifetime of being an adopted person, and also what existing relationships could offer.

Research on the perspective of fairness to birth parents was, however, still scant. Beth Neil explained in her ARI research that they are a hard to reach group.[27] Broadhurst and Luckock concluded from a small in-depth study in 2011 that processes were fair to those birth parents, and there were no substantial concerns raised in the parliamentary committee.[28] However by 2015, the strength of feeling about England practising 'forced adoption' was such that the European Parliament commissioned a report into the use of adoption without consent across Europe. It had become commonplace for even senior judges to comment that the UK was unusual or even unique in permitting non-consensual adoption.[29] On the contrary, however, Fenton-Glynn's report showed that all 28 EU Member States had legal mechanisms for ending parental rights and finding alternative caring arrangements for children in need, without parents' consent.[30]

3.2. THE FREEING STUDY[31]

This was a second report from the data in the Pathways study, to investigate the effectiveness of provisions for freeing for adoption which were introduced

---

26 Section 108 Social Services and Well-being (Wales) Act 2014; National Assembly for Wales Children and Young People Committee, *Inquiry into Adoption*, Cardiff 2012. See also H. Ottaway, S. Holland and N. Maxwell, *The provision and experience of adoption support services in Wales: Perspectives from adoption agencies and adoptive parents*, Cardiff University 2014.

27 E. Neil, *Supporting Direct Contact Study*, see C. Thomas, *Adoption for looked after children: messages from research*, BAAF, London 2013.

28 B. Luckock and K. Broadhurst, *Adoption cases reviewed: an indicative study of process and practice*, Department for Education, London 2013; House of Lords Select Committee on Adoption Legislation, *2nd Report of Session 2012–13. Adoption: Post-Legislative Scrutiny Report*, 6 March 2013. HL Paper 127.

29 For example, the President of the Family Division in *Re N (Children) (Adoption: Jurisdiction)* [2015] EWCA Civ 1112.

30 C. Fenton-Glynn, *Adoption without Consent*, European Parliament, 2015; and Update, 2016.

31 N. Lowe, with M. Borkowski, R. Copner, K. Griew and M. Murch, *Report of the Research into the use and practice of the Freeing Provisions*, HMSO, London 1993.

by sections 18–22 Adoption Act 1976. In essence, freeing was a mechanism whereby the court could make an order in favour of an agency that the child be freed for adoption, meaning the birth parents lost parental rights, with a proviso that they could apply to revoke the order if the child was not placed for adoption within 12 months.[32] The intention was to resolve doubts about adoption being the plan and enable any contest by the birth parents before a stage when adopters were matched and introduced to the child, and therefore remove any uncertainty that might exist in the minds of the birth parents, adopters or child as to the status of all parties and placements when the child physically moved in.

3.2.1. *Headlines from the Research*

The research team found that freeing provisions were not universally used, and some agencies never used them. In retrospect, this was perhaps unsurprising, given that a freeing application took an average of nine months in court and children could become attached to their short-term foster carers over extended periods. However, prior to the report, there was only anecdotal evidence of polarised opinions on whether to use freeing.

More than 80 per cent of applications were granted, with only one per cent being refused (the remainder had been adjourned or were withdrawn). The report was not conclusive that freeing had entirely failed in practice, because there was scope for benefit in a contested case being resolved by termination of parental rights before adopters were found.

3.2.2. *Developments*

Freeing was abolished by the 2002 Act, which introduced the separation of process into a placement stage and an adoption stage. Although a placement order can be made with regard to identified adopters, this is rare because it is only safe to begin matching and linking once the placement order has been secured. The new procedure was initially successful in avoiding various types of uncertainty that had arisen in earlier years, but judicial responses since 2013 to the introduction of the 26-week timetable have created new dilemmas.[33]

---

32 A tragic example of freeing orders going wrong is the case of *A and S v Lancashire County Council* [2012] EWHC 1689 (Fam), where infant brothers were freed for adoption in 2001, but never placed and had been 'statutory orphans', being moved around multiple unsuitable placements for 11 years and suffering 'irreparable damage'. They brought successful actions against Lancashire County Council under the Human Rights Act 1998.

33 See Judith Masson, 'Pathways to Adoption: From Long and Winding Road to Obstacle Course?' in this volume.

3.3. THE SUPPORT STUDY[34]

The Lowe and Murch studies reported in detail on the practical needs of the families they interviewed and any support they received, including financial allowances.

3.3.1. Headlines from the Research

A questionnaire was sent to all local authorities and voluntary adoption agencies in 1994 and data was gathered from the 115 who replied, relating to 1,557 children; 45 staff were interviewed. A second survey was also sent in 1995 to adoptive parents where the child was aged five or more when the placement became an adoptive one. (One-third of adopters were originally the children's foster carers). Forty-eight families were interviewed.

There was a disruption rate of about 10 per cent of the agency sample, with almost all of this occurring before an adoption order had been made. In the family sample, the disruption rate was six per cent. At the date of the survey, only 12 per cent of the children were still aged between six and nine years old; 50 per cent were aged 10 to 14 and 38 per cent were aged 15 or over. Nearly one-third of children were reported by parents as having learning difficulties, and a quarter had emotional and behavioural problems.

Findings included that many children had been poorly prepared before moving in; some adopters had not been given up-to-date information; there was wide variation in provision of financial and other support, with many adopters not knowing what was available; social workers felt that adoption services were under-resourced; and it seemed that availability of good adoption services was a lottery. Settling into school was often problematic, where there was little understanding of the child's situation.

The report concluded that a duty to provide adoption services should be made explicit and an education plan should be agreed for every child. A concept of partnership between adopters and agencies should be promoted, but there were too many agencies, with an 'overwhelming case for rationalisation'.[35]

3.3.2. Developments

The findings about difficulties faced by older children were reflected in the Selwyn disruption studies.[36] The Wales Adoption Cohort Study more

34 N. Lowe, M. Murch, M. Borkowski, A. Weaver, V. Beckford and C. Thomas, *Supporting Adoption: Reframing the Approach*, BAAF, London 1999.

35 R. Parker, above n. 8, p. 133.

36 J. Selwyn, S. Meakings and D. Wijedasa, *Beyond the Adoption Order: Challenges, interventions and adoption disruption*, BAAF, London 2015.

recently investigated the support needs of adoptive families in the first year of placement.[37] This national study collected data on all Welsh children placed for adoption in one year (2014–2015), surveyed adopters on their views and experiences, and conducted 40 in-depth interviews with adopters. The English government has invested to some extent in a support fund, and the National Adoption Service in Wales is promoting good practice in support provision.[38] A personal education plan is now prepared for every looked-after child and the importance of the role of schools in now recognised.[39]

3.4. ADOPTION AND SUPPORT FROM THE VIEWPOINT OF CHILDREN

The Thomas and Beckford study aimed to explore the views of older children on their understanding of adoption, their support needs and the extent to which they had been able to express their own views and, if so, how these had been responded to.[40] The authors noted that this was, as far as they knew, the only study on adoption from the point of view of children. Subsequent research incorporating views of children adopted from care has not been plentiful; this is summarised below.

3.4.1. Headlines from the Research

Of the sample of 41 children who had been selected through the interviews with parents in the *Supporting Adoption* study, 32 had been placed for adoption and nine had been adopted by foster carers. The average age of the children at placement was five years, and half of them were placed along with one or two siblings. The research focused on how they had been prepared for adoption, how they settled, their school life, the court process, and their links to their past. The picture was overall an optimistic one; these children were all in ongoing (and therefore, at the time, successful) placements. The views of children experiencing difficulties to the extent that meant families were disinclined to participate were not available. Although the methods developed by the researchers were effective in enabling the children to communicate openly and clearly about their current lives, it was a concern that they were not able to recall much about how they had

---

37 S. Meakings et al., 'Support needs and experiences of newly adoptive families: findings from the Wales Adoption Study' (2018) 42(1) *Adoption & Fostering* 58–75.

38 National Adoption Service, Annual Report 2016–2017.

39 Department for Education, *The Children Act 1989 guidance and regulations. Volume 2, Care planning, placement and case review*, 2015.

40 C. Thomas and V. Beckford with N. Lowe and M. Murch, *Adopted Children Speaking*, BAAF, London 1999.

been able to express their wishes and feelings at the early stages of the placement. This indicated a need for improved communication with the children when decisions are being made about them. They had felt excluded from the matching process and some had been conscious of very long delays between knowing the plan for them was adoption and progress with matching.

Duration of adopter recruitment and matching processes was a strong theme throughout these Department of Health studies. The children in this sample had been in placement for an average of two years and four months before the order was made. At the date of interview, their ages ranged from eight to 15.

The children said they had felt isolated and troubled when they were moved to their new environment, away from everything that was familiar to them. Moving school was particularly difficult. They had been fearful of 'going to court' but then usually enjoyed their 'celebration day'. Twenty per cent of the children had not had any life-story work carried out by agencies when (or since) they were placed. Those who did have life-story books valued them and looked at them repeatedly, although as most were just scrap books, the research team feared for their durability. Recommendations included that the books should be more physically robust in future. Almost two-thirds of the children had some form of contact with their birth families. Most of them had strong feelings about contact with their siblings, mothers and former foster carers. A third of the children had maintained some contact with the latter.

3.4.2. Developments

One of the recommendations made by the parliamentary committee in 2012 concerned the lack of data on the rate of adoption breakdown.[41] In response to mounting concerns about the long-term success of adoption, with some local authorities claiming breakdown rates of up to 25 per cent, the Department for Education (which had become the department responsible for children's services and adoption) commissioned an investigation into adoption disruption in England, followed by a similar piece of research commissioned by the Welsh Government. The resulting very comprehensive reports from Julie Selwyn and colleagues indicated relatively low breakdown rates but, importantly, a very high level of unmet needs of adoptive families, where a lack of support at earlier stages had manifested in challenging behaviour by adolescents. Although complete estrangement was rare, many families were staying together only through great efforts, against the odds. These studies included interviews with 12 young people who had left home before they turned 18. They were older than the DH sample, ranging from 16–23 at date of interview.[42]

---

41 House of Lords Select Committee on Adoption Legislation, above n. 28.

42 J. Selwyn et al., above n. 36.

The Biehal et al. study includes interviews with 37 children in adoptive homes and in long-term foster care. There was no difference in their psychological well-being according to type of placement.[43] Beth Neil's ongoing research on post-adoption contact has utilised a longitudinal study, which includes children's views and is being extensively used in social worker training.[44]

3.5. ADOPTION OR LONG-TERM FOSTERING?

A 15-month project began in January 2000 to examine the process which determined whether a looked-after child would be fostered or adopted.[45] The study compared three local authorities that appeared to make relatively high use of adoption as the plan, with three that looked low. Twenty case files were examined from each authority and a total of 26 social workers and managers were interviewed.

3.5.1. Headlines from the Research

The findings related to 113 children, roughly half where adoption was the plan and half, fostering. Only 61 per cent of the recorded details for these children included clear reasons for the plan. Age seemed the most influential factor, with children aged one to four being twice as likely to be the subject of an adoption plan as older children, whereas those aged five to nine were four times more likely to be fostered than adopted. Children who had emotional or behavioural problems or who had been subjected to abuse were more likely to be fostered than adopted. (This was based on a perceived inability to form attachments and consequent need for financial and therapeutic support.) Contact was a related factor, because the older the child, the more likely they would be to have a significant relationship with their birth family. The majority of the older children who had ongoing contact were subject to a fostering plan, in contrast with just under 60 per cent of the younger children who had ongoing contact. However, generally, patterns varied across the authorities. Policies were individualised amongst local authorities to an extent that suggested inefficiency as well as too much variation. Record-keeping, collection of statistics, and setting fostering allowances could have been more effective if centralised.

The interviews with local authority staff revealed both some confusion about policies and also inconsistent record keeping. The research team expressed

---

43 N. Biehal, S. Ellison, C. Baker and I. Sinclair, *Belonging and Permanence: outcomes in long-term foster care and adoption*, BAAF, London 2010.

44 See <http://contact.rip.org.uk/>.

45 N. Lowe and M. Murch, *The Plan for the Child: Adoption or long-term fostering*, BAAF, London 2002.

concern about flaws in the way adoption rates were measured by government. Another issue of concern was that despite age being the most significant factor, the authorities which made more use of adoption did not necessarily have younger looked-after populations. This study also highlighted the length of the adoption process (an average of two years between the plan and the order; and three years since becoming looked after). One-third of all the children had experienced four or more pre-adoption placements. There was a feeling that the goal of adoption as the child-rescue option had obscured the objectives of stable placement:

> It seems to us that it is often forgotten that the use of the rhetoric of permanence can be easily interpreted by the children and by their birth family as a threat to sever kinship ties which are important for the child's identity. Practitioners need, particularly with respect to the adoption of older children out of care, to stress the importance of the desired stability of future arrangements rather than the severance connotations associated with adoption.[46]

Interestingly, the book's conclusions include a section headed: 'The need to consider the full spectrum of options',[47] which is of course reflected in the judicial pronouncements about a 'global holistic evaluation' since the judgment in *Re B (A Child)*.[48] The authors referred to current political interest in adoption and risks of diverting attention from under-resourcing foster care and insufficient consideration of kinship placements. Even the concept of 'long-term fostering' was vague and not well-supported, seen by some as just a residual option. The research team recommended work on identifying positive reasons for its use.

3.5.2. Developments

As part of the Adoption Research Initiative, Biehal et al. compared adoption by strangers, by foster carers and long-term fostering in a study published in 2010.[49] This aimed to answer questions on how successful adoption and long-term fostering were, and how children perceived the emotional and legal security and sense of permanence offered. The authors explained the context of intense policy development and law reform under the Labour Government from 1997, including of course the Adoption and Children Act 2002, but also various policy programmes such as *Care Matters*, which aimed to improve the outcomes

46 N. Lowe and M. Murch, above n. 45, p. 147.
47 N. Lowe and M. Murch, above n. 45, p. 149.
48 [2013] UKSC 33. See *Re B-S (Children)* [2013] EWCA Civ 1146 [44].
49 N. Biehal et al., n. 43 above.

for children in the care system.[50] There had therefore been considerable change since the Lowe studies. However, similarly, they found that children were more likely to be adopted the younger they were, the less contact they had, and also according to which local authority area they lived in. Decisions on adoption seemed to be based on local policy, resources and practice cultures, as much as on children's needs.

4. THE ADOPTION RESEARCH INITIATIVE

In 2003, Rushton undertook a scoping review of existing research. He concluded, first, that there had been some studies about contact with birth family, but no research comprehensively examining the short- and long-term effects on the children and others of different forms of contact with the birth family. He pointed out that the design for such a study would need to produce evidence on the effect of contact itself while accounting for the many possible and confusing variables, and also include a prospective representative sample. He also noted that the views of adoptive parents and service providers had been much more frequently canvassed than the views of children or birth parents. There were gaps to be filled. He recommended planning longer-term prospective, longitudinal studies at that stage, to optimise all the activities generated by the Government's adoption agenda.[51]

A parliamentary committee was appointed to take evidence on the working of the 2002 Act from a range of individuals, groups and researchers.[52] It reported that no witnesses wanted large-scale legislative change. The major issues identified were delay and a shortage of adopters. However, the committee also recommended early intensive work with birth parents who have capacity to change. It found there was still variability in post-adoption support, and children felt they had not been listened to. It called for research on adoption breakdown, leading to the Selwyn studies.[53]

Nearly 10 years after the Rushton review, the *Adoption Research Initiative* was put in place to monitor and evaluate the implementation of the Act, following a new policy paper in 2012.[54] This comprised seven studies, some of which have been mentioned above. They were: Nina Biehal et al. comparing placement

---

50 J. Doughty, 'Care proceedings: is there a better way?' (2014) 26(2) *Child and Family Law Quarterly* 113–131.

51 A. Rushton, *The adoption of looked-after children*, Social Care Institute for Excellence Knowledge review 02, 2003, <http://www.scie.org.uk/publications/knowledgereviews/kr02.asp>.

52 House of Lords Select Committee on Adoption Legislation, above n. 28.

53 Selwyn et al., above n. 36.

54 Department for Education, above n. 15.

types; Harriet Ward on early decision-making on removal of children from birth parents; Elaine Farmer on family finding and matching; Julie Selwyn on planning and decision-making for black and ethnic minority children and (separately) on the inter-agency fee; Beth Neil on supporting birth parents and post-adoption support; and Alan Rushton on adoptive support programmes. They identified four common themes: permanence; family finding; adoption support overview; and contact. However, the Research Initiative noted some significant omissions, where studies had not been commissioned. First, unlike the 1990s research, systems were not covered, such as the role of independent reviewing officers in planning for permanence, preparation and assessment of adopters; and organisation of support services. Although research proposals had been received on these aspects, they had not been approved.[55] It was, however, ground-breaking in looking at the experiences of black and ethnic minority children and of birth parents. It also included the first study on special guardianship, which had been introduced in 2005. Thomas thought that there were two key limitations in the programme: only the Biehal study looked at long-term outcomes, and the children's perspective was missing.

5. CONCLUSION

This chapter has used five research reports as a framework to trace the development of adoption law and policy in the last 20 years. It may never be possible for research to provide the certainty that policy-makers and practitioners crave as an evidence base in making these difficult decisions.[56] But it remains essential that we do our best to inform ourselves by continuing to investigate what is measurable and that we listen to those people directly involved, both personally and professionally.

---

[55] C. Thomas, *Adoption for looked after children: messages from research*, BAAF, London 2013, p. 1.

[56] D. Quinton and J. Selwyn, 'Adoption: research, policy and practice' (2006) 18(4) *Child and Family Law Quarterly* 461–477.

PATHWAYS TO ADOPTION: FROM LONG AND WINDING ROAD TO OBSTACLE COURSE?

Judith MASSON

1. INTRODUCTION

In the late 1980s and 1990s, while he was Reader in Law at Bristol University and later as a Professor at Cardiff University, Nigel Lowe was a part of a research team which undertook three major studies on adoption.[1] The *Pathways to Adoption* study examined the operation of adoption law, highlighting the different routes to an adoption order and the time these took. It revealed a complex system and one with some very concerning features: there was 'avoidable delay'[2] and the process took too long for children; birth parents had no effective means of challenging adoption plans they objected to; and the legal process served adopters poorly.

The Adoption Act 1976 provided two pathways to adoption for children who could not be cared for in their families: an adoption agency could either apply

---

1 M. MURCH, N. LOWE, M. BORKOWSKI, R. COPNER and K. GRIEW, *Pathways to Adoption*, HMSO, London 1993; C. THOMAS, V. BECKFORD with M. MURCH and N. LOWE, *Adopted Children Speaking*, BAAF, London 1999; N. LOWE, M. MURCH, M. BORKOWSKI, A. WEAVER, V. BECKFORD and C. THOMAS, *Supporting Adoption: Reframing the Approach*, BAAF, London 1999.

2 R. PARKER, *Adoption Now – Messages from Research*, Wiley, Chichester 1999, p. 136.

to the court for an order to 'free for adoption' or place the child relying on the parents' agreement or a care order, which restricted the parents' right to remove their child. The freeing process also allowed parents, mainly single mothers, to give up their child quickly, before an adoption order could be made.[3] It also ensured that prospective adopters were protected from any challenge to their adoption, and that the reasonableness of the birth parents' refusal to consent was assessed without reference to the child's care in another family.

In practice, the pathways presented many difficulties. The time taken for the double process, freeing and adoption, was too long. Consequently, agencies continued to plan adoptions without freeing; in 1996, only 29 per cent of agency adoptions were preceded by a freeing order.[4] Without a freeing order, parents who opposed adoption were not pitted against the agency but against adopters, who had been assessed as suitable and were successfully caring for a child. The adopters were faced with presenting the case for dispensing with the parents' agreement but had no right of access to the agency's records.[5] Almost all orders were granted: whether this reflected agency decisions only to plan adoption where an order was certain, or a system unfairly skewed against birth parents' interests, was unclear.

This research contributed to the debates around adoption law which culminated in the Adoption and Children Act 2002. Adoption law was completely recast with the aim of producing a system which was fair to birth parents, protected adopters from the risk of contested adoption, and respected the rights of the three parties – parents, adopters and children. It also sought to achieve adoption more quickly, an aspect which grew in importance with evidence of the impact of delay on securing adoption[6] and the higher breakdown rates for late-placed children.[7]

This chapter examines the pathways to adoption laid by the 2002 Act. Focusing on the issues of fairness, risk and delay, it reviews current adoption law and practice. It concludes that new barriers, and attempts to surmount them, have produced a system that can operate unfairly against the interests of each of the parties to the adoption triangle, particularly the children, and remains prone to delay.

---

3 Report of the Departmental Committee on the Adoption of Children, (1972) Cmnd 5107.

4 G. Ivaldi, *Children Adopted from Care*, BAAF, London 1998.

5 M. Murch et al., above n. 1, p. 159.

6 J. Selwyn, W. Sturgess, D. Quinton and C. Baxter, *Costs and outcomes of non-infant adoptions*, BAAF, London 2006.

7 J. Selwyn, D. Wijedasa and S. Meakings, *Beyond the Adoption Order*, Department for Education, London 2014.

2. PLACEMENT ORDERS, REVOCATION OF PLACEMENT ORDERS, PLACEMENT AND ADOPTION

The Adoption and Children Act 2002 had four main aims: to simplify the adoption process; to require court approval of adoption plans and allow parents to challenge these before the process was initiated; to strengthen the focus on the child's welfare; and to avoid delay.[8] Local authorities planning adoption for children who have not been placed with them for adoption (relinquished) must obtain a placement order. Unless the child has no parent or guardian, the authority must establish that the child is suffering (or at risk of) significant harm, that making a placement order is in the child's best interests 'throughout his life'[9] and that there is no lesser intervention which meets this welfare interest.[10] Social workers and children's guardians are expected to explain the pros and cons of all 'realistic options' for a child in their care plan or assessment, and judges must similarly explain the reasons for the order they make.[11]

Examining the case for adoption before any steps are made towards placing the child is fair to parents (and relatives). Their capacity to meet the child's needs is assessed without reference to potential adopters; only their own suitability as the child's carers is in question. Children are exposed to various risks: a planned re-unification may fail, relatives may not provide a permanent home – these are inherent in any future-oriented process. The quality of decisions depends on the quality of evidence and assessments, and the abilities of those making them. A placement order is only a permission to place; there is a risk, particularly for older children, that no placement is found. Restricting the period for a search for adopters does not reduce this risk,[12] but the child's retention of the status of a child in care subject to regular reviews, and a duty on the local authority to apply to revoke the order where it is no longer in the child's interests, should do so.[13] Unlike children who were freed for adoption, those subject to placement orders are not in legal limbo[14] and remain in the care of the local authority.

Parents have further rights while their child is not yet placed for adoption. They can apply for leave to seek revocation of the placement order, but to obtain

---

8 *Re F (Placement Order)* [2008] EWCA Civ 439, [2008] 2 FLR 550 (CA), per Wall LJ, at para. 72.

9 Children and Adoption Act 2002, ss. 1(2) and 21(2), Children Act 1989, s. 31(2).

10 *Re B (A Child)* [2013] UKSC 33, *Re B-S (Children)* [2013] EWCA Civ 1146.

11 *Re B-S (Children)* [2013] EWCA Civ 1146, per Munby P at paras. 34–46.

12 Indeed, it may increase it. Although such limitations are sometimes included, there is no statutory power to add conditions to a placement order *Re A (Children)* [2013] EWCA Civ 1611.

13 Adoption and Children Act 2002, s. 24 and Adoption Agencies Regulations 2005, r. 36.

14 *A and S v Lancashire County Council* [2012] EWHC 1689 (Fam).

leave they must show a change of circumstances since the order was made.[15] This excludes simple attempts to retest the court's earlier decision. Fairness to parents justifies the possibility of their ending a placement plan before it has been implemented where they have improved their circumstances and it is in the child's best interests to do so. Once leave to seek revocation has been given, placement plans must be suspended unless the court grants the local authority permission to place the child.[16] It is not clear when (if ever) the court would be willing to do this; allowing a placement changes the welfare balance in the application and is unfair to the parents; refusing to do so delays the decisions for the child, risking the success of any placement (even re-unification) and their well-being.

In *Re F (Placement Order)*[17]the father failed to have his revocation application heard because the court delayed processing it and the child had been placed before leave could be granted. Consequently, it was refused; the father appealed, arguing that the restriction on placement should apply while an application was pending, to prevent a breach of his human rights. The majority of the Court of Appeal disagreed; if properly implemented, section 24 was Convention-compliant but all were highly critical of the local authority for placing the child after the father's solicitor had indicated the intention to apply for revocation. What the local authority had done was 'disgraceful, and must not be repeated'; there was no reason why judicial review should not be used to challenge such unlawful action.[18] Wall LJ set out how such situations should be handled. The father should seek an undertaking from the local authority not to place the child, and if this is not provided, apply for an injunction preventing the placement from the county court. If the local authority wanted to proceed with the placement in advance of the revocation hearing it could apply to the court for leave. Wilson LJ recognised that applications might be made merely to thwart placement arrangements and urged the development of good practice guidelines.[19] To ensure local authorities knew what it considered to be good practice, the Court of Appeal ordered wide circulation of the judgment. The Statutory Guidance now states, 'it is not appropriate for a local authority to proceed with the placement when it is aware of the application for leave … to do so … could be challenged by judicial review.'[20]

In *R (EL) v Essex County Council*[21] Charles J set out a 'duty of fairness', breach of which justified quashing the local authority's decision to place a child for

---

15 Children and Adoption Act 2002, s. 27(2), (3), *Re P* [2009] 2 FLR 1053 (CA).

16 Children and Adoption Act 2002, s. 24(5).

17 *Re F (Placement Order)* [2008] EWCA Civ 439 [2009] 2 FLR 550.

18 Per Wall LJ at paras. 93–94.

19 At paras. 113–115.

20 Department for Education, *Statutory Guidance on Adoption*, Department for Education, London 2014, para. 7.2.

21 *R (EL) v Essex County Council* [2017] EWHC 1041 (Admin).

adoption. It was not sufficient for the local authority merely to tell the mother that the child had been matched to prospective adopters because 'a race between an under-informed parent and an adoption agency is likely to be unfair.'[22] The local authority, giving the parent sufficient time to apply, had to tell the parent how to challenge the placement order and that it would proceed with its placement plan unless she obtained leave for a revocation application by a certain date.[23] The local authority's decision to bring forward the date of placement 'deliberately for welfare reasons' was unfair to the mother.

Placement is 'an emotional process,[24] involving introductions, meetings and temporary care which may extend over weeks.[25] The way this process is managed is very important in setting the foundation for the child's attachment to the adopters, long-term well-being and the success of the placement.[26] However, these court decisions treat placement as an event which occurs only when the child moves to the prospective adopters' home. Before that time parents who obtain leave to revoke can interrupt the process, which can then only continue with leave of the court. The child might be able to move to the prospective adopters' home as a foster child but it is easy to see that this too would be considered unfair to the parents.[27] Allowing the parents a second (or third)[28] opportunity to challenge the adoption plan once introductions have started is unfair to both the child and the prospective adopters. Treating placement as a process, and precluding any challenge from the beginning of the introductions would be fairer to all parties. Parents would still be able to seek revocation before the placement, and if the child did not remain with the prospective adopters, could make an application subsequently.

The final stage of the process is adoption, which requires a court order. The proposal in *Pathways to Adoption* that uncomplicated adoptions should be completed simply by registration was rejected on the basis that these could not be readily identified.[29] Adoptions require the parent's consent but the court may dispense with this at either the placement order or adoption stage where 'the welfare of the child requires' this.[30] A parent can oppose adoption where a

---

22 *R (EL) v Essex CC* at para. 49.
23 *R (EL) v Essex CC* at paras. 48, 60–61.
24 *R (EL) v Essex CC* at para. 40(i).
25 J. Selwyn et al., above n. 7, p. 125.
26 Family Futures, *Planning Transitions for Children Moving to Permanent Placement*, 2009, available at https://www.familyfutures.co.uk/wp-content/uploads/2015/06/Transitions-Practice-Paper.pdf>.
27 In *R (EL) v Essex CC* [2017] EWHC 1041 (Admin) this was permitted because the placement had been made. The court may well take a different view where leave for revocation was granted during the introductions.
28 Parents can argue against the order in the placement proceedings and appeal the decision (with leave) and seek revocation.
29 Above n. 1, p. 245.
30 Adoption and Children Act 2002, s. 52(1)(b).

placement order has been made or they have withdrawn their consent, but only with leave of the court.[31]

3. FOSTERING FOR ADOPTION AND ADOPTION BY FOSTER CARERS

Despite the Act, some children are placed without a placement order and adopted by their carers. Concurrent planning services recruit foster carers who support re-unification with parents but will adopt the child if this is not possible. These arrangements are agreed with parents, who accept that, if they cannot care themselves, a carer with an established relationship with their baby is best. Concurrent planning is a high risk and emotionally demanding endeavour for both carers and parents but reduces risks to babies of multiple placements, and gives adopters the opportunity to care for a child from early infancy. In practice, these services are available to few families, and few parents regain care of their child.[32] Concurrent planning is fair so long as parents and carers fully understand the arrangement, and parents are properly supported to maximise their chances of re-unification.

Concern to achieve 'early permanency' for children outside concurrent planning projects led to the introduction of 'fostering for adoption' (FfA).[33] This allows local authorities to place children in their care[34] for whom they are planning adoption, with prospective adopters who are also approved to foster. These placements can be made before the mother's consent can legally be given[35] and before a care plan for adoption is approved by the court. 'Placing children with foster carers who could become their adoptive parents offers many benefits to the child; it is the adults taking the risk that the placement will not be permanent.'[36] There is added risk if the arrangement places the parents and carers in direct conflict or leads courts to favour plans for adoption which they would not otherwise approve.[37] However, the decision in *Re T (Early Permanence Placement)*[38] makes it clear that the court's role remains determining

---

31 Adoption and Children Act 2002, s. 47(2), (5).

32 S. Laws, R. Wilson and S. Rabindrakumar, *Concurrent Planning Study Interim Report*, Coram, London 2012, available at <http://bit.ly/2urxHOl>.

33 Children and Families Act 2014, amending Children Act 1989, s. 22C; Department For Education, *Early Permanence Placements and Approval of Prospective Adopters as Foster Carers*, Department for Education, London 2014.

34 Including children looked after under Children Act 1989, s. 20: see C. Lynch, *Co-operation or Coercion?* Family Rights Group, London 2017.

35 When the child is six weeks old, Adoption and Children Act 2002, s. 52(3).

36 Department for Education, above n. 33, para. 14.

37 The strictures of the Supreme Court in *Re B (A Child)* [2013] UKSC 33, and the Court of Appeal in *Re B-S* [2013] EWCA Civ 1146 substantially reduce this risk.

38 *Re T (Early Permanence Placement)* [2015] EWCA Civ 983.

the principle of adoption for the child. The Court of Appeal overturned a decision to make the prospective adopters parties to care proceedings so they could argue against a plan to place a baby with his paternal grandparents. This risked diverting the court's attention from the principle of placement outside the family to a dispute between individuals.[39] Clearly, the risks of early permanence lie with the carers, not the parents; only those who can manage the potential return of the child to birth parents or other carers should be accepted for fostering to adopt.

During the first two years of its operation substantial use was made of fostering for adoption, with nearly 600 children placed in this way.[40] It is likely that many of these children were placed with carers who were already caring for their sibling. For these children, alternative adopters who might be a better match for the child are unlikely to be found. However, the fact that an older sibling required adoption does not mean this will be true for a younger one; parents do turn their lives around and the circumstance of relatives who were previously unable to offer care, can change.

Children who are not subject to a placement order and whose parents have not relinquished them for adoption may be adopted by foster carers who have cared for them for at least 12 months. Such adoptions are relatively rare: only just over 100 children are adopted without being subject to a placement order, or relinquished for adoption. Half of these children are over the age of 10 years and have been in care since early childhood;[41] for these children, adoption recognises their full membership of the family they live with. The risk to parents of losing a child in foster care through adoption is tiny; there is a far greater risk that a childhood in foster care will leave children with no permanent family.

As with other adoptions parental consent is necessary; consent can only be dispensed with where the Act allows.[42] These cases raise issues of comparing the merits of alternative carers, which the court avoided in *Re T*. Such decisions are made giving paramount consideration to the 'child's welfare throughout his life',[43] not fairness to the adults involved.

In *Re W*[44] a girl aged four-and-a-half years had originally been placed with a placement order, which was later revoked. After she had lived with the prospective adopters for more than three years, the court was faced with the stark choice between granting their adoption application or returning her to her

39 *Re T* [2015] EWCA Civ 983, at para. 53.
40 C. Lynch, above n. 34, p. 47. Over the same period nearly 10,000 children were adopted from care in England.
41 Department for Education, *Children Looked After National Tables*, SFR34, Department for Education, London 2015, Table E1.
42 Adoption and Children Act 2002, s. 52(1), and see above n. 30 and accompanying text.
43 Adoption and Children Act 2002, s. 1(2).
44 *Re W (A Child)* [2017] EWHC 829 (Fam).

father, with whom she had not lived since she was six weeks old. Both possible care arrangements involved risks to the child: adoption brought risks associated with not growing up in the biological family, and of adoption breakdown; return to her father carried the risks of breaking her attachments to her carers, the loss of the only family she had ever known and inability to establish new attachments, with negative effects for her emotional well-being.[45] Munby P accepted that the child's welfare was determinative.[46] To allow arguments about fairness to the father to be considered 'offends against the statutory principles and runs the risk of the welfare analysis being skewed and diverted from … its paramount focus.'[47] He accepted that the risks arising from removing the girl from the prospective adopters were more serious and more likely to occur, and made the adoption order. The longer the child spends with carers who seek adoption, and the more limited the contact with members of the birth family, the harder it is for a parent to make a case against adoption. Although parents can put the issue of contact to the court,[48] the timing of the adoption application is a matter for the prospective adopters.

4. RELINQUISHMENT

Relinquishment is the term used where parents ask an adoption agency to arrange their child's adoption. Such placements are sometimes referred to as 'voluntary' but the history of past practice reveals the pressures from family and society on parents to do this.[49] Far fewer babies are relinquished now[50] but women may still feel they must take this course. Attitudes to sex outside marriage, single parenthood and abortion continue to influence women's decisions, as does poverty and (lack of) access to abortion services; for some, adoption provides the only option for controlling their future.[51]

Parents may 'choose' to relinquish a child but may not be able reclaim the child to prevent adoption if they have a change of heart. Is this fair to them? Is it

---

45 Substantial expert evidence was given on all these points in the hearing.

46 An earlier decision in this case *Re W (Adoption Application: Reunification with Family of Origin)* [2015] EWHC 2039 (Fam), reached the opposite conclusion but was overturned on appeal, *Re H (A Child) (Appeal)* [2015] EWCA Civ 1284, [2016] 2 FLR 1173, because (inter alia) the judge misunderstood the expert's evidence on risk.

47 *Re W (A Child)* [2017] EWHC 829 (Fam), para. 89.

48 Children Act 1989, s. 34; Adoption and Children Act 2002, s. 26 only applies where there is a placement order.

49 D. Howe, P. Sawbridge and D. Hinnings, *Half a Million Women*, Penguin Books, London 1992.

50 In 2015–16, 130 children were adopted from care who were not subject to a care or placement order, Department for Education, *Children Looked After in England (Including Adoption) Year Ending 31 March 2016*, SFR41/16, Department for Education, London 2017, Table E1.

51 *A Local Authority v The Mother and Another* [2017] EWHC 1515 (Fam).

fair to their child? This must turn on: the information and counselling provided for parents; when in the adoption process the change is made; the circumstances in which agencies decide to pursue adoption; and the opportunities for parents to challenge decisions. These are all matters determined by statute, regulations and statutory guidance. 'The paramount consideration of the adoption agency must be the child's welfare throughout his life.'[52] If it wishes to continue with the adoption, the adoption agency must seek a placement order from the court;[53] only if the court accepts that a placement order would be proportionate can the adoption process continue.[54] Parents opposing placement proceedings need legal representation; currently (and unfairly) access to legal aid is more restrictive in these proceedings than in care proceedings.[55]

The degree of control a woman has over deciding to place her child for adoption can give rise to questions of fairness to the child, the father and the child's wider family. The child's access to information about his or her biological family and opportunities for placement within that family are dependent on the mother providing that information to the adoption agency. Adoption Agencies are required, 'so far as is reasonably practicable' to ascertain the wishes and feelings about the child's placement for adoption of the child's parents and 'any other person the agency considers relevant'.[56] They must also provide information and counselling, and where the agency knows the father's identity, this duty extends to fathers without parental responsibility (whose consent to the adoption is not required).[57] So once the mother identifies the father to the agency she risks the fact of her pregnancy and her plans for the child becoming known.

Statutory Guidance for adoption agencies advises, 'where it is in the child's best interests they must take all reasonable steps to trace and counsel the child's father, if his identity is known.'[58] Good practice guidance advises mothers that the father may seek parental responsibility, and of the limits on the secrecy of adoption.[59] Consequently, a mother cannot keep her plans confidential without limiting the information she provides to the agency. The courts have accepted they have 'no power to compel' mothers to provide information, and recognised

---

52 Adoption and Children Act 2002, s. 1(2).

53 Adoption Agencies Regulations 2005, reg. 38(1); Adoption and Children Act 2002, ss. 31, 32.

54 The tests in *Re B (A Child)* [2013] UKSC 33 and *Re B-S* [2013] EWCA Civ 1146 should apply to what has become a non-consenual adoption plan.

55 Only means and merits-tested is available but the children's minister has announced reform, see <http://bit.ly/2lWswD7>. However, changes have not yet been made to legal aid.

56 Adoption Agencies Regulations 2005 (2005 S.I. No. 389), reg. 14(1)(c).

57 Adoption Agencies Regulations 2005, reg. 14(3), (4).

58 Department for Education, above n. 20, para. 1.24.

59 CAFCASS and ADCS, *Good Practice Guidance for Adoption Agencies and Cafcass: Children Relinquished for Adoption* 2013. This document no longer appears on the ADCS website but remains on the cafcass policy website and can be accessed at <http://bit.ly/2I2WAb9> accessed 04.03.2018.

'a strong social need … to enable some mothers … to make discreet, dignified and humane arrangements for the birth and subsequent adoption of their babies, without their families knowing anything about it'.[60] However, Sloan argues that allowing adoption where care by the child's father or wider family might have been possible offends against the child's rights under the UN Convention on the Rights of the Child, Article 21.[61]

In *Re RA (Baby Relinquished for Adoption)*[62] the Latvian parents, who had lived and worked in England for many years, contacted the local authority seeking an adoption placement for the baby the mother was expecting and stating they did not want their family in Latvia to be told, or for the child to be placed there. After the local authority had approved the adoption plan and placed the child, it contacted the Latvian authorities, who traced and informed the grandmother. This action, which was not required by either domestic or international law was contrary to the parents' wishes. The grandmother offered to care and was assessed as suitable by the Latvian authorities. At a case management hearing in the adoption proceedings, the Cafcass children's guardian argued for a full assessment of the grandmother. The Latvian Central Authority indicated that they opposed adoption of their citizens in the UK, asserting the baby's right to maintain his Latvian identity. Cobb J ordered a full assessment of the grandparents and advised local authorities to seek the court's guidance about the enquiries they should make; the risk that this would add complications to straightforward cases was 'small but acceptable'.[63]

Even though the court is not required to establish whether there are other options for the child's care,[64] parents can only determine the enquiries the agency makes by withholding information. In fairness to those who wish to maintain their confidentiality but provide their child with a family history, parents should have control over the enquiries made.

5. CHALLENGING ADOPTION ORDERS

The scheme in the Adoption and Children Act 2002 gives parents multiple opportunities to challenge adoption plans. They can contest a plan for a

60 *Z County Council v R* [2001] 1 FLR 365, 366–367, per Holman J.

61 B. Sloan, 'Conflicting Rights: English Adoption Law and the Implementation of the Convention on the Rights of the Child' (2013) 25 *Child and Family Law Quarterly* 40, 58.

62 *Re RA (Baby Relinquished for Adoption)* [2016] EWFC 47.

63 *Re RA (Baby Relinquished for Adoption Case Management)* [2016] EWFC 25, per Cobb J at para. 51. An adoption order was finally made. It appears that withholding information is the only option for parents who do not want their family involved.

64 *Re JL and AO* [2016] EWHC 440 (Fam), per Baker J at para. 92(2) cf. *Re RA (Baby Relinquished for Adoption Case Management)* [2016] EWFC 25, per Cobb J at para. 50.

placement order; seek leave to appeal the order made; if they can show a change of circumstances, seek revocation of the placement order; seek leave to appeal refusal to revoke the placement order; if they can show a change of circumstances, seek to oppose the adoption; and appeal the adoption order. There are short time-limits for appeals but the court has ruled that permission for appeals out of time should be considered.[65] Whilst it is exceptional for parents to attempt to use all these opportunities, repeated challenges occur.[66] Most such cases reflect parents' determination to oppose and the design of the system, rather than uncertainty about children's needs or parenting capacity. It is at least arguable that allowing so many routes for challenge is unfair to all the parties involved: the birth parents, the child and the prospective adopters.

For parents, unfairness occurs because routes for challenge are not and cannot provide realistic opportunities to regain care of their child so long as decisions are (rightly) determined by the child's best interests. This is compounded by the notification of the date of the adoption hearing, which is easily misinterpreted as offering an opportunity to oppose the adoption.[67] The aim of adoption is developmental recovery'[68] for children who have suffered or been put at risk of significant harm before or after their birth, it is to be hoped that this starts at placement. The possibility of reclaiming a child naturally diminishes as the relationship with the parent weakens and that with the prospective adopters develops. A liberal approach to assessing changes in the parents' circumstances and granting leave to oppose gives false hope; successful challenge is very exceptional once a child has been placed.

Although the Court of Appeal acknowledged in *Re W* that adoptions will 'only in exceptionally rare circumstances' be prevented by parents opposing at the adoption order hearing,[69] subsequently, in *Re B-S*, it rejected that approach as too harsh and one that might make the possibility of challenge at this stage 'illusory'.[70] However, the fundamental issue for parents remains establishing that return to their care rather than a long-planned adoption will be in the child's best interests. The court's more liberal approach is likely only to increase the number of unsuccessful challenges and disappointed parents.[71] Even where

---

65 *Re H* [2015] EWCA Civ 583. This case finally ended in an adoption order, *Re W (A Child)* [2017] EWHC 829 (Fam).

66 B. Lucknock and K. Broadhurst, *Adoption Cases Reviewed: An Indicative Study of Practice and Process*, DFE-RR270, Department for Education, London 2013.

67 The right to be heard, FPR 2010, r. 14.15 does not include a right to oppose, which requires leave.

68 D. Quinton, *Rethinking matching in adoptions from care: A conceptual and research review*, BAAF, London 2012.

69 *Re W (Adoption Order: Set Aside and Leave to Oppose)* [2010] EWCA Civ 1535, per Thorpe LJ at para. 17.

70 *Re B-S* [2013] EWCA Civ 1146, per Munby P at paras. 68–72.

71 J. Masson, 'The quality of care proceedings reform' (2014) 36 *Journal of Social Welfare and Family Law* 82.

parents have made substantial improvements to their lives the risk to the child of breaking established relationships remains.[72] Where children have experienced substantial disruption before the adoptive placement, even a relatively short period with the adopters can make return to the parents too risky.[73]

Children unfairly carry the risks of all decisions, and of the reviews of those decisions. Apart from the risk that the wrong decision will be made, which cannot be eliminated, there are risks that delays arising from the review processes will prolong the period of uncertainty for the child, make the transition to an adoptive family more difficult, or even remove opportunities for adoption due to the child's increased age. Indeed, some adoption plans appear to have been challenged largely with the aim of preventing adoption, through delay.[74] Judges, who are generally alert to the injustice of allowing decisions about children to be made through the passage of time, appear to take little account of this when considering parental challenges or ordering re-hearings. More account should be taken of the real consequences for children than of supposed risks that a positive experience of childhood may in future become tainted by knowledge that the adoption process might have worked differently.[75]

The 2002 legislation intended to separate the approval of the adoption plan from the making of the adoption order, and so protect both parents and adopters. Prospective adopters are insulated from challenges at the early stages of adoption except where introductions are interrupted by a placement order revocation application,[76] but allowing parents to oppose adoption places the two families in direct conflict. In *Re B-S*, Munby P minimised the stressful effect on adopters and children of allowing parents to contest the adoption and warned judges against giving too much weight to it. The adopters' expectation of a smooth process will already have been disturbed by the application for leave, and 'firm case management' could ensure parental opposition did not delay the process.[77] This in no way recognises the profoundly upsetting effect of replacing an expected formality with a contested hearing.

When Parliament allowed for parental opposition at the final stage of adoption it cannot have intended to undermine a fundamental principle of the Act. All parties are harmed by challenges that can only reverse an adoption

---

72 This is the main welfare point in *Re SR* [2014] EWHC 1777 and *Re W (A Child)* [2017] EWHC 829 (Fam).

73 *Re AW* [2013] EWHC 2967 (Fam). In this case deception by the parents also raised questions about the extent to which the parents had changed.

74 For example, *Prospective Adopters v IA and Others* [2014] EWHC 331 (Fam) see also B. Lucknock and K. Broadhurst, above n. 66 and Wilson LJ's judgment in *Re W*, above n. 69.

75 The argument put on behalf of the father in *Re W (A Child)* [2017] EWHC 829 (Fam) at para. 189 ff. and *Re W (Adoption Application: Reunification with Family of Origin)* [2015] EWHC 2039 (Fam), per Russell J at para. 85.

76 *Re F* [2009] 2 FLR 550.

77 *Re B-S* [2013] EWCA Civ 1146 at para. 74 (ix).

process in the most exceptional circumstances. It is unfair to pretend otherwise, and for the courts to allow challenges which can only fail. Within a context where almost all adoption plans need court approval at the start, leave to oppose or appeal should be approached restrictively, considering whether the appellant has a realistic chance of achieving their ultimate goal, re-unification, not simply overturning the decision. Of course, this is not the current law, but it recognises that legal processes can harm and that no remedy is possible once facts have changed.

6. DELAY

Delay has been endemic in the child welfare system, with care proceedings averaging over 60 weeks in 2011.[78] Attempts to speed up the adoption process have included removing the role of adoption panels before placement orders are sought, monitoring the timeliness of local authority adoption practices and, most recently, imposing a 26-week time-frame for care proceedings.[79] Formally, the 26-week limit does not apply to decisions about adoption but most placement orders are made within care proceedings so they are affected by this constraint. Cutting the length of care proceedings has reduced the average time to complete adoptions.[80]

In the case of adoption plans, concerns about delay have been replaced by anxiety that the process is now too speedy, particularly in ruling out parents and kin. However, this appears to assume that local authority involvement starts when cases are brought to court, which is true for only a tiny minority. In the vast majority of families subject to care proceedings, social workers have been attempting to work to improve care and avoid proceedings for months.[81] Concerns about rushing to judgment may account for the spate of Court of Appeal decisions requiring clearer reasoning in care proceedings, allowing appeals to be made out of time and taking a more liberal approach to leave to oppose since 2013.[82] There also appear to be more cases where local authorities only succeed in having adoption plans accepted and obtaining a placement order after a second set of care proceedings.[83]

---

78 Family Justice Review, *Final Report*, Ministry of Justice, London 2011, p. 3.

79 Children and Families Act 2014, s. 14.

80 Adoption Leadership Board, *What Does Our Data Tell Us About What Is Happening In the Adoption System?* Adoption Leadership Board, London 2017.

81 J. Masson, J. Pearce and K. Bader, *Care Profiling Study*, Ministry of Justice Research Series 04/08, London 2008 <http://www.bristol.ac.uk/media-library/sites/law/migrated/documents/care-profiling-study-report.pdf> accessed 11.08.2017.

82 *Re B-S* [2013] EWCA Civ 1146, *Re H* [2015] EWCA Civ 583.

83 Observation from the data in the Outcomes for Children Before and After Care Proceedings Reform Study ESRC ES/M008541/1.

It is also clear that the discipline of 26 weeks is not applied to the process of considering appeals. Although the Court of Appeal continues to give priority to children cases and many appeals from the Family Court are now routed to the High Court, timeliness in the Court of Appeal remains very important for care and adoption cases heard by circuit judges and recorders.[84] Speedy decisions are particularly important where the case may have to be remitted for re-hearing. Data is not published for the length of court processes relating to adoption, or for appeals, so it is only possible to identify timelines where cases are reported and dates are given.

Appeals are not the only source of delay: listing difficulties (which are exacerbated by cases which require multiple hearings) and delays in the production of judgments have all contributed to the time parents, children and adopters have had to wait. For example, *SR* was removed under an emergency protection order in August 2011 but not made subject to a placement order until October 2012. She was placed for adoption the following month but the final adoption order was only made in April 2014.[85] *W*'s adoption was even longer drawn out, from her removal from her father at the age of six weeks at the end of 2012, her placement in January 2014 to the making of the adoption order in April 2017. As well as two separate appeals to the Court of Appeal, *W*'s parents and prospective adopters had to wait more than five months for the judgment.[86] A process which takes this long is not fit for its purpose of setting the course for the upbringing of very young infants.

7. CONCLUSION

Reform did not produce consensus about the use of adoption. Non-consensual adoption remains a highly controversial practice, not because of the outcomes achieved for children but because it prioritises the state's view of how children should be raised over the parents', irrevocably cuts legal ties to the birth family, and largely impacts on the most disadvantaged parents in society. Whilst there is near universal acceptance of the right to 'special protection' for children who cannot remain in their family in their own best interests,[87] there is far less willingness to accept that this should be done by a permanent arrangement, changing the child's legal identity, made without the parents' agreement.

For some of those involved, adoption remains an obstacle course but it is less clear than it was in the *Pathways to Adoption* study which children and

84 Practice Direction 30A Appeals, 06.04.2017.

85 *Re SR* [2014] EWHC 1777 (Fam). The Court of Appeal found fault with the judge's reasoning, *Re W* [2013] EWCA Civ 1177.

86 *Re W (A Child)* [2017] EWHC 829 (Fam), and see text accompanying above n. 44.

87 United Nations Convention on the Rights of the Child, Art. 20.

which prospective adopters might face this. Although placement without court approval may appear more risky because the court may not make a placement order, these orders do not guarantee a clear route to adoption. A small (but unknown) number of children and prospective adopters experience stressful delays and uncertainty in a process which holds out false hope to parents of reclaiming children who have already been placed. It is hard to avoid one of the conclusions of the study, that the adoption process is too elaborate. However, Lowe and his colleagues' view that separating adoption services from local authorities 'might help convert … a "last battle" into a new positive beginning for the child' seems overly optimistic. Whilst the function of adoption remains contentious there is unlikely to be agreement about the process.

CHILD ABUSE AND PUBLIC INQUIRY METHODOLOGIES

Trevor Buck

1. INTRODUCTION

Over the last 45 years, from the Maria Colwell inquiry to the current ongoing Independent Inquiry into Child Sexual Abuse (IICSA), public inquiries have assisted in the complex task of investigating and reporting on particular community and institutional cases of child abuse. They have contributed much to an increased public awareness of the nature and need for effective child protection services. But the record of public inquiries in this area is troublesome. Some commentators have pointed out the damaging effect that they can have on the social work and other caring professions engaged in this challenging work. Criticisms are also raised in relation to the poor implementation of inquiry recommendations and the delays and costs of inquiry processes. Above all, over the years, a consensus appears to have emerged that many of the 'lessons learned' have not been actioned, either at all or sufficiently. There have been repeated observations in inquiry reports of identical failings and weaknesses in child protection work that just seem to continue in the narratives from one inquiry to the next.

This chapter reviews the changing policy context and methodologies employed by public inquiries in this field and raises two important propositions for further consideration: first, that the ongoing IICSA inquiry provides an unprecedented opportunity to capture and disseminate fully and more deeply the emerging knowledge of the nature and impact of child abuse; secondly, that there is now a significant need to establish a permanent centralised unit in the UK – a Public Inquiries Office – as an independent non-departmental public body to support and maintain public inquiries in the child protection sector, and elsewhere.

2. THE DEVELOPMENT OF PUBLIC INQUIRIES INTO CHILD ABUSE

Both the number and scope of public inquiries that have examined the phenomenon of child abuse have increased since the landmark Maria Colwell inquiry.[1] If one counts the main forms of statutory and non-statutory inquiries, there have been around 80 such inquiries[2] since Colwell.

Although there had been some inquiries into child abuse issues before,[3] the Colwell inquiry did much to sensitise the public and professionals to the emerging and extensive problem of physical cruelty and neglect experienced by some children living in the community with parents and other carers. It also provided, arguably, a revision of society's assumptions about the 'blood tie' between children and their natural parents.[4] Growing public concern underlined the need to establish formal mechanisms of inter-professional collaboration to gain a holistic view of children's welfare. As with subsequent inquiries, Colwell was used as a government tool for policy change, prompted by pressure from families, politicians and the media.[5] This inquiry was followed, as have been several others, by changes in legislation.[6] Public pressure led to professionals' greater readiness to intervene and challenge parental authority.[7] Parton argued

1. T.G. Field-Fisher *Report of the Committee of Inquiry into the Care and Supervision Provided by Local Authorities and Other Agencies in Relation to Maria Colwell and the Co-Ordination between Them* (Chairman: T.G. Field-Fisher) HMSO, London 1974.
2. See House of Commons Health Committee, *The Victoria Climbié Inquiry Report*, Sixth Report of Session 2002–03, HC 570, 05.06.2003, p. 5, para. 7, and n. 60 below, Appendices 4 and 5.
3. See Home Office, *Report by Sir William Monckton KCMG KCVO MC KC on the circumstances which led to the boarding out of Dennis and Terence O'Neill at Bank Farm, Minsterly and the steps taken to supervise their welfare, etc*, (1945) Cmd 6636, Home Office, London. The Monckton report prompted reforms in the Children Act 1948 which shaped children's services in the post-war era.
4. P. Reder and S. Duncan, 'Making the most of the Victoria Climbié Inquiry Report' (2004) 3(3) *Child Abuse Review* 95, 96.
5. B. Corby, A. Doig and V. Roberts, 'Inquiries into child abuse' (1998) 20(4) *Journal of Social Welfare and Family Law* 377, 382.
6. Children Act 1975.
7. E. Munro, 'The impact of child abuse inquiries since 1990' in N. Stanley and J. Manthorpe (eds.), *The Age of Inquiry: Learning and Blaming in Health and Social Care*, Routledge, London 2004, pp. 75–91, 78.

that a dominant 'legalism' had appeared in the public discourse to explain the failures in child welfare.[8]

The Cleveland inquiry in 1988[9] provided public exposure of the emerging problem of, specifically, child sexual abuse. While Colwell and other inquiries had highlighted the failure of social workers and other professionals to intervene sufficiently, Cleveland emphasised the dangers of precipitate state intervention. The subsequent Children Act 1989 sought to rebalance the state's relationship with parental authority by circumscribing clearer boundaries to professional intervention. It was therefore unsurprising that the social work profession responded defensively in order to navigate the increasingly narrow territory perceived between over-zealous interventions in family life on the one hand, and over-cautious reticence to intervene on the other. More resources were allocated to increasing the accuracy of professional child assessments, to the detriment of funding other areas of child welfare.[10]

After Cleveland it seemed settled that such public inquiries would set, or reset, policy in this field, though some commentators noticed then that 'their defects have been overlooked.'[11] Hill pointed out some of the negative consequences of inquiries as a social mechanism for improving child protection, including their legalism, a model that would fail to analyse causes sufficiently. Further, he argued that the focus on the immediately precipitating events of an inquiry tended to distract from wider environmental and structural influences, and this in turn might reinforce individual pathological explanations for child abuse. Hill concluded that inquiries had had a disproportionate influence on setting the broad policy framework, which sometimes ran counter to basic principles of providing an integrated generic service for all stages of the life course.[12]

The arrival of a series of research projects into the child protection system in 1995[13] initiated the so-called 'refocusing debate'. The argument was that the professional attention given to preventing a child's death was limiting their resources to support families as a whole. It was concluded that there was a 'bias in service towards assessment rather than prevention and treatment'.[14] Thus there was a perceived need to refocus government policy from child protection to family support. While this was clearly not intended to produce binary and

8 N. Parton, 'Public Inquiries, Legalism and Child Care in England and Wales' (1989) 3(1) *International Journal of Law, Policy and the Family* 21, 32.

9 E. Butler-Sloss *Report of the inquiry into child abuse in Cleveland 1987* (1988) Cm 412, HMSO, London.

10 E. Munro, above n. 7, p. 89.

11 M. Hill, 'The Manifest and Latent Lessons of Child Abuse Inquiries' (1990) 20(3) *British Journal of Social Work* 197, 203.

12 Ibid., p. 210.

13 Department of Health, *Child Protection: Messages from Research*, HMSO, London 1995.

14 Ibid., p. 48.

mutually exclusive options, it did refocus professional attention from children at high risk to the assessment of all children in need. Reder and Duncan commented that, '[w]hile there was never an overt instruction for social services to refocus their work away from investigation, it is common knowledge that they understood that this was expected of them'.[15]

The 1990s also witnessed a shift in reliance on full public inquiries to 'Part 8 reviews'[16] of child death cases which could be conducted with greater privacy. Indeed, the perceived lack of value in child abuse inquiries was arguably the main reason why the Department of Health had introduced this procedure.[17] The policy refocus on family support also provided a suitable background for the development of more robust and early interventionist strategies, e.g. 'Sure Start',[18] which were introduced by the Labour government from 1997 to 2010.

The Climbié inquiry of 2003[19] refuelled concerns about child protection services generally. Lord Laming's report presented a picture of these services simply failing to safeguard children at a basic level, a lack of accountability, and failures in inter-agency working. It emphasised the need for a much clearer management grip on the assessment process, and provided credence for placing the protection of children at risk at the top of the hierarchy of social services priorities. The Laming recommendations prompted *Every Child Matters*[20] and the Children Act 2004, which established a fully accountable role of Director of Children's Services and local safeguarding children's boards, and highlighted the crucial role of information sharing as a means of child protection. Section 11 of the 2004 Act requires agencies to collect a very wide range of information about children's lives. The 2004 Act also harmonised with the then government's justifications for greater surveillance of the population, which some argue has struck the wrong balance between state power and private family life.[21]

---

15 P. Reder and S. Duncan, above n. 4, p. 104.

16 Later renamed 'serious case reviews' and 'child death reviews'. The current guidance is, HM Government, *Working together to safeguard children A guide to inter-agency working to safeguard and promote the welfare of children*, HMSO, London March 2015, pp. 72–91. For publications of case reviews, see <https://www.nspcc.org.uk/preventing-abuse/child-protection-system/case-reviews/>.

17 B. Corby, 'The costs and benefits of the North Wales Tribunal of Inquiry' in N. Stanley and J. Manthorpe (eds.), *The age of inquiry: learning and blaming in health and social care*, Routledge, London 2004, pp. 116–129, 117.

18 N. Glass, 'Sure Start: The Development of an Early Intervention Programme for Young Children in the United Kingdom' (1999) 13 *Children & Society* 257–264.

19 W.H. Laming, *The Victoria Climbié Inquiry: Report of an Inquiry by Lord Laming*, (2003) Cmnd 5730, The Stationary Office, London.

20 Chief Secretary to the Treasury, *Every Child Matters*, (2003) Cm 5860, The Stationary Office, London September 2003.

21 L. Devine, *The Limits of State Power & Private Rights: Exploring Child Protection & Safeguarding Referrals and Assessments*, Routledge, London 2017.

The emerging societal consciousness emanating from these public inquiries broadly describes an arc of increased awareness: from physical to sexual and emotional exploitation in the family home followed by increasing public concern with cases of abuse arising in 'institutional' settings. Clearly, this was not an entirely linear development. Previous criticisms of inquiries into child abuse in the community were that contexts, management and resources were frequently overlooked, but arguably this did not apply where the inquiry's terms of reference addressed the breadth and depth of an institutional setting such as children's homes. Public concern in relation to various children's homes around the country led to the establishment of a landmark inquiry set up under the Tribunal of Inquiry (Evidence) Act 1921 into certain children's homes in North Wales.[22] As with most of the previous inquiries, its principal impact provided further additions to the legal structure in the form of an independent children's champion for Wales.[23]

The arrival of IICSA in 2015, however, addressed very directly public concern about child abuse in a wide range of institutional settings. The inquiry has a very wide remit:

> To consider the extent to which State and non-State institutions have failed in their duty of care to protect children from sexual abuse and exploitation; to consider the extent to which those failings have since been addressed; to identify further action needed to address any failings identified; to consider the steps which it is necessary for State and non-State institutions to take in order to protect children from such abuse in future; and to publish a report with recommendations.[24]

3. INQUIRIES: POLICY PROCESSES AND METHODS

Alongside the policy developments in child protection services prompted by public inquiries, the nature of the inquiry process itself, deployed across various sectors, also came under scrutiny. Prior to the Inquiries Act 2005, the favoured model of inquiry was that established under the Tribunals of Inquiry (Evidence) Act 1921. In addition, there were over 30 other legislative provisions that authorised the establishment of a public inquiry; for example,

---

22 Department of Health, *Lost in Care: Report of the Tribunal of Inquiry into the Abuse of Children in Care in the Former County Council Areas of Gwynedd and Clwyd since 1974*, The Stationary Office, London 2000. See also B. Corby, 'The costs and benefits of the North Wales Tribunal of Inquiry' in N. Stanley and J. Manthorpe (eds.), *The Age of Inquiry: Learning and Blaming in Health and Social Care*, Routledge, London 2004, pp. 116–129.

23 Children's Commissioner for Wales Act 2001.

24 IICSA website: <https://www.iicsa.org.uk/terms-reference>.

the Climbié inquiry was established under three separate statutory powers.[25] There were, and remain, two principal models of public inquiry: statutory and non-statutory inquiries. The key differences are: that statutory inquiries provide powers to subpoena witnesses, administer oaths and order disclosure of documents, and operate under a presumption that hearings will take place in public; whereas non-statutory inquiries are reliant on the voluntary compliance of witnesses, they cannot take evidence on oath and there is no presumption of public access.

The Tribunals of Inquiry (Evidence) Act 1921 and the various bespoke legislative provisions were repealed by the Inquiries Act 2005, ostensibly to provide a new coherence to public inquiry activity. To a certain extent, the Inquiries Act 2005 was a robust answer to the criticisms raised in relation to the Saville (Bloody Sunday) Inquiry (1998–2010)[26] that it was, in effect, making judicial decisions, and was taking too long and was too costly. Another driver for reform was the Public Administration Select Committee (PASC) of the House of Commons which was also expressing interest in the subject. PASC had undertaken a 'Government by Inquiry' investigation in 2004 which triggered a government consultation 'Effective Inquiries'.[27] The Inquiries Act 2005 laid down all the key stages of the inquiry process from its establishment, the appointment of the chair and other panel members, the shape of evidential and other procedural rules, through to the submission of the inquiry report. In doing this, its proponents claimed it was codifying best practice from past inquiries, and bringing clarity to the respective roles of the Minister and chair, thus increasing transparency and accountability.

The Act clarifies that '[a]n inquiry panel is not to rule on, and has no power to determine, any person's civil or criminal liability'.[28] It does give inquiries full powers to seek out information within their terms of reference. Although the Minister cannot determine what evidence the inquiry can or cannot hear, executive influence over the public inquiry is retained and, some would argue, enhanced. The Minister has a discretionary power to initiate a public inquiry where '(a) particular events have caused, or are capable of causing, public concern, or (b) there is public concern that particular events may have occurred'.[29]

---

25 Children Act 1989, s. 81, National Health Services Act 1977, s. 84 and the Police Act 1996, s. 49.

26 Saville Inquiry, (2010) *Report of the The Bloody Sunday Inquiry*, <http://webarchive.nationalarchives.gov.uk/20101017060814/http://report.bloody-sunday-inquiry.org/>.

27 See Department for Constitutional Affairs, *Effective Inquiries*, DCA Consultation Paper 12-04, DCA Corporate Communications, London, 6 May 2004; and, House of Commons Public Administration Select Committee, *Government by Inquiry*, First Report of Session 2004–05, HC 51-I, The Stationary Office, London February 2005.

28 Inquiries Act 2005, s. 2(1).

29 Ibid., s. 1.

The Minister appoints the chair, and other panel members if required.[30] The Minister signs off the terms of reference of the inquiry, albeit that s/he must consult the chair, or the proposed chair, before doing so,[31] and may amend the terms of reference 'if he considers that the public interest so requires'.[32] The Minister may also suspend or end an inquiry before the report emerges,[33] and has considerable potential power to control witness attendance and document disclosure via 'restriction notices'.[34] The Joint Committee on Human Rights thought that this legislation 'risked compromising the independence of an inquiry'.[35]

Although it is recognised that the decision to initiate an inquiry is a political one, there is also recognition that independence is a core value of the public inquiry. Consequently, too much pressure by the Minister on the inquiry panel to restrict costs and/or produce a report without delay, as experienced prior to arrival of the Iraq War inquiry (2009–2016) report,[36] or trying to influence the content of the report in any way, will undermine the rationale of a public inquiry. There are more procedural details contained in secondary legislation in the form of the Inquiry Rules.[37] The Rules have been criticised as lacking an appreciation of the practical realities of inquiry proceedings and as being too prescriptive, thereby inhibiting the flexibility of the chair to direct the procedure and conduct of the inquiry.[38]

4. INDEPENDENT INQUIRY INTO CHILD SEXUAL ABUSE (IICSA)

Theresa May, then Home Secretary, launched the Independent Inquiry into Child Sexual Abuse on 7 July 2014. This followed many months of scandals involving celebrities and other figures in authority.[39] Initially, this was a

30 Ibid., s. 4.

31 Ibid., s. 5(4).

32 Ibid., s. 5(3).

33 Ibid., ss. 13 and 14.

34 Ibid., s. 19.

35 Joint Committee on Human Rights, Eighth Report of Session 2004–05, *Scrutiny: Fourth Progress Report*, HL Paper 60, HC 388, The Stationary Office, London March 2005, pp. 42–47.

36 Chilcot Report, *The Report of the Iraq Inquiry*, Report of a Committee of Privy Counsellors, HC 264, The Stationary Office, London July 2016.

37 Inquiry Rules, SI 2006/1838.

38 In particular, there is concern about Rule 13 (warning letters). Ministry of Justice, *Memorandum to the Justice Select Committee: Post-Legislative Assessment of the Inquiries Act 2005*, (2010) Cm 7943, The Stationary Office, London October 2010, paras. 66–69.

39 P. Wintour, 'Theresa May vows child abuse inquiry will take on the establishment', *The Guardian*, 08.07.2014.

non-statutory inquiry, but following the resignations of the first two chairs,[40] Theresa May established the inquiry under the Inquiries Act 2005 on 4 February 2015, and it was formally opened by a newly appointed (third) chair, Dame Lowell Goddard, a New Zealand judge, on 9 July 2015, who noted some weeks later that this was 'the most ambitious and wide-ranging inquiry ever established under the Inquiries Act.'[41] Unfortunately her enthusiasm for the inquiry's breadth did not last long, and in a brief statement, released in August 2016, Dame Lowell said the inquiry was beset with a 'legacy of failure' and offered her resignation to Amber Rudd, the Home Secretary. She stood down on 4 August 2016 and was replaced by the fourth chairwoman, but this time a non-judicial appointment, Professor Alexis Jay. She was already a panel member to the inquiry and had led a well-regarded Independent Inquiry into Child Sexual Exploitation in Rotherham, South Yorkshire, in 2014.[42] She has 30 years' experience in social work.

This rather bad start to IICSA, relating to the appointment of a suitable chair, illustrates that the appointment of a judicial figure to chair an inquiry no longer automatically guarantees public confidence in the inquiry process. As with some other inquiries,[43] it is perhaps unsurprising that those inquiries which engage the interest and passions of significant sections of the public, require more thorough-going signs of the absence of bias and pro-active commitment to get to the truth of the matter in hand. Professor Jay has fought off critical voices calling for a narrowing of the inquiry's terms of reference. The wide scope of the inquiry has driven the development of an extensive organisational architecture to provide the appropriate support and direction.[44]

IICSA has gathered together a range of working methods and strategies that reflect a radically different approach to the paradigm public inquiry model that focused on an interrogation of particular facts, witnesses and expert opinions in a court-like adversarial setting. IICSA accommodates legal forensic activity but

---

40 Baroness Butler-Sloss, a retired senior judge, resigned days after her appointment (07.07–14.07.2014), following public concern that she had failed to take into account a family conflict of interest. Fiona Woolf (05.09–31.10.2014), a City lawyer and former president of the Law Society, faced questions about her links with Lord Brittan, a Conservative peer whose role in dealing with child abuse in the 1980s was likely to be scrutinised.

41 Dame Lowell Goddard, General Investigations Hearings transcript, 26.07.2016, p. 3. Available at: <https://www.iicsa.org.uk/sites/default/files/documents/2016-07-26-general-matters-relating-to-investigations-transcript.pdf>.

42 Independent Inquiry into Child Sexual Exploitation in Rotherham (1997–2013), 21.08.14. <http://www.rotherham.gov.uk/downloads/file/1407/independent_inquiry_cse_in_rotherham> accessed 01.03.2018.

43 *Hansard, Grenfell Tower Fire: Written Statement*, HCWS18, 29.06.2017. The statement announced the appointment of retired Court of Appeal judge Sir Martin Moore-Bick to chair the inquiry to be established under the Inquiries Act 2005.

44 See generally <https://www.iicsa.org.uk/how-we-work>.

it is also attempting to do much more. The Inquiry has set up three key projects: the Truth Project; the Public Hearings Project; and the Research and Analysis Project. Each has distinctive and complementary roles aimed at revealing systemic issues and informing future improvement. The Truth Project enables victims and survivors to provide information, in private sessions in different regions of England and Wales, about their experience in a safe environment. It is not a formal, fact-finding exercise, but instead provides an opportunity for victims and survivors to express their experiences of childhood sexual abuse in an institutional context. Where appropriate, allegations may be referred to the police for investigation. At the time of writing the Truth Project has heard over 800 victims and survivors.[45] This approach mirrors the well-regarded model adopted in the private hearings of the ongoing Australian Royal Commission of Inquiry into Institutional Responses to Child Sexual Abuse.[46] Public hearings will formally hear evidence, including from witnesses on oath. At the time of writing, following public hearings on the child migration programmes of the UK government, the IICSA issued its first investigation report which stated:

> ... it is the overwhelming conclusion of the Inquiry that the institution primarily to blame for the continued existence of the child migration programmes after the Second World War was Her Majesty's Government (HMG). This was a deeply flawed policy, as HMG now accepts. It was badly executed by many voluntary organisations and local authorities, but was allowed by successive British governments to remain in place, despite a catalogue of evidence which showed that children were suffering ill treatment and abuse, including sexual abuse.
>
> The policy in itself was indefensible and HMG could have decided to bring it to an end, or mitigated some of its effects in practice by taking action at certain key points, but it did not do so.[47]

The report recommends that the government establishes a redress scheme for the 2,000 child migrants that are alive today along with further institutional apologies and a recommendation that the responsible institutions should have robust systems in place to preserve migrants' records.[48]

Finally, the Research and Analysis Project, overseen by the Academic Advisory Board, is intended to help scope and define future investigations and assist in publishing original research in the field. It has already run numerous

---

45 See <https://www.iicsa.org.uk/news/inquirys-truth-project-opens-rochdale>.

46 See <https://www.childabuseroyalcommission.gov.au/>.

47 Independent Inquiry into Child Sexual Abuse, *Child Migration Programmes Investigation Report*, IICSA, March 2018, p. viii.

48 Ibid., pp. 150–152.

seminars and produced several valuable rapid evidence assessments.[49] It can be seen that although a senior judicial figure may have the relevant experience and legal forensic knowledge to run public hearings, the skill-sets required in such a wide-ranging inquiry are much broader.[50]

The inquiry has launched no fewer than 13 investigations into a broad range of institutions.[51] One of Professor Jay's first actions was to order an internal review of the Inquiry's approach to its investigations.[52] She also authorised a restriction order under the Inquiries Act 2005[53] to protect the anonymity of complainants who allege child sexual abuse in the course of the inquiry's deliberations. As with several recent public inquiries, the inquiry website provides a huge amount of information in relation to the inquiry processes and is producing live streaming and full transcripts of hearings. It is clear that efforts are being made to strengthen the inquiry's communication strategy.[54]

The establishment and operation of IICSA is clearly extensive in scope and requires the careful formation of good working relationships with its various constituencies and stakeholders. It also requires a prudent management of resources, expertise and skills not seen on quite the same scale before in public inquiry work in this field. Some, if not all, of its initial teething problems, could have been better managed had it received more organised and timely organisational support. So often, in public inquiries generally, when the final report is issued, inquiry staff are transferred to other jobs and/or returned to their civil service departments. When the next inquiry is launched there is then a need to reinvent the administration and management of the inquiry process once more. The next section considers a proposal, which has been on the public agenda since 2004, to address this 'reinventing the wheel' phenomenon to support public inquiry work in the child abuse field and more generally.

---

49 E.g. C. Fisher, A. Goldsmith, R. Hurcombe and C. Soares, *The impacts of child sexual abuse: A rapid evidence assessment*, IICSA Research Team, Independent Inquiry into Child Sexual Abuse, July 2017.

50 See, J. Beatson, 'Should judges conduct public inquiries? (2003–2004) 37 *Israeli Law Review* 238, 251.

51 Accountability and Reparations; Cambridge House, Knowl View and Rochdale; Children in Custodial Institutions; Children Outside the UK (including Child Migration Programmes case study, see n. 47 above); Child Sexual Exploitation by Organised Networks; Institutional Responses to Allegations Concerning Lord Janner; Lambeth Council; Nottinghamshire Councils; Residential Schools; The Anglican Church; The Internet; The Roman Catholic Church; and Westminster.

52 See: Independent Inquiry into Child Sexual Abuse, *Report of the internal review*, IICSA, December 2016.

53 Inquiries Act 2005, s. 19(2)(b). See <https://www.iicsa.org.uk/key-documents/969/view/restriction-order-complainant-witnesses-child-migration-programmes_2.pdf>.

54 A point that was in need of attention, according to Dame Lowell Goddard in her written evidence to the Home Affairs Select Committee. Home Affairs Committee, *The Work of the Independent Inquiry into Child Sexual Abuse*, Eleventh Report of Session 2016–17, HC 636, 24.11.2016, p. 18.

5. A PUBLIC INQUIRIES OFFICE

Over the last decade, public inquiries in many fields have been established with much wider terms of reference and greater public expectations of engagement and influence in the processes involved. The increased complexities and range of communities participating in inquiries have in turn enhanced their tendency to exert greater influence in shaping public policy agendas. IICSA, the Chilcot Inquiry,[55] and the upcoming Grenfell Tower Inquiry[56] are all examples of inquiry activity that call for a much more sophisticated construction and co-ordination of organisational and other support to ensure that they deliver the public good that is expected of them. It is argued here that the development of a permanent Public Inquiries Office would address some of the weaknesses in inquiry establishment, operation and implementation. A brief reflection on the provenance of this, as yet unimplemented, proposal is instructive and salutary when read against the background of IICSA's teething problems referred to above.

PASC's 'Government by Inquiry'[57] and the Labour Government's subsequent consultation in 2004[58] had suggested the possibility of having a dedicated inquiries unit, mainly focused on the contribution that it could perform in terms of co-ordinating the setting-up and running of new inquiries. It was envisaged that such a unit could, inter alia, advise on possible candidates to chair inquiries, get an appropriate secretary in place as soon as possible, and ensure that the terms of reference were clearly drafted and correctly focused. The proposal picked up much support. The government's response in 2004 was positive and promised further consideration. The most authoritative legal practitioner's work on public inquiries also acknowledged the 'strong arguments for the creation of a centralised unit'.[59]

A House of Lords Select Committee, established in 2014 to undertake a post-legislative scrutiny of the Inquiries Act 2005, noted however, that 'it is not clear to us whether, in nearly a decade, there has been such further consideration'.[60] Various expert witnesses provided robust support for the proposal. The Council on Tribunals thought a dedicated central inquiries unit would be 'a great asset' and 'could provide valuable advice and experience and so avoid the need to

55 Chilcot Report, above n. 36.

56 *Hansard*, above n. 43.

57 House of Commons Public Administration Select Committee, above n. 27.

58 Department for Constitutional Affairs, above n. 27.

59 J. Beer, *Public Inquiries*, Oxford University Press, Oxford 2011, para. 12.53. See also T. Buck, 'Public Inquiries – continuity, change, and institutional infrastructure' in M. Elliott and R. Thomas (eds.), *Public Law*, 3rd edn., Oxford University Press, Oxford 2017, pp. 751–755.

60 House of Lords Select Committee on the Inquiries Act 2005, *The Inquiries Act 2005: post-legislative scrutiny*, Report of Session 2013–14, The Stationary Office, London, HL Paper 143, 11.03.2014, para. 167.

re-think the core structural and administrative issues afresh each time.'[61] One witness, Lee Hughes, whose experience was recognised as unrivalled by the Committee, commented:

> With this reinventing the wheel issue, even on the inquiries I have done, it is very dispiriting two or three years down the line to do another inquiry and find that everything you set up before has been dismantled and you have to do it all again. It is quite wasteful of public money just to go through the procurement exercise to get your IT in yet again, whereas if you had one department responsible for delivering the inquiries you could get call off contracts arranged and that kind of thing. We are not talking about billions of pounds here but we are talking about millions, so there are great savings to be made.[62]

Other witnesses with recognised expertise in public inquiry work opined that 'a dedicated sponsoring department for inquiries would be invaluable.'[63] The Centre for Effective Dispute Resolution (CEDR), produced reports which recommended the creation of a central inquiries unit.[64] It recommended that such a unit could not only be a repository for information about previous public inquiries, but also a watchdog for the implementation of inquiry recommendations. It commented in its 2015 report:

> We have found that most Inquiry Chairs have this desire and are keen to share their views with others, however, there is currently no mechanism for this, meaning that every new Inquiry has to start essentially from scratch. This is ultimately a waste of both financial and non-financial resources, and causes delay to the progress of the Inquiry and possibly to the effectiveness of some Inquiries. An Independent Inquiries Office which acted as a repository of experience and lessons learnt would be a great benefit.[65]

The House of Lords Select Committee, having considered various possible departmental homes for such a unit, had concluded that it should be established as an executive non-departmental public body (NDPB) and accommodated within Her Majesty's Courts and Tribunals Service (HMCTS), an executive

---

61 Ibid., para. 166.

62 Lee Hughes, House of Lords Select Committee on the Inquiries Act 2005, above n. 60, para. 168.

63 Michael Collins, Judy Kemish and Ashley Underwood QC, the Secretary, solicitor and counsel respectively, to the *Azelle Rodney Inquiry* (2010–2013). House of Lords Select Committee on the Inquiries Act 2005, above n. 60, para. 169.

64 K. Mackie, *Public Inquiries – Proposals for a Design Rethink, Centre for Effective Dispute Resolution (CEDR)*, December 2012, p. 20. Available at: <https://www.cedr.com/docslib/Public_Inquiries_-Proposals_for_a_Design_Rethink_-_December_2012.pdf>.

65 K. Mackie and F. Way, *Setting up and running a public inquiry: guidance for chairs and commissioning bodies*, Centre for Effective Dispute Resolution (CEDR), January 2015, p. 72.

agency of the Ministry of Justice, to serve both statutory and non-statutory inquiry work.[66] It was envisaged that the new unit should include assistance with premises, infrastructure, IT, procurement and staffing and should work to the chairman and secretary of the Inquiry.

However, the policy of the Coalition Government in 2010 and subsequent governments has been for the Cabinet Office to retain what appears to be a light touch co-ordinating role. This is performed by the 'Propriety and Ethics Team' based in the Cabinet Office,[67] though it is questionable whether the predominant culture of this team is suitable to provide any further developmental reforms.[68] The prudence of staying with the current arrangement was questioned by the House of Lords Select Committee in 2014:

> Officials in ... [the Propriety and Ethics] team may be well placed to advise on persons to be appointed to the inquiry panel or as assessors, and the terms of appointment; but there is nothing to suggest that they are the repositories of knowledge about the practicalities of setting up an inquiry. There is indeed nothing to suggest that such a repository exists anywhere in central government.[69]

At the time of writing it would seem unlikely that the proposal will be reactivated for serious consideration. Even the finalisation of the Inquiries Guidance recommended by the Select Committee in 2014 still remains in draft form only.[70]

6. CONCLUSION

It has been argued in this chapter that the ongoing IICSA inquiry, though bedevilled with a difficult start in relation to the appointment of a suitable chair and other matters,[71] nevertheless provides an emerging model of a public inquiry in terms of both structural and tonal values that could be of great benefit to future inquiry work in the child protection field and elsewhere. The breadth

---

66 House of Lords Select Committee on the Inquiries Act 2005, above n. 60, para. 174.

67 See <https://www.gov.uk/government/people/sue-gray>.

68 See further, C. Cook, 'The most powerful person you've never heard of', policy editor Newsnight, *BBC News*, 10 July 2015. Available at: <http://www.bbc.co.uk/news/uk-politics-33431580>.

69 House of Lords Select Committee on the Inquiries Act 2005, above n. 60, para. 167.

70 Cabinet Office, *Inquiries Guidance: Guidance for Inquiry Chairs, Secretaries and Sponsor Departments* (Draft) (c. 2012–13). Available at: <https://www.parliament.uk/documents/lords-committees/Inquiries-Act-2005/caboffguide.pdf>.

71 See S. Laville and O. Bowcott, 'Counsel to child sexual abuse inquiry suspended amid "leadership concerns"', *The Guardian*, 28 September 2016. Available at: <https://www.theguardian.com/society/2016/sep/28/ben-emmerson-counsel-child-sexual-abuse-inquiry-sacked-concerns-over-leadership>.

of IICSA, along with its innovative three-strand strategic format, marks a radical rebalancing of the approach taken in previous public inquiries concerning child abuse. As Professor Jay has remarked, '[i]t was apparent to me and the Panel that the Inquiry could not be delivered through a traditional public inquiry approach alone'.[72] However, it is not inconceivable that IICSA will achieve a more durable presence, particularly if further investigations are added to the current workload. The way in which IICSA is being developed provides new opportunities, amongst other things, to capture the voices of victims and survivors of child abuse in institutional and other settings in an organised way that will inform not only the evidence base for particular investigations but also the generic knowledge base that has the potential to transform child protection service practice. More thoughtful and intense approaches to the collation and collection of data should far surpass the current formal requirements for inquiries to ensure that their legal obligations to preserve their 'public records'[73] are met.

Alongside the developments in IICSA, it can be seen that the arrival of a permanent Public Inquiries Office would provide the required organisational framework to support it and other similar major inquiries that deal with increasingly complex subject-matters. Relevant staff members in a Public Inquiries Office could be seconded to particular inquiry teams, like IICSA. Indeed, this would reflect, to an extent, the cross-fertilisation of staff from one inquiry to another that currently exists. A Public Inquiries Office would provide continuity in the knowledge gained from one inquiry to the next, and develop flexibly to accommodate the changing requirements of individual inquiries driven by their different subject-matters. Such an Office could advise on chair and panel membership, the administrative implications of remit formulae, legal issues, time-lines, costs and the various potential methodologies of approach. To be credible, such a body would not be directly sponsored by a government department. Instead, to maintain its independence and impartiality, it should be financed directly by a Parliamentary vote and could be accountable to the House of Commons Public Administration and Constitutional Affairs Select Committee. The potential public good generated by the consequent increase in knowledge and depth of understanding of the nature and impact of child abuse would seem to far outweigh the costs and delay objections that have recently accompanied major public inquiry work.

72 Independent Inquiry into Child Sexual Abuse, above n. 52, (Foreword) p. 4.
73 As defined by Schedule 1 of the Public Records Act 1958.

LOWE AND THE INHERENT JURISDICTION

Richard WHITE

It is a privilege to have the opportunity to contribute to a *festschrift* for Professor Nigel Lowe. He is one of four people who have been a major influence in the development of my professional life.

I first met Nigel in 1976 in Somerset House in what was then the Principal Registry of the Family Division. I was representing the London Borough of Camden on one of the early local authority wardship applications before Senior Registrar Norman Turner in a very pleasant room overlooking the Thames.

Nigel was engaged in some initial research on wardship. As I recall we asked for the Registrar's permission (or leave as it would then have been called) to discuss the case outside court. We really did take the protective nature of the jurisdiction seriously in those days.

That chance meeting led to a writing (and teaching and research and even tennis) partnership over 40 years. It led more immediately to the co-writing and publication of the first edition of *Wards of Court* in 1979.[1] I say co-writing but in reality it was an opportunity for Nigel to coach a junior partner on legal research and academic writing. I like to think that I contributed with a little knowledge about the workings of local authorities and by emphasising the need for such works to be accessible to practitioners, legal and non-legal. It was one of life's odd coincidences that the opportunity to prepare the first edition occurred when I broke a leg. As a result I spent many research hours cloistered in the law library at Bristol University.

The history and scope of wardship was of course at that time relatively unexplored. Mr Justice Cross (as he then was) wrote briefly about the subject in 1967, noting that the only book of reference had last been published in 1926. We know that the origins of wardship date from feudal times. The case law provides a fascinating insight in the social history of our treatment of children over the centuries.

1 N. LOWE and R.A.H. WHITE, *Wards of Court*, 1st edn., Butterworths, London 1979.

Oddly enough I had represented a party in wardship proceedings in the Chancery Division during my articles in 1970, the year before such proceedings were transferred to the Family Division. In spite of my briefing of Richard Scott (who was later a Law Lord) the case never explored the jurisdictional intricacies of a Scottish element, as we did later.

In the 1970s and 1980s the growth area for wardship was its use by local authorities to meet the shortcomings of the Children Act 1948 and the Children and Young Persons Act 1969. Such were the complexities of, and advances in the use of, the jurisdiction that we had to produce a second edition in 1986. I seem to recall that we foresaw a market given the discussions that took place during those years about new legislation.

Looking back 28 years, the provisions in the Children Act 1989 were of course intended to obviate the need for wardship and permit the lower courts to have wider powers. In the local authority context, the intention was to ensure that courts applied more specific criteria for the removal of children and their subsequent treatment in care. It proved to work in relation to child protection in the local authority context. In the private law arena the creation of a family court jurisdiction across three levels empowered the lower courts to make prohibited steps orders and specific issue orders so as to deal with some of the disputes which had previously been reserved to the High Court.

Initially, local authorities used to issue wardship proceedings automatically, because we knew no better. That had the benefit of giving the child the immediate protection of the status, but could also be a hindrance to taking urgent decisions to promote the child's welfare. Nigel recognised that the inherent jurisdiction of the High Court was not exclusively vested in wardship. Although it had provided a convenient machinery for exercising the powers of the jurisdiction outside of wardship, there was scope for invoking the jurisdiction outside of wardship. This proved to be the case.

Wardship has of course across the five decades since the 1970s fulfilled many roles in promoting the welfare of children. Over the years, at first wardship and later the inherent jurisdiction had to address the legal complexities of our developing world. What I think we saw latterly was that the High Court provided an experienced judicial vehicle with a high level of expert representation for investigating and managing novel legal problems. Frequently this led to specific legislation to deal with the specific problem. Consider in particular surrogacy, adoption and permanent placement of children away from their birth family, deprivation of liberty and international child abduction.

Our focus on the use of the wardship jurisdiction in relation to the particularly vulnerable group of 'minors' extended as the legal confraternity became aware of the possibilities of the broader concept of the inherent jurisdiction for other concerns relating to vulnerable groups. These could not have been foreseen by the architects of the Children Act 1989: such as relations with the media, forced marriage, female genital mutilation, medical treatment and end-of-life decisions, and now radicalisation. What we have seen over recent years in particular is its use in cases with a foreign element, on which the President will elaborate in the next chapter.[2]

Meanwhile of course, Nigel was also producing the acknowledged leading work on *Contempt of Court*,[3] which had its own complex relationship with wardship. And then later he became the acknowledged expert on child abduction.

So what of the future? I venture to suggest that there is life in the old dog yet. As the President wrote in *Re M (Wardship: Jurisdiction and Powers)*,[4] commenting on the jurisdiction, 'despite its antiquity, [it] has shown, is showing, and must continue to show a remarkable adaptability to meet the ever emerging needs of an ever changing world'.

The one area which perhaps should be explored remains embryonic. In *Paton v Trustees of British Pregnancy Advisory Service* Sir George Baker, who wrote the Foreword to our first edition in the year that decision was reported, commented that 'a foetus cannot in English law have any right of its own at least until it was born and has a separate existence from the mother'.[5]

In 1979 we did not contemplate such a high level of alternative families or, significantly, their methods of production. I remain surprised that we have not found a way to make the courts available for resolving the consequent pre-birth disputes which must arise.

2 See Sir James Munby, 'Wards of Court' in this volume.

3 G.J. Borrie and N. Lowe, *The Law of Contempt*, 1st edn., Butterworths, London 1973.

4 *Re M (Wardship: Jurisdiction and Powers)* [2015] EWHC 1433 (Fam), [2016] 1 FLR 1055, [32].

5 *Paton v Trustees of British Pregnancy Advisory Service* [1979] QB 276, 279,

WARDS OF COURT

James MUNBY

Nowadays we tend – rightly – to think of Nigel Lowe as being, par excellence, an international family lawyer. Indeed, in that part of the Academy he stands preeminent, with an enviable international reputation. But we forget at our peril that, 40 or so years ago, he cemented his scholarly reputation with two outstanding books on two very different areas of domestic law. First, in 1973, and written in collaboration with Gordon Borrie, came *Contempt of Court*. Then, in 1979, and written in collaboration with Richard White, came *Wards of Court*.

These two works, albeit on very different subjects, had a number of things in common. Both dealt with highly technical topics. Both dealt with topics with a long and complex history, where knowledge and analysis of the historical hinterland was key to understanding and explaining the current law. Both dealt with topics where the existing literature was distinctly elderly. In 1973, the most recent work on contempt of court was the third edition of Oswald's *Contempt of Court*, published in 1910. In 1979, as Sir George Baker P pointed out in his Foreword to the first edition of *Lowe & White*, the only book of reference on wards of court was the fourth edition of *Simpson on Infants*, published in 1926. And both have stood the stern test of time.

Borrie & Lowe is now in its fourth edition, published in 2010. It continues to stand high in what is now, because of the popularity of the subject, a more populated field of legal publishing. *Lowe & White*, perhaps because wardship occupies a more specialised niche, has seen nothing more recent than the second edition, published in 1986. That is a matter of keen regret because, as I recently had occasion to remark,[1] it remains 'a book of high authority although we rejoice in the continued vigour of both its authors.' Down the years I have on a number of occasions gently chided Nigel for his failure to produce what would be so valuable, an up-dated edition. I am always met with the characteristic, self-deprecating smile which, while not seeking to challenge the justice of my observation, indicates that it is unlikely to be heeded. Perhaps, if he and Richard White are too busy on other important ventures to undertake the task themselves, they could find some suitably youthful and energetic academic to produce the new edition which would be so very welcome.

1 *Egeneonu v Egeneonu* [2017] EWHC 43 (Fam), [2017] 4 WLR 100, [2017] 2 FLR 1181, para. 26.

Each edition of *Lowe & White* was published at an interesting time in the long history of wardship. When the first edition, stating the law as at August 1978, was published, the vitally important decisions of the House of Lords in *A v Liverpool City Council and Another*[2] and *In re W (A Minor) (Wardship: Jurisdiction)*,[3] still lay in the future. By the time the second edition, stating the law as at October 1986, was published, although the direction of travel had been indicated by the House of Lords, the other important jurisdictional feature of the current law – section 100 of the Children Act 1989 – had not yet been enacted.

The authors of *Lowe & White* were alert to the issue. In the Preface to the first edition, they wrote

> Recent trends indicate that the jurisdiction is being increasingly used to review decisions already made by other courts or bodies. We are concerned that continued expansion might not only overload the wardship jurisdiction itself but might also undermine the rest of the child welfare system. Although the exercise of the wardship power can be justified on the basis of the paramountcy of the ward's welfare the extent to which such a principle should be applied is questionable. It may be that the current increase in the conflict between wardship and other jurisdictions will be seen as detrimental to the interests of children generally. If so, some limitation of the principle that the welfare of the ward is paramount should be considered.

In the Preface to the second edition, by contrast, they said this:

> When we completed the first edition we were concerned at the possibility that the jurisdiction would be swamped and thereby lose its attractions. Nine years on and following two major cases in the House of Lords our concern is that the appellate courts are too keen to restrict the jurisdiction, to the extent that wardship is in danger of failing to provide the protection that it has extended to infants for many centuries. The House of Lords may be considering this area again this autumn and it is hoped that they will reverse the trend to vest almost absolute power in administrative bodies.

Increasingly, down the years, the true impact of the *A v Liverpool City Council* principle in relation to wardship has been recognised and its wide ramifications explored in an ever-lengthening line of authorities.[4] But the troubling questions raised by *Lowe & White* remain live today, more than 30 years on.[5]

---

2 *A v Liverpool City Council and Another* [1982] AC 363, HL.

3 *In re W (A Minor) (Wardship: Jurisdiction)* [1985] AC 791, [1985] FLR 879.

4 For a recent survey see *In re a Ward of Court (Wardship: Interview)* [2017] EWHC 1022 (Fam), [2017] 3 WLR 593, [2017] 2 FLR 1515, paras. 11–13. For the most recent reported example of the application of the principle see *Re X (A Child) (No. 5)* [2017] EWHC 2141 (Fam).

5 See Sir J. Munby, 'Children across the justice systems: The 2017 Parmoor Lecture to the Howard League for Penal Reform', London, 30 October 2017, [2017] *Family Law* 1303, 1305–1306, 1309–1310.

One of the marks of the true quality of a textbook is the frequency of its citation in reported cases. *Lowe & White* stands high on this index of quality. No doubt the search could be extended, but confining myself to what is reported in the *Family Law Reports* we find that *Lowe & White*, then in its first edition, was cited as long ago as in *Regina v D* [1984] FLR 300. Its most recent citation was in *Re A Ward of Court* [2017] EWHC 1022 (Fam), [2017] 2 FLR 1515. There were many in the intervening years.

Perhaps of even more significance is the number of occasions when the analysis in *Lowe & White* has been central to the judge's reasoning and thus to the eventual outcome. Can I take three of my own judgments to illustrate just how invaluable *Lowe & White* has been?

In *Kelly v British Broadcasting Corpn*,[6] the question was whether the media required the leave of the wardship judge before interviewing a ward of court and publishing or broadcasting the interview. Pressed with dicta of Russell LJ, with whom Cross LJ agreed, in *In re T (AJJ) (An Infant)*,[7] suggesting that such leave might be required, and having referred to what I described as the 'useful discussions' to be found in *Lowe & White* and in *Borrie & Lowe*, I said this:

> Recognising, as I do, the vast experience of wardship which both Russell and Cross LJJ had in the days when wardship was still in the Chancery Division, I have to say that I share the same doubts and uncertainties as to what exactly it was they had in mind which are expressed in *Lowe & White* [and] *Borrie & Lowe*, [neither of which] seem to evince much enthusiasm for what Russell LJ said.

In the event I preferred the view of the Academy to the judicial dicta.

Egeneonu v Egeneonu[8] was a curious case raising the esoteric question whether contempt of court in relation to a ward of court is a criminal or a civil contempt – the question being raised in the context of a wish to obtain the extradition of the alleged contemnor from the country to which he had fled. So the case raised a number of issues lying at the intersection between the law of wardship and the law of contempt. The judgment contains extensive citations from, and, in its ultimate conclusions, closely follows the analysis in, *Lowe & White*, which I described as being 'invaluable, and as it seems to me accurate.' I set out a number of passages in *Lowe & White* 'which I accept as an accurate statement of the law.'

In *In re a Ward of Court (Wardship: Interview)*,[9] the question was whether an officer of the Security Service required the leave of the wardship judge before interviewing a ward of court. There was much authority, starting with the

6 *Kelly v British Broadcasting Corpn* [2001] Fam 59.
7 *In re T (AJJ) (An Infant)* [1970] Ch 688.
8 [2017] EWHC 43 (Fam), [2017] 4 WLR 100.
9 *In re a Ward of Court (Wardship: Interview)* [2017] EWHC 1022 (Fam), [2017] 3 WLR 593.

decision of Booth J on 16 December 1986, in *In re S (Minors) (Wardship: Police Investigation)*,[10] that, as she put it, 'if the police are to interview … wards then leave of the court must first be given.' Now this was rather curious, given the 'very striking and … very telling fact', as I pointed out, that the authors of *Lowe & White*, setting out to state the law as at 1 October 1986,

> are, seemingly, unaware of any principle that police interviews with a ward of court require judicial approval. Chapters 5 and 8 contain detailed discussions of the 'no important step' principle, but are bare of any suggestion that it extends to police interviews. Specific discussion … under the heading 'Interviewing the ward' is as illuminating for what it does *not* say as for what it does.

My conclusion was that there is not and never has been any principle or rule that judicial consent is required before the police can interview a ward of court; that Booth J was wrong to hold that there was; and that the subsequent authorities, where the point was not in fact argued, take the matter no further. From this it followed that an officer of the Security Service does not require the leave of the wardship judge before interviewing a ward of court.

Mention of the Security Service brings out what is perhaps the key point about the wardship jurisdiction: the need, despite its venerable age, for it to adapt to the ever-evolving needs of our ever-changing society. In this connection, I need to bring out two aspects of practice in recent years which exemplify just how adaptable the wardship jurisdiction can be; as it has to be.[11]

The first example relates to the many new problems – or newly recognised problems – which wardship has had to address: medical treatment issues; abduction; forced marriage; female genital mutilation; and, most recently, radicalisation and terrorism. These may arise entirely unexpectedly, rapidly and in the most acute form. Few would have predicted in January 2015 the emergence of radicalisation and terrorism as a focus of *family* justice, or the demands which they would impose on the law and practice of wardship. Yet by the autumn of that year, such was the number of these cases which had arisen in previous months, I had had to issue, on 8 October 2015, *Guidance on Radicalisation Cases in the Family Courts*.

The second example relates to the utility, in a system of family justice where jurisdiction is usually founded on the child's habitual residence, of the fact that the wardship jurisdiction is exercisable, irrespective of the child's habitual residence, and irrespective of where the child may be, in relation to any child who is a British national.

---

10 *In re S (Minors) (Wardship: Police Investigation)* [1987] Fam 199.

11 See in relation to all this *Re M (Wardship: Jurisdiction and Powers)* [2015] EWHC 1433 (Fam), [2016] 1 FLR 1055, and *In re B (A Child) (Reunite International Child Abduction Centre and others intervening)* [2015] EWCA Civ 886, [2016] UKSC 4, [2016] AC 606.

As both Roger Casement and William Joyce ultimately discovered to their cost, a British subject (see *The King v Casement*[12]) or someone travelling on a British passport (see *Joyce v Director of Public Prosecutions*[13]) has a duty of allegiance to the Crown wherever he may be, whether in this country or abroad. As Darling J said in *Casement*,[14] 'the subjects of the King owe him allegiance, and the allegiance follows the person of the subject. He is the King's liege wherever he may be'.

The correlative of this – I put the matter generally and without descending into detail or identifying any qualifications to what I am about to say – is that the Crown has a protective responsibility for its subjects wherever they may be. The significance of this for the wardship jurisdiction is that the Crown's protective duty as *parens patriae*, in relation to children, extends, in the case of a child who is a British subject or who, although not a British national is travelling on a British passport, to protect the child wherever he may be, whether in this country or abroad.[15]

Thus, as is well recognised in the authorities, the court may make a child who is a British subject a ward of court even if the child, at the time the order is made, is outside the jurisdiction. Recent examples include *Re KR (Abduction: Forcible Removal by Parents)*,[16] *Re B, RB v FB and MA (Forced Marriage: Wardship: Jurisdiction)*[17] and *Re M (Wardship: Jurisdiction and Powers)*.[18]

The purpose of such an order is to protect the child, not least by facilitating the child's hopefully speedy return to the jurisdiction. In the days of Lord Palmerston, the Briton imperilled abroad had merely, in echo of the Roman of old, to assert *civis britannicus sum* to find rescue at hand. The days of gunboat diplomacy are, at least in this context, long gone. Modern 'soft power' is exemplified by the sonorous words which appear in every British passport:

> Her Britannic Majesty's Secretary of State Requests and requires in the Name of Her Majesty all those whom it may concern to allow the bearer to pass freely without let or hindrance, and to afford the bearer such assistance and protection as may be necessary.

Judicial comity properly bridles at the use of a word such as 'require' in an English order directed to a foreign court. A wardship order relating to a British

---

12 *The King v Casement* [1917] 1 KB 98.

13 *Joyce v Director of Public Prosecutions* [1946] AC 347.

14 At 137.

15 See *In re P(GE) (An Infant)* [1965] Ch 568, applying the principle in *Joyce v Director of Public Prosecutions* [1946] AC 347.

16 *Re KR (Abduction: Forcible Removal by Parents)* [1999] 2 FLR 542.

17 *Re B, RB v FB and MA (Forced Marriage: Wardship: Jurisdiction)* [2008] EWHC 1436 (Fam), [2008] 2 FLR 1624.

18 *Re M (Wardship: Jurisdiction and Powers)* [2015] EWHC 1433 (Fam), [2016] 1 FLR 1055.

child abroad which seeks the assistance of the foreign authorities, whether judicial or otherwise, is couched in language designed to minimise all risk of offence. It 'respectfully requests' their assistance: see the forms of order in *Re KR (Abduction: Forcible Removal by Parents)*[19] and in *Re M (Wardship: Jurisdiction and Powers)*.[20]

The utility of this aspect of the wardship jurisdiction was strikingly demonstrated in the latter case, where a wardship order made at 2.15pm on 5 May 2015, and 'respectfully requesting' the assistance of the 'judicial, police, security, immigration and other authorities in Moldova,' led to the family being detained on its arrival in Moldova an hour later and returned to this country only two days later.

On this aspect of the matter I said:

> I wish to place on record my gratitude and thanks, as President of the Family Division of Her Majesty's High Court of Justice and Head of Family Law in England and Wales, for the prompt assistance the court has received from the public authorities of the Republic of Moldova. The Republic is a sovereign state within which, of course, I have no authority at all. The English court must always be astute to ensure that no order it makes could possibly be construed as an interference with the sovereign rights of another State. These are matters to be dealt with in accordance with the well-established principles of international comity between friendly States. That is why the order I made was deliberately expressed in terms of this court 'respectfully requesting' the assistance of the various public authorities in Moldova to which I referred. I am, as I have said, very grateful for the assistance afforded to the English court by the Republic of Moldova.

How far does this extend? What of the future? Who can say what future exigencies may require? In the same case I hazarded some tentative thoughts:

> I have no doubt that the jurisdiction was properly exercised in both *Re KR* and *Re B*, just as I have no doubt that it can properly be exercised in the circumstances with which I am here faced. This is not the occasion, and there is no need for me, to explore the range of circumstances in which it may be appropriate to make a child who is outside the jurisdiction a ward of court. I merely observe that cases such as this demonstrate the continuing need for a remedy which, despite its antiquity, has shown, is showing and must continue to show a remarkable adaptability to meet the ever emerging needs of an ever changing world. I add that the use of the jurisdiction in cases where the risk to a child is of harm of the type that would engage Articles 2 or 3 of the Convention – risk to life or risk of degrading or inhuman treatment – is surely unproblematic. So wardship is surely an appropriate remedy, even if the child has already left the jurisdiction, in cases where the fear is that a child has been taken

[19] *Re KR (Abduction: Forcible Removal by Parents)* [1999] 2 FLR 542.
[20] *Re M (Wardship: Jurisdiction and Powers)* [2015] EWHC 1433 (Fam), [2016] 1 FLR 1055.

> abroad for the purposes of a forced marriage (as in *Re KR* and *Re B*) or so that she can be subjected to female genital mutilation or (as here) where the fear is that a child has been taken abroad to travel to a dangerous war-zone. There is no need for me to go any further, so I need not consider whether there are other kinds of situation where a child who is already abroad should be made a ward of court or whether wardship is an appropriate remedy where the risk to the child is of harm falling short of harm of the type that would engage Articles 2 or 3 of the Convention.

What I there referred to as the remarkable adaptability of wardship to meet the ever-emerging needs of an ever-changing world was something of which the authors of *Lowe & White* were very conscious. For both editions contain interesting discussions of how the use of wardship had changed down the years and how it might be expected to develop in future.

On one level, human nature being what it is, very little changes. And in that sense, the principles applied by the wardship court are timeless. Thus, there is enduring relevance in what Lord Eldon LC said in *Wellesley v Duke of Beaufort*: 'it has always been the principle of this court, not to risk the incurring of damage to children which it cannot repair, but rather to prevent the damage being done.'[21]

His words are as apposite today as they were some 190 years ago and as I am sure they will be 100 years hence.

Two hundred years ago, Lord Eldon was familiar with the use of wardship to protect impressionable teenagers from the follies of youth. Everything has changed, but nothing changes. 'Hot pursuit' in the days of Lord Eldon would have been of the coach and four labouring over Shap Fell carrying the teenage heiress and her unsuitable paramour to the Scottish border and the blacksmith's forge at Gretna Green. Today, pursuit is of the aeroplane and bus carrying the would-be teenage jihadist to the border between Turkey and Syria. But the approach remains and must remain as Lord Eldon put it all those years ago.

[21] *Wellesley v Duke of Beaufort* (1827) 2 Russ 1, 18.

PART II

INTERNATIONAL FAMILY LAW

JUDGING PARENTAL CHILD ABDUCTION: WHAT DOES IT MEAN TO ADOPT A CHILDREN'S RIGHTS-BASED APPROACH?

Kathryn HOLLINGSWORTH and Helen STALFORD

1. INTRODUCTION

Nigel Lowe's work in the field of international family law has been groundbreaking, not just because of his achievements in gathering, synthesising and analysing unique data on cross-border family movement over the past two decades, but because of his efforts to bring children's perspectives and experiences to bear on that process.[1] Similarly impressive has been his success in bridging the gulf between academic scholarship and legal practice; his work is a primary reference point for any serious lawyer working on cross-border family cases.[2]

---

1 See for example N. LOWE and V. STEPHENS, 'Children's Welfare and Human Rights under the 1980 Hague Abduction Convention – the ruling in Re E' (2012) 34 *Journal of Social Welfare and Family Law* 125; N. LOWE and M. NICHOLLS, *International Movement of Children: Law, Practice and Procedure*, 2nd edn., Jordans, Bristol 2016.

2 A search of cases on Westlaw found 29 references to Nigel Lowe's work, 25 of which were to his work on the international movement of children.

In this chapter, we pay tribute to these efforts by analysing recent cross-border child abduction cases for their compatibility with a children's rights-based approach to judging. It is of some regret that Nigel could not be involved in our recent *Children's Rights Judgments* project.[3] This project involved over 50 children's rights scholars and practitioners who revisited 28 existing judgments involving children, from a range of different jurisdictions and legal contexts, and re-wrote them from a children's rights perspective.[4] In the process, we identified five strategies for achieving a judgment that is more faithful to our understanding, as academic scholars, of a children's rights-based approach. First, judges can utilise to better effect the formal legal tools which give effect to children's rights, including (but not confined to) the UN Convention on the Rights of the Child (CRC).[5] Second, a children's rights judgment can draw on scholarly insights to address theoretical tensions, conceptual challenges, and prevailing presumptions which stymie the resolution of cases in ways that best protect children's rights.[6] The third strategy relates to the legal processes leading up to the judgment, which should maximise children's participation by endorsing and conforming with, where appropriate, child-friendly, participatory procedures.[7] The fourth and fifth elements concern *how* judgments are written; their form rather than their substance. Specifically, the narrative employed should seek to centralise the child's perspective and voice; and children should be acknowledged as one of the audiences for legal judgments,[8] such that child-appropriate language, structure and style should be used, either in the primary judgment itself or in an additional 'child-friendly' version. Where some or all of these strategies are employed, the likelihood of a children's rights-compliant

---

3 Funded by the Arts and Humanities Research Council Network Grant BH141351 and published in H. Stalford, K. Hollingsworth and S. Gilmore (eds.), *Rewriting Children's Rights Judgments: From Academic Vision to New Practice*, Hart Publishing, Oxford 2017.

4 The collection includes two rewritten parental abduction cases: the Australian case *RCB as Litigation Guardian of EKV, CEV, CIV and LRV v The Honourable Justice Colin James Forrest of the Family Court of Australia & Others* [2012] HCA 47 (rewritten by Brian Simpson with a commentary by Rhona Schuz), and *Povse v Austria*, Application no. 3890/11, ECtHR, 18 June 2013 (rewritten by Lara Walker with a commentary by Ruth Lamont).

5 It also involves maximising regional and domestic rights protection, including the EU Charter of Fundamental Rights (CFR), the European Convention on Human Rights (ECHR), the Human Rights Act 1998 (HRA), and the common law, as well as other relevant international treaties.

6 Nigel's empirical and statistical work on child abduction has been particularly influential in challenging some of the presumptions in parental abduction cases. See below, n. 25.

7 See especially *Guidelines on Child-Friendly Justice*, Council of Europe 2010 and, more recently, the *Guidelines on Children in Contact with the Justice System*, produced by the International Association of Youth and Family Judges and Magistrates, IAYFJM 2017.

8 See E. Rackley, 'The Art and Craft of Writing Judgments: Notes on the Feminist Judgment Project' in R. Hunter, C. McGlynn and E. Rackley (eds.), *Feminist Judgments: From Theory to Practice*, Hart Publishing, Oxford 2010.

outcome is increased and the law is more likely to fulfil its communicative and standard-setting function to respect children as rights-holders.

The analysis in this chapter is informed by our review of 30 recent abduction cases (first instance and appellate decisions) involving children's objections to return,[9] which have been decided since the first Supreme Court decision concerning the Hague Abduction Convention.[10] The cases are evaluated for their compatibility with some of the strategies identified above as indicative of a children's rights judgment. The chapter begins with a brief exploration of the conceptualisation and protection of children's rights in cross-border parental child abduction cases. It sets out some of the context-specific constraints that confront judges in such cases, before examining, in sections 3, 4 and 5, how – if at all – the courts have navigated these constraints to produce judgments that are either reflective of, or antithetical towards, our understanding of a children's rights-based approach. We argue, by reference to this sample of cases, that, even within the seemingly restrictive confines of abduction proceedings, there remains not just greater scope, but a greater necessity for courts to engage with children's rights on a procedural, substantive and communicative level than is currently the case.

2. IS IT POSSIBLE TO ADOPT A CHILDREN'S RIGHTS-BASED APPROACH TO CHILD ABDUCTION CASES?

Child abduction cases invoke numerous children's rights concerns that nearly all states are duty bound to respect by virtue of their ratification of the CRC. This includes, most prominently, a right to maintain regular contact with both parents.[11] Other rights – including the rights to exercise and maintain

---

9 See Art. 13 of the Hague Convention on the Civil Aspects of Child Abduction: 'The judicial or administrative authority may also refuse to order the return of the child if it finds that the child objects to being returned and has attained an age and degree of maturity at which it is appropriate to take account of its views'; The Hague Convention 'child objections' exceptions apply also to intra-EU abduction cases. See Art. 11(2) of Council Regulation (EC) No. 2201/2003 of 27 November 2003 concerning jurisdiction and the recognition and enforcement of judgments in matrimonial matters and the matters of parental responsibility, repealing Regulation (EC) No. 1347/2000, OJ L338, 23.12.2003 (commonly referred to as Brussels IIA). For a justification of our focus on this category of exceptions to return, see below, text at nn. 32–33.

10 *Re E (Children)* [2011] UKSC 27. Cases were selected via a search conducted on 22 August 2017 of (1) the *Family Law Reports*, using keywords 'child objecting to return', 'child objections defence' and 'child's objection' and; (2) *Westlaw*, using 'Hague Convention on the Civil Aspects of International Child Abduction 1980' in the legislation field *and* 'objections' (in the keyword field); and (separately) 'child objections' in the case title.

11 See especially Arts. 9(1), 9(3) and 10(2) CRC; Art. 8 ECHR; and Arts. 7 and 24 CFR.

cultural identity,[12] to education,[13] to the highest attainable standard of health,[14] and to freedom of association – are also likely to be engaged.[15] Insofar as these rights are put at risk by the abrupt and non-consensual removal of children from their place of habitual residence, it is not surprising that the international legal framework governing such proceedings (notably the 1980 Hague Abduction Convention) shares a long and closely aligned history with the CRC.[16] In the same vein, the Brussels IIA Regulation is explicit in its aims 'to ensure respect for the fundamental rights of the child as set out in Article 24 of the Charter of Fundamental Rights of the European Union' (CFR).[17] This cross-pollination between abduction law and children's rights law relates not only to the substantive rights listed above, but also to provisions pertaining to children's procedural rights.[18] Indeed, of the cases we analysed, six made explicit reference to Article 12 CRC or Article 24 EU Charter to guide their discussion of the currency of the child's participation in decisions around return.[19]

Notwithstanding the clear correspondence between Hague/Brussels IIA and international children's rights instruments, evidence of judges bringing children's rights to bear on child abduction proceedings appears more limited in practice. We attribute this less to indifference on the part of the judiciary to activate children's rights, and more to the fact that children's rights are mediated through a different policy lens in child abduction cases. That policy lens is one of automatic return to avert any legal advantage that parents might gain from

---

12 Art. 8 CRC.

13 Art. 28 CRC.

14 Art. 24 CRC.

15 Art. 15 CRC.

16 Indeed, the discussions that informed the 1980 Hague Convention inspired several provisions of the CRC, and in turn, the CRC provided the basic principles around which subsequent private international law instruments of the Hague Conference were constructed. See further A. Dyer, 'The Contribution of the Hague Children's Conventions to the Protection of Human Rights' [2012] *International Family Law* 7.

17 Art. 24 CFR is inspired heavily by Arts. 3, 7 and 12 CRC. See further R. Lamont, 'Article 24 of the Charter of Fundamental Rights of the European Union' in S. Peers, T. Hervey and A. Ward, *The EU Charter of Fundamental Rights* Hart Publishing, Oxford 2014, pp. 661–691.

18 Art. 9(2) CRC enshrines the right of all parties, including children, to participate in family justice proceedings and make their views known. Art. 6 (right to a fair trial) ECHR has also been interpreted to reinforce children's right to participate in family justice proceedings.

19 *Re M (Children) (Abduction: Child's Objections)* [2015] EWCA Civ 26, per Black LJ at para. 17; *AVH v SI, SIV* [2014] EWHC 2938 (Fam), per Cobb J at para. 18; and *F v M, B (by his Litigation Friend)* [2015] EWHC 3300 (Fam), per Cobb J at para. 64. Note some cases merely cite previous case law referring to the same principles but stop short of any more in-depth analysis. See for instance *Re KP (Abduction: Child's Objections)* [2014] EWCA Civ 554, [2014] 2 FLR 660; and *X v Y, Z Police Force, A, B and C (by their Children's Guardian)* [2012] EWHC 2838 (Fam), both of which cite Lady Hale *In re M and another (Children) (Abduction: Rights of Custody)* [2007] UKHL 55; and *LCG v RL* [2013] EWHC 1383 (Fam), per Cobb J citing Wilson in *Re W (Abduction: Child's Objections)* [2010] EWCA Civ 1165, [2010] 2 FLR 1165 at para. 110.

unlawfully removing children from their established environment and from the care of their other parent.

The hard and fast nature in which this rule has been applied has been subject to some academic criticism on grounds that it can undermine children's welfare,[20] but there are persuasive children's rights-based reasons to support it. First, returning the child as quickly as possible to the parent/environment from where they were taken (usually abruptly) is, in many cases, the most effective means of minimising any trauma.[21] Related to this, abduction proceedings are about restoring the status quo, so that ultimate decisions concerning parental responsibility can be disposed of in the country/jurisdiction with which the child has the closest connection, in a manner that is most sensitive to the child's cultural and social circumstances.[22] Moreover, in many cases, an extensive welfare assessment will have already been undertaken prior to the child's wrongful removal, usually in private family proceedings seeking to resolve custody/access issues between the parents. To suggest that that should be supplanted by a renewed assessment in a foreign jurisdiction, in the absence of the same wealth of information/evidence that would have been available to the original court, is likely to undermine rather than reinforce the child's best interests. Finally, return is more likely to facilitate the child's contact with both parents. The policy of return is therefore widely accepted by the judiciary as entirely compliant with a children's rights-based approach.[23]

The concern, however, is that the arguments against focusing on the individual child's best interests, coupled with a desire to promote mutual recognition and respect between jurisdictions, have entrenched presumptions about the nature and effects of child abduction and fuelled widespread judicial resistance to actively engaging children's rights principles and processes where it is most appropriate and necessary. This, we argue, not only belies the close correspondence that the abduction regulation framework has with international children's rights norms, but also stifles critical, evidenced debate around the extent to which the child abduction framework actually protects children. Even leading proponents of the 1980 Hague Convention have noted that the success of the Convention

---

20 R. Schuz, *The Hague Child Abduction Convention: A Critical Analysis*, Hart Publishing, Oxford 2014; P. McEleavey, 'Judicial Communication and Co-operation and the Hague Convention on International Child Abduction' (2012) 2 *International Journal of Procedural Law* 36–53; and H. Stalford, *Children and the European Union: Rights, Welfare and Accountability*, Hart Publishing, Oxford 2012, ch. 4.

21 Aligning with the 'no delay' principle in the Children Act 1989.

22 Explanatory Report by Elisa Pérez-Vera, para. 22, available at <https://assets.hcch.net/upload/expl28.pdf>; J. Chamberland, 'Whither the 'Best Interests of the Child' in the 1980 Child Abduction Convention?' (March 2012) Special Issue *International Family Law* 27.

23 See for example *F v M, B (by his Litigation Friend)*, above n. 19, para. 66ff (Cobb J).

is not to be measured by the number of children returned.[24] Certainly, more recent evidence has challenged some of our thinking about the effectiveness of the law in responding to the reality of abduction experiences. The original 1980 Convention responded to an assumption that most abductors were fathers seeking to change the custody arrangements that, at the time, favoured mothers (at least in Western states) by taking them to another jurisdiction. But data, including that gathered by Nigel Lowe, has revealed that over 70 per cent of abductions globally are perpetrated by mothers, most of whom are the primary carer of the child.[25] A significant rise in international migration and relationship formation is now more likely than before to trigger return migration of the mother with her child without permission following relationship breakdown, often enabling her to draw on the emotional and financial support of family and community networks[26] or to escape an allegedly violent partner.[27] The policy of automatic return, therefore, 'potentially places some children at risk of harm, but realistic alternatives to the Convention remedy have not been seriously considered.'[28]

We argue, as have others,[29] that there is much more scope within the abduction framework to respond to such cases in a way that is more closely informed by children's rights principles and processes, particularly in relation to the right to be heard. We add a new dimension to existing critiques by identifying how typical cases either perpetuate poor practice or, conversely, engender a more meaningful rights-based approach. Our analysis focuses specifically on proceedings where

24 W. Duncan, 'The International Family Law Lecture 2010: Is It Time For A Protocol?' (2010) 1 *Journal of Family Law and Practice* 4.

25 In 2015, 73% of taking persons were the mother of the child and, in 91% of cases, the sole or joint primary carer. 24% of abductors are fathers and the remaining 3% are grandparents, institutions or other relatives., See N. Lowe and V. Stephens, *Part I: A Statistical Analysis of Applications Made in 2015 under the Hague Convention of 25 October 1980 on the Civil Aspects of International Child Abduction – Global Report* (Preliminary Document No. 11A. Revised version, February 2018), Permanent Bureau of the Hague Conference, The Hague 2018. Available at: <https://www.hcch.net/en/publications-and-studies/details4/?pid=6545&dtid=57>. Published to inform the 7th Meeting of the Special Commission on the Practical Operation of the 1980 Hague Child Abduction Convention and the 1996 Hague Child Protection Convention (October 2017).

26 For detailed empirical evidence of this see L. Ackers and H. Stalford, *A Community for Children?: Children, Citizenship and Migration in the European Union*, Ashgate, Aldershot 2004.

27 M. Weiner, 'International Child Abduction and the Escape from Domestic Violence' (2000) 69 *Fordham Law Review* 593; H. Keating and A. Reddaway, 'Child Abduction: Would Protecting Vulnerable Children Drive a Coach and Four through the Principles of the Hague Convention?' (1997) 5 *International Journal of Children's Rights* 77.

28 R. Lamont, 'International Family Law' in R. Lamont (ed.), *Debates in Family Law*, Routledge, Oxford forthcoming 2018.

29 R. Schuz, above n. 20; R. Lamont, 'Free Movement of Persons, Child Abduction and Relocation within the European Union' (2012) 34 *Journal of Social Welfare and Family Law* 231, H. Stalford, above n. 20.

the child's objection to return is raised pursuant to Article 13 of the Hague Convention,[30] and includes cases where the judge followed the child's wishes as well as those where return was nonetheless ordered. The child objection 'defence' is one of only four exceptions to the general policy of return,[31] and we selected this type of case for our analysis for two reasons. First, where one of the exceptions to return applies, judges have a larger discretionary space within which to take account of children's rights, including their individual best interests.[32] Secondly, the child objection defence is arguably the most 'child-centric' of the Hague exceptions since it expressly requires a judge to take account of the child's views and wishes (where the child is of sufficient age and maturity), reflecting one of the four underpinning principles of the CRC.[33] The next section interrogates more closely the nature and extent of judicial engagement with children during abduction proceedings as an initial indicator of their potential to produce a children's rights judgment.

3. CHILD-FRIENDLY PROCEDURES? AN ANALYSIS OF HOW CHILDREN'S OBJECTIONS ARE PRESENTED TO THE JUDICIARY

The *Children's Rights Judgments* project sought to reinforce the importance of participatory procedures to achieving a child rights-based judgment insofar as: 'Ensuring that the child's voice is heard, including through the facilitation of her participation, helps to mitigate the many ways in which the views and experiences of the child … are silenced or distorted through legal proceedings.'[34]

Article 12 CRC is an obvious reference point in this regard, since it requires that States Parties shall assure to the child who is capable of forming his or her own views the right to express those views freely in all matters affecting him or her, and that those views should be given due weight in accordance with the child's age and maturity. To achieve this, the child has to be given the opportunity

---

30 Above n. 9.

31 See Art. 12 (that more than a year has passed and the child is settled in the new environment) and the 'defences' in Art. 13: (a) that the left-behind parent/carer consented or later acquiesced to the child's removal; and (b) that there is a grave risk of harm to the child or s/he is placed in an intolerable situation.

32 See, for example, Lady Hale, *In re M and another (Children) (Abduction: Rights of Custody)*, above, n. 19, para. 46.

33 See Lord Wilson in *In re LC (Children) (Reunite International Child Abduction Centre Intervening)* [2014] UKSC 1, para. 48 (*Re LC*). Note that the obligation to hear the child's voice is not confined to objection cases; see for example, Lady Hale's child-focused approach to determining the child's habitual residence in *Re LC* (para. 57 ff).

34 K. Hollingsworth and H. Stalford, 'Towards Children's Rights Judgments' in H. Stalford, K. Hollingsworth and S. Gilmore (eds.), above n. 3 at 76.

to be heard in any judicial and administrative proceedings affecting him or her, either directly, or through a representative or an appropriate body.

Thus, the extent to which Article 12 is, in practice, a child's *right* during legal proceedings very much depends on whether those exercising discretion – judicially, professionally or administratively – act in a manner that is compatible with the spirit of this provision.[35] Objection cases, which are fundamentally concerned with the voiced wishes and feelings of the child, offer a fertile testing ground for Article 12. Indeed, there is an established jurisprudence pointing to the importance of child participation in Hague Convention proceedings, which is cited recurrently in the cases we analysed.[36] The most notable, perhaps, is Lady Hale's guidance in *Re D (A Child) (Abduction: Rights of Custody)*, a case concerning an eight-year-old boy who had been in England for nearly four years following removal by his mother from Romania.

> When applying Articles 12 and 13 of the 1980 Hague Convention, it shall be ensured that the child is given the opportunity to be heard during the proceedings unless this appears inappropriate having regard to his or her age or degree of maturity … the principle is in my view of universal application and consistent with our international obligations under Article 12 of the United Nations Convention on the Rights of the Child … It erects a presumption that the child will be heard unless this appears inappropriate.[37]

In the same vein, Thorpe LJ, in *Re G (Abduction: Children's Objections)*, emphasised that hearing from children in international family proceedings should extend to direct meetings with the trial judge 'in carefully arranged conditions'.[38]

In analysing our sample of 30 objection cases, we looked at the opportunities available to children of different ages and abilities to present their views and objections to the judiciary. Our sample included a range of approaches, most of which evidenced a clear willingness on the part of the judiciary to support a participatory process, although only a minority of judges went as far as Thorpe LJ's recommendation in *Re G* and met with the child. In eight cases, the child was joined as a party to proceedings,[39] including one case on appeal,[40]

---

35 Ibid., paraphrasing Jane Williams' re-write of *P-S (Children)* [2013] EWCA Civ 223, in H. Stalford, K. Hollingsworth and S. Gilmore (eds.), above n. 3, at 159.

36 Most notably: *Re D (A Child) (Abduction: Custody Rights)* [2006] UKHL 51, *Re M (Children)* above n. 19; and *Re LC*, above n. 33. On the explicit reference to Art. 12, see again n. 19 above and surrounding text.

37 *Re D*, ibid., para. 58.

38 *Re G (Abduction: Children's Objections)* [2011] 1 FLR 1645.

39 See for example *Re S (Child Abduction: Joinder of Sibling: Child's Objections)* [2016] EWHC 1227 (Fam); *NP v JP* [2015] EWHC 2551; and *X v Y, Z Police Force*, above n. 19.

40 *Re KP*, above n. 19.

where the judges reiterated the emotional, practical and ethical value of involving young people as parties to proceedings.[41] There were two cases in which the child's application to be joined to proceedings was turned down.[42] These cases involved some balancing up of the value of children's direct participation in the process with the potential risk that exposure to such proceedings might pose to their welfare. For instance, in *LCG v RL*,[43] Cobb J's decision to refuse a 12-year-old girl's application to be joined was upheld on appeal on the grounds that the child, described as 'mature', had already expressed her views 'forcefully and intelligently' through the Cafcass officer, and that there could be nothing gained from exposing her to the 'potentially damaging effects of court proceedings between her parents over her future'.[44]

Unsurprisingly, therefore, in the majority of cases analysed, the child's views were communicated to the court by a Cafcass officer's report only, and, consistently with other types of family proceedings, these were relied on heavily by the judge.[45] However, further scrutiny of the process by which the child's views and objections were elicited raises some questions as to the reliability of Cafcass accounts as a proxy for direct testimony from children. Where details were provided in the judgments, Cafcass officers met children on two occasions on average, for approximately one hour, sometimes less. In other cases, the Cafcass officer did not have sufficient time to review the child's files, impeded on at least one occasion by the language barrier.[46] Such evidence is tantamount to not hearing the child at all, and reinforces the findings of Beaumont et al.'s research that in only 20 per cent of abduction cases heard under Brussels IIA are children really heard.[47]

It confirms also the concerns of other commentators regarding the hefty influence of welfare reports and the inadequacy of these as a medium for representing children's views in abduction proceedings. Schuz, for example, bemoans the 'filtering' potential of Cafcass reports in a process where conveying nuanced, often subtle distinctions between express objections and mere

---

41 Reiterated by Lady Hale in *Re LC*, above n. 33.

42 *LCG v RL*, above n. 19 (see the appeal in the Court of Appeal [2013] EWCA Civ 1058; *Re LC* (CA) hereafter); *Re U-B (A Child)* [2015] EWCA Civ 60.

43 *LCG*, above n. 19.

44 *Re LC* (CA) above n. 42, per Black LJ.

45 See for examples, *X v Y, Z Police Force*, above n. 19; and *Re LC (Habitual Residence: Grave Risk of Harm)* [2014] EWFC 8, [2015] 1 FLR 1019; and *Re H (A Child: Summary Return: Child's Objections)* [2012] EWHC B32 (Fam) in which the judges set a lot of store by the experience of the Cafcass officers concerned.

46 *Re D (Children)* [2011] EWCA Civ 1294.

47 P. Beaumont, L. Walker and J. Holliday, 'Conflicts of EU Courts on Child Abduction: The Reality of Article 11(6)–(8) Proceedings Across the EU' (2016) 12 *Journal of Private International Law* 211.

preferences is all-important for founding an objection to return.[48] Others have pointed to the specific complexities of abduction proceedings, which warrant clear explanations so that the child is aware of the nature and scope of the judicial discretion and the high threshold required to rebut the presumption of return. The judgment of Thorpe LJ sets out this obligation in more detail in *Re J (Abduction: Children's Objections)*, a case involving three children aged 10–15 abducted from Poland:

> These children understandably felt themselves to be vulnerable and lost in a complex legal landscape. They needed to understand that the proceedings in this jurisdiction were brought under an international instrument and were essentially summary in character. They needed to understand that they were habitually resident in Poland and that accordingly the Polish court had primary jurisdiction ... They needed to understand that any profound investigation of their future would be determined by the paramount consideration of their welfare and that the task of assessing that was for the Polish judge ... They needed to understand that a summary return order might be a transient order dependent on the outcome of the mother's application for custody and relocation.[49]

The limitations of relying solely on the welfare report are compounded in the context of England and Wales, where cuts in resources to social welfare services, coupled with an increasing number of public care applications, have placed unprecedented pressure on court and family welfare services.[50] This inevitably limits the extent to which Cafcass officers can engage in a meaningful assessment of the child's wishes and welfare.[51]

Some of the cases analysed supported a blend of approaches, providing more than one opportunity for the child to present his or her objections to the judge:[52] Cafcass reports were, in three cases, coupled with a letter to the judge from the young person;[53] and, in four cases accompanied by a face-to-face meeting

48 R. Schuz, 'The Hague Child Abduction Convention and Children's Rights' (2002) 12 *Transnational Law and Contemporary Problems* 393.

49 *Re J (Abduction: Children's Objections)* [2012] FLR 457, para. 39.

50 Sir James Munby, P, '15th View from the President's Chambers: Care Cases: the Looming Crisis', [2016] *Family Law* 1227.

51 The Children's Society, The National Children's Bureau and Children and Young People Now, 'Cuts that Cost: Trends in Funding for Early Intervention Services', National Children's Bureau 2015.

52 In line with the judicial guidance issued by the Court of Appeal in *Re KP*, above n. 19, para. 53.

53 Cobb J quotes at length from the letter written to him by 'S' in his judgment on *Re S*, above n. 39. See also *Re KP*, above n. 19; and *B v B (Abduction: Child with Learning Difficulties)* [2011] EWHC 2300 (Fam).

with the judge.[54] Some first instance judgments were also appealed on grounds of procedural irregularity relating to hearing the child.[55] But such cases were in the minority; direct meetings with children remained the exception rather than the norm, and usually only occurred at the instigation of the child rather than the judge. Certainly, there was limited evidence of any proactive attempts on the part of the judiciary to invite children to meetings. Persistent (and, in many cases, unfounded) fears of exposing the child to additional trauma,[56] coupled with a desire to expedite decision-making and to avoid a 'multiplicity of representation',[57] perpetuate widespread judicial resistance to supporting anything more than participation by proxy.

Such preoccupations risk obscuring the purpose and effects of children's participation. As the jurisprudence itself points out, direct participation is not just about clarifying issues for the judge but about ensuring that the various factors that have to be taken into account in reaching a decision are understood by the child.[58] Furthermore, judicial practice guidelines issued in 2010 and updated in 2012 suggest that direct participation should be the default preference in family proceedings.[59] This guidance is supported (and, one would hope, informed) by abundant research attesting to the fact that engaging children more sensitively and directly in judicial decision-making achieves not just better process, but more durable outcomes, leading to fewer appeals, greater levels of compliance,[60] and less trauma.[61]

Whilst hearing children might present challenges to the judiciary in abduction cases, giving weight to those views is another leap altogether. Of the cases we

---

54 *C v V* [2016] EWHC 559 (Fam); *Re F (Abduction: Acquiescence: Child's Objections)* [2015] EWHC 2045 (Fam); *B v B*, ibid., and *Z v Y* [2013] EWHC 3381 (Fam).

55 For example, see *Re M (A Child)* [2014] EWCA Civ 1519, at para. 54; and *Re D (Children)*, above n. 46; *Re KP*, above n. 19.

56 See for example *Re M (A Child)*, ibid.

57 *Re LC* (CA), above n. 42 at para. 40.

58 *Re NB (A Child Residence)* [2014] Lexis Citation 19, per Alex Verdan QC para. 10; *Re F (Child's Objections)* [2015] EWCA Civ 1022, per Black LJ para. 58.

59 *Guidelines for Meeting Children who are Subject to Family Proceedings* [2010] 2 FLR 1872. Followed by *Guidelines in Relation to Children Giving Evidence in Family Proceedings* [2012] 2 FLR 456. These latter guidelines were issued following the Supreme Court decision in *In re W (Children) (Family Proceedings: Evidence)* [2010] UKSC 12 where it was held that there was no longer a presumption, or even a starting point, against children giving evidence in family proceedings. See also *Re KP*, above n. 19, para. 20ff.

60 It is perhaps no coincidence that return orders are notoriously difficult to enforce, even following an unequivocal order. See further P. Beaumont, M. Danov, K. Trimmings and B. Yüksel (eds.), *Cross-Border Litigation in Europe*, Hart Publishing, Oxford 2017; and P. Beaumont, K. Trimmings, L. Walker and J. Holliday, 'Child Abduction: Recent Jurisprudence of the European Court of Human Rights' (2015) 64 *International and Comparative Law Quarterly* 39.

61 For a detailed analysis of the evidence to this effect, see A. Daly, *Children, Autonomy and the Courts: Beyond the Right to be Heard*, Brill, Leiden 2017.

analysed, eight (fewer than one-third) persuaded the judge that their objections were such that return should not be ordered.[62] We turn now to consider why, having overcome the many obstacles to actually being heard, judges remain so ill-inclined to allow such views to override the general policy of return.

4. SUBSTANTIVE JUDICIAL ASSESSMENTS OF CHILDREN'S OBJECTIONS TO RETURN: GIVING DUE WEIGHT

As already noted, a key component of children's right to be heard is the obligation on the part of decision-makers to give their views due weight, in accordance with the child's age and maturity (Article 12(1) CRC). Given the high premium placed on expediting the swift return of abducted children to their place of habitual residence, it is perhaps not surprising that the approach to objections cases in England and Wales remains overwhelmingly defensive, imposing a high threshold of persuasiveness and clarity for children's objections to be weighted in favour of non-return. Specifically, since the Court of Appeal judgment in *Re M (Abduction: Child's Objections)*,[63] it has been standard practice to deal with such cases in a series of interrogatory stages, with each stage placing the child on the evidential back foot.

The first stage considers whether the child's expressed views really do amount to an objection to being returned, rather than a mere preference. The case law we analysed was conflicting in terms of the threshold that had to be reached to establish a persuasive objection. Cobb J, in *F v M, B (by his Litigation Friend)*,[64] suggested that the threshold in this regard is fairly low, whereas judges in other, factually similar, cases required an unequivocal expression of dissent. The approach of HHJ Bellamy in *Re F*, for instance, is heavily endorsed in other cases:

> There is a qualitative difference between a preference and an objection. In this context an 'objection' means a wholesale objection to returning to the country of habitual residence. Invariably such a child cannot think of anything positive to say about that other country.[65]

---

62 *SP v EB* [2014] EWHC 3964; *Re K (A Child) (Hague Convention: Child's Objections)* [2014] EWCA Civ 1364; *Re LC* (CA), above n. 42; *X v Y, Z Police Force*, above n. 19; *B v B*, above n. 53; *CB v CB* [2013] EWHC 2092 (Fam); *K v B*, above n. 58; *Re H*, above n. 45.

63 *Re M (Abduction: Child's Objections)* [2007] 2 FLR 72.

64 Above n. 19, para. 50, citing authority in *Re W (Minors)* [2010] EWCA Civ 520 and *Re M (Republic of Ireland) (Child's Objections)* [2015] EWCA Civ 26.

65 Above n. 54, para. 101, supported by *Re M (Children) (Abduction: Child's Objections)* [2015] EWCA Civ 26, at para. 41.

Yet in a number of other cases, judges interpreted a more 'balanced' view as a sign of the child's maturity, such that they were willing to take any accompanying objections at face value.[66]

Significantly, some judges in the sample reviewed recognised that the propensity of children to express their objections in persuasive terms depends heavily on the manner in which those views are elicited; namely how the child is questioned by intermediaries, and the circumstances surrounding those meetings. Indeed, Cafcass officers in four of the cases analysed were heavily criticised for failing to probe whether the child was objecting or simply expressing a preference, or to inform the child of the importance of expressing their views in the unequivocal terms required for an objection.[67]

A second evidential obstacle that children have to overcome is the requirement that they demonstrate a high degree of independence from the views of parents. A number of the cases doubted the authenticity and independence of the child's expressed objections, concluding that they were heavily influenced by one or other parent. In *Re F*, for instance, the judge declined to set any store by the child's views, suggesting that they had been 'coloured' by those of the father.[68] In *RB v DB*[69] Mostyn J confidently rejected the authenticity of the children's views on the basis that they were simply too mature:

> It is perfectly obvious to me that both children, and in particular D, are speaking in unnaturally adult language, leading one to the inevitable conclusion ... and that is so often the case and is almost an unavoidable really [sic] ... that their views have been to some extent either consciously or unconsciously inculcated in them by their carer, namely their father.

Can the judge justify imposing such a high threshold of persuasiveness, insight, independence and rationality on the child before giving weight to his or her views, when the reasonableness and coherence of the parents' demands are rarely subject to such scrutiny? Quite apart from the fact that the judge had not met any of the children in this case, such an approach paints an oversimplified picture of the dynamics of parent/child relationships. To suggest that children should remain impervious to the expressed views and feelings of their parents is unrealistic and unfair. Judges' perspective on this point might change if they considered evidence from the body of work on relational theory that tells us that we are all, to some degree, a product of our relationships, expressing thoughts

---

66 See for example *Re U-B* above n. 42, para. 21, *X v Y, Z Police Force*, per Baker J, above n. 19; and *CB v CB*, per Peter Jackson J, above n. 62.

67 For examples see HHJ Bellamy in *Re F*, above n. 54, para. 59; Theis J in *MR v HS* [2015] EWHC 234 (Fam); Thorpe LJ in *Re D (Children)*, above n. 46; and Cobb J in *F v M, B (by his Litigation Friend)*, above n. 19, para. 41.

68 Above n. 54, para. 120 (HHJ Bellamy).

69 *RB v DB* [2015] EWHC 1817 (Fam), para. 22.

and feelings that are inevitably influenced by those closest to us.[70] A judgment that brings such theoretical intelligence to bear might resemble that of Baker J in *X v Y, Z Police Force, A, B and C (by their Children's Guardian)*.[71] In recognising that the child in question laboured under some parental influence, the judge in this case did no more than acknowledge an inescapable feature of the human condition, but this did not inhibit his ability to conclude that the child's views were genuinely his own.

Of course, judges have to be alert to situations in which the child forms an opinion only on the basis of partial 'facts', conveyed by only one parent, which deliberately and unfairly vilifies the other parent or indulges either parent's own selfish needs. Equally, the courts want to avoid situations in which the child is unable to express her own (differing) views for fear of reprisals from the parent/s or, more likely, for fear of hurting a parent that they love. But concerns of parental influence should be treated with some caution; rather than aspiring to an artificial expression of independent thought, courts should point to ways of disentangling the wishes of the various parties and interrogating further the views of the child, if necessary through appropriate expert intervention and assessment.[72] Some of the other judgments achieved this through critical interrogation of the Cafcass officer's conclusions and experience, and a more nuanced perspective on what responses and behaviour might be reasonable to expect of a child in such circumstances.[73] Indeed, in *K v B*, the fact that the child sought the support of others (in this case his friends) and discussed the matter 'appropriately' with them, reinforced, for the judge, his conclusion that the child did in fact object.[74]

Once it is established that there is an independent and unequivocal objection, the judge then has to be satisfied that the child is of sufficient age and maturity for their views to be taken into account. Whilst the sample of cases analysed presented a relatively liberal attitude towards hearing the views of children of a range of ages[75] and abilities,[76] the perennial reminder that such views have to

70 For examples, see F. Kelly, 'Conceptualising the Child Through an "Ethic of Care": Lessons for Family Law' (2005) 1 *International Journal of Law in Context* 375; J. Herring, *Relational Autonomy and Family Law*, London, Springer 2014. *Children's Rights Judgments* proposes that judges should engage with such theoretical perspectives more readily as a means of testing and critically reflecting upon their deeply entrenched presumptions. See further K. Hollingsworth and H. Stalford, above n. 34 at 74–75.

71 Above n. 19, at para. 48ff. See also Black LJ in *Re F (Child's Objections)*, above n. 54.

72 H. Stalford and S. Byrne, 'Human Rights, Children's Rights and Family Law' in R. Lamont, (ed.), *Debates in Family Law*, Routledge, Oxford forthcoming 2018.

73 See again *X v Y, Z Police Force*, above n. 19.

74 Above n. 58, para. 17.

75 See for example *F v M, B (by his litigation Friend)*, above n. 19 in which Cobb J goes to some effort to consider the 'actual words' of a child of seven in reaching his decision.

76 *B v B*, above n. 53 concerned the objections of a 14-year-old boy with Asperger's syndrome.

meet a high threshold to render them determinative undermines the significance of this otherwise promising feature of abduction case law. A children's rights-based approach at this stage would resemble that of Peter Jackson J in *CB v CB*[77] to the effect that a child who expresses a mature and insightful opinion 'deserves respect', and that sound reasons should be given to dissent from what they say rather than the converse. And yet, it is telling that so many others dwell on Lady Hale's assertion that hearing the child is not to be confused with giving effect to his views,[78] virtually conceding that their consideration of the views of the child is a tokenistic nod to the perceived need to make the child merely *feel* part of (rather than genuinely influence) the process. The skepticism expressed by Peter McEleavey almost a decade ago, therefore, still pervades the case law:

> The uneasy balance between the principle of return and the subsidiary aim of respect for the views of children will ... most likely continue. Such an outcome should scarcely be surprising since for all the progress made in recent years in advancing children's rights, these two objectives will always remain uncomfortable bedfellows.[79]

Having overcome these 'gateway' hurdles, the child still remains subject to the judge's discretion to direct or refuse a return. A key judicial reference point is Lady Hale's guidance in *Re M and another (Children) (Abduction: Rights of Custody)*,[80] which lists a range of considerations that need to be taken into account in exercising this discretion, relating not only to the child's welfare and the soundness of the child's objections, but to the overarching policy of the Hague Convention.[81] This provides an important opportunity in which judges could engage in a more individualised assessment of what is in the child's best interests, through more forensic consideration of the various rights that might be disrupted by a decision to remain or return to the country of habitual residence. Surprisingly few of the judgments actually achieve this, though. Many of the first instance cases analysed imply only a superficial consideration of the social, familial, cultural and educational impact of return on a child, even where such issues are expressly raised by the child.[82] Virtually none of the cases alluded to the corresponding provisions of the CRC or other human rights instruments to support such an assessment.

---

77 Above n. 62, para. 25.

78 Above n. 32, para. 46.

79 P. McEleavey, 'Evaluating the Views of Abducted Children: Trends in Appellate Case-law' (2008) 20 *Child and Family Law Quarterly* 230, 254.

80 Above n. 19.

81 Reinforced by Sir Mark Potter P, in *DL v H* [2009] EWHC 3074 (Fam) para. 66.

82 See for instance Black LJ's criticism of Judge Bellamy's failure to consider the child's welfare and education in any depth in *Re F (Child's Objections)* above n. 58. A similar criticism could be levelled at the first instance judge in *In re KK, VK and AK v CC* [2013] NI Fam 6 (Maguire J).

5. CRAFTING A CHILDREN'S RIGHTS JUDGMENT: THE IMPORTANCE OF FORM

Our analysis of recent objections cases demonstrates a mixed judicial approach to the conformity with children's rights principles in the process, reasoning and outcome. We turn now to a related, yet under-explored, aspect of a children's rights judgment: the *way* in which judges craft their opinions – the style, tone, structure, choice of facts and language employed. The 'art and craft'[83] of judgment writing – including the narrative or 'story' that is created[84] – is important because it is how judges (consciously or not)[85] seek to convince their audience that they have reasoned and decided correctly, and it can thus be highly revealing of judicial attitudes towards children and their rights. Examining the *form* of a judgment is, therefore, another lens through which to assess its children's rights compatibility and we conclude our chapter by embarking on such an analysis of our sample cases. We do this for three reasons. First, judgments have an important communicative value. How they are written sends powerful messages about children's status as rights-holders (including to children themselves) and the respect the law confers upon them.[86] Second, and relatedly, judgments that are specifically written *for* children, in a 'child-friendly' manner, better conform with the rule of law and children's access to justice. Finally, we suggest that the conscious adoption of a children's rights-based approach to *how* the judgment is written can shape *what* is written: that is, a judge who regards the child as a potential audience and who centralises him or her in the narrative is more likely to reach a children's rights-based outcome, substantively and procedurally.

5.1. EXPLORING NARRATIVE IN ABDUCTION CASES

Prima facie, the summary nature of abduction proceedings does not lend itself to the creative use of narrative as a strategy to give effect to children's rights. In most of these cases, judicial discretion is limited by at least three factors: the narrow focus on the jurisdictional question arising from the return objective; the limited yet often contested nature of the evidence before the court which

---

83 See E. Rackley, above n. 8.

84 E. Rackley, above n. 8 and P. Brooks and P. Gewirtz (eds.), *Law's Stories: Narrative and Rhetoric in the Law*, Yale University Press, New Haven CT 1996. Applied in a children's rights context see K. Hollingsworth and H. Stalford, above n. 34 at 79.

85 It would seem some judges are alive to the importance of narrative: in our sample, see HHJ Jenkins in *B v B*, above n. 53.

86 See generally, K. Hollingsworth and H. Stalford, above n. 34 at 78–84; and on rights as recognition see J. Anderson and A. Honneth, 'Autonomy, Vulnerability, Recognition and Justice' in J. Christman and J. Anderson (eds.), *Autonomy and the Challenges to Liberalism: New Essays*, Cambridge University Press, New York 2005.

constrains the judge's freedom to construct different 'stories' or versions of the facts;[87] and by the imperative to expedite proceedings – as Black LJ observes:

> The interests of children are generally best served if the courts determine cases with as little delay as possible and judges therefore do not have the luxury of time … this court must be realistic about what can be achieved in the time allowed and on the material that is available within the constraints of this summary process.[88]

It may be challenging for judges to craft a tailored, children's rights-focused narrative within such restrictive temporal constraints. Nonetheless, the cases we analysed exposed wide differences in approach, suggesting that even in summary proceedings such constraints are not insurmountable. A first and simple children's rights technique that is unaffected by the abduction-specific context is for judges to use a pseudonym for the child, rather than simply an initial. Conferring a name on the child recognises their status as a moral actor rather than a 'thing' or proprietary interest about which others are making decisions, and the effect is to remind us that at the heart of the case is a specific, very real, child.[89] It is especially important in abduction cases not to lose sight of the individual child, given that the overall policy is one based on presumptions about what is in the best interests of children in general (swift return to the country of habitual residence) and which is aimed at prioritising the interests of *all* children by deterring abduction. That said, only five of our 30 sample cases used a name for the child/ren concerned.

A second marker of a children's rights-based approach in the judgment's form, is the extent to which the child's experiences are centralised in the narrative, ensuring that it is the child's perspective and not that of adult others (particularly parents) that informs the reasoning and outcome.[90] It also reminds the audience of who and what is at stake and has a respect-conferring function for the child as the central legal subject.[91] How this is done can be subtle yet powerful. For example, consistent with her approach in other cases, Black LJ opens her account of the facts in *Re U-B* with the child as the primary subject ('[t]his appeal concerns E … E's parents separated when he was about 18 months old').[92] Contrast this with Davis LJ in the same case who mentions the child only

---

87 Particularly, as noted above, the child's version of events, which in most cases will be heard only through the Cafcass filter.

88 *Re U-B.*, above n. 42, para. 34.

89 See M. Freeman, '*Re T (A Minor)*' in H. Stalford, K. Hollingsworth and S. Gilmore (eds.), above n. 3, ch. 13; and Lady Hale's plenary lecture at the Family Congress and Children's Rights Conference, Dublin, 5 June 2017.

90 See K. Hollingsworth and H. Stalford, above n. 34 at 79ff.

91 See J. Anderson and A. Honneth, above n. 86.

92 Above n. 42. See also, for example, *Re K*, above n. 62; *B v B*, above n. 53; and *CB v CB*, above n. 62.

three times in eight paragraphs and, consistent with the majority of the judges in our other cases,[93] it is the parental perspective that is foregrounded. This emerges most starkly when he asks us to '[i]magine her [the mother's] feelings' when the English court refuses the child's return; and yet no plea is made to empathise with the child.[94]

Children's marginalisation in the narrative is evident also in *LCG v RL* where the children themselves feature little in Cobb J's account of the facts, and certainly do not provide the lens through which those facts are told. Instead, the children's perspective is confined to the consideration of their objections later in the judgment. The narrative can act as a signifier – and a shaper – of what is to come and so it is perhaps not unsurprising when a return order is made against the children's objections. In the appeal of this decision in the Supreme Court, Lady Hale observed that:

> [t]he relevant reality is that of the child, not the parents. This approach accords with our increasing recognition of children as people with a part to play in their own lives, rather than as passive recipient of their parents' decisions.[95]

Although written in the context of determining habitual residence, Lady Hale's statement has a wider application in abduction cases (and elsewhere). Such strong rhetoric is important for the message it sends to the lower courts for their determination of future cases (ensuring that the judicial mind is focused on the child), and also for the message it sends to children themselves (demonstrating that she or he has been taken seriously).[96] It also serves to emphasise the inter-relationship with other aspects of a children's rights judgment and in particular the importance of the child's participation, either through separate representation or judicial interview. Only if the child's voice is genuinely heard can her perspective be reflected in the judgment.

Other, seemingly minor, stylistic choices are also significant. Parker J's decision not to use the possessive pronoun in *C v V* and, instead, to refer predominantly to 'the mother' or simply 'mother' rather than 'the boys' mother' or 'their mother', was not unusual and reflects wider practice in family law. But

---

93 Of the 30 judgments, we identify 10 as adopting the child's perspective to some degree, and the rest are told from the adult point of view or a mixed perspective.

94 Para. 49. The differences between these judges in particular may reflect the variation in professional background and experience in abduction cases which may inform the narrative. H. Stalford and K. Hollingsworth, 'Judging Children's Rights: Tendencies, Tensions, Constraints and Opportunities' in H. Stalford, K. Hollingsworth and S. Gilmore (eds.), above n. 3, ch. 2.

95 *Re LC (SC)* above n. 33, para. 87.

96 See also Black LJ in *Re F*, above n. 58, para. 45: 'No one suggested the children should be split. I have treated them as a single entity, even though I am conscious that they all have their own individual personalities and views'.

omitting the possessive pronoun has the effect of literally removing the child from the narrative. Indeed, the whole judgment in *C v V* is rather striking for its tone and choice of language. For example, when describing the 14/15-year-old boy giving evidence she said:

> L's demeanour in the case was very much the active engaged combatant rather than a frightened sad young person. ... If I am not entitled to make these observations about L's presentation, they are not the foundation of my conclusions, and I would have come to the same conclusion without them.[97]

Parker J explicitly recognises that her observations are not relevant to the decision, yet she nonetheless chooses to present this image of the child, revealing presumptions about the 'ideal', enfeebled way that a child fearful of his stepfather should conduct himself in court. A similar tone is evident in *Z v Y* where a distinctly authoritarian and judgmental attitude is adopted towards the child and her views. It is suggested, for example, that the girl has been 'inappropriately empowered'; that she is 'dredging up flimsy rationalisations' for her objections; that the short-term harm she will suffer does not go beyond normal 'teenage angst'; and that the child's use of a crude phrase (which the Cafcass officer refers to as 'unfortunate') was 'offensive and rude, particularly for a well brought up girl from a conservative country'.[98] This can be contrasted with Black LJ's discussion of the child's participation in Court of Appeal proceedings in *Re LC (Children)*. Although she did not think the child should have been present, she used respectful language towards the girl, including commending her on how she conducted herself.[99]

Structure and fact-selection are yet other ways in which children can be brought to the forefront or, indeed, sidelined in a judgment. In *Re F*, Black LJ presents the children's letters to the court before the Cafcass report, thus ensuring that it is their unfiltered voices that are heard first.[100] She also implicitly criticises the first instance judge for failing to include some of the 'stronger comments' of objection made by the children.[101] In the Supreme Court decision in *Re LC*,[102] Baroness Hale avoids such pitfalls by quoting the children verbatim, using their

97 Above n. 54, para. 50.

98 Above n. 54, para. 35, per Parker J.

99 Above n. 42. However, we might ask whether even seemingly positive statements such as this perpetuate a view that children must conform to adult standards of 'good behaviour' in order to be listened to and respected.

100 Above n. 58.

101 See also Cobb J who, citing Black LJ in *Re F*, explicitly notes in *F v M, B (by his Litigation Friend)* above n. 19 that he has looked at *all* of the child's comments and that he has 'tried as far as possible to concentrate on the actual words used by L, not the descriptions given by reporters', para. 35.

102 *Re LC* (SC) above n. 33.

exact language and thus allowing their authentic voice to be heard to a greater degree than had occurred in the lower courts. Both cases reinforce our argument that the strategies for achieving a children's rights judgment are inter-related and mutually supportive: a judge can only construct a narrative that centralises the child if the child is able to participate; but even when the child is directly heard, the judge must actively adopt a children's rights-based approach to ensure those views are *fully* and *accurately* conveyed in order to reach a children's rights-compatible outcome. Facts might be used in other ways too. For example, again in *Re LC*, Baroness Hale provides more detail about the child than we read in the lower court judgments, including the observation that the child, T, had always wanted to go to Oxford University. Prima facie this was not relevant to the case but it helps to provide a fuller picture of this individual child, whilst also hinting at her ambition and intelligence, perhaps to support giving her views greater weight.

5.2. THE AUDIENCE FOR ABDUCTION CASES: WRITING A CHILD-FRIENDLY JUDGMENT

The second aspect of the 'art and craft' of a children's rights judgment is a consideration of whom the judgment is written *for*. Different courts write for different audiences (an appeal court, a lower court, the public, the legislature, etc.). In family court proceedings in particular, where the personal relationships at the heart of the dispute are likely to be on-going and highly emotive, there is a strong imperative that those involved in the proceedings – not only the (adult) parties but the affected child/ren as well – understand the outcome and (hopefully) the reasoning so that the decision can be accepted as fair and can be subsequently enforced. The obligation for judgments to be written in a way that can be understood by those affected is founded in rule of law principles and access to justice. For children, this duty finds partial expression in the Council of Europe's *Child-Friendly Justice Guidelines*, though it is an obligation imposed on the child's lawyer or guardian (to communicate the decision to the child in language adapted to the child's level of understanding) rather than on the judge.[103]

Examples of 'child-friendly' judgments are starting to emerge in England and Scotland,[104] but are still rare. In parental child abduction cases, the legal framework and the practical and emotional issues they involve can be complex

[103] Council of Europe, *Guidelines on Child-Friendly Justice* (Council of Europe, 2010), para. 75.

[104] *Re A (Fact-Finding Hearing: Judge Meeting with Child)* [2012] EWCA Civ 185; *Re A: Letter to a Young Person*, [2017] EWFC 48; *Lancashire County Council v M and Others* [2016] EWFC 9 (Peter Jackson J); *Mr Patrick (a pseudonym) Pursuer against Mrs Patrick (a pseudonym)* [2017] SC GLA 46 (Sheriff Aisha y Anwar). See also the fictive examples in H. Stalford, K. Hollingsworth and S. Gilmore (eds.), above n. 3, chs. 13, 17, and 18.

and confounding for the parties involved; yet for the judiciary, especially in first instance decisions, the law is relatively settled and thus the need for intricate legal reasoning is reduced. Both of these factors provide a strong imperative for judges to write *for* the parties and, moreover, to write child-friendly judgments for the children affected (whether they have party status or not). This imperative is further heightened in objections cases where, in most instances, the child is regarded as of sufficient age and maturity to make objections and to have those objections taken into account. These children should, therefore, be regarded as also having sufficient capacity to understand an appropriately drafted judgment that clearly explains the decision-making process and the outcome.

It is perhaps surprising then that none of the cases we reviewed was obviously written for the child concerned. Some of the judgments were written in a simpler, clearer and more accessible way (Black LJ's judgments stand out); and there is evidence that some of the judges direct some of their comments to the child, with a view to ensuring the child understands their reasoning, including Cobb J, in *LCG v RL* ('I wish T to know that I understand and respect her views. She is plainly a bright and determined young person').[105] But even here, where there is a clear recognition of the value of children understanding the decision, the judgment is not written in a child-friendly manner. Indeed, there are examples of cases being actively child *un*friendly. Parker J likes to use old-fashioned phrases (she refers to a mother being 'confined' after giving birth) and, as noted above, the tone of her judgment is less than sympathetic to the children; indeed, one might imagine that if they did read what and *how* she wrote about them, their view of the law and faith in the legal system could be somewhat damaged.[106] There are also examples of abstruse phrases and language unlikely to be understood by children (or, indeed, by most adults), perhaps best exemplified by Mostyn J's idioms and similes ('without wishing to pile Ossa upon Pelion' and 'as plain as a pike staff'!).[107] Other judgments are cold, detached, legalistic and thus unlikely to be accessible to a child.[108]

Of course, there are a number of potential barriers to writing a child-friendly judgment in abduction cases, not least: linguistic (does the child speak the same language?); cultural (are there significant generational differences between the judge and the child that act as a barrier?); ethical (are there factors that have influenced a decision to which it would be inappropriate or traumatic to expose the child?); temporal (do judges have time to compose a child-friendly version when time is of the essence?); and procedural (will a child-friendly version satisfy the appeal court or will two judgments have to be written?). But none of these factors is insurmountable and in the cases we analysed, where not only

105 Above n. 19, para. 108.
106 See also *C v V* and *Z v Y*, above n. 54.
107 *SP v EB*, above n. 62.
108 E.g. *RB v DB*, above n. 69; *M (A Child)*, above n. 55.

is the child the focus of the judgment but s/he has also objected to her return, the arguments in favour of child-friendly judgments, or at least child friendly versions, are strong.

6. CONCLUSION

International child abduction cases present an important opportunity and, indeed, a need to reflect on how a children's rights-based approach to judgment-writing can be achieved. Our relatively modest analysis of 30 recent child objections cases in England and Wales suggests there is a great deal of variation in the extent to which judges are able and willing to engage with the factors that we have identified as characteristic of such an approach. In most instances, despite the constraints imposed by the summary nature of the process and the presumption in favour of return, there is greater scope for judges to more comprehensively reason, decide and compose children's rights judgments. This speaks not only to the substantive outcome, but also to ensuring that children's voices are adequately heard during proceedings, that their wishes are conveyed accurately and given due weight, that the narrative centrally positions the child ensuring that it is her reality (in the words of Lady Hale) which informs the reasoning, and that the judgment is drafted in a way respectful of, and comprehensible to, children. This is especially true in objection cases, where the discretion available to judges once the gateway criteria have been satisfied provides a unique opportunity to elaborate more fully and explicitly on the full range of children's rights that are disrupted by child abduction or, indeed, by an order for return.

Notwithstanding the practical and legal constraints, some of the cases in this area offer an encouraging lesson in how to apply children's rights principles, but as Black LJ notes in *Re KP*:

> courts in this jurisdiction are … still feeling their way forward in order to determine how best to hear the voice of a child who is the subject of an application under the Hague Convention. What is, or is not, the appropriate channel through which a child is heard will differ from case to case, and the manner in which the task is undertaken will depend on the developing skill and understanding of the judge and the other professionals involved … Our collective understanding of these matters … is still, to an extent, in its infancy.[109]

We hope that the insights gained from the *Children's Rights Judgments* project and tested out here will assist judges, in some way, in this endeavour.

---

[109] Above n. 19, para. 52.

JUDICIAL ACTIVISM: A 20-YEAR EVOLUTION

Mathew THORPE

The development of international family law, initiated by the 1980 Hague Abduction Convention and progressed by a number of other European and global instruments, led to the rapid rise of litigation in the many domestic courts of transnational jurisdiction. In the 1990s the younger judges felt the urge to communicate directly with a judge in the other court seised and a corresponding sense of frustration if prevented from doing so.

This natural development was not restricted to cross-border family proceedings. It was an equally prominent feature of international insolvency practice. Mr Justice Baragwanath of the New Zealand High Court drew attention to this developing trend, which he labelled 'Judicial Activism'. I learned from him and was able to repay him with my experience in international family proceedings, which were not his sphere.

It has been said that the earliest reported case recording direct judicial collaboration was the Canadian case of *D v B*, decided on 17 May 1996 in the Superior Court of Quebec. In our law reports direct judicial communication seems to make its first appearance in the case of *Re HB (Abduction: children's objections)* [1998] 1 FLR 422. I was in the court together with Lady Justice Butler-Sloss and Sir John Vinelott. At first instance Wall J had endeavoured to establish direct communication, an endeavour which we supported. Another strong supporter of direct judicial communication in the Family Division was Singer J, who tackled the topic head on in his judgment in *Re MJ (Abduction: international judicial collaboration)* [2000] 1 FLR 803.

But these judicial pronouncements must be set in a much broader context. The 1980 Abduction Convention depended for its function on the creation and operation of Central Authorities, one in each state party to the convention. This was mandated. But the text of the Convention more or less took for granted the effective operation of judicial authority. That this was not a safe given was subsequently to be demonstrated by innumerable return applications malfunctioning in the courts of many states party to the Convention. As the mesh of countries operating the Convention steadily advanced and enlarged it became increasingly evident that the successful operation of the Convention depended not only upon the effective work of the Central Authorities but also upon the effective work of the judges. It was vital for the judges to understand and correctly apply the law, a goal they were unlikely to achieve without specialist skills. Not only must the judges be specialists in the law, but they must also be past masters in its practice and procedures. No doubt these realities persuaded the Hague Conference to host the first residential conference for judges of the states party to the 1980 Convention.

The conference was convened in the summer of 1998 at De Ruwenberg in the Catholic South of the Netherlands. At that date there were some 50 states party to the Convention and approximately half sent judges to contribute. Expertly guided by the Deputy Secretary General, the much esteemed Professor William Duncan, very valuable work was done. From this gathering stemmed the INCADAT website and the Judges' Newsletter, but its greatest achievement was the tentative creation of the Hague International Judicial Network. I say tentative because the proposal came from the United Kingdom. It was fiercely opposed by France. Thus it might have been stillborn. But I believe it survived thanks to strong support from Australia and New Zealand and the fact that France's opposition attracted no ally.

Having survived this uncertain baptism, it was given concrete existence by the nomination of specialist judges by the few states initially supporting the project.

This early development coincided with developments in Europe. 2001 saw the arrival of the Regulation creating the European Judicial Network for Civil and Commercial Law. In the same year came the prototype of what was to come, namely the short-lived Brussels II Regulation. In 2003 this matured into the Brussels IIA Regulation which, with its commencement in March 2005, brought family law into the heart of the work of the European Judicial Network. What gradually, almost inevitably, emerged were two parallel networks, one global, one European. Obviously the individual judge served both functions where applicable. It would have made no sense to have had one judge on the Hague Network and a different judge on the European Network.

As the Hague international network grew in strength and numbers, so it became necessary to develop a code of judicial practice and conduct. Such developments were shaped by debate at Special Commissions, which in their resolutions were broadly supportive of the existence and function of the judicial network and direct judicial communication. But something more focused was needed, and in a joint venture the European Commission and the Permanent Bureau organised the 2009 Joint EC–HCCHC conference on Direct Judicial Communications on Family Law Matters and the Development of Judicial Networks. This was a creative partnership venture. The Hague Conference provided the expertise and convened the judges. The Commission funded the event at its premises in Brussels.

Specifically, the conference was designed to bring to fulfilment the preparatory work that had been done by each of the partners. The European Commission was certainly not averse to innovation. It had published its 'Practice Guide for the Application of the New Brussels II Regulation' on 1 June 2005. The Guide had been drafted by an expert group, including Singer J. Thanks to his experience, the Guide cautiously endorsed the scope for judges to talk to each other across jurisdictional boundaries. Under the heading 'How should the judges communicate?', in considering Article 15 transfers, there appeared:

> Article 15 states that the courts shall co-operate, either directly or through the Central Authorities, for the purpose of the transfer. It may be particularly useful for the judges concerned to communicate to assess whether in the specific case the requirements for a transfer are fulfilled, in particular if it would be in the best interests of the child. If the two judges speak and/or understand a common language, they should not hesitate to contact each other directly by telephone or e-mail. Other forms of modern technology may be useful, e.g. conference calls. If there are language problems, the judges may rely on interpreters. The Central Authorities will also be able to assist the judges.

Whilst this now seems unremarkable, in the summer of 2005 it was a ground-breaking statement and certainly not uncontentious. There were still influential senior judges, even family specialists, who saw danger ahead on this road. There was even an academic who published an article accusing us of breaching our judicial oath.

On the global stage, the Fifth Special Commission in October and November 2006 had included in its conclusions a recommendation that a statement of principles and good practice in direct judicial communication should be prepared with the advice of an expert group drawn principally from the judiciary.

We who were appointed to the Expert Group met first in July 2008 in The Hague, where we discussed and revised a preliminary draft. It was this text which was the working document considered by the much larger congregation of judges at the Brussels conference in the following January, which I have recorded above. Although difficulties emerged in the fundamentally important areas of judicial independence and natural justice, the draft was approved with further revisions.

We, the Expert Group, met again in The Hague in June 2010 and what we agreed was put to the Sixth Special Commission in June 2011. Once approved, it was published with all the authority of the Hague Conference.

As is not uncommon with the products of the Hague Conference, it has a lengthy title, thus: 'Emerging Guidance regarding the development of the International Hague Network of Judges and General Principles for Judicial Communications, including commonly accepted safeguards for Direct Judicial Communications in specific cases, within the context of the International Hague Network of Judges'. The guide has met an important need. It answers the questions of the critical opponent. It guides the tyro or enthusiast who seeks reassurance as to the legitimate and the orthodox.

The balance of authority between the European Union and the Hague Conference was not left in doubt. Regulations expressly stated their priority over Conventions. Article 11 of Brussels IIA effectively amended the 1980 Abduction Convention when operated between two EC Member States. At the Special Commissions in The Hague after 2003 the European Commission appeared as a substantial presence at the table. It then introduced the discipline of a preliminary coordinating meeting for Member States' representatives at which a line was settled for that day's business from which Member States should not depart.

There were also tensions within some delegations as policy officials excluded judges from debate or imposed a policy line on the judge. From these and other experiences there grew the desire for occasional residential conferences for judges who were nominated members of the Hague Network. I was able to secure the support of the Ministry of Justice and of the Foreign and Commonwealth Office to host the first at Cumberland Lodge in July 2013. The second became possible in Hong Kong in September 2015 in conjunction with the Third Children's Forum there and the following Commonwealth Judicial Conference in Sydney. The Seventh Special Commission in October created the opportunity for the next meeting of the Network.

Let me step back from any further consideration of the detail and simply observe that there has been a movement of forces all in the same general direction.

- There was the stream of judicial pronouncements from the bench in reported judgments, increasingly creative and positive.
- There was the contribution of the judges in their quasi-diplomatic role, arguing the case for activism at Commissions and Conferences, as well as creating through the Expert Group the 'Emerging Guidance'.
- There was the parallel and supportive activity of the European Commission through the European Judicial Network.
- There was the spectacular growth of the International Hague Network from single figures at the turn of the century to well over 100 judges, representing over 70 jurisdictions, in modern times.

This is a history of harmony since, apart from the earliest days, there has been no real dissent and there is not a single case in which miscarriage of justice has resulted from an abuse of the general principles governing direct judicial communication.

So we have seen the specialist family judges of the world united in their more or less passionate support for direct judicial collaboration. This support is expressed not only by the trial judges but also by the most influential courts, such as the Court of Justice of the European Union and the Supreme Court of the United Kingdom. We should also note the flexibility of the tool. Although originally and principally for use in child abduction cases, it has in this jurisdiction been used in cases involving intercountry adoption, maintenance, care proceedings in two jurisdictions, the validity of marriage and a divorce forum dispute. There would be no sense or logic in restricting its use. It is a tool of general utility. The only, and perhaps theoretical, argument against its validity is the absence of any legislative reference. Obviously the concept long post-dated the 1980 Convention. During the long negotiation of Brussels IIA, culminating in agreement in 2003, the tool was comparatively new to the world. So whereas the Regulation mandated the meetings of the Contact Points and the Central Authorities, there is nothing that requires a Member State to send its network judge to the meetings of the European Judicial Network.

But now at last legislative legitimacy may be in sight. In particular, I draw attention to Recital 44 in the Council's proposals for the text of Brussels II Recast, which, in detailing channels of communication, gives equal status to Central Authorities, Network Judges and Contact Points. In the articles themselves the role of the European Judicial Network is explicit in Article 14(6) and Article 79(2).

Of course, these are only proposals and we must wait to see how they emerge from the process of negotiation by 27 Member States. Whatever may result it is a political acknowledgment from the Commission. It is a thoroughly realistic and modern acknowledgement. It is to be much applauded. It would remove the pedantic argument, much advanced in the early days, that in the domestic law of the particular state there was no legal basis for the nomination or function of the network judge.

I write as a retired judge to record my memory of what was a substantial growth in the responsibility of the specialist judges worldwide. Without that growth our power and influence would have withered.

But, you may ask, what does this record have to do with the career of Nigel Lowe? My answer is that we have all drawn on his great authority.

First his statistical research, prepared for successive Special Commissions, established not only the scale of Convention applications worldwide but also trends, such as duration of proceedings, use of mediation, the sex of the abductor, the percentage of return orders, the frequency with which the Article 13(b) objection was invoked, and outcomes once invoked. The guidance that his statistical research offered was and is crucial to the quasi-diplomatic and advisory work of the specialist judges worldwide.

Secondly, we specialist judges, just as much as specialist practitioners, have been heavily reliant on his great work (with Mark Everall and Michael Nicholls): *International Movement of Children*. How did we manage before its arrival in 2003? He, appreciating the ever-increasing volume and complexity of international family law (caused in part by competition between the law-makers to stake out their territories), saw the need to survey the whole territory in a single volume. The standing and reputation of his work grew steadily and, as new laws and trends flowed in, we became increasingly anxious for news of a second edition. In 2016 this (by Nigel and Michael Nicholls) arrived, 50 per cent fatter than the first, and we rejoiced. However Brexit is resolved, we are sure to need a third edition to explain a new legal order for the protection of children moving across European borders.

Throughout Nigel has worked quietly, courageously and always with great authority and with great modesty. Now has come the time for us to acknowledge our great debt to him and our great gratitude.

GLOBALISATION OF ADJUDICATION IN INTERNATIONAL FAMILY LAW: SERVING INTERNATIONAL FAMILIES BY PRODUCING INTERNATIONAL SOLUTIONS

David HODSON[1]

1. OVERVIEW

The number of international families has grown hugely, with the trend likely to continue with increased mobility of labour and travel. But they have been ill served by family law which remains stoically, and sometimes jingoistically, national. The international family laws which do exist sometimes work well but are too often dependent upon national interpretations and resources. This cannot continue. It is for the community of international family lawyers to debate and find solutions and then persuade both national governments and international organisations of their importance. Justice and fairness requires it.

---

[1] DAVID HODSON OBE MICArb is an English solicitor, mediator, arbitrator, an Australian qualified solicitor and barrister and a part time deputy family court judge in London (DDJ at the CFC). He is a co-founding partner of The International Family Law Group LLP, a specialist practice in Covent Garden, London, (www.iflg.uk.com) serving the interests of international families and their children. He is editor and a primary author of *The International Family Law Practice*, 5th edn., Jordans, Bristol 2016, England's leading textbook on international family law. He is an honorary professor at Leicester University and a visiting professor at the University of Law. He was awarded the OBE for services to international family law. He can be contacted at dh@davidhodson.com.

2. THE LIVES OF INTERNATIONAL FAMILIES

There are now very many international families.[2] These families live in an international community. Some are totally immersed in an entirely expat community within a country. Some adopt some aspects of the country, perhaps dependent upon the term of years they are likely to be living in that country. Some live entirely within the national community but may have one family member who maintains ongoing connections with the home country. There are national families with ongoing connections with other countries such as holding property or pensions abroad. International families are very varied. They share the distinctive quality of an overall lesser connection with home countries. This plays out in various aspects of their life.

Some work for international employers, with international terms of employment which include real risks of international travel or relocation as contract terms. They may be paid from abroad or indeed be paid in a country abroad. They may build up a pension abroad. These kinds of international families will be distinctly more comfortable with international currencies, transferring funds abroad and holding funds abroad. They are likely to be at least bilingual. Their children are more likely to be at international schools studying for internationally recognised exams, and in turn more likely to be meeting other children of other nationalities. They will live digital lives in order best to maintain contact with family and friends. They will be familiar with international developments either in their home countries or generally across the globe, for the simple reason that these developments affect them more than national families.

Into this mix comes the 'third culture kid' (TCK), the child raised in a culture, perhaps even just a country, which is not that of the birth or nationality of his or her parents. These are often children of diplomats, military or multinational corporate employees, moving every few years, some of whom are now adults. They have far less affinity with their parents' nationality and sometimes refer to their passport nationality, their birth nationality and their present nationality. Whilst some return home on adulthood, many continue the transnational life

---

2 The EU, inevitably the most transient set of countries because of the freedom of movement and of labour, estimates there are around 122 million marriages in the EU, of which around 16 million (13%) are considered 'international' (couples of different nationalities, couples living apart in different countries or living together in a country other than their home country). There were more than 1 million divorces in the 27 EU Member States in 2007, of which 140,000 (13%) had an 'international' element. Figures from Eurostat, EU statistics agency and further here: <http://ec.europa.eu/eurostat/statistics-explained/index.php?title=Marriage_and_divorce_statistics&oldid=295538>. This ignores those many international families who are unlikely to seek access to private civil law remedies, e.g. refugees, who themselves have distinctive legal needs not addressed here.

of their parents and form relationships with those of other nationalities. In turn they are raising the second-generation TCKs who have often only the most tenuous personal connections with any particular nation or nationality culture.

When seeking professional services, these international families invariably look to advisers with an international presence. When seeking solutions to problems affecting their family, they inevitably look for international solutions because that is the life they lead and where in other aspects of their life, commercial and corporate arrangements exist.

Specifically, such international families are often unwilling to accept an entirely national, perhaps even nationalistic and certainly national-centric, outcome.

Too often these international families have no constituency,[3] no lobbying group, little uniformity for representational purposes and indeed may have little direct interest in the affairs of the country in which they may be presently living beyond their own interests. It's little wonder that pressures for reform must come from lawyers seeing a wide range of international problems, not the families themselves.

3. THE PROBLEMS WITH INTERNATIONAL FAMILY LAWS

The experience of international families when they seek assistance from what they presume is some sort of international law is that it either does not exist or exists inadequately for the most part. They find directly conflicting national laws on outcomes, jurisdictions, stays, divorce, child support, financial arrangements and working out the best arrangements for children. They find laws which favour the first party to break up the marriage and favour the wealthier party. They find some judges inexperienced in dealing with international cases and lawyers without international experience. They find difficulties in international enforcement. Most sad of all, too often they find general jingoistic nationalism and favouritism.

Reform has been slow. Impetus has come from the EU and the Hague Conference. Each has, however, fallen foul of different national interpretations. Neither has any effective policing in respect of, for example, non-compliance, slow process or nationalistic favouritism. There are other problems.

Any reform at EU level does not include the USA and Canada, the former Commonwealth countries, the Emirates and other parts of the Middle East, China and Japan; leading non-EU international family law countries, which will

3 France is rare in giving a constituency to its citizens in London.

soon include the UK. The EU is openly expansionist with its concepts of universal application of its laws and exclusive competency in international arrangements.[4] First, this is not universally welcomed and a number of EU countries have resented the frustration of their sovereign powers to enter into arrangements with non-EU countries with which they have close connections in different areas of personal and commercial life.[5] Secondly, this is not reciprocated. The EU may demand that some or all Member States apply the law of another jurisdiction including the laws of countries outside the EU, but countries outside the EU will not reciprocate necessarily and apply the law of the EU Member State in identical circumstances. Australia will not apply the law of an EU Member State even if that EU Member State in identical circumstances would apply the law of Australia. Thirdly, expansionism of its laws and concepts fails to acknowledge that its success thus far has been as a consequence of the power to impose laws on EU Member States.[6] This will not be possible outside EU borders, where cooperation and collaboration will be needed. One success of the EU has been the CJEU as the final Court of Appeal on matters of EU law. Even here, it has struggled with long delays, invariably 18 months, with only occasional use of its fast track[7] or abbreviated process.[8] Fundamentally it is a court of final appeal and not a first instance court of a supranational nature.

The Hague Conference on Private International Law[9] created the original international family law, with the 1980 Child Abduction Convention being the first significant multi-international law and still probably the one most referred to and most regarded across the world. Unlike the EU, which has been able to impose laws on EU Member States, The Hague works through cooperation, collaboration and consultation. It covers a far wider range of jurisdictional traditions, cultures and systems. It embraces a much greater range of economies and therefore resources available for judicial systems and processes. Cultural and religious elements are more significant across The Hague countries than the EU. But these potential weaknesses, in contrast to the EU, are its very strengths. A frustrating slowness, inevitable with consultation and collaboration, leads however to far greater acceptance and adherence by its signatories. Its flexibility

---

4 Opinion 1/03, CJEU 7 February 2006, ECLI:EU:C:2006:81.

5 E.g. Case C-399/12 *Germany v Council*, ECLI:EU:C:2014:2258.

6 UK and Denmark have opt-outs.

7 Art. 105.1 Rules of the Procedure of the Court of Justice [2012] OJ L265, as amended on 18 June 2013 [2013] OJ L173, and on 19 July 2016 [2016] OJ L217.

8 Art. 95.1 ibid.

9 HCCH (the Hague Conference) is the preeminent organisation in the area of private international law. It was formed in 1893 to 'work for the progressive unification of the rules of private international law'. It has done so by creating and assisting in the implementation of multilateral conventions including harmonising conflicts of law. 82 countries are members of the Hague Conference, inclusive of EU Member States by virtue of the EU being a member.

has prompted significant co-working between judges in separate countries operating Hague laws, with specialist co-working between experts in reviewing legislation and making proposals. Its primary weaknesses include the lack of any overall court to consider interpretations of Hague law and of any real centralised policing of failures of implementation. There is no doubt that the role of The Hague will be paramount for the future for international families and is their best hope short of any other innovations. Indeed, any innovations are most likely to be successful coming from The Hague or working through existing Hague mechanisms.

The heart of the matter, and inevitable starting point, is where any proceedings should take place. Here lies a chief frustration for the international family familiar with cross-border life and solutions. They find it incredible that they cannot come to a solution until at least two nation states – with which they may have a relatively passing, even historic, connection – have engaged in a dispute about forum, when their own concern is overall resolution. They find jurisdictional criteria to be out of touch with the realities of international life.[10] This is probably the core issue for going forward for the longer-term future

4. SOME PRESENT SOLUTIONS

As forum is the invariable starting point, this should be the focus for solutions. In fairness to the EU, it recognised this in the late 1990s and introduced in March 2001 a radical solution.

In Brussels II, from March 2001, the EU dealt with the issue of forum on divorce, subsequently extended to maintenance[11] and soon extended to marital property,[12] by saying that whichever party was first to commence proceedings secured those proceedings in that national jurisdiction, whatever might be the weakness of the connections with that jurisdiction and the strength of the connections with any other jurisdiction. There had to be some connectedness,[13] but this was widely drafted, and many international families found themselves with two or more countries in which the proceedings could be commenced. Although warned by English lawyers in consultation in the late 1990s of the

10 Such as requiring only one habitual residence in law whereas some have clearly two home bases e.g. Dublin and Belfast, London and Paris.

11 Council Regulation (EC) 2009/4 of 18 December 2008 on jurisdiction, applicable law, recognition and enforcement of decisions and cooperation in matters relating to maintenance obligations.

12 Council Regulation (EU) 2016/1103 of 24 June 2016 implementing enhanced cooperation in the area of jurisdiction, applicable law and the recognition and enforcement of decisions in matters of matrimonial property regimes.

13 Art. 3.

consequences of the race to court, which have proven to be the case, the EU has maintained this law despite a subsequent change to Brussels IIA, and most recently has refused any reforms in the new Brussels IIA Recast, to be introduced in 2019. Whilst its stance has brought clarity and certainty, it has been at a high cost through the adverse impact on mediation, pre-litigation negotiations and reconciliations in saving 'saveable' marriages. No other group of countries has such a law.[14] It is compounded by the uncertainty of what it means to be the first to 'commence proceedings'[15] and the significant difference in practice as to speed between countries. It has been described as arbitrary and unfair.[16]

The EU belatedly recognised the problems and has said the answer is applicable law. It does not matter where the proceedings are if the country applies the law with which the couple have the closest connection. This could be a resolution. Its difficulty is that in practice countries apply another law through their own rose-tinted nationalistic glasses. It works best between civil law countries and inadequately with discretion-based common law jurisdictions. It can cause delays and increase costs dependent upon the process for ascertaining the relevant applicable law. It causes perceived injustice where one court may grant one particular outcome in a case and then an hour or a day later in another case hand down a totally different outcome on the same facts, simply because of applying a different law. It only works if the competing countries both operate adherence to applicable law. The EU tried over several years and several pieces of draft legislation to impose this approach on all EU Member States but eventually those Member States, aware of the need for legislation for harmonisation and clarity on applicable law, entered into what was then a unique enhanced cooperation arrangement.[17]

If applicable law was supported and rolled out globally, with adherence to the relevant national law, then it could answer the problem. Politically and legally this is unlikely. It is not the solution.

Arbitration schemes have been created to deal with forum disputes, using arbitrators with a distinctive international experience. This is quite probably an important way forward.[18]

---

14 T. Oldham, 'Why a new Uniform Equitable Distribution Jurisdiction Act is needed to reduce forum shopping on divorce litigation' (2015) 49 *Family Law Quarterly* 359.

15 See Case C-173/16 *MH v MH*, ECLI:EU:C:2016:542.

16 *L-K v K (No. 3)* [2006] EWHC 3281 (Fam), [2007] 2 FLR 741 and *Re N (Jurisdiction)* [2007] EWHC 1274 (Fam), [2007] 2 FLR 1196.

17 Council Regulation (EU) 2016/1103 of 24 June 2016 implementing enhanced cooperation in the area of jurisdiction, applicable law and the recognition and enforcement of decisions in matters of matrimonial property regimes.

18 See the International Family Law Arbitration Scheme, set up by Patrick Parkinson and the author, for arbitration in forum disputes, with specialist arbitrators and (fundamentally) an arbitrator not from a country with which either party is presently connected i.e. a neutral one. <https://internationalfamilyarbitration.com/>.

Another solution is common threads or legal terminology across the world e.g. the 'best interests of the child' test. This appears in many national laws and some international laws but carries widely differing cultural and other understandings. The international family invariably understands the cultural differences because these will have intruded already on to their family life in many ways. They are often way ahead of the family lawyers and justice process in comprehending this obstacle. What they cannot accept are other differences of a more nationalistic nature intruding on what should be a fairly straightforward exercise in analysing best interests. It is found in the frequent difficulties in coming to some international consensus in respect of child relocation, one of the most dominant elements for the lives of international families. Almost 40 years on from the 1980 Hague Convention, it is also found in the still re-occurring difficulties in the acceptance that 'best interests', in the context of child abduction, means the return of the child to another signatory state for resolution of matters concerning the child in that state. International family lawyers find clients absolutely bemused and amazed that these differences still exist in our increasingly closer international community. A solution of one terminology as basic as 'best interests of the child' has not thus far found the success that should have been expected.

Another solution has been increased co-working between judges. This is found in the European Judicial Network. It has been distinctively found in the network of Hague Convention judges, predominantly in the child abduction context.[19] More generally, specialist judges often have direct contacts in other jurisdictions. Undoubtedly this has hugely helped the implementation of international laws, alongside international judicial cooperation between judges dealing with any particular case. Overall, this has undoubtedly been beneficial for international families and international law. It may be a key to the future.

Some innovative countries have gone even further for disputes within their borders. The Dubai International Financial Centre (DIFC) is an international free zone in Dubai, established in 2004. The Centre was created to ensure that global investors and issuers of capital with a regional capital market set in an international environment could operate easily in Dubai. It has a separate jurisdiction with its own system of laws, based largely on English common law, and its own courts, the DIFC Courts. In 2011 its jurisdiction was expanded,[20] which allowed any parties to use the DIFC Court to resolve commercial disputes. This opened up the possibility of avoiding the United Arab Emirates

---

19 See Mathew Thorpe, 'Judicial Activism: A 20-Year Evolution', in this volume.

20 Following the signing of Dubai Law (No. 16) of 2011 Amending Certain Provisions of Law (No. 12) of 2004 Concerning Dubai International Financial Centre Court.

court system and allowing parties to opt for an English-based, common law court. The DIFC Courts are courts of the UAE and, as such, are party to a series of treaties which support the enforcement of foreign decisions in the UAE. The DIFC Courts have also signed memoranda of guidance, mainly on reciprocal enforcement, with a number of courts and authorities including the Commercial Court of England and Wales. Whilst these memoranda do not have binding legal effect on judges and do not constitute a treaty or legislation, they promote a mutual understanding of the laws and judicial processes for enforcement in each party's desired jurisdiction. There are no reported plans to expand the DIFC Courts jurisdiction further. Nevertheless, this model might well prove a way forward in family law. Other countries have a similar outlook, e.g. Singapore.

Resolution of disputes for international families need not be confined to the judicial process. Arbitration has been highly successful in the corporate and shipping realm. It is starting to work well in a few jurisdictions in family law where arbitration schemes have been created to deal with forum disputes using arbitrators with distinctive expertise. Arbitration enjoys one of the leading international conventions namely the New York 1958 Arbitration Convention, allowing reciprocal enforcement often broader than existing measures through court orders. It allows reservations and most signatories have entered reservations for family law. This is a key way forward for change by national governments to help international resolutions in the family law context.

A crucial element is marital agreements with cross-border effectiveness. Marital agreements and relationship agreements are usual in the culture of many countries. They are transportable and include choice of jurisdiction or law clauses. For the family which does not know where they may be if, sadly, the relationship breaks down, they are an obvious solution. Some countries automatically enforce them. This gives the security and confidence which the international family wants. But there are problems. First, the countries where marital agreements are normal are invariably those which do not insist on independent legal advice before they are executed. This can cause unfair outcomes or unfair circumstances in which the agreement was entered into with one party being under duress and/or not having knowledge of their separate rights and entitlements. Some countries by contrast, especially in the common law tradition, have very strong preconditions on entering into these agreements to protect the more vulnerable party. There is across the world a huge chasm on this issue. Secondly, some countries do not treat marital agreements as automatically binding. They will be taken into account and usually given weight. But these countries are also the most likely to have little difficulty holding an agreement to be unfair and then to substitute another outcome. Whilst this might be good in equity and morality, in the broader global sphere it does not help the reputation of and confidence in these agreements. Thirdly, there is confusion created by a wide range of ways of drafting these agreements when they come to be implemented in another, perhaps quite different, jurisdiction. However, undoubtedly this is a possible key way forward.

5. SOME THINKING ABOUT FUTURE SOLUTIONS

Much academic thinking has been devoted to other areas of law, and family law's challenge is to adapt and apply. But international family problems are not unique. Provided we are not precious about the distinctive family dynamic of the work (and there are certainly some distinctive issues pertaining to children), what is happening elsewhere can be borrowed.

Laurence R. Helfer and Anne-Marie Slaughter contributed hugely to this discussion in their article 'Towards a Theory of Effective Supranational Adjudication',[21] probably foundational reading on finding a way forward. They asked, from the American perspective, whether the European experience of supranational adjudication could be transplanted beyond Europe. They went on to develop a 'checklist' of factors that enhance the effectiveness of supranational adjudication. They distinguished between those factors that are within the control of Member States; those that are within the control of the judges themselves; and those that may be beyond the control of either states or judges. After developing the checklist, they used it to analyse the practice of the United Nations Human Rights Committee (UNHRC). Although it was established expressly as a committee of experts rather than a court, they found analysis of its practice revealed that it had become increasingly 'court-like'. They found little difficulty in the concept of supranational adjudication. This meets exactly the expectations of international families and the way forward. This was two decades ago but set the ground work.

Perhaps a primary contribution to the debate has been a special edition of the *Utrecht Law Review* of June 2007 on *Adjudication in the globalising context*. This has inspired the author in his own thinking over the past decade. A number of articles were written about different aspects, some from a national perspective looking outwards and some from the international perspective looking forwards. It is essential reading in finding solutions. Space here does not allow a greater exposition and a simplistic summary would not do it justice. But the conclusion bears repeating:

> The developments described in this special issue are not restricted to one country, or to one region. Adjudication is undergoing rapid changes as a result of globalization,

---

[21] L.R. Helfer and A. Slaughter, 'Towards a Theory of Effective Supranational Adjudication' (1997–1998) 107 *Yale Law Journal* 273.

> but also because major institutions like the IMF and the World Bank foster policies for improving court functioning, judicial quality and integrity. As a result, the law, but also the courts and judicial organizations, have to adapt. Adjudication needs strategic management in order to be able to respond to societal and technological developments; courts and judicial organizations also need to adapt for the same reason. As a result, adjudication and judicial organization have become participants in local, national and global processes of change. Judges and court management will, as a result, have to live up to increasing demands and pressures for juridical and organizational development. Judges and courts need to demonstrate that they can fulfil their societal roles in an infinitely enlarged environment: The World.[22]

The authors anticipate not only national courts adjudicating in international matters but some supranational judicial structures.

Oreste Pollicino continued this approach, looking at the impact of the then enlargement of the European Union (EU) on the judicial interaction between the EU and Member States' legal orders.[23] The distinctive element was the constitutional courts of the new accession countries, based on their post-war political past, looking at the context in order to evaluate the reciprocal influences between the two sides, supranational and national.

A few years after the above *Utrecht Law Review* special issue, but in the same periodical, looking at contract law, Anne Keirse argued that employing a solely national approach to contract law is no longer a sustainable preference given European developments' increasing influence on national law. She called for all stakeholders to partake in further debate concerning the future of contract law in the Member States.[24] A similar call is needed in family law.

Finally, Geert De Baere's edited volume on *The Contribution of International and Supranational Courts to the Rule of Law* accepts that international and supranational courts are increasingly central to the development of a transnational rule of law.[25] The book examines the manner in which and the extent to which international courts and tribunals contribute to the rule of law at the national, regional, and international levels.

There are other contributions. There cannot be any progress without a good understanding of the debate and thinking so far on this issue from academia.

---

22 A.M. Hol and P.M. Langbroek (eds.), 'Introduction' (2007) 3(1) *Utrecht Law Review* 1, 7.

23 O. Pollicino, 'The New Relationship between National and the European Courts after the Enlargement of Europe: Towards a Unitary Theory of Jurisprudential Supranational Law?' (2010) 29(1) *Yearbook of European Law* 65.

24 A. Keirse, 'European Impact on Contract Law: A Perspective on the Interlinked Contributions of Legal Scholars, Legislators and Courts to the Europeanization of Contract Law' (2011) 7(1) *Utrecht Law Review* 34.

25 G. De Baere (ed.), *The Contribution of International and Supranational Courts to the Rule of Law*, Edward Elgar, Cheltenham 2016.

6. SOME WAYS FORWARD

What could the future look like? What could be the way forward?

A clear global theme is private autonomy, the right and entitlement of individuals and couples to take decisions for themselves for their futures. Private autonomy is respected by legislators, the judiciary and by the couple themselves. It also recognises what the couple have accomplished in reaching the agreement and the decisions themselves. In family law it is found in marital and other family agreements. But this private autonomy clashes with keenness to protect vulnerable parties from duress, misrepresentation and unfairness. Here is judicial paternalism versus the individual keenness to reach private agreements. Contract law principles can be applied. However, the family courts may have higher requirements in the context of a domestic arrangement than might be the case in a civil contract at arm's length and where there may be greater involvement of lawyers or other professional advisers. The primary difference across the world is between those countries who are quite content to have either no representation or joint representation, i.e. no *separate* independent legal advice, and those which insist upon it. But amongst the latter, the position is softening in places. In June 2017 an expert group recommended that the Hague Conference look into private agreements.[26] Admittedly this recommendation was in the children law context but it is hoped this will inform the debate.

Presuming there can be progress and some unanimity accepted amongst leading jurisdictions, two elements arise. First, there must be more standardisation and uniformity in the content of these agreements: it is inefficient and unhelpful that agreements are drafted afresh each time. Of course couples will want distinctive elements but the author has argued that European law reform organisations need to create half a dozen pro forma precedent models of marital agreements, identified as such, e.g. 'model agreement No 3', which can therefore be understood by all who may then subsequently implement it. This will produce more clarity and certainty. No other economically efficient model would have tailor-made agreements almost every time. Thus far the plea has fallen on deaf ears. Secondly, these agreements can operate in a supranational form, and already do so. They may be informed by national awareness of what might be fair and reasonable but they are not tied to this. Thirdly, they can include choice of adjudication rather than choice of jurisdiction or law. It is this third element which could lead the way forward.

A number of countries have limited, 'ticketed' judges for distinctive areas of work where they have international effect. The concern is to limit the judges

[26] <https://assets.hcch.net/docs/1c688fd7-631d-4bb3-9597-e2c7a975839a.pdf>, with a meeting anticipated March 2018.

whose decisions will have international implications. Sometimes these are judges sitting in the so-called 'Senior Courts',[27] whose decisions have international enforceability as distinct from some first instance courts. In the past when international cases were fewer, some countries commendably restricted these cases to a couple of court locations and a restricted cache of judges.

It is a short step from two parties with independence and real choice entering into an agreement with a degree of precision about the intended outcome but perhaps with a saving of adjudication on particular elements, to go to a small group of judges internationally certified or authorised to hear these matters. Disputes on jurisdiction would then be irrelevant, as these judges would in essence be handling the marital agreement, in one of several forms, and applying the intention of the parties regarding an overriding fairness objective, to be internationally stated, albeit with the outcome in a national law order, fully recognised and enforced internationally. This could be through adjudication in court or in arbitration.

There would need to be an important debate to hear from those countries anxious about fairness such as provision for each party's needs. This debate has not happened in any global sense rather than regional discussions. One side will have to give way. This will intrude on legal past traditions. This is further reason why the discussion must be global rather than regional. It might well be that more couples than presently anticipated would admit that each party's needs should be taken into account if circumstances are different to those at the time of the entering into the agreement. This global discussion can be best undertaken under the auspices of the Hague Convention. Although this future may be some time away, planning must start soon.

In a similar way in respect of children, with the distinctive importance of listening to the voice of the child and the universal criteria of the best interests of the child, some supra-adjudication is far more likely to produce an outcome with international acceptance than the singular national outcome. It will be more acceptable to other countries and to the family involved. Future justice systems will work with technology, with use of online courts whereby the parties are only present through some updated version of Skype. This will facilitate supranational adjudication.

This process overcomes the concerns caused by applicable law because it will significantly follow the couple's wishes. It overcomes the dispute on forum because national law is not being applied and the judge is empowered and authorised to adjudicate on the supranational intentions. It meets precisely the lifestyle and needs of this kind of international family. It fits already with the foundations laid by international judicial networks. It can be underpinned

27 Senior Courts Act 1981.

by international enforcement through an extension of existing mechanisms on international enforcement either of court orders or of arbitration awards. The lawyers working within the system are increasingly in place with international family law expertise. The experience will create and inform a similar process for those without agreements.

There may be other ways forward. But existing ways are not working, will not work and are only causing frustration for those whom they are intended to serve, namely international families and their children. Global discussion and commitment is needed. This model builds on existing successful components to help produce global adjudication for international families and a truly international family law.

CREATING INTERNATIONAL FAMILIES: PRIVATE INTERNATIONAL LAW AND THE INDUSTRY OF PARENTHOOD

Claire FENTON-GLYNN

When discussing international child law, few authors are more eminent than Nigel Lowe. His exceptional writing on the international movement of children, including his work with the Permanent Bureau of the Hague Conference on Private International Law, the European Union and the Council of Europe, establishes him at the top of any reading list on the topic. In particular, his writing on parental child abduction, and its international regulation, has provided a benchmark for scholars that follow. In honour of his work on this important issue, this chapter will consider how the Hague Conference can continue its work in the field of international family law, focusing in particular on the confluence and congruence between regulation of intercountry adoption and international surrogacy.

1. THE CHANGING GLOBAL PICTURE

In the late 1980s, the international community was struggling to deal with the implications of intercountry adoption. A demand for adopted children in the West led to a 'mass exportation' of children from developing nations, accompanied by a thriving and lucrative industry for agencies and intermediaries. In response to this phenomenon, and the problems associated with it, the 1993 Hague Convention on Protection of Children and Co-operation in Respect of Intercountry Adoption was drafted. The aim of the Convention was not to harmonise, but to regulate, thus establishing a system of co-operation to prevent the abduction, sale of, or traffic in children under the cover of adoption. Unlike earlier conventions pertaining to children drafted by the Hague Conference, the 1993 Convention had the explicit aim of protecting the fundamental rights of children. For example, while the 1980 Convention on the Civil Aspects of International Child Abduction noted in its preamble that 'the interests of children are of paramount importance in matters relating to their custody', the objectives of the Convention were to 'secure the prompt return of children' and 'ensure … rights of custody and access'. Though the provisions may have had the intended effect of ultimately promoting the interests of the child, the focus of the convention was on civil regulation, rather than fundamental rights. The 1993 Convention, on the other hand, instead of simply establishing common provisions on jurisdiction, applicable law and recognition of orders, went further to establish safeguards to ensure that intercountry adoption takes place in the best interests of the child.[1]

Under the auspices of the Convention, intercountry adoption continued to grow, but in a much more regulated and ethical manner. In 2004, over 45,000 children were placed for intercountry adoption throughout the world, with almost 23,000 travelling to adoptive parents in the USA alone. By 2015, however, the total annual number had dropped to just over 12,000 globally – fewer than China had placed in 2004[2] – and a new phenomenon of international surrogacy was on the rise, leaving politicians, judges and academics facing new, complex, legal dilemmas.

There are many similarities between the phenomena of intercountry adoption and international surrogacy, and thus in the way we might choose to regulate them. Indeed, the Hague Conference itself has suggested that the 1993 Convention, with its combined nature as 'a human rights instrument, an instrument for judicial and administrative co-operation and a private international law instrument'[3] may provide a starting point for considering how to approach international surrogacy arrangements. The remainder of this chapter will explore the similarities in adoption and surrogacy, but also highlight the divergences, and how these may affect the approach that the international community takes to tackling the manifold difficulties posed by the growing industry of international surrogacy.

---

1 Although I have argued elsewhere that the Convention does not fully achieve this aim. See C. Fenton-Glynn, *Children's Rights in Intercountry Adoption: A European Perspective*, Intersentia, Antwerp 2014.

2 P. Selman, *Global Statistics for Intercountry Adoption: Receiving States and States of Origin 2004–2015* (2017), <https://assets.hcch.net/docs/a8fe9f19-23e6-40c2-855e-388e112bf1f5.pdf>.

3 Hague Conference on Private International Law, *A Preliminary Report on the Issues Arising from International Surrogacy Arrangements* (2012), <https://assets.hcch.net/docs/d4ff8ecd-f747-46da-86c3-61074e9b17fe.pdf>, at para. 50.

2. THE CONVERGENCE AND DIVERGENCE OF INTERCOUNTRY ADOPTION AND INTERNATIONAL SURROGACY

When deciding whether to start investigating the feasibility of a convention on adoption, the Hague Permanent Bureau put forward three bases for consideration:

(i) a dramatic increase in international adoptions which had occurred in many countries since the late 1960s to such an extent that intercountry adoption had become a worldwide phenomenon, involving migration of children over long geographical distances and from one society and culture to another very different environment;
(ii) serious and complex human problems, partly already known but aggravated as a result of these new developments, partly new ones, with among other things manifold complex legal aspects; and
(iii) insufficient existing domestic and international legal instruments, and the need for a multilateral approach.[4]

As with intercountry adoption in the 1980s, international surrogacy is going through a period of rapid expansion, becoming a worldwide phenomenon. While global statistics are not available, a 2014 study by the Hague Conference concluded that the number of international surrogacy arrangements taking place globally has 'grown significantly (if not, dramatically) over the past five years and is continuing to grow', estimating that several thousand children are being born each year to intending parents from all regions of the world.[5]

This global movement of children is also causing significant legal difficulties, both for the children themselves and also for the surrogate and commissioning parents. We have seen numerous reports of children who once born are not permitted to travel to the country of origin of the commissioning parents;[6] cases where the commissioning parents are not recognised as legal parents in their home country, leading to cases of 'limping parenthood', where different individuals are recognised as parents in different jurisdictions;[7] children who

---

4 G. Parra-Aranguren, *Explanatory Report on the Convention on the Protection of Children and Co-operation in Respect of Intercountry Adoption* (undated), <https://assets.hcch.net/upload/expl33e.pdf>, at para. 6.

5 Hague Conference on Private International Law, *A Study of Legal Parentage and the Issues Arising from International Surrogacy Arrangements* (2014), <https://assets.hcch.net/docs/bb90cfd2-a66a-4fe4-a05b-55f33b009cfc.pdf>, at para. 129.

6 See, for example *D v Belgium*, Application no. 29176/13, ECtHR, 11 September 2014; *Union of India v Jan Balaz* (2015-10-121) Supreme Court of India, 14 October 2015.

7 See, for example, *Mennesson v France*, Application no. 65192/11, ECtHR, 26 June 2014. This case was heard simultaneously with *Labassee v France*, Application no. 65941/11, ECtHR, 26 June 2014.

are left stateless;[8] and cases where children are taken away from commissioning parents and placed for adoption, as the surrogacy arrangement is contrary to domestic law.[9]

Also, similarly to intercountry adoption, surrogacy has seen a cyclical effect in primary countries of origin, where countries rise in prominence, before being shut down due to concerns surrounding exploitation, only to be replaced with a new jurisdiction offering more relaxed regulation and fewer legal safeguards. In relation to intercountry adoption, this was seen most poignantly in Romania, where large numbers of adoptions and widespread corruption in the 1980s and 1990s led to a moratorium on intercountry adoption in 2001, but has since been seen also in countries such as Guatemala, Russia and Vietnam. The same phenomenon is now being seen in destination countries for 'reproductive tourism': for example, Thailand, India, and Nepal – all once prominent hubs for commissioning parents – have in the last two years dramatically restricted accessibility of surrogacy for foreigners. The new Thai law now only permits surrogacy where the surrogate is related to one of the spouses, while the Government of Nepal has announced that exit permits will no longer be granted to children born to surrogates.[10] In India, where reproductive technology techniques were once a multi-billion-dollar industry,[11] the 2016 Surrogacy (Regulation) Bill currently going through parliament would restrict commissioning parents to Indian citizens using a surrogate who is a close relative.[12]

These features of surrogacy – the rapid growth of an industry, uncertainty of legal status, and rise in reproductive tourism – demonstrate the necessity of multilateral action, as there was in the early 1990s for intercountry adoption. The Hague Conference itself has referred to this as a 'human rights imperative'.[13] Current legal instruments are either non-existent, or at least inadequate to deal with the new and emerging problems, and, given the ease with which commissioning parents can cross borders, international co-operation is crucial.

---

8 See, for example, *Re X and Y (Foreign Surrogacy)* [2008] EWHC 3030 (Fam).

9 See, for example, *Paradiso and Campanelli v Italy*, Application no. 25358/12, ECtHR, 24 January 2017. In this case, the European Court of Human Rights found that there was no violation of Article 8 when the child was removed from the commissioning parents, as there was no genetic connection between them, and the social relationship between the child and parents was insufficient to constitute protected 'family life' under the Convention.

10 Hague Conference on Private International Law, *Background Note for the meeting of the Experts' Group on the Parentage/Surrogacy Project* (2016), <https://assets.hcch.net/docs/8767f910-ae25-4564-a67c-7f2a002fb5c0.pdf>, at para. 22.

11 As estimated by the Confederation of Indian Industry. See Liz Bishop, 'India's new surrogacy laws are only part of the equation' (14 March 2013) <http://monash.edu/news/show/indias-new-surrogacy-laws-are-only-part-of-the-equation>.

12 See <http://www.prsindia.org/billtrack/the-surrogacy-regulation-bill-2016-4470/>.

13 See Hague Conference on Private International Law, *The Desirability and Feasibility of Further Work on the Parentage/Surrogacy Project* (2014), <https://assets.hcch.net/docs/6403eddb-3b47-4680-ba4a-3fe3e11c0557.pdf>, at para. 19.

Despite these similarities, however, there are also manifest differences between the regulation of surrogacy and intercountry adoption, which cannot be taken lightly. The first problem lies in the wide divergence between different regulatory approaches to surrogacy. While it is true that there were 'serious and complex human problems' relating to intercountry adoption before the Hague Convention, these were different in nature to the problems besetting surrogacy. Adoption itself is a practice that is explicitly recognised in Article 21 of the UN Convention on the Rights of the Child,[14] and the challenge facing states was to ensure that adequate safeguards were in place to regulate best practice. In relation to surrogacy, states are deeply divided as to whether the practice itself is an inherent violation of human rights, let alone the mechanics of how it should be carried out and in what circumstances.

States' responses to surrogacy can be seen to fall into four categories. First, are those jurisdictions such as France, Germany, Austria, Switzerland, and Italy where surrogacy is expressly prohibited, no matter what form it takes. In these jurisdictions, both altruistic and commercial surrogacy are seen as intrinsic wrongs – offending the principle of the inviolability of the human body as well as the inalienability of personal status – which should be prohibited whether or not the surrogate herself wishes to enter into the arrangement.[15] This position was also taken by the European Parliament in a resolution on the EU's *Annual Report on Human Rights and Democracy in the World*, when it stated that it:

> condemns the practice of surrogacy, which undermines the human dignity of the woman since her body and its reproductive functions are used as a commodity; considers that the practice of gestational surrogacy which involves reproductive exploitation and use of the human body for financial or other gain, in particular in the case of vulnerable women in developing countries, shall be prohibited and treated as a matter of urgency in human rights instruments.[16]

Despite prohibiting surrogacy within their own territory,[17] these states are in many cases simply exporting the problem, with couples or individuals resident

---

14 Although this is prefaced by the proviso 'States Parties that recognize and/or permit the system of adoption'.

15 For a more comprehensive discussion of the law and practice of different jurisdictions, see K. Trimmings and P. Beaumont, *International Surrogacy Arrangements*, Hart Publishing, Oxford 2013.

16 European Parliament Resolution of 17 December 2015 on the Annual Report on Human Rights and Democracy in the World 2014 and the European Union's policy on the matter (2015/2229(INI)), <http://www.europarl.europa.eu/sides/getDoc.do?type=TA&language=EN&reference=P8-TA-2015-0470>.

17 Though even then, it may be that the practice is simply pushed underground. Since surrogacy does not necessarily require medical assistance (for example, traditional surrogacy involving 'DIY' insemination), it can be difficult to effectively police.

in these states travelling to other jurisdictions to achieve their desire to become parents. This 'reproductive tourism' in turn leads to conflicts of laws, and these states have had to struggle with whether, and to what extent, they recognise the parenthood and civil status of the child born out of a surrogacy arrangement that is contrary to their own strict laws.

Second, there are some jurisdictions which have not yet legislated explicitly on the issue of surrogacy, instead trying to cobble together solutions from general rules on legal parenthood and adoption – for example, Belgium, the Czech Republic, the Netherlands. In such states, there is a lacuna in the law, often leaving medical institutions to determine the conditions for treatment, and parenthood or civil status is not guaranteed, leaving children, women and families in a state of uncertainty.

Third are those states where surrogacy is permitted and regulated by law. This can take the form of pre-approval of the arrangement, where the prospective commissioning parents and surrogate must present their arrangement for approval before medical treatment can go ahead – for example, Greece, Israel and South Africa; or may consist of ex post facto procedures to transfer legal parentage from the surrogate to the commissioning parents, provided certain criteria are met – as seen in the United Kingdom and Hong Kong. In these jurisdictions, surrogacy is not an intrinsic wrong, but merely a contextual one – it is not inherently a violation of human rights, but can lead to such if it is not adequately regulated.[18]

Finally, there are states that take a free market approach to surrogacy, for example Russia, Ukraine, and some states in the USA. In these states, commercial surrogacy is permitted and practised, and there is no domicile or residence requirement for the intending parents. The existence of such permissive regimes raises difficulties for all other jurisdictions trying to prohibit or strictly regulate surrogacy, as commissioning parents can simply travel to another jurisdiction that is willing to provide the treatment.

These differing positions on the very nature of surrogacy arrangements not only lead to conflicts of laws when commissioning parents cross borders to find jurisdictions with more permissible and accessible regimes, but also mean that there is very little common ground between the different systems on which to draw when trying to undertake multilateral co-operation, or devise an international convention. So what, then, can the Hague Conference do in this area? Can it repeat the success of the 1993 Adoption Convention in the field of surrogacy?

---

[18] See C. Fenton-Glynn, 'Outsourcing Ethical Dilemmas: Regulating International Surrogacy Arrangements' (2016) 24(1) *Medical Law Review* 59.

3. THE FORM AND CONTENT OF POSSIBLE INSTRUMENTS

There are two separate issues that need to be addressed by the international community in relation to international surrogacy. The first concerns legal and civil status – the recognition of the child within the family. The second concerns the potential violations of the rights of surrogates and children in the process of gestation and transfer to commissioning parents.

In relation to the former, the rights of the child are very clear – the right to identity, to nationality, and to legal certainty. Article 7 of the UN Convention on the Rights of the Child requires that all children shall have the right to acquire a nationality, and that states must ensure that the child is not left stateless. Moreover, Article 8 requires that states preserve the child's identity, including nationality, name and family relations, without unlawful interference. This has been recognised by the European Court of Human Rights in the case of *Mennesson v France*,[19] where it was held that a refusal to recognise the commissioning parents as legal parents in France was a violation of the child's right to respect for private and family life under Article 8 of the European Convention on Human Rights. The Court observed that Article 8 encompasses the right to establish details of one's identity, as well as the recognition of the legal parent–child relationship. The manifest need for international co-operation in this area was also recognised by the Hague Conference, which acknowledged a 'children's rights imperative to work concerning legal parentage'.[20]

On the other hand, when considering the latter – the process of gestation and transfer of the child – the situation is much more contentious. While the 1993 Adoption Convention was able to integrate human rights considerations to a certain extent, as discussed above, surrogacy operates in a completely different ethical and political space than intercountry adoption. States remain deeply divided as to how to respond to surrogacy, both in legal and cultural terms. Finding a middle ground between those states that view surrogacy as a violation of the dignity of women and as the commodification of children, and those that allow commercial surrogacy for the highest bidder seems unrealistic. Moreover, surrogacy involves reconceptualising the idea of parenthood, challenging traditional assumptions concerning the mother–child bond, and womanhood in general, with little guidance from the international human rights instruments as to how the rights of children, women, and families, as well as the interests of the state, should be analysed and balanced.

---

19 Above n. 7.

20 See Hague Conference on Private International Law, *The Desirability and Feasibility of Further Work on the Parentage/Surrogacy Project* (2014), <https://assets.hcch.net/docs/6403eddb-3b47-4680-ba4a-3fe3e11c0557.pdf>, at para. 19.

At a very basic level, the Hague Conference could draft a convention that requires mutual recognition of parental status across jurisdictions in cases of surrogacy. This could take the form of automatic transposal of birth certificates, or if an added layer of scrutiny is deemed necessary in the area of surrogacy, recognition of judicial decisions concerning parenthood. As with the 1993 Adoption Convention, where adoptions are recognised by operation of law in other Contracting States, a Surrogacy Convention could simply require that where the competent authority has made a declaration of parenthood following a surrogacy arrangement, such parenthood should be recognised in all other states. As with the Adoption Convention, this could be subject to a public order exception – see Article 24, stating that '[t]he recognition of an adoption may be refused in a Contracting State only if the adoption is manifestly contrary to its public policy, taking into account the best interests of the child.'

This appears to fit with the approach of both prohibitive and regulatory receiving states outlined above, in that no matter how the state views the surrogacy process, once the child is born, the parenthood of the commissioning parents must be recognised, and the best interests of the child must be the primary consideration. This can be seen in the French approach following *Mennesson v France*,[21] as well as the position of the German Federal Court,[22] the Spanish authorities,[23] and English High Court.[24] A simple Surrogacy Convention such as this may be able to draw a wider number and range of signatories, no matter what their view on the practice of surrogacy is.

One problem with this approach is that a Convention that recognises parenthood across borders for children born of surrogacy, but not that of children born through natural reproduction or other artificial reproductive techniques, would not only be artificial, but also a missed opportunity. The more significant issue, however, is the fact that such a simple Convention only solves

---

21 See Cour de Cassation, Ruling no. 619 (3 July 2015), <https://www.courdecassation.fr/cour_cassation_1/in_six_2850/english_2851/the_transcription_7252/ruling_no._619_32234.html>.

22 Bundesgerichtshof Beschluss XII ZB 463/13 (10 December 2014), <http://juris.bundesgerichtshof.de/cgi-bin/rechtsprechung/document.py?Gericht=bgh&Art=pm&Datum=2014&Sort=3&nr=69759&linked=bes&Blank=1&file=dokument.pdf>.

23 See P. Orejudo Prieto De Los Mozos, 'National Report: Spain' in K. Trimmings and P. Beaumont, *International Surrogacy Arrangements*, Hart Publishing, Oxford 2013; Hague Conference on Private International Law, *The Parentage/Surrogacy Project: An Updating Note* (February 2015), <https://assets.hcch.net/docs/82d31f31-294f-47fe-9166-4d9315031737.pdf>, at para. 3; P. Beaumont and K. Trimmings, 'Recent Jurisprudence of the European Court of Human Rights in the area of cross-border surrogacy: is there still a need for global regulation of surrogacy?' (University of Aberdeen, Working Paper 2015/2, revised by Working Paper No. 2016/4 'Recent jurisprudence of the European Court of Human Rights in the area of cross-border surrogacy: is there still a need for global regulation of surrogacy?').

24 See C. Fenton-Glynn, 'The Regulation and Recognition of Surrogacy in English Law' (2015) 27(1) *Child and Family Law Quarterly* 83.

half the problem, while sweeping the rest of the issue under the proverbial rug. While it would protect the civil status of children, it does little more than codify the existing situation in most jurisdictions, which already recognise parenthood as a matter of course in any case (even if they have to bend the rules to do so).[25] Moreover, while providing this recognition, it ignores the wider implications for the industry as a whole, and the potential exploitation and commodification occurring in the course of the transaction. This is precisely what has occurred in England: the English courts, faced with a child already being cared for by the commissioning parents, have dealt with the situation that they *can* control – civil status – rather than that which they cannot – the potential exploitation of women and commodification of children overseas. They are being forced to close their eyes to potential violations of the latter, in order to ensure respect for the former. In this respect, the focus has been on the tangible – the child before them – rather than the intangible of a woman in another jurisdiction. Under such a model, practices that are considered exploitative by the domestic authorities continue to go unchecked, with domestic authorities left with no way to control or regulate the circumstances under which a surrogacy is undertaken. It only solves half the problem – that of the child's identity – while neglecting the rights of those involved with the arrangement.

This would be a form of regularisation, rather than regulation,[26] and in doing so, it risks legitimising practices that domestic authorities deem contrary to human rights principles. Where a government enters into an international treaty saying that it will recognise the effects of a surrogacy arrangement, it sends the message that it is a legitimate transaction. Any treaty in this area will be seen as prescribing acceptable practice, and giving international authority for this.

For this reason, such a treaty would risk much, while achieving little. In practice, states are already providing this recognition, driven by the paramountcy of children's rights and ensuring the right to identity. Although this may be accomplished in a haphazard way on a case-by-case basis, without the guarantee of a clear legal route, it achieves the practical result of protecting children's rights, while retaining the power of the law to send a message that certain practices remain unacceptable.

A bolder proposal would be to try to tackle both the issues relating to civil status *and* to provide a framework of regulation to protect the rights of women and children involved in the practice. This is where the 1993 Adoption Convention could provide the foundation. The Adoption Convention provides guaranteed

---

25 Ibid.

26 This concept is used by EEKELAAR when discussing the law's role in divorce (J. EEKELAAR, *Regulating Divorce*, Clarendon Press, Oxford 1991). Whereas regulation attempts to direct society's actions, taking a more interventionist approach, regularisation is more fatalistic, accepting that the phenomena will happen regardless of what the law does, and confines the legal process to ensuring that the legal process does not add to the harm (at p. 142).

recognition of parenthood (Articles 23, 24 and 26), and the ability of the child to travel to the destination country (Articles 17 and 18). It establishes a framework for co-operation and exchange of information between states (Article 7), while allocating responsibilities between them (Articles 4, 5, 15 and 16). Furthermore, it requires the regulation of agencies and of profit-making, ensuring that the industry that had grown up around the practice was scaled back to state-run or non-profit institutions (Articles 9 to 12).[27]

Likewise, a Surrogacy Convention could provide recognition of the status of parenthood (and subsequent nationality) and a guarantee that the child would be able to travel to the commissioning parents' home jurisdiction once the surrogacy arrangement was certified. It could provide safeguards concerning minimum acceptable medical standards, as well as a regulation of agencies and middlemen, and the profits they are making. It could further allocate responsibility for ensuring the suitability of the commissioning parents to their state of residence, while the state of residence of the surrogate is given responsibility for ensuring that she has given her free, voluntary and informed consent to the process.

The sticking point with such a model of convention lies with questions as to the enforceability of the surrogacy contract, the identity of the legal parent(s) at birth, and whether the surrogate can change her mind and decide to keep the child. These are issues for which the 1993 Adoption Convention cannot provide a framework.

If the instrument were to allow commercial surrogacy (which would indicate that there should be some form of contractual enforceability, and recognition of the commissioning parents as legal parents), this would severely limit the number of countries willing to ratify the agreement. While countries where international surrogacy *takes place* are predominantly those that allow commercial surrogacy, very few jurisdictions where the *commissioning parents reside* permit this – in fact, it is this very difference that drives the international surrogacy industry. It is interesting to note that some destination jurisdictions which previously fell within this category – for example, India, Thailand and Nepal – have now recently amended their laws to adopt a much more restricted approach, as discussed above. These jurisdictions now require an affiliation between the commissioning parents and the surrogate, as well as residence or citizenship, effectively disbanding their lucrative industry in reproductive tourism.

On the other hand, if the Convention prohibited commercial surrogacy, allowing only reasonable expenses, it would severely limit its scope. Those entering into international surrogacy arrangements are unlikely to be doing so on an altruistic basis, meaning that they would fall outside the scope of the instrument, and we would be left facing the same difficulties of what to do when an agreement falls outside the scope of our existing legal framework.

[27] Although it did, unfortunately, leave room for approved, non-accredited bodies under Article 22, as a result of pressure from the United States of America.

Moreover, in either case, any instrument that regulated surrogacy, rather than simply regularising the position of children involved in the practice, would be anathema to those jurisdictions with prohibitive approaches. States that view surrogacy as an intrinsic or inherent wrong, no matter how it is carried out, would certainly refuse to be party to such an instrument, leaving yet another gap in protection.

This leaves the Hague Conference at an impasse. Neither convention appears to be a viable option, yet multilateral co-operation is vital. Every year, more and more commissioning parents are entering into international surrogacy, and more and more children are born into legal uncertainty. One solution might be for the Hague Conference to consider drafting soft law instruments – for example, guidelines for good practice – although this too would have the difficulty of having to decide what position to adopt on commercialisation, exploitation and parenthood, risking alienation of states with conflicting values. Another solution would be for the Hague Conference to step out of the arena for the meantime, leaving it to other players to establish a baseline before beginning its work. One way to do this would be for individual states themselves to start small, introducing bi-lateral agreements, trying to establish common ground before attempting to find universal consensus. Europe is already seeing movement in this area, through not political but judicial action, with the rulings of the European Court of Human Rights requiring minimum safeguards. It may be that more regional co-operation in this area is needed before an international consensus can be found.

4. CONCLUSION

International surrogacy has many similarities to intercountry adoption, and as such, there is much to learn from the 1993 Adoption Convention and the framework of regulation it provides. At the same time, we must also be careful not to read too much into its success, as surrogacy raises unique and complex issues that go beyond those faced by the international community in the 1990s.

What we need to recognise is that the disparity in laws in different jurisdictions goes beyond simple regulatory variations, but is at heart a dispute over alternative conceptions of human rights. Does surrogacy always exploit women? Does it commodify children? Does giving birth make someone a parent? And is parenthood something that can be alienated by contract? These questions are ones that must be answered by human rights bodies, and principles enshrined in human rights treaties. We are asking too much of the Hague Conference – a body concerned with private international law – to sort out these complex differences.

While the 1993 Adoption Convention did have the aim of protecting the fundamental rights of children, in that case it was clear what those rights were – it was simply a matter of creating a framework of recognition and co-operation to regularise this across jurisdictions. Surrogacy does not have this same baseline; it does not have this same common ground. In the current state of international diversity, trying to create a private international law convention would be akin to trying to put a square peg in a round hole. The Hague Conference is an exceptional international body, which has achieved great things, but there are limits to its abilities. Instead, it is time for human rights institutions – the United Nations, the Council of Europe and other regional organisations – to step up in the area of surrogacy. Only then can the Hague Conference fulfil its function.

ISSUES IN INTERNATIONAL DIVORCE CASES

Rebecca Bailey-Harris

1. INTRODUCTION

Freedom of movement within an area of freedom, security and justice is one of the political pillars of the European Union and underpins its regime of Regulations.[1] But international mobility of individuals and families is by no means confined to the European Union: it is worldwide. Many 'international' families have links to more than one country, whether within the EU or without. Against the background of high rates of marriage breakdown, the mobility of individuals and their families has posed considerable challenges for the rules of private international law. Clear jurisdictional rules on access to courts are required and the reciprocal recognition and effective enforcement of orders between countries is of vital importance.

Both EU law and national law within the UK jurisdictions have responded to the challenge. This chapter will address recent developments and current issues in rules on international jurisdiction and the recognition and enforcement of orders in divorce and ancillary financial matters. In addition to issues which have arisen to date, the UK now faces the immense legal challenges posed by the process of exiting the EU. The European Union (Withdrawal) Bill published on

1 E.g. Council Regulation (EC) No. 2001/2003 (Brussels IIA) Recital (1).

13 July 2017 gives rise to many issues of constitutionality and interpretation,[2] and it will no doubt be subject to close scrutiny and lively debate in both Houses of Parliament. The Bill's implications in the field of divorce and ancillary matters will be addressed in this chapter, albeit that a high degree of speculation is inevitable at the time of writing.

2. JURISDICTION IN DIVORCE

Developed legal systems require connecting factors as the prerequisite for an individual's access to courts. Subject to provisions enabling prorogation (choice of court), the connecting factors embodied in jurisdictional rules are underpinned by the policy of deterring 'forum-shopping', and divorce law is no exception.[3] Neither EU law nor the domestic laws of UK jurisdictions permit prorogation of jurisdiction for divorce.[4] Jurisdictional rules for divorce are based on the principle of a genuine connection between an individual and the country of which the courts are invoked. Rules must strike a balance between the flexibility required by family mobility and the need for legal certainty.[5]

The jurisdiction of a court to entertain a divorce petition is stated in section 5(2) of the Domicile and Matrimonial Proceedings Act 1973. The court has jurisdiction either under Council Regulation (EC) No. 2201/2003[6] or, if no court of a Member State has jurisdiction under the Regulation, under the residual domestic law jurisdiction based on the domicile of one party. The residual jurisdiction cannot be invoked against a person habitually resident in or a national of another EU Member State; in the case of the UK and Ireland, domicile replaces nationality.[7]

Article 3 of Brussels IIA founds jurisdiction on habitual residence (in various permutations) and common nationality or common domicile. It provides:

> 1. In matters relating to divorce, legal separation or marriage annulment, jurisdiction shall lie with the courts of the Member State:
>
> (a) in whose territory:
> - the spouses are habitually resident, or

---

2 M. Elliott, 'The EU (Withdrawal) Bill: Initial Thoughts', 14 July 2017, <https://publiclawforeveryone.com/2017/07/14/the-eu-withdrawal-bill-initial-thoughts/>.

3 *Z v Z (Divorce: Jurisdiction)* [2010] 1 FLR 694 at [42].

4 Contrast the prorogation of jurisdiction in civil matters under Council Regulation (EU) No. 1215/2012 (Brussels I Recast) Art. 25 and in matters relating to maintenance under Council Regulation (EC) No. 4/2009 (the Maintenance Regulation), Art. 4.

5 A. Borras, Explanatory Report on Council Regulation (EC) No. 1347/2000, 28 May 1998 ([1998] OJ C221/27) paras. [27]–[32].

6 Hereinafter referred to as Brussels IIA.

7 Brussels IIA Art. 6.

- the spouses were last habitually resident, insofar as one of them still resides there, or
- the respondent is habitually resident, or
- in the event of a joint application, either of the spouses is habitually resident, or
- the applicant is habitually resident if he or she resided there for at least a year immediately before the application was made, or
- the applicant is habitually resident if he or she resided there for at least six months immediately before the application was made and is either a national of the Member State in question or, in the case of the United Kingdom and Ireland, has his or her 'domicile' there;

(b) of the nationality of both spouses, or, in the case of the United Kingdom and Ireland, of the 'domicile' of both parties.

2. For the purposes of this Regulation, 'domicile' shall have the same meaning as it has under the legal systems of the United Kingdom and Ireland.

These grounds are alternatives and there is no priority or hierarchy: hence it is common for the courts of more than one Member State to have jurisdiction. The rules for resolving conflicts between competing jurisdictions are addressed below.

The concept of habitual residence has given rise to some issues of interpretation, since Brussels IIA does not itself define the concept for the purposes of Article 3.[8] To date there has been no judgment of the Court of Justice of the European Union (CJEU) on the interpretation of habitual residence in Article 3.[9] There is, however, case law at national level within the EU on habitual residence in Article 3. The case law emphasises that an autonomous interpretation must be adopted, for obvious reasons of uniformity. The definition adopted in the UK is: 'The place where the person has established, on a fixed basis, the permanent or habitual centre of his interests, with all the relevant factors being taken into account for the purpose of determining such residence'.[10]

---

8 Nor for the purposes of Arts. 8, 10 or 15.

9 By contrast there is CJEU case law on the interpretation of the habitual residence of a child under Arts. 8 and 10: *Re A (Area of Freedom, Security and Justice)* [2009] 1 FLR 1, Case C-497/10 PU *Mercredi v Chaffe* [2011] 1 FLR 1293.

10 This definition is derived from the Borras Report (above n. 5) para. [32], applied by the Cour de Cassation in *Moore v McLean* iv 1ère 14 December 2005 (B No. 506), cited with approval by Singer J in *L-K v K (No. 2)* [2006] EWHC 3280 (Fam), [2007] 2 FLR 729 at [42], Munby J in *Marinos v Marinos* [2007] 2 FLR 101 at [29] and Ryder J in *Z v Z (Divorce: Jurisdiction)* [2010] 1 FLR 694 at [38]. The Borras Report formulation was based on decisions of the European Court of Justice in contexts other than divorce – principally, social security: Case 76/76 *Silvana Di Paulo v National Employment Office* [1977] 2 CMLR 59, Case C-297 *Rigsadvokaten v Nicolai Christian Ryborg* [1991] ECR I-1943, Case C-102/91 *Doris Knoch v Bundenstadlt für Arbeit* [1992] ECR I-4341, Case C-452/93 *Pedro Magdalena Fernandez v Commission*, [1994] ECR I-4295 esp. at para. [22] and Case C-90/97 *Robin Swaddling v Adjudication Officer*, [1999] 2 FLR 184 esp. at paras. [29] and [30].

According to the case law, the interpretation of habitual residence for the purposes of Article 3 involves not a purely quantitative evaluation of the time spent by a person in a particular place[11] but instead a qualitative evaluation of all the facts pertaining to an individual's links with a place. An individual's centre of interests is identified by taking into account all relevant factors, including both objective connecting factors and intention.[12] For the purposes of Article 3 a person may have only one habitual residence at a given date – wholly consistent with there being only one centre of interests.[13] In *Tan v Choy*[14] the Court of Appeal identified habitual residence under Article 3 as requiring the satisfaction of three tests: (1) that there is a permanence or stability in the residence of the individual in the relevant territory (2) that this location is the centre of the person's interests and (3) the individual has, at the time, no other habitual residence.

The qualitative approach to identifying an individual's centre of interest has the benefit of flexibility and fact-sensitivity, but may be open to some criticism on the ground of unpredictability. Furthermore, the judicially developed test for identifying the habitual residence of an adult individual for the purposes of Article 3 differs from that applied to children for the purposes of Articles 8 and 11.[15] Is this difference unavoidable, or an undesirable complexity?

An unresolved issue on the interpretation of Article 3 goes to the nature and strength of the connecting factor between an individual and a Member State, which could make a difference to the outcome as to jurisdiction. Is there a distinction to be drawn between 'habitual residence' and 'residence' as terms used in Article 3?[16] There are contrary *obiter dicta* in the case law at first instance.[17] The Court of Appeal in *Tan v Choy* did not consider it necessary to

---

11 Contrast the earlier interpretation under domestic law: *Ikimi v Ikimi* [2001] 2 FLR 1288.

12 Intention means the reasons for a party's actions: *V v V (Divorce: Jurisdiction)* [2011] 2 FLR 778.

13 *Marinos*, above n. 10, at [38]–[43], *Munro* at [47], *Z v Z* at [42], in contrast to the position under domestic law in *Ikimi v Ikimi* [2001] 2 FLR 1288 where the Court of Appeal held that a person may have two habitual residences simultaneously.

14 *Tan v Choy* [2014] EWCA Civ 251, [2015] 1 FLR 492 at [31].

15 For Arts. 8 and 10 habitual residence means the place that reflects some degree of integration by a child in a social and family environment: see n. 9 above and *Re A (Jurisdiction: Return of Child)* [2014] 1 FLR 111, *Re B (A Child) (Habitual Residence: Inherent Jurisdiction)* [2016] 1 FLR 561.

16 See Art. 3 indents 3, 5 and 6.

17 Munby J in *Marinos*, above n. 10, at [45]–[49] (different concepts), Bennett J in *Munro* at [48]–[54] (same concept). In *V v V (Divorce: Jurisdiction)* [2011] 2 FLR 778 at [42], [43], [47] Peter Jackson J preferred the approach in *Marinos*.

decide the point on the facts, but Aikens LJ in *obiter dicta* put forward no less than three possible interpretations:[18]

> I would accept that there could be legitimate debate as to what is the precise construction of Article 3(1)(a) indent five [of Brussels II Regulation]. It seems to me that there are (at least) three possible constructions. First, it could mean that the person seeking to found jurisdiction has to be 'habitually resident' in the territory concerned at the date the proceedings are started and he also has to have 'resided' there for at least a year before the relevant proceedings are started. Secondly, it could mean that the person seeking to found jurisdiction has simply to have been 'habitually resident' for one year prior to the start of the proceedings. Thirdly, it could mean that the person seeking to found jurisdiction has to establish that he/she is 'habitually resident' at the time the proceedings are started and that this fact is proved by establishing that he/she has 'resided' in that territory for at least a year immediately before the proceedings were started ('... application was made').

Domicile is an available ground of jurisdiction in Article 3.1(b) Brussels IIA (common domicile) and under the residual domestic law jurisdiction in the Domicile and Matrimonial Proceedings Act 1973 section 5(2)(b) (domicile of one party). Where habitual residence is unclear or both parties are habitually resident overseas, domicile will provide the only available jurisdictional link. Family law practitioners have in recent years witnessed an increasing resort to domicile as the foundation of divorce jurisdiction, usually by the party who perceives a juridical advantage in the potential outcome of ancillary financial remedy proceedings.[19] The tenacity of the domicile of origin in English law provides a jurisdictional link even where an individual's real connection with this country may be slight – and the real connection (which should underpin jurisdictional criteria in matters of personal status in order to discourage forum-shopping) is questionable. The tenacious quality of the domicile of origin is well established in the authorities. In *Barlow Clowes International Ltd v Henwood*[20] Arden LJ stated:

> There is a strong line of case law, binding on this court, that the domicile of origin is tenacious. Thus, for example, Lord Macnaghten in *Winans v Attorney-General* [1904] AC 287 at 290 held that the character of domicile of origin 'is more enduring, its hold stronger, and less easily shaken off' than domicile of choice.

18 [2015] 1 FLR 492 at [30].

19 E.g. the lack of jurisdiction in respect of maintenance where the divorce petition is based on the domicile of only one party: Maintenance Regulation Art. 3(c).

20 *Barlow Clowes International Ltd v Henwood* [2008] EWCA Civ 557, [2008] BPIR 778 at [85].

Winans is not the only venerable case regularly cited in contemporary domicile cases: other older favourites are *Bell v Kennedy*[21] and *Udny v Udny*.[22]

Cases where domicile is disputed require a careful application to the evidence, both written and oral, of the highly technical (and some would say archaic) doctrines of domicile at common law. In *Barlow Clowes* Arden LJ stated:[23]

> A finding as to domicile requires a careful evaluation of all the facts. This point is illustrated by a memorable passage from the judgment of Mummery LJ in *Agulian v Cyganik* [2006] 1 FCR 406 at [46(1)]:
>
> > 'Positioned at the date of death in February 2003 the court must look back at the whole of the deceased's life, at what he had done with his life, at what life had done to him and at what were his inferred intentions in order to decide whether he had acquired a domicile of choice in England by the date of his death. Soren Kierkegaard's aphorism that "Life must be lived forwards, but can only be understood backwards" resonates in the biographical data of domicile disputes.'

Courts routinely cite the classic text *Dicey, Morris & Collins on the Conflict of Laws* for the applicable principles.[24] The distinction between domicile of origin and domicile of choice assumes great importance, particularly in respect of how easily or otherwise such a domicile is lost. Recent examples of the meticulous exercise undertaken at trial are *Divall v Divall*[25] and *U v J (No. 2) (Domicile)*.[26] Cases are routinely listed in the High Court for three to four days. Such litigation is self-evidently costly (ill affordable by all save the very wealthy) and its outcome is unpredictable, given the importance of oral evidence.

The question whether domicile should continue as the sole alternative to habitual residence in divorce jurisdiction is now subsumed within the pressing general question of what will be jurisdictional grounds for divorce post Brexit. Importantly, Article 3 of Brussels IIA is part of our domestic law by direct application of the Regulation[27] and applies whether or not a divorce has an international dimension. The significance of this was recognised by the House of Lords European Union Committee Report *Brexit: justice for families,*

---

21 *Bell v Kennedy* (1868) LR 1 Sc & Div 307.

22 *Udny v Udny* (1869) LR 1 Sc & Div 441.

23 [2008] BPIR 778 at [16].

24 See e.g. *Barlow Clowes*, above n. 20 and *Ray v Sekhiri* [2014] 2 FLR 1168.

25 *Divall v Divall* [2014] 2 FLR 1104, Moor J: '*The common law concept of domicile is notoriously elusive*'.

26 *U v J (No. 2) (Domicile)* [2017] EWHC 449 (Fam) (2017) 47 *Family Law* 497.

27 By Art. 288 of the Treaty on the Functioning of the European Union, EU Regulations are of direct operation in every Member State, without the need for any implementation in domestic legislation, as explained in *EDG v RR (Enforcement of Foreign Maintenance Order* [2015] 1 FLR 270 and *MP v PS (Enforcement Procedure under the Maintenance Regulation: Reference to CJEU)* [2017] 1 FLR 394.

individuals and businesses.[28] The Hague Convention on the Recognition of Divorces and Legal Separations 1970 is not a satisfactory fall-back: there are only 20 contracting states and in any event the Convention does not contain any provisions on jurisdiction. Is the substance of Article 3 of Brussels IIA and of the Domicile and Matrimonial Proceedings Act 1973 section 5(2)(b) to be replicated in the domestic law of this country, or should it be replaced? If the latter, with what? The European Union (Withdrawal) Bill seeks to enact the substance of EU Regulation law into domestic law[29] with effect from the day of exit (probably 29 March 2019). The Bill confers extraordinary powers on Ministers of the Crown to modify retained EU law through regulations[30] subject to a sunset clause imposing a two-year time-limit[31] and subject to a degree of Parliamentary control.[32] Subject to these 'Henry VIII powers' (according to the Government, not to be exercised in relation to policy matters), it is to be assumed that any reform of international family law matters after EU Regulations are enacted into domestic law on exit day will be a matter for the usual Parliamentary process for primary legislation, including involvement of the Law Commission.

Some see Brexit as an opportunity for constructive reconsideration of the jurisdictional grounds for divorce in this country. For example, a group of practitioners with EU experience has published a paper for discussion,[33] which suggests consideration of the following grounds: joint habitual residence, habitual residence of the respondent, habitual residence of the petitioner for six months before and as at the date of the petition, sole domicile of either party, and sole nationality of either party and a greater connection with England and Wales than any other country within the UK. The addition of nationality (with or without an additional criterion) is an interesting possibility. Nationality is currently not available as a jurisdictional ground under Article 3 of Brussels IIA in the UK and Ireland.[34] Nationality as a ground of divorce jurisdiction has usually been associated with civil law countries, but within the common law 'family' it is for example a ground of divorce jurisdiction in Australia.[35] When speculating on divorce jurisdiction in the UK after Brexit, it is interesting to note that the European Commission's recent proposal for a recast of Brussels IIA recommends no substantive changes to the divorce provisions of the Regulation.[36] The UK

28 House of Lords European Union Committee Report 17th Report, Session 2016–17, *Brexit: justice for families, individuals and businesses* HL Paper 134.

29 As 'retained EU law': Clause 3.

30 Clause 7.

31 Clause 7(7).

32 Clause 7.

33 EU Law Working Group, Divorce Jurisdiction after Brexit, *Family Law Week*, 7 March 2017.

34 Brussels IIA, Art. 3.1(b) and (2); *Re N (Jurisdiction)* [2007] 2 FLR 1196 (Art. 3.1 does not permit both nationality and domicile to found jurisdiction for UK and Irish citizens).

35 Family Law Act 1975 (Cth) s. 39(3): nationality of either party.

36 *Proposal for a Council Regulation on jurisdiction, the recognition and enforcement of decisions in matrimonial matters and matters of parental responsibility and on international child*

decided to opt into the negotiations on the reform proposals, notwithstanding the result of the referendum on 23 June 2016. It is not known when the recast Regulation will come into force, but it appears unlikely that it will be in force prior to the UK's formal exit from the EU in March 2019.[37]

A final note of concern relates to the likelihood and timetable of any considered law reform process. Divorce jurisdiction is a matter of policy, which cannot be within the scope of subordinate legislation to be deal with by the executive under the European Union (Withdrawal) Bill. However, the enormity of the overall legislative challenge posed by Brexit gives little confidence as to the time and priority to be accorded to the future of grounds of jurisdiction in divorce. It may be that provisions brought into force as 'retained EU law' on exit day will in reality endure for many years and not simply for an undefined transitional period. Thus the substantive provisions of Brussels IIA as it stands on exit day will be retained, notwithstanding the revision of that Regulation by the remaining Member States of the EU[38] and without the benefit of conclusive interpretive guidance from the CJEU on concepts such as habitual residence. According to the European Union (Withdrawal) Bill, CJEU judgments after the date of exit will not be binding on courts in this country[39] and the mechanism for reference to the CJEU for preliminary ruling on a question of interpretation will cease to exist. However, the Bill currently provides[40] that a court or tribunal 'need not have regard to anything done after exit day by the European Court … but may do so if it considers it appropriate to do so'. This apparently unfettered discretion has, at the date of writing this chapter, already given rise to much controversy. The issue will no doubt give rise to much debate when the Bill is considered in both Houses of Parliament.

Those who hope that Brexit will provide an opportunity to consider reform of the grounds for jurisdiction in divorce may yet be disappointed. On 22 August 2017 the Government published a policy paper *Providing a Cross-border Civil Judicial Cooperation Framework – A Future Partnership Paper*. The relatively brief paper (11 pages) is to form the basis of negotiations and sets out 'key issues of the Government's vision' for the new, deep and special partnership' to be built with the EU. The issues addressed are in essence those of the rules on jurisdiction, and on reciprocal recognition and enforcement of judgments in civil matters, including family law. The level of analysis is superficial, the greater

abduction(recast) COM(2016) 411/2; C. Honorati, 'The Commission's proposal for a recast of Brussels IIa Regulation' [2017] *International Family Law* 97; N. Lowe, 'Some reflections on the options for dealing with international family law following Brexit' (2017) 47 *Family Law* 399.

37 N. Lowe, above n. 36 at 400.

38 See n. 35 above.

39 Clause 6.

40 Clause 6(2).

part of the content being devoted to description of current Regulations and other international instruments including Hague Conventions and the Lugano Convention 2007, as well as political rhetoric. The Government's essential policy, set out in three paragraphs,[41] is to preserve the status quo in the substance of the rules and to recognise that the direct jurisdiction of the CJEU ends when the EU Treaties cease to apply in the UK. Other international instruments are summarily dismissed because 'they would not generally provide the more sophisticated and effective interaction, based on mutual trust between legal systems, that currently benefits both EU and UK business, families and individual litigants'.[42] A number of questions immediately spring to mind. If the current benefits of EU membership are so invaluable, why leave? Will the continuation of the status quo on exit be politically acceptable to the EU, in particular given the UK's stance on the CJEU?[43] Is the proposal workable even on its own terms, without the vital interpretative role of the CJEU and the undeniable reality that EU Regulations will evolve over time and leave the substance of laws applied in the UK far behind? At the time of writing the negotiations between the UK and the EU are just beginning and the future is at large.

3. AVOIDING THE POTENTIAL CONFLICT OF COMPETING DIVORCE PROCEEDINGS

Where the courts of two countries have jurisdiction over divorce proceedings in respect of the one marriage, the potential for conflicting judgments is self-evident. The traditional approach of the law of England and Wales (and of many other common law countries) is to resolve the potential conflict by application of the principle of *forum conveniens* to identify the jurisdiction in which the case should be determined. Paragraph 9 of Schedule 1 to the Domicile and Matrimonial Proceedings Act 1973 and the inherent jurisdiction[44] give the court discretionary power to determine whether there is a more appropriate forum, considering all relevant factors and the classic authorities *Spiliada Maritime*

41 Paras. 18–20.

42 Para. 18.

43 On 23 August 2017 the Government published *Enforcement and Dispute Resolution: A Future Partnership Paper*. The paper confirms that the direct jurisdiction of the CJEU must end on the date of withdrawal from the EU. The Government will 'engage constructively to negotiate an approach to enforcement and dispute resolution which meets the key objectives of the UK and the EU, underpinning the deep and special and partnership we seek' (Executive Summary, para. 5). Beyond such political rhetoric the paper contains little more than a superficial description of a range of options. It does not address the major political question of whether the UK's proposals will work without the CJEU being the ultimate tribunal for dispute resolution.

44 The operation of which is expressly saved by DMPA 1973, s. 5(6)(b).

Corporation v Cansulex[45] and *de Dampierre v de Dampierre*.[46] Which proceedings were instituted first in time is a relevant but not a decisive consideration.

The approach of EU law to resolving potential conflict of judgments in competing jurisdictions is completely different. The simple rule of *lis pendens* accords absolute priority to the court first seised. Thus in respect of concurrent proceedings Article 19 of Brussels IIA provides (so far as is material to this chapter):

> Article 19
>
> *Lis pendens and dependent actions*
>
> 1. Where proceedings relating to divorce, legal separation or marriage annulment between the same parties are brought before courts of different Member States, the court second seised shall of its own motion stay its proceedings until such time as the jurisdiction of the court first seised is established.
>
> ...
>
> 3. Where the jurisdiction of the court first seised is established, the court second seised shall decline jurisdiction in favour of that court ...

The same *lis pendens* rule applies in respect of the same causes of action brought in different EU jurisdictions in matters of maintenance.[47]

Brexit raises the question of which approach to concurrent divorce and ancillary maintenance proceedings should be adopted in this country post exit from the European Union. On exit day, the *lis pendens* provisions of Article 19 of Brussels IIA and Article 12 of the Maintenance Regulation will become part of domestic law as retained EU law.[48] But should this provision thereafter continue or be reformed? This writer favours the rule which accords absolute priority to the court first seised.[49] It has the great merit of simplicity and is ultimately founded on a high degree of comity and mutual respect between states. The *forum conveniens* approach has – like any discretionary power – the disadvantage of unpredictability and thus engenders costly litigation. But others take the contrary view and favour the flexibility of the *forum conveniens* approach, criticising the 'first in time' rule as encouraging an unseemly rush to court and discouraging a mediated settlement.[50] The important policy decision

---

45 *Spiliada Maritime Corporation v Cansulex Ltd* [1987] AC 460.

46 *de Dampierre v de Dampierre* [1988] AC 92.

47 Maintenance Regulation Art. 12. Art. 13 confers discretionary power to stay a related action.

48 European Union (Withdrawal) Bill Clause 3.

49 Thorpe LJ in *Wermuth v Wermuth (No. 2)* [2003] 2 FLR 1029 para. [3]; R. Bailey-Harris and J. Wilson QC, 'Brexit: To Hell in a Handcart – Episode II' (2016) 46 *Family Law* 692 at 693.

50 D. Hodson, 'Brexit: England and Wales as a global family law leader or EU-emasculated?' (2016) 46 *Family Law* 572 at 573; G. Smith, 'The Brexit debate: project fear – no fear' (2016) 46 *Family Law* 696 at 699.

as to which approach to adopt will have to be taken at some stage after EU law becomes domestic law as received EU law at the date of exit. The issue is a challenging one not only as to its substance but also from the perspective of the relationship with other countries. Countries in the common law tradition which adopt the *forum conveniens* approach do not apply it uniformly.[51] Importantly, if the *forum conveniens* approach were to be adopted, how would that operate in cases involving parallel proceedings in a UK jurisdiction and in one of the remaining 27 EU Member States, which continue to adopt the *lis pendens* rule of first in time? The two systems simply do not fit together. One would predict that the *lis pendens* approach would in practice frequently win the race against the discretionary *forum conveniens* approach where the court in the *lis pendens* jurisdiction is first seised. That court would simply proceed with the divorce and there would be no marriage to dissolve in the *forum conveniens* jurisdiction, even were the latter to determine that it should not stay its proceedings. This foreshadows the acute problem of lack of reciprocity highlighted in the next section.

The Government's negotiating paper *Providing a Cross-border Civil Cooperation Framework*, published on 22 August 2017 as explained above,[52] advocates the continuation of the substance of EU jurisdictional rules. It must therefore be assumed that the Government supports the continuation of the 'first in time' approach to the resolution of potential conflicts of jurisdiction (although no discussion is contained in the paper). The political acceptability to the EU of the Government's position remains to be seen.

4. RECOGNITION AND ENFORCEMENT OF DIVORCE AND ANCILLARY FINANCIAL ORDERS

The EU Regulations enshrine the principle of automatic recognition and enforcement of orders in all Member States. The policy and political significance of this scheme cannot be too strongly emphasised: it reflects the mutual respect between Member States which is the essence of the special 'family' of the EU. Brussels IIA and the Maintenance Regulation contain a regime of mutual recognition and enforcement of orders throughout the EU,[53] regardless which

51 As illustrated by *Peng v Chai* [2017] 1 FLR 318, the *forum conveniens* approach adopted by Malaysian courts (following the High Court of Australia in *Voth v Manildra Flour Mills Pty. Ltd.* (1990) 171 CLR 538) differed from that adopted by English courts and no issue estoppel arose.

52 Above, nn. 41–42.

53 Brussels IIA Chapter III; Maintenance Regulation Chapter IV.

Member State the order was made in, subject to limited exceptions.[54] Recognition is the condition precedent to enforcement. The consequential enforcement procedures applied under the laws of each Member State treat an order as if it were an order made in the receiving state.

Reciprocal enforcement of orders is of enormous significance in the family law context, where the rights of individuals and their children are engaged. The Maintenance Regulation has been criticised for its complexity, but nevertheless the mechanism for reciprocal enforcement of orders which it sets up is very much in the interests of maintenance creditors: children's financial rights are an important aspect of their welfare rights.[55] To remove reciprocity with European countries after Brexit poses serious issues for families. The European Union (Withdrawal) Bill aims to retain EU Regulations on exit day as domestic law provisions, but it cannot deliver reciprocity. Professor Lowe has rightly labelled it the 'so-called unilateral option'.[56] The House of Lords European Union Committee Report was very concerned about the preservation of reciprocity.[57] Reciprocal enforcement and recognition of orders (in all areas of law) will be a matter for political negotiation between the UK and the EU. At the time of writing a government policy is not discernible and the general impression of practitioners and academics is that international family law matters will have a low priority. Gavin Smith[58] has proposed that the UK's first step should be to confirm that all EU judgments (whether divorce, children or financial) would continue to enjoy recognition and be entitled to enforcement in the UK, on precisely the same terms as they do under existing EU law. The result may be highly desirable but there are real questions about its political acceptability and of what the EU may demand in return, for instance in terms of the UK's acceptance of applicable law.[59]

The advantages of a virtually automatic system of recognition and enforcement of orders are self-evident. By contrast, where recognition of orders depends on the national laws of each recognising country, such laws require a link such as nationality, residence or domicile between the individual and the

---

54 Where recognition is manifestly contrary to public policy or principles of natural justice have been breached or where judgments are irreconcilable: Brussels IIA Art. 22 (for judgments relating to divorce, separation or annulment); Maintenance Regulation Art. 24.

55 The cases cited in n. 28 above concerned enforcement of child maintenance orders; see further Case C-283/16 *MS v PS* [2017] 1 FLR 1163.

56 Above n. 36, at 399.

57 Above n. 28, at 28–31, 40–41.

58 Above n. 50, at 696.

59 For example, the UK has not opted into the applicable law provisions in Chapter III of the Maintenance Regulation, nor into Council Regulation (EU) No. 1259/2010 (Rome III) on applicable law in divorce. Would this be a possible requirement posed by the EU in future negotiations?

country in which the order to be recognised was made. Thus section 46 of the Family Law Act 1986 provides that recognition of foreign divorces granted in countries outside the EU requires a connecting factor of habitual residence, domicile or nationality with the country granting the divorce. Absent a governing international instrument, it is for each country to determine the recognition criteria, and uniformity is difficult to achieve.

To what extent could international instruments other than EU Regulations post Brexit be relied on to secure recognition and reciprocal enforcement of divorce and maintenance orders after Brexit? The Hague Convention on the Recognition of Divorces and Legal Separations 1970 provides recognition rules but contains no provisions on jurisdiction. The EU is party to the Hague Convention on the International Recovery of Child Support and Other Forms of Family Maintenance 2007. The Hague Convention does not currently operate within the EU because the EU Maintenance Regulation takes precedence, and can only be used between a Member State and a non-Member State. The 2007 Hague Convention's main focus is reciprocal enforcement of family maintenance orders and it contains no provisions on jurisdiction. Opinion is divided on the extent to which the Hague Conventions or the Lugano Convention 2007 are capable of filling the gaps left by the demise of the EU Regulations after Brexit.[60]

The Government's paper *Providing a Cross-border Civil Judicial Cooperation Framework*[61] proposes continuation of the substantive provisions of EU Regulations on reciprocal recognition and enforcement of judgments, and rejects other international instruments as inferior in the 'interaction' they can afford. The political challenges which the UK's proposals will meet in negotiations have been highlighted earlier in this chapter. The refusal to accept the direct jurisdiction of the CJEU (reiterated in the paper *Enforcement and Dispute Resolution*) may well prove to be the reef on which negotiations founder. Only time will tell.

5. CONCLUSION

The private international law rules applying to families currently stand at the crossroads. The finer issues of interpretation arising over the last decade are now dwarfed by the fundamental challenge posed by Brexit. Whether Brexit is viewed as a positive opportunity or an unmitigated disaster, the enormity of the task ahead cannot be doubted. Lord Judge has recently observed: 'The Brexit

60 D. Hodson, above n. 50 at 574–575; G. Smith, above n. 50 at 697; cf. N. Lowe, above n. 36 at 404; House of Lords European Union Committee Report, above n. 28 at 28–31, 38–39, 43–44.

61 See nn. 41–42 above.

negotiations will be monumental: so will the Parliamentary processes which will give effect to the results of the negotiations'.[62]

According to Professor Mark Elliott:[63]

> Leaving to one side any questions about the merits or otherwise of the decision to leave the EU, what needs to be done between now and exit day is nothing short of a herculean task ... In political terms, the Withdrawal Bill is being presented as the epitome of the taking back of control and the restoration of 'sovereignty' that has been so fetishized by some. But it actually demonstrates something very different. It serves as a stark reminder of the way in which the banal rhetoric that has characterised – and that continues to characterise – much of the political debate in this area is now beginning to meet brutal legal and constitutional reality.

The two policy papers published in late August 2017 *Providing a Cross-border Civil Judicial Cooperation Framework* and *Enforcement and Dispute Resolution* advocate continuation of the substance of EU Regulations while disavowing the direct jurisdiction of the CJEU as the ultimate interpreter and arbitrator. The political naïveté of the UK's stance may well be exposed in the negotiations with the EU which at the time of writing are just beginning.

Professor Nigel Lowe in whose honour this chapter is written has been one of the greatest contributors of his generation to the jurisprudence of international family law. It remains to be seen what landscape his successors will survey.

62 Lord Judge, 'Legislating Brexit', *Counsel*, July 2017, 24–25.
63 Above n. 2.

NON-JUDICIAL DIVORCE IN FRANCE: PROGRESS OR A MESS?

Frédérique FERRAND

1. INTRODUCTION

Who could have predicted that in 2016 France would open a new path for consensual divorce in which the family judge would no longer have a role to play? Nobody expected such a radical change so soon.

In 1998, sociologist Irène Théry suggested introducing non-judicial divorce.[1] But it was too early for such a radical change.[2]

---

1 I. THÉRY, *Couple, filiation et parenté aujourd'hui*, Editions Odile Jacob, Paris 1998.

2 Even though some lawyers and judges admit that the family judge cannot dedicate much time to each consensual divorce proceeding. The scrutiny of the spouses' consent and of the child's interest is therefore limited, especially as most minor children do not request to be heard by the court in non-contentious divorce proceedings, see R. BARTHÉLÉMY, 'Divorce sans juge: interrogeons nos pratiques! – Le point de vue de l'avocat', *Droit de la Famille* n°. 7–8, Jul. 2016, dossier 27.

In 2007,[3] it was suggested that the notary public should record the consensual divorce of spouses. But in 2008 the *Guinchard* Commission[4] on desirable justice reforms did not support this proposal, as they considered that it would hinder the important task of the family judge to protect the weaker spouse and the minor children.

A new suggestion was made in 2013 by the *Delmas-Goyon* report '*Le juge du 21ème siècle*'.[5] The report suggested that consensual divorce should be granted by a new *greffier juridictionnel* (a new position that did not yet exist);[6] this would be a high-ranking court clerk to whom some judicial functions should be transferred in order to relieve the judges of part of their workload. They could grant consensual divorce (*divorce par consentement mutuel*) notwithstanding the existence of minor children of the spouses and without regard to the composition of the spouses' assets (immovable property, etc.). According to proposal no. 47,[7] this new *greffier juridictionnel* would also have to scrutinise the spousal agreement, at the time of divorce, with regard to the fairness of the divorce consequences and the child's best interest.[8] Scholars criticised this proposal.[9]

Because of this history, nobody expected new discussions so soon about a possible out-of-court divorce. When the Draft Bill on Justice in the Twenty-First Century was presented by the former minister of justice, Christiane Taubira, not a single provision mentioned non-judicial divorce, since divorce did not initially fall within the scope of the Draft Bill. However, after the Bill was brought before Parliament (on 31 July 2015), the Ministry of Justice presented numerous subsequent amendments. One of them suggested the introduction of a non-judicial consensual divorce. On 12 July 2016, the Parliamentary Assembly (*Assemblée Nationale*) passed the law on the modernisation of justice of the twenty-first century. In October 2016, the Second Chamber (*Sénat*) withheld consent regarding non-judicial consensual divorce in cases where the spouses have minor children. However, as the *Assemblée Nationale* always has the final say, the Draft Bill was enacted on 12 October 2016. Law Act no. 2016-1547 of 18 November 2016 *de modernisation de la justice du XXIème siècle*[10] came into force on 1 January 2017. Article 50 of the law creates a new private

3 *Rapport du Conseil de modernisation des politiques publiques*, 12.12.2007. See also J.-R. Binet, 'Divorce sans juge: nouvelle tentative, nouveau débat', *Droit de la Famille* n°. 2, Feb. 2014, repère 2.

4 *Rapport S. Guinchard, L'ambition raisonnée d'une justice apaisée*, Doc. française, Paris 2008.

5 *Rapport Delmas-Goyon, Le juge du 21ème siècle, Un citoyen acteur, une équipe de justice*, Dec. 2013, <http://www.justice.gouv.fr/publication/rapport_dg_2013.pdf>.

6 *Rapport Delmas-Goyon*, above n. 5, p. 33 and proposals 45–54, pp. 102–114.

7 *Rapport Delmas-Goyon*, above n. 5, p. 106: Proposals 47 and 49.

8 See the discussions within the commission *Rapport Delmas-Goyon*, above n. 5, p. 107.

9 See J.-R. Binet, above n. 3: the new Law Act only aims at an optimisation of the prompt mass processing of family cases.

10 *Journal Officiel (JO)* of 19.11.2016.

divorce procedure. Procedural provisions enacted by Decree no. 2016-1907 of 28 December 2016 were integrated in the Code of Civil Procedure (CPC, Articles 1144–1148-2).

2. CONTENTS OF THE LAW ACT NO. 2016-1547 OF 18 NOVEMBER 2016 ON THE MODERNISATION OF JUSTICE IN THE TWENTY-FIRST CENTURY

The purpose of the new Law Act on the Modernisation of Justice in the Twenty-First Century is to make court proceedings simpler, quicker and more efficient. It also promotes alternative mechanisms of dispute resolution.

In family law, the reforming law aims to give the spouses more freedom with regard to marriage breakdown. Marriage is increasingly understood as a contract[11] and less as an institution.[12] This contract can be terminated by a spousal agreement without the interference of any state body such as a court.

The true reason for this sudden unexpected introduction of non-judicial divorce into French law seems to be practical and pragmatic: the government hopes to stop the work overload among family judges. At first, there was also real concern that the government would use this as a strategy to reduce legal aid expenditure (*aide juridictionnelle*), but this fear was misplaced as, according to the new Law Act of 18 November 2016, either of the spouses can apply for free legal advice (*aide juridique*) even if the divorce process is not judicial.[13]

The Constitutional Council (*Conseil constitutionnel*)[14] ruled that extrajudicial divorce did not infringe the principle of equal treatment or any other constitutional provisions.

Article 229 of the Civil code, which lists the different grounds for divorce, has been supplemented with a new paragraph. The new kind of divorce is now regulated in a specific part of the Civil code, which contains only four new articles (Articles 229-1–229-4 Civil code). A governmental decree[15] of 28 December 2016 clarifies some procedural details.

---

11 Compare B. Beignier, 'Balises pour un divorce contractuel', *Droit de la Famille* n°. 7–8, Jul. 2016, repère 7. – V. Égea, 'Déjudiciarisation du divorce: brèves observations relatives à l'acte d'avocat', *Droit de la Famille* n°. 7–8, Jul. 2016, dossier 29: the Draft Bill is a 'mutation profonde du droit de la famille, basculant sans cesse vers une plus grande privatisation' (n. 4) spricht. – C. Brunetti-Pons, 'Un divorce "sans juge" pour un droit déréglé', *Droit de la Famille* n°. 7–8, Jul. 2016, dossier 28, n. 14.

12 See N. Baillon-Wirtz, 'La déjudiciarisation précipité du divorce par consentement mutuel', *JurisClasseur Pratique G* 2016, n°. 653, p. 1114.

13 See also Art. 1144-5 CPC.

14 *Conseil constitutionnel*, 17.11.2016, n°. 2016-739 DC, *Journal Officiel (JO)* of 19. 11.2016.

15 *Décret* n°. 2016-1907 of 28.12.2016, *Journal Officiel (JO)* of 29.12.2016.

2.1. WHEN IS A PRIVATE DIVORCE LEGALLY POSSIBLE?

According to Article 229-2 of the Civil code, there are two situations in which divorcing spouses cannot agree on their divorce and its consequences in a private deed countersigned by two solicitors (*acte sous signature privée contresignée par avocat*) and must apply to the court:

1. a minor child of the spouses has been informed about his/her right to be heard[16] by the family judge and wants to make use of this right;[17] or
2. one of the spouses is placed under a legal protection regime such as guardianship or trusteeship (*tutelle, curatelle*).[18]

In all other situations, private divorce is legally possible. Several aspects appear to be problematic. First is the fact that the parents themselves have the duty to inform the child about his/her right to be heard and that no true guarantee is provided that the information has actually been given and understood. Secondly, it is not appropriate that the child's wish to be heard by the family judge leads to the redirecting of the divorce process, which then cannot remain extrajudicial and must be brought before court. In the child's interest, the modern law-maker strives for a clear separation between the divorce consequences relating to the spouses and the consequences with regard to the children. This is not the case in Law Act no. 2016-1547 of 18 November 2016 since the child's wish to be heard shall necessarily lead to a court divorce proceeding. Another question is who shall decide whether the child has the capacity of understanding (*capacité de discernement*) that is a necessary legal prerequisite to be heard by the family judge? The parents themselves? And what will happen if the parents follow their child's wish to be heard, apply for divorce before the court and the family judge later decides that the child does not have the capacity of understanding required for a hearing? Will the divorce process remain judicial? Probably, since for the transfer of the proceedings to the court, Article 229-2, paragraph 1° of the Civil code only requires the child's wish to be heard, not a positive answer of the family judge.[19]

Must the spouses use the non-judicial divorce process if they agree on the divorce and all its consequences and do not have minor children (or their minor children do not wish to be heard)? It would have been preferable to leave them an

16 See Art. 388-1 Civil code.

17 Yet, this would probably seldom happen. The ministry of justice indicated that in 2015 in 65,875 consensual divorce court proceedings, only 25 children expressed the wish to be heard by the family judge, see S. Thouret, 'Le nouveau divorce par consentement mutuel ou le divorce sans juge', *Actualité Juridique Famille (AJ Famille)* Dec. 2016, p. 569.

18 In such a case, no judicial or non-judicial consensual divorce is allowed by the Civil code.

19 See S. Thouret, 'Le nouveau divorce par consentement mutuel ou le divorce sans juge', *AJ Famille* Dec. 2016, p. 569.

option between a private divorce and an application before court in order to let the family judge scrutinise the agreement and approve it (*homologation*). However, the final version of Article 229-1 reads: 'where the spouses agree upon divorce and its consequences, they shall lay down the contents of their agreement in a private deed countersigned by their solicitors and set up under the conditions laid down in Article 1374'. This wording must[20] be interpreted as meaning that if the spouses agree on the divorce and on all its consequences, they cannot apply for divorce by mutual consent before the court and can only use the new extra-judicial divorce process (except in the two situations previously mentioned in which private divorce is not allowed). This interpretation is confirmed by the new Article 229 of the Civil code, which expressly limits a consensual divorce court order to the case in which the minor child has expressed his/her wish to be heard by the family judge. It is highly questionable to exclude any option and to *oblige* the spouses to divorce extra-judicially as soon as they agree on all the divorce consequences. This suggests that the overriding goal of the reform was to reduce the caseload of the family courts. Moreover, wouldn't it be more appropriate to let the choice of the divorce process/proceeding depend on the joint decision of the spouses and not on the expressed wish of the child to be heard or not? This expressed wish could even bring some economic advantages to the spouses, since they may appoint a joint solicitor in the case of *judicial* divorce by mutual consent.[21]

Several legal provisions[22] have been adjusted, such as Article L. 111-3 of the *Code des procédures civiles d'exécution* (Code of enforcement proceedings), which contains a comprehensive list of enforcement orders (*titres exécutoires*) under French law. The private divorce deed that is signed by the spouses and countersigned by two solicitors becomes an enforcement order when it is filed in the original records of a notary public.

2.2. DIVORCE PROCESS AND CONSEQUENCES

2.2.1. *The Role of the Spouses, of the Solicitors and of the Notary Public*

Pursuant to the new Article 229-1 of the Civil code, the spouses shall lay down the content of the agreement in a private document, which they must then sign[23]

20 See S. THOURET, above n. 17, p. 568 (it is not a '*divorce optionnel*').

21 See Art. 250 Civil code.

22 See e.g. *Code pénal* (criminal offence of *délit d'abandon de famille*, Art. 227-3 Criminal code. The offence – non-payment of maintenance for at least two months – is also committed if the duty of maintenance was laid down in the spousal private divorce agreement).

23 The spouses receive (by registered letter) a draft agreement from their lawyers and must wait until the reflection period of two weeks has elapsed (Art. 229-4 para. 1 Civil code). The reflection period runs from the receipt of the draft agreement by the spouse. Lawyers and spouses sign the agreement together during a final meeting (Art. 1145 para. 1 CPC).

and have countersigned by the two solicitors. They must also meet other formal requirements provided in Article 1374[24] of the Civil code. Each spouse must appoint a solicitor ('*assistés chacun par un avocat*') who will take care of the spouse's interests; the written agreement must be filed with the records of a notary public;[25] and the notary public must check whether all the legal requirements are met (new Article 229-2, paragraphs 1–6 of the Civil code[26]). Pursuant to the new Article 229-3 of the Civil code, the agreement entered upon by the spouses (*convention*) must contain the following items:[27]

1. name, surname, profession, place of domicile, nationality, date and place of birth of each spouse, date and place of the marriage celebration and, where relevant, the same information relating to the spouses' children;
2. name and professional address of the two solicitors who have been appointed by the spouses;
3. a reference to the spouses' agreement on the divorce and its consequences as laid down in the agreement;
4. the terms of the comprehensive settlement of all divorce consequences, in particular whether a '*prestation compensatoire*' (compensatory benefit)[28] should be paid by one spouse to the other;
5. information relating to the division of matrimonial property (the division must be made in a notary deed if there are immovables to be divided) or the statement that no division of property has to take place; and
6. a reference to the fact that the minor child has been informed[29] by his/her parents about his/her right to be heard by the family judge but does not want to make use of this opportunity.[30]

---

24 Art. 1374 Civil code: the private deed countersigned by the solicitors of each party or by the solicitor of all parties proves, between themselves as well as against their heirs and successors, that the parties have written and signed the deed. The statute does not require such a private deed (*acte contresigné par avocat*) to be handwritten.

25 On request of the spouses, one of the lawyers sends the divorce deed and the annexes (forms for each minor child ...) to the notary public within seven days of the signing. The notary must file the deed within two weeks from its receipt (Art. 1146 CPC).

26 See also Art. 1144-1 CPC (the private deed mentions the name of the notary who will file it) and Art. 1144-5 CPC (the written agreement should indicate how the divorce fees will be divided; in the absence of any indication, each spouse shall pay half). Each spouse keeps a copy of the deed and the third one is sent to the notary public.

27 If one of these required elements is missing, the agreement is null and void (*à peine de nullité*). See J. Casey, 'Convention de divorce par consentement mutuel', *AJ Famille* Feb. 2017, pp. 96–104.

28 See also Art. 1144-3 CPC (the value of the assets or rights allocated as compensatory benefits shall be indicated in the private deed).

29 If a child has no capacity of understanding, it should be mentioned in the private deed that for this reason, no information could be provided to the child (Art. 1144-2 CPC).

30 The child has to fill in and sign a form. *Arreté* of 28.12.2016 provides a template for such form. Each minor child must complete a form, see Art. 1144 CPC. If a child refuses, private divorce is not possible.

The agreement becomes enforceable (*force exécutoire)* when it has been filed in the records of a notary public (paragraph 2).[31] The fees to be paid to the notary public should be kept low (€50).

The notary public must check that the agreement was signed only after termination of the reflection period and verify whether all required annexes have been attached to the deed.[32] This is a mere formal check,[33] which means that the solicitors will bear the responsibility for the contents of the divorce agreement.

2.2.2. *Are Appeals Available?*

Since the divorce process is extra-judicial, no specific means of recourse are provided by the law. However, one does wonder whether a spouse could seek the annulment of the divorce agreement on the ground of a defect of consent or of legal incapacity. It would lead to huge legal uncertainty[34] if the divorce could be nullified. Could the divorce consequences be challenged before the court by one of the spouses if they have not been scrutinised by the family judge? Since private divorce is a contract between the spouses, it is logical to admit that one of the spouses is entitled to make use of the nullity grounds provided by general contract law and that a third party could also, in some cases,[35] challenge the agreement.[36] In the context of *judicial* consensual divorce, the French Court of cassation has ensured that agreement on the divorce consequences cannot be easily challenged, particularly in setting the principle of the indivisibility of the granting of divorce and of the judicial approval of the agreement on the divorce consequences.[37] An application to reopen proceedings (*recours en révision*),[38]

---

31 See also Art. 229-1 para. 3 Civil code.

32 See S. David and R. Brunet, 'Le role du notaire dans le nouveau divorce par consentement mutuel', *AJ Famille* Jan. 2017, pp. 31–40.

33 Notaries expressed their concern about a merely formal scrutiny, see G. Bonnet, 'Divorce sans juge – Le point de vue du notaire', *Droit de la Famille*, n°. 7–8, Jul. 2016, dossier 2, n. 6. According to *Circulaire* of 26.01.2017, the notary should draw the lawyers' attention to a clause which is contrary to the *ordre public*. See also C. Brenner, 'Le nouveau divorce par consentement mutuel: retour à l'an II?', *JCP G* 2017, n°. 195, pp. 342–345.

34 Some scholars suggest that the divorce declaration should not be subject to further action for voidance where it has been filed by the notary public, see H. Fulchiron, '"L'après-divorce sans juge": remise en cause et modification de la convention passée par les époux', *Droit de la Famille*, n°. 7–8, July 2016, dossier 32, n.12.

35 A spouse's creditor could e.g. bring an '*action paulienne*' (*actio pauliana*, revocatory action) if the agreement on the divorce consequences affects his/her rights, see S. Thouret, 'Quelles voies de recours dans le nouveau divorce par consentement mutual?', *Droit de la Famille*, n°. 7–8, Jul. 2016, dossier 30, n. 5.

36 See S. Thouret, above, n. 35.

37 See E. Fortis, *Répertoire civil Dalloz*, 'Divorce (Cas de divorce)', n°. 326.

38 Cass. civ. 1, 5.11.2008, n. 07-14.439, *Bull. civ.* I, n. 247; *Droit de la Famille* 2008, comm. 170 V. Larribeau-Terneyre.

a claim for nullity on the ground of a defect or a lack of consent,[39] on the ground of the legal incapacity of one spouse and of a huge economic imbalance in the regulation of the divorce consequences (*lésion*)[40] have all been rejected by the Court of Cassation.

3. CRITICISM

The law reform introducing private divorce in France has been subject to numerous critical assessments.[41]

3.1. IS PRIVATE DIVORCE REALLY CHEAPER?

It was argued that private divorce would reduce the spouses' costs of proceedings. However, it is not certain that this is the case. There are no specific official tariffs for solicitors in France (unlike in Germany) and lawyers' fees are decided by the lawyers themselves but require a written agreement between the lawyer and the client. In the framework of non-judicial consensual divorce, the spouses must appoint one lawyer each and a notary public. Before the law reform came into force, spouses who agreed on the divorce and its consequences could appoint one single joint lawyer; this is no longer possible. Therefore, cost savings should not be expected.[42]

Does private divorce reduce costs for the state? In 2008, the *Guinchard* report indicated that cost saving to the benefit of the state would be modest because it would mean abolishing only a few judicial positions. Moreover, the law reform provides for legal aid if one or both the spouses have a low income. Therefore, it can be concluded that private divorce will not reduce the state expenses relating to legal aid (*aide juridictionnelle* before court or *aide juridique* for non-judicial divorce).

---

39 See E. Fortis, above n. 37, n.° 331 and Cass civ. 2, 13.11.1991, n.° 90-17.840, *Bull. civ.* II, n.° 303.

40 Cass. civ. 1, 3.03.2010, n.° 08-70.214 and 08-12.395.

41 See e.g. C. Brunetti-Pons, above n. 11.

42 Critically, C. Brunetti-Pons, above n. 11, considers whether the law reform will lead to a 'class divorce' depending on the spouses' economic situation (the wealthy would choose a quick private divorce, whereas the other spouses would go to court for financial reasons). State courts' costs are very low in France.

3.2. LEGAL CERTAINTY FOR THE SPOUSES?

Before the law reform of 2016, the family court granted consensual divorce only after ensuring that both spouses consented to the divorce[43] and that the divorce consequences sufficiently took into account the spouses' and the children's interests[44] (this is still the case in consensual divorce proceedings if a minor child wishes to be heard). Some lawyers argue that this scrutiny is more theoretical than real,[45] as family courts are overloaded with cases, but it is nevertheless a safeguard to prevent major imbalance or unfairness in the agreement, which the 'stronger' spouse may impose on the weaker one. This guarantee no longer exists in non-judicial consensual divorce, and so there is now a risk that the stronger spouse might impose his/her views regarding the divorce consequences, which could be unfair or unbalanced.[46] Whether the reflection period of two weeks legally imposed on the spouses before they may sign the divorce agreement can be regarded as a protection is doubtful.[47]

The new private divorce carries some major risks for the spouses. Until 2016, French law and case law made it difficult to invalidate a spousal agreement on the divorce consequences once they had been approved (*homologué*) by the family judge. With the law reform, the spousal agreement on the divorce and its consequences becomes a contract,[48] which does not need any court approval. This contract will be governed by general contract law,[49] which means that legal provisions of the Civil code relating to defects of consent (mistake, fraud, duress), incapacity, infringement of public order or major change of circumstances should apply.[50] For example, the new Article 1195 introduced

---

43 Art. 232 para. 1 Civil code: '*Le juge homologue la convention et prononce le divorce s'il a acquis la conviction que la volonté de chacun des époux est réelle et que leur consentement est libre et éclairé*'.

44 Art. 232 para. 2 Civil code: '*Il peut refuser l'homologation et ne pas prononcer le divorce s'il constate que la convention préserve insuffisamment les intérêts des enfants ou de l'un des époux*'. See M. Juston, 'Le divorce par consentement mutuel sans juge : une opération sans chirurgien. – Le point de vue d'un magistrat', *Droit de la Famille* n°. 7–8, Jul. 2016, dossier 25, n. 10 *et seq*.

45 For a different opinion, see M. Juston, above n. 44, n. 12.

46 C. Brunetti-Pons, above n. 11: '*Le projet de loi supprime … tout contrôle judiciaire de la pesée des intérêts de chacun des époux*'.

47 In a *Circulaire* of 26.01.2017, the Ministry of Justice defends the view that the agreement is binding on the spouses. The spouses are free to opt for a court proceeding as long as their divorce agreement has not been filed in the originals section of the notary (Art. 1148-2 CPC).

48 But a specific one, see F. Chénedé, 'Divorce et contrat. A la croisée des réformes', *AF Famille* Jan. 2017, pp. 26–29.

49 See V. Égéa, 'Déjudiciarisation du divorce: brèves observations relatives à l'acte d'avocat', *Droit de la Famille* n°. 7–8, Jul. 2016, dossier 29. Compare J. Casey, 'Le nouveau divorce par consentement mutuel, une réforme en clair-obscur', *AJ Famille* Jan. 2017, p. 17.

50 H. Fulchiron, above n. 34.

in 2016 in the Civil code,[51] which allows an adjustment of contract terms or even the termination of a contract by a court decision where there is a major change of circumstances (*imprévision*),[52] should normally apply to spousal contracts on the consequences of divorce. Legal certainty will be weaker.[53]

What will happen for example if a spouse does not indicate all his/her assets so that the liquidation and property distribution between the spouses is incomplete? One can assume that the Court of Cassation will stick to its case law, which allows, under specific circumstances, that one spouse can claim an order for supplemental sharing (*action en complément de partage*).[54]

Is judicial scrutiny of the spousal agreement on the divorce consequences absolutely necessary? According to solicitors,[55] it is not true that spouses reach balanced and fair agreements only because they fear the family judge's scrutiny. Solicitors also play a decisive role to help the spouses to achieve fair solutions. They can use collaborative law, mediation or also a new process created by Law Act no. 2010-1609 of 22 December 2010: '*procédure participative assistée par avocats*'[56] (an amicable procedure carried out with the lawyers' assistance: a contract is signed between the parties and their lawyers before or during the court proceedings and the aim is to find an amicable solution to the dispute through negotiation). Some solicitors defend the view that the new private divorce is a '*valorisation*' of their task to provide advice to the spouses to enable them to reach amicable, balanced and fair agreements. The new consensual divorce law requires solicitors to give helpful and strong advice. Otherwise, they could be held liable for their mistakes.[57] They must thoroughly discuss the possible contents of the divorce agreement and the legal consequences with their clients, and formulate the contract as accurately as possible. Article 66-3-1 of Law no. 71-1130 of 31 December 1971 on the legal profession states that the lawyer who countersigns a private deed certifies thereby that they have fully informed their client about the legal consequences of the transaction.[58]

---

51 Contract law reform, see *Ordonnance* n°. 2016-131 of 10.02.2016.

52 See Art. 1195 Civil code. More optimistic, see J. Casey, 'Le nouveau divorce par consentement mutuel', above n. 49, pp. 24–25.

53 See J. Casey, above n. 49, p. 14.

54 See e.g. Cass. civ. 1, 20.11.2013, n°. 12-21.621.

55 See R. Barthelemy, 'Divorce sans juge: interrogeons nos pratiques! – Le point de vue de l'avocat', *Droit de la Famille* n°. 7–8, Jul. 2016, dossier 27.

56 See Arts. 2062–2068 Civil code and Arts. 1542–1564-4 CPC (*Code de procédure civile*).

57 See G. Barbe, 'Vers un divorce personnalisé, à perfectionner …', *Gazette du Palais* 17.05.2016, pp. 9–10.

58 '*En contresignant un acte sous seing privé, l'avocat atteste avoir éclairé pleinement la ou les parties qu'il conseille sur les conséquences juridiques de cet acte*'.

3.3. WHAT ABOUT THE CHILDREN'S BEST INTEREST?

As spousal agreements on divorce and its consequences are no longer subject to court scrutiny before they become applicable, we can but hope that divorcing parents will reach agreements on parental responsibilities (child maintenance, residence, exercise of contact rights) that are in accordance with the child's best interest.[59] Certainly, Article 373-2-13 of the Civil code was amended and extends to private divorce and the parent's and the attorney general's right to request, at any time, from the family court a modification of the spousal agreement with regard to the exercise of parental responsibilities and to child maintenance. This, however, does not replace a preliminary check of the compatibility of the agreed divorce consequences with the child's best interest.[60] One could of course object that the same applies to children whose parents are not married: if the parents agree on the exercise of parental responsibilities and/or child maintenance, the agreement is not subject to any court scrutiny.[61] But this agreement is not an enforceable order, whereas the spousal divorce agreement filed with a notary public is enforceable.[62]

A further major problem lies in the possible 'instrumentalisation' of children.[63] The parents have a duty to inform their children about their right to be heard by the family judge. To certify that such information has been provided, the parents must present a form to the child, who has to sign and tick a box (I want to be heard by the judge: yes or no). Parents may not necessarily know that they must fulfil this duty. Their solicitors must inform them and check whether the parents have fulfilled their duty towards the minor children. But the law does not require the information to be given to the children in the presence of the solicitors. The parents could present the form to the child and ask them to tick the box 'no' without any further explanation.[64]

The legal provision places a heavy responsibility on the child's shoulders: to oblige their parents to divorce before a court if the child expresses their wish to be heard. Private divorce should only be allowed in the absence of minor children. A scholar suggested that the following distinction[65] be made: if the spouses have minor children, the agreement on the divorce consequences should

---

59 Critically, see H. Fulchiron, 'L'enfant dans le divorce sans juge', *Droit de la Famille* n°. 7–8, Jul. 2016, dossier 31, n. 3; Ph. Buratti, 'Réflexions sur l'arreté du 28 décembre 2016', *AJ Famille* Jan. 2017, p. 30.

60 See C. Brunetti-Pons, above, n. 11.

61 The family court is seised only if the parents cannot reach an agreement.

62 See H. Fulchiron, 'Le divorce sans juge, c'est … pour bientôt!', *Droit de la Famille* n°. 9, Sep. 2016, repère 8.

63 See H. Fulchiron, above n. 62.

64 See also N. Baillon-Wirtz, above n. 12, p. 1116.

65 See e.g. B. Beignier, above n. 11.

always be subject to court scrutiny and approval ('*homologation*'). If the spouses do not have minor children, a fully private divorce agreement without any court scrutiny would be acceptable.

Judicial scrutiny of the spousal agreement with respect to the exercise of parental responsibilities and child maintenance should be required. The approval process ('*procédure d'homologation*') would not necessarily require the spouses to appear before a court. One could imagine that the spouses would send a written request for approval together with a copy of the divorce agreement. The family judge could order the spouses' personal appearance if this seems necessary before approving or rejecting the agreement.[66]

4. CONCLUSION

Until 2016, French divorce law could definitely not be described as 'revolutionary'. The previous law reform (Law Act no. 2004-439 of 26 May 2004 *relative au divorce*) kept various divorce grounds and endeavoured to promote a peaceful break-up by promoting spousal agreements subsequently approved (*homologués*) by the family judge.

By contrast, the most recent Law of 18 November 2016 has made a huge and ill-thought-out step towards the privatisation of divorce. Whether an extra-judicial consensual divorce is appropriate where spouses have minor children is highly questionable. The protection of the weaker spouse (e.g. the wife who is a victim of domestic violence or simply economically weaker than her husband) is no longer safeguarded. Moreover, there is concern that numerous disputes relating to the divorce consequences could occur:[67] they would be subject to general contract law, which has been recently amended in France and allows numerous court interventions. Was divorce reform worth all these risks?

---

66 A very similar process has just been abolished in England and Wales (s. 41 Matrimonial Causes Act 1973 repealed by s. 17 Children and Families Act 2014).

67 See S. Thouret, 'L'après-divorce conventionnel: vers le retour du juge!', *AJ Famille* Jan. 2017, pp. 42–45.

THE ISTANBUL CONVENTION: IS DOMESTIC ABUSE VIOLENCE AGAINST WOMEN?

Jonathan HERRING

1. INTRODUCTION

Nigel Lowe and International Family Law have gone together, well, rather better than love and marriage, for many decades. Family lawyers know that if you have a tricky question on international family law Nigel is the person to ask. The depth of his knowledge, the warmth of his support, the gentleness of his spirit, and his passion for the subject are an inspiration to all.

Recent international human rights instruments have recognised the category of Violence against Women (VAW). Most notable is the UN Declaration on the Elimination of Violence Against Women. The VAW approach emphasises that women are subject to violence in a range of contexts and that this should be understood as having especial significance because it is *against women*. Feminist scholars see VAW as a key aspect of patriarchy. This chapter focuses on one particular question which has arisen for European family lawyers and that is whether it is helpful to see domestic abuse as VAW.

The focus of this discussion will be the Istanbul Convention, which plays a major role in the European response to crimes against women. In this chapter I will criticise the Convention for separating out domestic abuse from VAW. I will argue that this masks a crucial aspect of domestic abuse: that it contributes to patriarchy.

Of course, in saying this I am not for a moment denying that within intimate relationships women are violent to women; that women are violent to men; or that men are violent to other men. But I will argue that in some of these cases that violence lacks the patriarchy-supporting dimension that needs to be recognised. That dimension is downplayed by grouping all violence within intimate relationships into a single category.

This chapter will start with a description of the definition of domestic abuse in the Istanbul Convention and will clarify the issue being discussed. It will then explore why it is important that domestic violence is explained as VAW, before looking at the difficulties in doing so.

2. THE ISTANBUL CONVENTION

The Istanbul Convention draws together European legal policies on violence against women. I will not seek to set out all the terms of the Convention. There is much that is admirable and helpful in it. My focus is on its gender-neutral definition of domestic abuse.

It is no secret that that there was fierce dispute over the definition of domestic abuse when negotiating the Convention and that the gender-neutral definition was a compromise between competing points of view.[1] The Task Force on Violence against Women and the European Committee on Crime Problems were both working on the issue and were required to work together on the drafting of the Convention. The former was looking at VAW generally, while the latter was looking at domestic violence and was keen to ensure the law took seriously cases where men were the victims of violence in intimate relationships and cases of violence within same-sex relationships. Not surprisingly the Task Force sought a VAW definition, while the Committee sought a gender-neutral definition. The Committee won the argument.

This is apparent from the Convention's full title: *Council of Europe Convention on Preventing and Combating Violence Against Women and Domestic Violence*, which clearly separates domestic violence from 'violence against women'. It indicates that under the convention there can be domestic abuse which is not

[1] S. Kiymaz Bahçeci, *Safe From Fear Safe From Violence*, Council of Europe, Brussels 2013.

violence against women. This is also made clear in the definition of domestic abuse in Article 3(b):

> all acts of physical, sexual, psychological or economic violence that occur within the family or domestic unit or between former or current spouses or partners, whether or not the perpetrator shares or has shared the same residence with the victim.

That definition does not restrict the understanding of domestic violence to cases where the victim is female or to cases where the perpetrator is male. This is clearly a deliberate policy and is in marked contrast to Article 3(a), which defines gender-based violence:

> a violation of human rights and a form of discrimination against women and shall mean all acts of gender-based violence that result in, or are likely to result in, physical, sexual, psychological or economic harm or suffering to women, including threats of such acts, coercion or arbitrary deprivation of liberty, whether occurring in public or in private life.

The distinction between the terminology VAW and domestic violence is all the more surprising given the Convention's preamble, which demonstrates a clear awareness of the gendered impact of VAW generally. It includes the following statements which are in line with standard VAW analysis of domestic abuse for the past few decades:

> Recognising that violence against women is a manifestation of historically unequal power relations between women and men, which have led to domination over, and discrimination against, women by men and to the prevention of the full advancement of women;
>
> Recognising the structural nature of violence against women as gender-based violence, and that violence against women is one of the crucial social mechanisms by which women are forced into a subordinate position compared with men;
>
> ...
>
> Recognising that women and girls are exposed to a higher risk of gender-based violence than men;
>
> Recognising that domestic violence affects women disproportionately, and that men may also be victims of domestic violence ...

This makes it all the more striking that domestic abuse is separated out and defined in gender-neutral language, outside of the category of VAW.

The text of the Convention is not completely unambiguous. Article 2(1) states: 'This Convention shall apply to all forms of violence against women, including domestic violence, which affects women disproportionately.' This seems to imply that domestic violence can be a form of VAW. This is also reflected in Article 2(2), which states: 'Parties are encouraged to apply this Convention to all victims of domestic violence. Parties shall pay particular attention to women victims of gender-based violence in implementing the provisions of this Convention.'

These provisions seem to acknowledge that there is something special about domestic violence in cases where women are the victims, sufficient to mean that 'particular attention' should be paid to such cases. However, the requirement that 'particular attention' is paid to such cases seems a very weak requirement. Read as a whole, the Convention is clear that domestic abuse is best seen as a category on its own, even though some instances of it may be regarded as VAW.[2] It is that approach I will criticise in this chapter.

3. DOMESTIC ABUSE AND PATRIARCHY

To clarify the nature of the argument I am making I draw on the seminal work of Michelle Madden Dempsey on the definition of domestic abuse.[3] She developed a sophisticated approach which draws on the intersection of three concepts: violence; domesticity; and patriarchy. She separates out 13 different ways in which these concepts could intersect (violence and domesticity, but no patriarchy; violence and patriarchy, but no domesticity and so forth). She argues that it is only at the intersection of the three concepts that we have 'domestic violence in the strong sense': '[A] violent act occurring in a domestic context, which tends to sustain or perpetuate patriarchy and is, all things considered, unjustified.'[4] Other intersections of the concepts can amount to domestic violence, but only in the weak sense. For example:

> [A] violent act occurring in a domestic context, which does not tend to sustain or perpetuate patriarchy but is, all things considered, unjustified. I will refer to this concept as 'domestic violence in its weak sense'.[5]

To emphasise, the claim is not that violence in the home which does not sustain or perpetuate patriarchy is not domestic violence, but that it is only so in a 'weaker sense'. She explains the significance of this distinction in later writing:

> when a prosecutor is faced with two sets of cases that are otherwise identical in all salient respects (that is, other things being equal), there is an important value to be realized

---

2 Although *Bălşan v Romania*, Application no. 49645/09, para. 79, describes the case (involving domestic violence) as one of violence against women.

3 M. Madden Dempsey, *Prosecuting Domestic Violence*, Oxford University Press, Oxford 2009.

4 Ibid. at 209.

5 Ibid. at 211. Other combinations do not amount to domestic violence in any sense: e.g. an act which is violent but outside the domestic context.

> in targeting cases of domestic violence in its strong sense for aggressive prosecution and, in comparison, declining to target cases of domestic violence in its weak sense for equally aggressive prosecution.[6]

This is not, therefore an argument that cases outside the 'strong sense' of domestic abuse are not domestic abuse, or that they should not be taken seriously or have resources devoted to them. It is rather a claim that there is a particular wrong in strong domestic violence cases (namely the sustenance and perpetuation of patriarchy) that is not present in other cases.

Broadly, I agree with Madden Dempsey's analysis.[7] Cases of domestic abuse which sustain or perpetuate patriarchy engage a very particular wrong and should be separated from other cases. To explore this claim further I will start by explaining the nature of patriarchy before then exploring how patriarchy is sustained or perpetuated by domestic abuse and how domestic violence is sustained or perpetuated by patriarchy. That will explain why cases of strong domestic abuse contain a special kind of wrong which justifies their being separated from other cases, and hence why the Istanbul Convention is in error in not identifying clearly the very particular wrong of domestic abuse as a crime against women, which perpetuates patriarchy.

3.1. WHAT IS PATRIARCHY?

Much has been written on the definition of patriarchy[8] and I will only sketch an outline of it. Michelle Madden Dempsey defines patriarchy in this way: 'a collection of social forms which constitute a structural inequality, whereby men hold systematic social power in society more generally.'

Patriarchy is a range of forces which restrict the ability of women to access valuable resources and exercise their options. This can be through active misogyny (hatred of women) but also through a failure to value the work or characteristics of women. It can be expressed in a range of ways: from sex discrimination where barriers are put in place; to social resources which favour men over women; to sexual harassment in the street which discourages women from accessing public spaces; to a devaluing of care which is predominantly performed by women. It involves denying women access to resources they need to live valuable lives. Patriarchy works to restrict women to domestic spaces and deny them access to

---

6 M. Madden Dempsey, 'Response to Commentators' (2014) 8 *Criminal Law and Philosophy* 557, 559.

7 I do not agree with the details of some of her observations on the nature of violence or domesticity, but those are not important for the question in this chapter.

8 S. Walby, *Theorizing Patriarchy*, Oxford University Press, New York 1990.

economic, material and public resources. The argument in this chapter is that patriarchy supports and is supported by domestic abuse. As the United Nations Special Rapporteur on Violence against Women puts it: 'violence is not an isolated incident targeting vulnerable women but a systematically used tool of patriarchal control to ensure that "women stay in their place."'[9] This claim will now be explored further.

3.2. HOW DOMESTIC ABUSE SUSTAINS PATRIARCHY

As explained, patriarchy is about denying women access to socially valuable goods, restricting their choices and devaluing them as women. In this section I seek to explain the role that domestic abuse plays in supporting patriarchy.

First, domestic abuse reinforces the messages sent more broadly by patriarchy that women should be subservient to men and are inferior to them. The Convention on the Elimination of All Forms of Discrimination against Women, General Recommendation 19, states that domestic abuse is based on 'traditional attitudes by which women are regarded as subordinate to men.' Gender stereotypes typically underpin domestic abuse. Consider, for example, this incident in the American case, *State v Norman*:[10]

> John Norman asked Judy Norman to make him a sandwich; when Judy brought it to him, he threw it on the floor and told her to make him another. Judy made him a second sandwich and brought it to him; John again threw it on the floor, telling her to put something on her hands because he did not want her to touch the bread. Judy made a third sandwich using a paper towel to handle the bread. John took the third sandwich and smeared it in Judy's face.

Accounts of domestic abuse commonly involve behaviour which is designed not just to humiliate a partner, but to reinforce a particular role for women (e.g. as home-maker) and a particular status (e.g. as lesser than men).[11] This echoes similar messages found in advertising, street harassment and the media.

Second, domestic violence reinforces the practical barriers that exist to restrict women's access to the labour market and reinforces traditional roles for women. Evan Stark reports how domestic abuse may intensify when women

9 Y. Ertürk, 'Violence Against Women: From victimization to empowerment'. Paper presented at the ESCAP forum 'Where's the Power in Women's Empowerment?', Bangkok, Thailand, 4 August 2008.

10 *State of North Carolina v Norman* 366 SE 2d 586, 588 (NC App 1988).

11 E. Stark, *Coercive Control*, Oxford University Press, Oxford 2007.

seek to gain independence, by for example finding employment.[12] Consider, for example, the comments of two women who had tried to start a course of study in the hope of pursuing a career:

> Things really started to go down hill when I went to university, there's no doubt about that ... I don't think there'd been any need for him to be violent to me [to that point in the relationship] because he had me so much in his control in other ways, financially, at home with the children.[13]
>
> He almost burnt my work one time – three years of research and writing. He had lots of my papers out in the garden and the incinerator was burning. I had to beg and plead and agree to various conditions to get it off him.[14]

Third, domestic abuse is often used to deny access to an autonomous life, by restricting movement, association with friends and economic independence. Mary Ann Dutton and Lisa Goodman, examining the experiences of victims of domestic abuse, have explored the forms of coercion and see these as covering nine areas of control: 'personal activities/appearance', 'support/social life/family', 'household', 'work/economic/resources', 'health', 'intimate relationship', 'legal', 'immigration', and 'children'.[15] Evan Stark comments on the role of control in domestic abuse: 'Perpetrators commonly spy on or stalk partners even when they are living together and control their access to and means of transportation, monitor them at work, and use beepers, cell phones, or human proxies to monitor their activities.'[16] These combine with other patriarchal forces restricting access to public spaces.

Fourth, behind all these points is the idea that domestic violence is best understood as a relationship of coercive control, which over time diminishes women's autonomy. Psychologist Mary Ann Dutton explains:

> Abusive behaviour does not occur as a series of discrete events. Although a set of discrete abusive incidents can typically be identified within an abusive relationship, an understanding of the dynamic of power and control within an intimate relationship goes beyond these discrete incidents.[17]

---

12 Ibid.

13 L. Kelly, *Surviving Sexual Violence*, Polity Press, Bristol 1988, 129.

14 Ibid.

15 M. Dutton and L. Goodman, *Development and Validation of a Coercive Control Measure for Intimate Partner Violence*, US Department of Justice, Washington 2006 p. 3.

16 E. Stark, 'Commentary on Johnson's "Conflict and Control: Gender Symmetry and Asymmetry in Domestic Violence"' (2006) 12 *Violence Against Women* 1019.

17 M. Dutton, 'Understanding Women's Response to Domestic Violence' (2003) 21 *Hofstra Law Review* 1191, 1204.

The impact of this is that, as Rachel Pain argues, domestic violence results in 'chronic fear which builds up over the long term and leads to significant trauma and negative effects on health and wellbeing.'[18] This means that victims become frightened to break out of the traditional roles that their abusers demand of them.

3.3. HOW PATRIARCHY SUSTAINS DOMESTIC ABUSE

In this section I explore how domestic abuse is sustained by and supported by patriarchy. Ruth Gavison[19] explains: 'When women are battered at home, it is not because each particular victim has triggered an unfortunate "individual" tragedy ... Social structures are involved, social structures which are not simply "natural". They are person-made, and they benefit males.'

The refusal to link gender and domestic violence reinforces the notion that domestic abuse is simply a private matter; that family life should a privileged sphere in which the state does not intervene. Domestic abuse is not just supported by patriarchy's conceptions of the private. Michelle Madden Dempsey explains:

> the patriarchal character of individual relationships cannot subsist without those relationships being situated within a broader patriarchal social structure. Patriarchy is, by its nature, a social structure – and thus any particular instance of patriarchy takes its substance and meaning from that social context.[20]

The arguments just given make the case for identifying cases of domestic violence which promote patriarchy as inflicting a very particular kind of wrong which deserves isolating and focusing upon. The wrong produced is not simply one toward the individual victim but is a broader social wrong, in reflecting and reinforcing patriarchy. Further, the solution to that wrong is not responding to a misguided abuser, but challenging the wider social attitudes the behaviour reflects.

4. THE CASE FOR GENDER NEUTRALITY

There are two primary arguments used in support of a gender-neutral definition of domestic violence. The first is that it makes it clear that men can be the victims

[18] R. Pain, *Everyday Terrorism: How Fear Works in Domestic Abuse*, Scottish Women's Aid, Edinburgh 2016.

[19] R. Gavison, 'Feminism and the Public/Private Distinction' (1992) 45 *Stanford Law Review* 1, 3.

[20] M. Madden Dempsey, 'Towards a Feminist State' (2007) 70 *Modern Law Review* 908, 909.

of domestic abuse at the hands of women or their male partners; and women can be the victims of domestic abuse at the hands of female partners. The second is that the focus on VAW, particularly in the context of domestic violence, essentialises the experiences of women in unhelpful ways. I will explore these arguments now.

4.1. VICTIMS OF DOMESTIC ABUSE OUTSIDE THE HETEROSEXUAL CONTEXT

One of the major arguments against domestic abuse as VAW is that it sidelines cases of violence in domestic relationships outside the male on female context. One practical consequence of the VAW model is said to be that victims of domestic violence who do not fit the VAW model are not able to access the legal and social support services that should be available to them. Julie Goldscheid writes:[21]

> Heterosexual, gay, trans men and trans women are subjected to sexual assault as well as intimate partner violence at rates that are difficult to quantify, though no doubt are higher than commonly recognized. The woman-specific frame erases the experiences of these survivors and excludes them from services as well as from legal and other forms of redress.

This is a somewhat strange argument. At least, it is not addressing the argument made above, which is that non-patriarchal domestic abuse can be domestic abuse, but in a weaker and significantly different sense from patriarchal domestic abuse. The 'woman-specific frame' does not erase the experience of other victims any more than targeting child abuse erases the victims of adult victims of domestic abuse. It simply identifies a particular wrong which is not present in non-patriarchal domestic abuse. As Johnson argues, only a 'cartoonish' version of the VAW argument would suggest it denies there is violence in other contexts.[22] Perhaps the most that can be said is that the VAW approach carries a danger of being understood in a superficial way and if that is done it can have harmful consequences. But, that could be said of almost any argument.

Second, is the claim that to use the VAW model for domestic abuse would be statistically misleading. Bennett Capers[23] argues: 'one in three women have

---

21 J. Goldscheid, 'Gender Neutrality and the "Violence Against Women" Frame' (2014) City University of New York Academic Works. <http://academicworks.cuny.edu/cl_pubs/60>.

22 M. Johnson, 'Gender and Types of Intimate Partner Violence: A Response to an Anti-Feminist Literature Review' (2011) 16 *Aggression and Violent Behavior* 289, 299.

23 B. Capers, 'Real Rape Too' (2011) 99 *California Law Review* 1259, 1259.

experienced domestic violence. But the number for men is not that different: one in four. The term "violence against women" obscures this.' This is a view that depends very much on the definition of domestic abuse that is used. If one uses simply a question in surveys of whether one's partner has ever used physical force against you there is little difference, but such an approach is over-simplistic. For example, it draws no distinction between cases where force was used in self-defence or the start of an attack. Michael Johnson[24] in his powerful analysis demonstrates that when the focus is on 'intimate terrorism', which he defines as 'violence enacted in the service of taking general control over one's partner', that is very much a male preserve. He accepts that in cases of what he calls 'situational couple violence' or 'mutual violence', force used in self-defence, anger or frustration, or a situation where each party is equally abusing the other, there is less of a marked gender difference.[25]

Before moving on to further arguments, I think there is an issue raised by these points, which a VAW approach needs to develop. That is that if, as I have argued, the VAW approach is primarily justified in terms of looking at conduct that reflects and promotes patriarchy, we should not assume that only male-on-female violence does this. It seems plausible that some same-sex and female-on-male violence could reflect and reinforce patriarchal attitudes. Part of patriarchy is the promotion of heteronormativity and that can certainly play a role in same-sex violence.[26] And even among same-sex couples we can see a difference between gay and lesbian couples, indicating that gender norms may be playing a role.[27] Clearly this issue requires more research and analysis, but I accept that in so far as the VAW approach may indicate that only violence against women reinforces patriarchy, that may be inaccurate. The terminology 'patriarchy-reinforcing violence' may, therefore be preferable to VAW, although the latter is so well established in the legal and political sphere it is probably best to stick with it.

4.2. PROBLEMS WITH THE CATEGORY 'WOMEN'

A second set of objections to the VAW paradigm is to the terminology of 'women' in its definition.

---

24 M. Johnson, above n. 22.

25 J. Hamberger and B. Larsen, 'Men's and Women's Experience of Intimate Partner Violence: A Review of Ten Years of Comparative Studies in Clinical Samples' (2015) 30 *Journal of Family Violence* 699.

26 M. Madden Dempsey, above n. 3, ch. 7.

27 C. Donovan and M. Hester, *Domestic Violence and Sexuality*, Policy Press, Bristol 2006.

4.2.1. *Definitions of Sex*

First, it is claimed that the distinction between men and women is fictitious. That simply in biological terms although it is commonly assumed that everyone falls into the box of male or female, sexual categorisation is a far more complex matter than this and it would be better to see sex as a scalar property or even abandon the concept altogether. The VAW model, it is said, reinforces the binary sex model which we should be seeking to dismantle.[28]

Although I have written strongly in favour of the dismantling of the male/female binary as a scientific category this does not require us to abandon the concept as a social construction.[29] The truth is that although we cannot be readily broken down into male and female, society still does so. People are categorised, designed to be male or female and that is a reality that we need to challenge. The VAW model can acknowledge that we are looking at violence against *those categorised and treated as women* and who suffer disadvantages as they are so labelled, without having to accept that these labels are correctly given.

4.2.2. *Intersectionality*

The more profound claim, I believe, comes from intersectionality.[30] Julie Goldschied[31] complains that the VAW paradigm has a problem in focusing on gender alone:

> This single axis of focus obscures the complexities of survivors' experiences and fails to take into account the variability in survivors' experiences of abuse based on structural factors other than gender, such as race, immigration status, class, and gender identity.

Responding to such challenges, there is now a growing body of literature promoting intersectionality.[32] Traditional feminist approaches assumed one could write about the experiences of 'women', but in reality this presented the voice of powerful women, typically said to be white, middle-class women, and

---

28 D. Rosenblum, 'Unsex CEDAW, or What's Wrong With Women's Rights' (2011) 20 *Columbia Journal of Gender and Law* 98.

29 J. Herring and P.-L. Chau, 'Defining, Designing and Assigning Sex' (2002) 16 *International Journal of Law, Policy and the Family* 327.

30 K. Crenshaw, 'Mapping the Margins: Intersectionality, Identity Politics, and Violence Against Women of Color' (1991) 43 *Stanford Law Review* 1241.

31 J. Goldscheid, above n. 21.

32 A. Gruber, 'Neofeminism' (2013) 50 *Houston Law Review* 1325.

silenced the other voices of non-mainstream women.[33] So, the argument goes, it makes no sense to talk about VAW because there is no unifying feature of womanhood that we can identify. The experience and impact of domestic abuse on women depends on so much more than their sex; it depends on race, class, religion, poverty, sexuality, disability and so forth.

Again there is a danger of over-simplifying the VAW claim. Few feminist commentators would suggest that patriarchy is the only social influence in town. The real challenge of the intersectionality claim is whether the consideration of these other factors is such that to talk of 'women' loses all meaning. Sharon Cowan[34] correctly asks the question:

> So do we need patriarchy (as defined by Madden Dempsey or otherwise) to understand domestic violence? If we take it out of the equation, do we lose an important distinction between men's and women's violence? Would we lose more than we gain – that is, would we lose an understanding of domestic violence as grounded in existing societal gender power imbalances?

The problem with the intersectional challenge is that if it is true that sex has lost its meaning as a category, that must also be true for the other categories under discussion (such as race and class) and, if so, we fall back on looking at the characteristics or combination of characteristics of each individual. Your experience of domestic abuse is unique because only you have the particular combination of characteristics that make you. Doing so, however, would rob individuals of characteristics that form a sense of community or cohesion. Part of the value of humanity is identifying with others in communal endeavours, rather than seeking always to emphasise what separates us. We can surely do both: to recognise common groupings of humanity, while at the same time accepting there are differences too.

It is, therefore, preferable not to ditch the concepts of race or sex, but rather make them more tentative. There are important unifying characteristics of those identified as being a woman and also important differences. Even more to the point, even if our actual identities are important combinations of intersections, patriarchy treats women as an homogenous group. A good example can be in some forms of pornography where the woman is stripped of all identity save sexual organs; or street harassment, where the sole identifying characteristic noted by the sexual harasser is the person's sex. So, when patriarchy is described

---

33 S. Choudhry, 'Towards a Transformative Conceptualisation of Violence Against Women – A Critical Frame Analysis of Council of Europe Discourse on Violence Against Women' (2016) 79 *Modern Law Review* 406.

34 S. Cowan, 'Motivating Questions and Partial Answers: A Response to Prosecuting Domestic Violence by Michelle Madden Dempsey' (2014) 8 *Criminal Law and Philosophy* 543.

as the oppression of women, feminists are not having to accept patriarchy's understanding of women as an homogenous group, but can understand that that there are social forces and attitudes that categorise a set of people as women and subject that group to disadvantages. That approach can be taken, even while accepting much of the intersectional challenge. Lena Gunnarsson[35] writes,

> there are no discrete racial, gender and class parts at the level of concrete identity; nevertheless, the structures of race, gender and class have distinct existences insofar as they exercise their causal force on our lives in ways relatively independent from each other.

For law, political interaction and policy engagement categories must inevitably be used. The nature of bureaucracy requires categorisation. The danger of abandoning categories such as gender in the face of the intersectional challenge is that it can lead to failure to challenge structures.[36] Iris Marion Young[37] explains that we need tools for 'understanding how and why certain patterns in the allocation of tasks or status recognition remain persistent in ways that limit the options of many women and of most people whose sexual and intimate choices deviate from heterosexual norms.' Without the use of concepts such as patriarchy we lose these.[38]

5. CONCLUSION

This chapter has looked at the question of whether domestic abuse should be categorised as violence against women. There are some legitimate reasons for opposing that. It might be seen to imply that domestic violence in same-sex couples or by women against men does not exist or should not be taken seriously; or it might be seen to imply that domestic violence should only be understood in terms of gender and that issues of race, class or disability play no role. I have argued however, that such concerns would be based on a misunderstanding of the VAW argument. Further, that there are very good reasons for separating out and highlighting violence that sustains or perpetuates patriarchy. Doing so identifies a very particular wrong, significantly strengthens the reasons why the state must take steps to challenge it, and highlights the best ways of responding to it.

---

35 L. Gunnarsson, 'A defence of the category "women"' (2012) 11 *Feminist Theory* 23.

36 J. Conaghan, 'Intersectionality and the Feminist Project in Law' in J. Conaghan and D. Cooper (eds.), *Law, Power and the Politics of Subjectivity: Intersectionality and Beyond*, Routledge, Abingdon 2008.

37 I. Young, 'Lived Body vs Gender: Reflections on Social Structure and Subjectivity' (2002) 15 *Ratio* 410.

38 L. Gunnarsson, above n. 35.

NATIONALITY AND MIGRATION STATUS IN INTERNATIONAL CHILDREN'S LAW

Ann Laquer Estin

1. GLOBAL CHILDHOODS

Children belong to families, to communities, to nations and to the world, and sometimes these different types of belonging lead to conflicts. The reality of globalisation is that children's lives are dynamic: they move with their families, they move to join new families, and they move independently. They move with and without documentation or permission, in and out of countries where they hold citizenship. Sometimes children stay put while their parents move away, for work or for love, by choice or compulsion. As a result of this movement, a child's sense of identity and belonging may be layered and complex.

For international family law, the reality of children and families in motion creates two sets of problems. The first is addressed by conflict of laws rules on jurisdiction, choice of law, and recognition of judgments, which attempt to assign decision-making responsibility to one of the multiple places where a child has significant ties. In international cases, the Hague Children's Conventions rely on habitual residence as the primary connecting factor for assigning jurisdiction and for other purposes. This approach recognises that older notions of domicile and nationality are no longer adequate to define the connections between people and places. Yet the use of habitual residence has risks as well. It may tend to freeze the status quo, even for children and families with deeper ties to other places. There is the potential in these cases for the inquiry into habitual residence to become the whole analysis, defining where children will remain, rather than just its first step.

A second set of legal problems in these cases, less well explored, comes from the laws governing citizenship, immigration, and asylum that regulate cross-border movement. There may be considerable tension between the lived experience of children and their families and the hard realities imposed by these rules. This tension surfaces in immigration cases,[1] but it is also a factor in parental responsibility and child abduction disputes. With its focus fixed on habitual residence, however, international family law sometimes fails to notice the central role of nationality and immigration status in many parenting disputes.

1.1. ADOPTION, CHILD WELFARE AND IDENTITY RIGHTS

The question of 'where children belong' lies at the heart of many international children's issues, but has been most directly addressed in intercountry adoption and child welfare cases. The UN Convention on the Rights of the Child (CRC) and other human rights instruments safeguard children's rights to protection of their family relations and their identity, including their nationality.[2] This is related to, but distinct from, the family law problem of where and with whom children will live.

In the context of adoption, there is a growing awareness that internationally adopted children can belong to multiple places. The CRC and the Hague Adoption Convention embrace a subsidiarity principle, based upon the conviction that it is ordinarily best for children to remain in the place where they have ties of family, nationality, and cultural heritage.[3] From the perspective of receiving countries and families, we understand the importance of assuring that adopted children have full membership rights, including secure residence, and ideally nationality. At the same time, we have come to recognise the importance of respecting a child's identity in relation to his or her birth family and country

1 E.g. *ZH (Tanzania) v Secretary of State* [2011] UKSC 4.

2 GA Res. 44/25, UN GAOR 44th Sess., Supp. No. 49, at 167, UN Doc. A/RES/44/49 (20.11.1989); 1577 UNTS 43, Arts. 7–10.

3 CRC Art. 21(b); Hague Convention on Protection of Children and Co-operation in Respect of Intercountry Adoption (1993) Preamble, Art. 4.b.

of origin. Internationally-adopted children may want a dual affiliation: to have full citizenship in their new country, while maintaining ties to their country of origin.

In child welfare cases, the UN Guidelines for the Alternative Care of Children suggest that a child should be maintained 'as close as possible to his/her habitual place of residence, in order to facilitate contact and potential reintegration with his/her family and to minimize disruption of his/her educational, cultural and social life.'[4] Child welfare laws in many countries recognise a preference for placing a child in need of care with other family members when this is possible, but these placements are more complex when those family members live in another country.[5] The claims of nationality in this context are underscored by consular agreements, which may require notice to the child's country of citizenship when a guardian has been appointed for a non-citizen child.[6]

The proposed recast of the Brussels IIA Regulation,[7] which pays greater attention to the need for cooperation in cross-border placements, includes a new recital referencing the family and identity rights of the CRC. It states: 'In particular, when considering solutions, due regard should be paid to the desirability of continuity in a child's upbringing and to the child's ethnic, religious, cultural and linguistic background.'[8]

For some children who are separated from their families of origin, a 'best interests' approach suggests they should remain in their place of habitual residence, despite the absence of nationality or legal migration status there. In the US, a child in this situation is eligible for Special Immigrant Juvenile immigration status if a court finds that 'reunification with one or both of the [child's] parents is not viable due to abuse, neglect, abandonment, or a similar basis found under State law' and that it would not be in the child's best interest to be returned to the child or parent's country of nationality or previous habitual residence.[9] International law recognises that children may be independently eligible for asylum, and many unaccompanied children arriving in Europe and the US have claims that argue strongly against forcing their return to a prior habitual residence. Some unaccompanied children have parents who may have

---

4 GA Res. 64/142, UN Doc. A/RES/64/142, para. 11 (24.02.2010). See also CRC Art. 20(3).

5 E.g. *Matter of N*, below n. 50.

6 E.g. Vienna Convention on Consular Relations, 596 UNTS 261 (Entered into force 19.03.1967) Art. 37.

7 Council Regulation (EC) No. 2201/2003 of 27 November 2003 concerning jurisdiction and the recognition and enforcement of judgments in matrimonial matters and the matters of parental responsibility (Brussels IIA).

8 Proposal for a Council Regulation on jurisdiction, the recognition and enforcement of decisions in matrimonial matters and the matters of parental responsibility, and on international child abduction (recast), COM(2016) 411 (final), Recital 51.

9 8 USC §1101(a)(27)(J).

encouraged them to leave, but in other cases children and their parents disagree as to where they should reside.[10]

The importance of children's nationality rights was further highlighted by European Court of Human Rights (ECtHR) decisions addressing the rights of children born from surrogacy arrangements.[11] Beyond the problem of defining parent–child relationships, the ECtHR noted the risk that children without settled parentage might be unable to obtain nationality in the country that is their home. Moreover, depending on the circumstances, a child in this situation could be stateless if it is not possible to obtain nationality through the parent who intends to raise the child.[12]

1.2. IMMIGRATION ISSUES IN PARENTING DISPUTES

Although questions of nationality and belonging are also common in cross-border parenting disputes, they have been less openly acknowledged in this setting. In some families, citizenship and immigration status issues make it impossible for both parents to live in reasonable proximity to their child. This is particularly true in the US, where parents of minor citizen children have no special access to a residence visa on this basis. In contrast, following a series of decisions from the European Court of Justice,[13] and the ECtHR,[14] EU countries do recognise derivative residence rights for parents and primary carers, which can help provide solutions in difficult cases.

In the EU, the tension between habitual residence and nationality is embedded in the jurisdictional provisions for divorce under Brussels IIA,[15] but this does not extend to disputes regarding parental responsibilities, for which jurisdiction is based primarily on the child's habitual residence.[16] A court may exercise jurisdiction based on nationality in a narrow range of cases in which parents agree,[17] or when another court, with jurisdiction based on habitual residence, has determined that a court in the child's place of nationality would be better placed to hear the case.[18] In the US, a uniform jurisdictional law for

---

10 Canadian and US courts have addressed the intersection of refugee law with the Abduction Convention, in cases involving parents seeking return of children who had been granted asylum. See below n. 42.

11 See *Mennesson v France*, Application no. 65192/11, ECtHR 26 June 2014; *Labassee v France*, Application no. 65941/11, [2014] ECHR 185.

12 In *Mennesson* and *Labassee*, above n. 11, the children had US citizenship, by virtue of their birth in the US, so they were not stateless.

13 E.g. Case C-34/09 *Gerardo Ruiz Zambrano v Office national de l'emploi*, ECLI:EU:C:2011:124.

14 E.g. *Jeunesse v Netherlands*, Application no. 12738/10, [2014] ECHR 1036.

15 Brussels IIA, Art. 3.

16 Brussels IIA, Art. 8.

17 Brussels IIA, Art. 12.

18 Brussels IIA, Art. 15.

parental responsibility cases gives jurisdictional priority to the child's Home State, defined as 'the State in which the child lived with a parent or a person acting as a parent for at least six consecutive months immediately before the commencement of a child-custody proceeding,' without regard to nationality or immigration status.[19]

2. LITIGATING PARENTAL RESPONSIBILITIES

Globalisation has increased the numbers of both expatriate families living in places where they lack citizenship ties, and mixed-status families with members who have different nationalities or immigration statuses. Along with the complex and varied challenges that these situations present as a matter of immigration law, they complicate the work of international family lawyers in cases involving children.

2.1. CUSTODY AND ACCESS

Courts hearing transnational custody and relocation disputes sometimes encounter immigration problems that could prevent a child from having regular access to both parents. In the US, a parent's lack of legal immigration status is sometimes seen as relevant in assigning parental responsibilities,[20] and it may be considered when courts impose restrictions on removing a child from the jurisdiction, in order to reduce the risk of abduction.[21] Conversely, other cases have given parents permission to relocate when, among other factors, their immigration status did not allow them to remain in the United States.[22]

2.2. RELOCATION DISPUTES

A significant subset of relocation disputes involve a parent who seeks to return 'home' with a child, to a place where the parent has greater social and family support. This was the context of several leading decisions that allowed

19 Uniform Child Custody Jurisdiction and Enforcement Act §102(7).

20 E.g. *Rico v Rodriguez*, 120 P.3d 812 (Neb. 2005); cf. *Orantes v Orantes*, 381 S.W.3d 758 (Ark. 2011); *Custody of ALR*, 830 N.W.2d 163, 172–173 (Minn. Ct. App. 2013). See D. Thronson, 'Custody and Contradictions: Exploring Immigration Law as Federal Family Law in the Context of Child Custody' (2008) 59 *Hastings Law Journal* 453.

21 See e.g. UCAPA § 7(a)(9) and (10); Tex Fam Code Ann § 153.502(b).

22 E.g. *Marriage of Abargil*, 131 Cal.Rptr.2d 429, 432 (Cal. Ct. App. 2003); see also *JM v GH*, 175 Cal.Rptr.3d 371 (Cal. Ct. App. 2014).

international relocation, including *Payne v Payne*[23] in the UK and *U v U*[24] in Australia. These particular rulings have been overturned or modified, with more recent judgments adopting an open-ended or 'holistic' approach, balancing all relevant factors and giving paramount consideration to the child's welfare.[25]

Although it is often not clear what weight courts give to migration status and nationality, relocation to the country where the child and both parents share nationality and family ties seems much less likely to present difficulties than moving a child so that one parent can pursue an educational or employment opportunity or follow a new spouse or partner. The US and Canadian cases generally bear out this intuition, although there are obviously many other important factors.[26]

3. ABDUCTION CONVENTION DISPUTES

Cases under the Hague Convention on the Civil Aspects of International Child Abduction (Abduction Convention) require a determination of the child's habitual residence. The nationality of parents or children is not directly relevant, with good reason: Nigel Lowe's statistics show that a majority of taking parents were returning to a country of which they were nationals.[27] But citizenship and migration status are significant to the circumstances in which families find themselves when litigation begins. In many cases, entirely apart from the issues being litigated, the real problem facing the family is an immigration barrier that could entirely prevent one parent from being able to live with or visit the child.[28] For this reason, courts sometimes consider nationality or migration status in determining a child's habitual residence, in their analysis of whether a child has become settled in a new country, or in decisions regarding several of the exceptions to the presumption of return.

---

23 *Payne v Payne* [2001] EWCA Civ. 166.

24 *U v U* 191 ALR 289, 2002 WL 2017079 (2002).

25 In the UK, see *Re C (Internal Relocation)* [2015] EWCA Civ. 1305 and *Re F (International Relocation Cases)* [2015] EWCA Civ. 882. In Australia, changes were enacted in 2006. See generally P. Parkinson, 'The Realities of relocation: Messages from judicial decisions' (2008) 22 *Australian Journal of Family Law* 35.
For New Zealand, see M. Henaghan, 'Case Note: *Kacem v Bashir*: Relocation in the Supreme Court of New Zealand – The Best Interests of the Child' (December 2010) *New Zealand Family Law Journal* 375.

26 E.g. *Abargil*, above n. 22, *Lenz v Lenz*, 79 S.W.3d 10 (Tex. 2002); *Osmanagic v Osmanagic*, 872 A.2d 897 (Vt. 2005). For Canada, see R.D.A. Thompson, 'Heading for the Light: International Relocations from Canada' (2011) 30 *Canadian Family Law Quarterly* 1.

27 N. Lowe and V. Stephens, 'Global Trends in the Operation of the 1980 Hague Abduction Convention' (2012) 46 *Family Law Quarterly* 41, 50.

28 E.g., *Mota v Castillo*, below n. 34; *Gonzalez-Caballero v Mena*, below n. 39; *In re Mikovic*, 541 F.Supp.2d 1264 (M.D. Fla. 2007). See also R. Schuz, *The Hague Child Abduction Convention: A Critical Analysis*, Hart Publishing, Oxford 2013, p. 289.

3.1. DETERMINING HABITUAL RESIDENCE

Consider how the Abduction Convention operates in the setting of an expatriate family whose current residence is not the place of their shared family roots, identity, or nationality. The US circuit courts of appeal are divided on the proper approach to determining habitual residence, particularly when a child's parents have different intentions regarding the child's move to a new place. The decision in *Mozes v Mozes*[29] offers an extensive discussion of the question, and is often cited for an approach that gives strong weight to the last 'shared parental intent' regarding a move. But the problem facing the court in *Mozes* was a very specific one: despite having spent a successful year in California, this was an Israeli family, with much stronger ties to that country than to the US (where they had only temporary visas), no economic base, and no extended family. Viewed from the children's perspective, it seems highly unlikely that returning them to Israel could be characterised – to paraphrase Elisa Perez-Vera – as tantamount to taking them out of the family and social environment in which their life has developed.[30]

Mozes presents an interesting contrast to an earlier case, *Feder v Evans-Feder*,[31] which involved an expatriate American couple with a troubled marriage and a four-year-old child, who had spent a few months living in Australia when the parents' relationship finally collapsed. The mother returned with the child to the US, and when the father commenced Hague return proceedings, the trial court found that the child's habitual residence had not shifted to Australia during their six months there, noting the child's strong ties to the US including maternal and paternal grandparents. The appellate court reversed this decision, however, and 20 years later this decision is sometimes cited as precedent for a 'hybrid' approach weighing both acclimatisation and parental intent. From the child's perspective, however, it seems highly unlikely that moving him from Australia, where his only local tie consisted of attending a nursery school several days a week for six months, could be said to have deprived him of the family and social environment in which his life had developed. The decision gave force to the Abduction Convention, but the result seems primarily to have served the global ambitions of the father, who had 'worked for four different employers in ten different cities in seven different countries on four different continents in the past twenty years.'

---

29 *Mozes v Mozes*, 239 F.3d 1067 (9th Cir. 2001).

30 E. Pérez-Vera, *Explanatory Report on the 1980 Hague Child Abduction Convention*, Permanent Bureau of the Hague Conference on Private International Law, HCCH Publications, The Hague (1982) para. 11 (English translation). <https://assets.hcch.net/upload/expl28.pdf>.

31 *Feder v Evans-Feder*, 63 F.3d 217 (3rd Cir. 1995).

Among the US cases, *Feder* may be an outlier. Other decisions suggest that, when parents share a nationality and family home, there is a gravitational pull toward that place that makes it more difficult to argue that the child has established a new habitual residence somewhere else. In the case of an expat family, this has a certain intuitive appeal, but the pull for home has caused real mischief in abduction disputes involving mixed-status families. The problems are particularly acute when the parents and children have deep ties to more than one place, and the parents themselves have strong, and opposite, preferences.

For cases involving mixed-nationality families, the most common risk is that a court asked to return a child from one of the child's home countries will not give fair weight to the child's ties in the other. An example from the US is *Ruiz v Tenorio*,[32] which concluded that a US–Mexican family had not become habitually resident in Mexico despite living there for almost three years. This decision has been appropriately criticised as an extreme version of the 'shared parental intent' approach. The court had almost nothing to say about the children's family and social environment in Mexico, and made no mention of the children's views. *Ruiz* is one of many cases, from different countries, in which courts seem to have prioritised a child's ties to the forum in determining habitual residence.

Cases such as *Ruiz* reflect the risk that Perez-Vera described, in the context of 'best interests' determination, that authorities will express particular cultural and social attitudes that derive from the subjective value judgements of a given national community.[33] Courts seem more likely to make the *Ruiz* mistake, of discounting the importance of the child's other home, than the *Feder* mistake of ignoring the larger family context of global movement.

Nationality and immigration status may factor directly into the habitual residence determination in mixed-status family cases. For example, consider the case of a child with a non-citizen parent who is not permitted to live in the country where the child resides. This is familiar ground in immigration law, but the problem belongs to family law as well. If the family was living in the US and one parent was deported, that fact would not change the child's habitual residence, but it would likely be a major consideration for the court in deciding on the child's best interests.

Coming from the other direction, *Mota v Castillo*[34] involved a young family who planned to relocate from Mexico to the US. The father went first, entering without inspection, sending support home to his family and then funds to smuggle them across the border. The mother succeeded in getting their child into the US, but she was blocked several times in her own attempts to cross and was finally arrested and deported. When the mother filed Hague return proceedings

---

32 *Ruiz v Tenorio*, 392 F.3d 1247 (11th Cir. 2004).

33 E. Perez-Vera, above n. 30, para. 22.

34 *Mota v Castillo*, 692 F.3d 108 (2d Cir. 2012).

in the US, the court found that the US had not become child's habitual residence during the period while the mother was attempting to enter, and also that she had not consented to the child relocating without her.

3.2. WHEN IS A CHILD WELL-SETTLED?

Immigration status issues also surface in disputes over whether a child has become sufficiently settled after a year or more in a new place to trigger the exception to return under Article 12 of the Abduction Convention. When a taking parent has removed or retained the child in the parent's home country, it will typically be easier to establish the kinds of ties that suggest the child has become well-settled. Conversely, if the parents have a shared family history in the country of habitual residence, it may be harder to argue that the child has become settled somewhere else. In particular, when a taking parent or child has no legal immigration status it is more difficult to conclude that the child is settled. Four of the US Courts of Appeals have ruled on this issue, uniformly concluding that immigration status is a relevant factor, but not determinative.[35]

The child's perspective is particularly important here. This was pointed out in Baroness Hale's judgment in *Re M*,[36] which involved two girls brought secretly from Zimbabwe to the UK. By the time return proceedings were commenced more than two years later, they had strong objections to returning there. Despite what might seem to be the claims of home or nationality, they clearly felt themselves to be settled in Britain. In a dramatic example of children's objections to return, the US case of *Sanchez v RGL*[37] concerned three children from Mexico who requested asylum in the US based on family and gang-related violence, even as their mother sought their return to Mexico under the Abduction Convention.

3.3. EXCEPTIONS TO RETURN

Beyond the questions of habitual residence and whether a child has become settled in a place, immigration status may play a role in determining whether a parent has acquiesced or consented to the child's relocation pursuant to Article 13(a).[38] It may also be relevant in deciding whether return would place the child in an intolerable situation pursuant to Article 13(b), particularly when

---

35 See *Alcala v Hernandez*, 826 F.3d 161 (4th Cir. 2016); *Hernandez v Garcia Pena*, 820 F.3d 782 (5th Cir. 2016); *Lozano v Alvarez*, 697 F.3d 41 (2d Cir. 2012) aff'd in part 134 S.Ct. 1224 (2014); *In re B del CSB (minor), Mendoza v Miranda*, 559 F.3d 999 (9th Cir. 2009).

36 *Re M and another (Children) (Abduction: Rights of Custody)* [2007] UKHL 55.

37 *Sanchez v RGL*, 761 F.3d 495 (5th Cir. 2014).

38 E.g. *Mota*, above n. 34, and *Gonzalez-Caballero*, below n. 39.

a forced return would separate the child from a primary caretaking parent who is not legally permitted to live in the child's country of habitual residence. More unusually, the question whether a child or taking parent has a valid asylum claim may be considered in the context of Article 13(b) or the human rights exception under Article 20.

For example, *Gonzalez-Caballero v Mena*[39] concerned a child born to an unmarried Panamanian mother and US-citizen father. The child lived exclusively with her mother in Panama, with the father acknowledging paternity and sending clothing and support from the US, until the mother found herself in a difficult personal and financial situation when the child was two-and-a-half years old. Although she made arrangements for the child to travel to the US to live with the father, she later brought Hague return proceedings. The court ultimately rejected the mother's argument that she had consented only to a temporary visit unless she could immigrate as well.[40] When a parent's 'conditional consent' theory is rejected, the result may be that the parent loses his or her Hague Abduction claim and is left with no possibility of travelling to see the child in the child's new home.

Cases in which immigration issues would prevent a taking parent from returning with or having contact with the child might give rise to an intolerable situation under Article 13(b). Although this issue does not seem to have been addressed in the US case law, Rhona Schuz reports decisions from Australia, South Africa, and Switzerland that consider this problem.[41] In at least one of these cases, return to the US was refused after the child's mother was denied a visa.

Asylum claims suggest that denial of a return order might be appropriate under the 'grave risk of harm' provision in Article 13(b), or the human rights exception in Article 20.[42] In *Sanchez v RGL*, three brothers from Mexico were taken into care after requesting asylum at the US border based on their fear of family and gang violence.[43] After the trial court granted their mother's petition for return under the Abduction Convention, an asylum officer granted their asylum petition. On appeal, the court concluded that although the grant of asylum did not override the Hague return order, the evidence presented in the asylum matter should be considered in determining whether to enforce the return order. In a similar situation, the Ontario Court of Appeal held in

---

39 *Gonzalez-Caballero v Mena*, 251 F.3d 789 (9th Cir. 2001).

40 See also *Moreno v Basilio Pena*, 2015 WL 4992005 (S.D. N.Y. 2015) (unreported) (left-behind parent consented to parent in US obtaining Lawful Permanent Resident status for child).

41 See R. Schuz, above n. 28, p. 289.

42 See A. Estin, 'Protecting Child Welfare in Abduction and Asylum Proceedings' (2016) 41 *North Carolina Journal of International Law* 793; M. Bailey, 'Canada's Conflicted Approach to International Child Abduction', Queen's Law Research Paper Series 2015-072 (May 2016) at 8–9.

43 *Sanchez*, above n. 37.

AMRI v KER that courts must construe Articles 13(b) and 20 in a manner that takes into account the *non-refoulement* principle of international refugee law.[44]

4. CONCLUSION

The challenges for globalised families and children cross the traditional boundaries of international law, family law, and immigration and citizenship law. Ideally, each of these bodies of law should be shaped and mobilised to protect the best interests of children, with courts and decision-makers adopting a child-focused perspective, rather than prioritising abstract public policies or adult interests. But the reality today is that the rules in these distinct fields complicate and contradict each other. Beyond the framework of legal rules, therefore, an adequate response to globalised childhood requires an appreciation for children's attachments to multiple nations and communities, and a commitment to equal respect for all children and families.

Two recent judgments by Baroness Hale, writing for the UK Supreme Court, suggest the complexity of these issues and help point the way forward. In *Re KL (A Child)*,[45] the parents of KL had met and married in Texas, where KL was born. His father was a US citizen, and his mother a Ghanaian national with indefinite leave to remain in the UK. When the father was deployed to Afghanistan, the mother removed KL to London. This removal provoked a serious tangle of litigation in both countries, under both the Abduction Convention and the courts' general family law jurisdiction. When the Supreme Court ruled in the case, KL was seven years old. He had lived for substantial periods of time in both countries, and was used to travelling back and forth, but was also 'confused and upset by the conflict between his parents, and his conflict of loyalties to them.'[46]

In her judgment, Baroness Hale affirmed a contested determination that the child was habitually resident in the UK, acknowledging that other courts might disagree.[47] The judgment went on to consider whether the child should be returned from the UK to Texas pursuant to the court's inherent jurisdiction. At the close of her judgment, Baroness Hale wrote:

> The crucial factor, in my view, is that this is a Texan child who is currently being denied a proper opportunity to develop a relationship with his father and with his country of birth. For as long as the Texan order remains in force, his mother is most unlikely to allow, let alone encourage, him to spend his vacations in America with his father.

---

44 *AMRI v KER* (2011) 106 O.R.3d 417 (Ont. CA).
45 *Re KL (A Child)* [2013] UKSC 75.
46 [2013] UKSC 75, para. 34.
47 For the US appellate court judgment, see *Larbie v Larbie*, 690 F.3d 295 (5th Cir. 2012).

> Whilst conflicting orders remain in force, he is effectively denied access to his country of origin. Nor has his mother been exactly enthusiastic about contact here. The best chance that K has of developing a proper relationship with both of his parents, and with the country whose nationality he holds, is for the Texas court to consider where his best interests lie in the long term. It is necessary to restore the synthesis between the two jurisdictions, which the mother's actions have distorted.[48]

Writing for a unanimous court, Lady Hale's judgment separated the use of habitual residence as a jurisdictional principle from the larger and more difficult problem of where the child's best interests lay. Her analysis framed the challenge in terms of protecting the child's significant ties, rather than simply freezing the status quo. The fact that the United States was KL's country of origin and country of nationality was understood to matter for the purposes of determining his best interests.[49]

The second illustration comes from *Re N (children)*,[50] which considered child protection proceedings commenced in the UK for very young children of Hungarian and Roma descent. There was no question but that the British courts had jurisdiction on the basis of the children's habitual residence. But although the children had never lived there, their parents had returned to Hungary, and the children had ties of nationality and descent and a large extended family there. The question was whether proceedings should be transferred to Hungary under Article 15 of the Brussels IIA Regulation.[51] The court concluded that the transfer to Hungary would not be in the children's best interests, but the judgment observed that it was a 'very live issue' as to whether in the long term the girls would be better off living in Hungary, and noted some ways that this might be accomplished even with the English court exercising jurisdiction.[52]

With respect to the question: where (in the world) do children belong?, the answer is often: both here and there. Children's identity rights, and their right not to be separated from their parents, define the challenge before us: to consider both the depth of a child's ties to his or her place of habitual residence, and the strength of that child's connections elsewhere. Our goal should be to recognise

---

48 [2013] UKSC 75, para. 36.

49 In the US, left-behind parents often prefer to file Hague return proceedings in federal courts, which do not have jurisdiction in family law. The conclusion that a child is habitually resident in the US therefore ends the proceeding, and a left-behind parent must bring a new action in a State court to address parental responsibilities and the child's residence.

50 *Re N (children)* [2016] UKSC 15. See also Case C-428/15 *Child and Family Agency v JD*, ECLI:EU:C:2016:819; see generally N. Lowe and H. Setright, 'Transferring the problem – how article 15 of the revised Brussels II Regulation operates in the public law context' [2017] *International Family Law* 13.

51 A similar question could arise under Article 8 of the 1996 Hague Child Protection Convention.

52 Notably, Baroness Hale has also encouraged us to pay greater attention to family law issues in the context of migration laws: B. Hale, 'Families and the law: the forgotten international dimension' (2009) 21 *Child & Family Law Quarterly* 413.

the claims of 'home', and still appreciate that children may belong in more than one family, and more than one place. We need to look across borders to consider the availability of parents and also wider family resources. In this assessment, we need to acknowledge immigration issues for all family members as part of the 'reality testing' of a relocation proposal or parental responsibility determination.

No one can determine a priori whether living as an expatriate with both parents is better or worse for a child than living in a place that is home in a deeper sense without regular access to both parents. Children can do well – or poorly – in either situation. This dilemma reminds us, however, of the fundamental importance of considering these disputes from the child's own unique perspective whenever possible.

THE DEVELOPMENT OF CHILD PROTECTION ACROSS INTERNATIONAL BORDERS FOR CHILDREN AT RISK OF HARM

Ruth LAMONT

1. INTRODUCTION

In 2004, Professor Lowe, with Everall and Nicholls, noted that international disputes over children had seen a 'noticeable and welcome increase in judicial cooperation.' Children's cases needed 'bold and decisive action' to ensure decisions were made with the minimum of delay and uncertainty.[1] The field of international family law, and the study of the development and use of the law have been heavily shaped and influenced by the contribution of Professor Lowe. These statements proved prescient of the future developments of international disputes relating to children. The increasing number of disputes and the volume of case law and legislation originating from the European Union (EU) and Hague Conference on Private International Law have required new approaches to resolving disputes. The activity of the EU in particular has encouraged greater increase in judicial cooperation and trust, facilitated and supported by the valuable contributions from Professor Lowe's research.

In 2004, *International Movement of Children* raised the question of jurisdiction in England and Wales over public law proceedings with an

---

1 N. LOWE, M. EVERALL and M. NICHOLLS, *International Movement of Children: Law, Practice and Procedure*, Jordan Publishing, Bristol 2004, viii.

international dimension. This was raised as an issue in relatively few cases by this time, but the Family Law Act 1986 contained no jurisdictional rules for such cases, applying as it did only to private law proceedings.[2] Where a child at risk had a link to another jurisdiction, it was unclear what should be the jurisdiction rule to enable the English child protection system to intervene to protect a child.[3] However, the impact of the Brussels IIA Regulation[4] has meant that children who are habitually resident in England and Wales are subject to English public law care proceedings[5] if identified as being at risk of serious harm. The adoption of the EU measures has provided greater certainty in the assumption of jurisdiction[6] and, as suggested above, has also encouraged closer cooperation between judicial authorities in the Member States. Whilst the rules adopted in the Brussels IIA have provided some clarity on the ground of jurisdiction in public law cases, the circumstances in which private international family law rules may be used in disputes have become increasingly complex. This chapter will consider the circumstances in which public law assumes an international dimension, and the way in which these disputes are resolved. It will also consider the potential impact of the UK's withdrawal from the EU, if the Brussels IIA Regulation is no longer binding in the UK.

2. THE COMPLEXITIES OF CROSS-NATIONAL CHILD PROTECTION

The impact of rising levels of migration has affected children in a variety of personal circumstances. The internationalisation of family law, and regulation between different countries of children and their relationships, has developed significantly over the last 30 years.[7] The circumstances of modern family life have changed as an international dimension has become increasingly prominent and, whilst private family law has traditionally been the focus of regulation, the state has also become an actor in international family law. Lowe identified

2 N. Lowe, M. Everall and M. Nicholls, *International Movement of Children: Law, Practice and Procedure*, Jordan Publishing, Bristol 2004, 192–194.

3 *Re R (Care Proceedings: Jurisdiction)* [1995] 1 FLR 711; *Re M (A Minor) (Care Orders: Jurisdiction)* [1997] Fam 67.

4 Regulation 2201/2003 concerning jurisdiction and the recognition and enforcement of judgments in matrimonial matters and the matters of parental responsibility [2003] OJ L338.

5 Art. 8, Brussels IIA. Case C-435/06 *C.*, ECLI:EU:C:2007:714.

6 N. Lowe and M. Nicholls, *International Movement of Children: Law, Practice and Procedure*, Jordan Publishing, Bristol 2016, 44.

7 D. Bryant, Foreword in N. Lowe and M. Nicholls, *International Movement of Children: Law, Practice and Procedure*, Jordan Publishing, Bristol 2016, v.

this possibility emerging in the 1990s,[8] but in the twenty-first century resolving conflicts between national authorities trying to protect a child is a rapidly developing and complex field of practice.

Migration flows between the Member States of the EU, and particularly immigration from other Member States into the UK, has meant that children who are not UK nationals may be subject to English child protection proceedings. The fundamental freedom of workers within the EU extends to the worker but also to members of their family, awarding them a right of residence in the host Member State.[9] Free movement rights have encouraged migration of families within the EU.[10] Migration may affect the law governing the family if children develop links to the host state. After parents relocate to another Member State for work, or for other reasons, and either bring their child along with them, or give birth to a child in England, they may be subject to the national family laws of the host state.

The state is under a positive obligation arising from Articles 3 and 8 of the European Convention on Human Rights (ECHR) to protect children from harm,[11] to prevent inhuman and degrading treatment, and to respect a child's private and family life. These obligations will apply to all children, not just those who are nationals of the country concerned.[12] In England and Wales, this means that the public authorities are obliged to take action under Part IV of the Children Act 1989 if a child is at risk of harm. If the child has only a limited connection to England and Wales, the steps taken may be limited to emergency intervention through an interim care order. If, however, the child has a strong link to this jurisdiction, substantive action may be taken to determine the child's future. The links the child and the family may have to another country raise the issue of which legal system should resolve the future provision for the child, in their best interests, allowing for the fact that national substantive law on child protection may vary greatly from state to state.

The circumstances giving rise to state involvement in the family may be a failure to provide appropriate care for the child, placing them at risk of significant harm,[13] abuse of the child[14] or, in some cases, abandonment of a child

---

8 N. Lowe, M. Everall and M. Nicholls, *International Movement of Children: Law, Practice and Procedure*, Jordan Publishing, Bristol 2004, 192.

9 Directive 2004/38 on the right of citizens of the Union and their family members to move and reside freely within the territory of the Member States [2004] OJ L158/1.

10 Eurostat 'Migration and Migrant Population Statistics' available at: <http://ec.europa.eu/eurostat/statistics-explained/index.php/Migration_and_migrant_population_statistics#Migrant_population>.

11 *E v UK*, Application no. 33218/96 (2006) 36 EHRR 31.

12 *Maumousseu v France*, Application no. 39388/05 (2010) 51 EHRR 35.

13 *Norfolk County Council v VE* [2015] EWFC 30.

14 See *Re D (Habitual Residence)* unreported, 11 November 2014, Family Court of East London, where an 11-year-old girl displayed sexualised behaviour.

by the parent returning to their state of origin.[15] In some circumstances, the parents may be complicit in exposing the child to harm through the process of migration. In *Re S (Care Proceedings: Jurisdiction)*[16] the child had been trafficked from Romania to England by her father, in an operation in which her mother was complicit. Her father was convicted of child trafficking offences and the child had been made subject to an interim care order in England. An application was subsequently made by the mother under the Hague Convention on the Civil Aspects of International Child Abduction 1980 for the return of the child to Romania. There was a suggestion that the child might be re-trafficked once returned, although the Romanian authorities did not regard this as a risk, and the child wished to return to Romania. This case demonstrates the complex circumstances in which questions of jurisdiction over the child's welfare may arise; the child clearly had links to Romania that meant its court was the appropriate one to take welfare decisions, but securing the child's return to that country could put them at further risk of harm. In other examples, the parent themselves may have been trafficked, affecting their ability to care for the child and the child's welfare.[17]

The ease of movement between international jurisdictions in the modern world and the impact on families was first identified with the increasing incidence of parental child abduction.[18] As well as giving parents the opportunity to travel with their child to attempt to escape the other parent, the availability and relative cheapness of international travel have led to specific attempts by parents to avoid intervention by the state in the family through social services. Parents who have been notified that their child is likely to be subject to care proceedings when they are born, or whose child has come to the attention of social services may seek to travel to another country to avoid further intervention.[19] The proliferation of online advice services for parents includes material and journalistic reporting highlighting this possibility.[20] 'Forcedadoption.com' states in its 'Golden Rules':

> You must never disobey a court order by taking abroad a child already in care, but if you are pregnant and threatened neither a court nor the 'SS' [Social Services] can stop you leaving the country before the baby is born! If the children are already with you, but you feel menaced by social services try to leave the country BEFORE any notice of care proceedings is served on you.[21]

---

15 *Leicester City Council v S and others* [2014] EWHC 1575 (Fam).

16 *Re S (Care Proceedings: Jurisdiction)* [2008] EWHC 3013 (Fam).

17 See *Re HA (A Child) (Brussels IIA: Article 15)* [2015] EWHC 1310 (Fam).

18 N. Lowe and A. Perry, 'International Child Abduction: the English experience' (1999) 48 *International and Comparative Law Quarterly* 127, 134.

19 *Lancashire County Council v T and Others (Habitual Residence: Care Proceedings)* [2014] EWHC 3321 (Fam).

20 For example: <http://www.ectopia.org/>.

21 Available at: <https://forced-adoption.com/detailed-golden-rules/>.

Such advice promotes the possibility of manipulating jurisdiction over legal proceedings designed to protect children. The advice is also entirely legally accurate, despite the tone, which is very hostile to state intervention and the role of social services and the court. It fails to acknowledge or clearly address the fact that investigation is required by law if a child is identified as being at risk of significant harm, and therefore some risk must already be posed to the child in question.[22] Other online resources are more balanced in their assessment of fleeing abroad as a resolution to intervention by social services, whilst raising this as an option for parents. Prevent Intervention Now states:

> Fleeing from social services is the most extreme option that you can take in deciding how to deal with their intervention. It is a huge upheaval, you will not only be leaving behind your home, probably a lot of your possessions but also, most importantly family and friends. You may be removing your child from school, from grandparents, their friends, the clubs they attend and ultimately the safe environment they call home. You are giving up a lot, but as many parents who have successfully fled will confirm, the fear of an even greater loss – that of your children – makes the sacrifice of material things and even extended family a price worth paying. Just to be clear, *we do not encourage you to flee.*[23]

There is online material to challenge and question the suitability of such advice through resources such as the Transparency Project[24] or the Child Protection Resource,[25] which provide critique and practical information about the child protection and adoption systems in England. However, the development of social media and online forums means that the availability of such information is more widespread and difficult to authoritatively and consistently destabilise. The problem of hostile and frightened parents seeking a route out of state intervention to protect their children by relocating means that this is a very powerful and appealing narrative.

Advice to relocate abroad has largely been specific to the role of English social services and child protection, and in particular the English practice of using adoption from care, without the consent of the birth parents, as a means of providing long term for the child.[26] This has been pejoratively labelled as the practice of 'forced adoption'. In the UK, the former Liberal Democrat MP John Hemming has commented on what he regards as a system that

---

22 Children Act 1989, s. 47(1).

23 <http://www.preventinterventionnow.org/fight.html/>.

24 <http://www.transparencyproject.org.uk/>.

25 <http://childprotectionresource.online/>.

26 R. Lamont and C. McGlynn, 'Cross-border Care and Adoption Proceedings in the European Union' (2016) 38 *Journal of Social Welfare and Family Law* 94, 99.

encourages and incentivises adoption.[27] However, across Europe, there has been significant political controversy attached to the English adoption system. Complaints have been addressed by the Latvian Parliament to the UK Parliament and to the British Embassy in Slovakia, and a petition was presented to the European Parliament advocating 'abolition' of adoption without consent.[28] Subsequent research by Fenton-Glynn has identified that all of the Member States of the European Union permit some form of adoption without parental consent, although the mechanism may vary.[29]

Despite this reality, the controversy attaches specifically to English law and practice on child protection, and highlights the challenges of protection of children in different legal systems. It is entirely legitimate that national legal systems differ in the way they address child protection and manage adoption, as long as they do not breach human rights standards, and English law is compliant with the rights expressed in the ECHR.[30] Cases of cross-national child protection throw legal divergence into a sharp relief, as it becomes clear that national systems may deal with cases quite differently. By contrast, there may be concern that a child at risk would not be provided for by a foreign system in the same way, or with the same level of support, as by the known domestic legal system.[31] Even commonly agreed concepts, such as the best interests of the child, may be interpreted and applied differently in national legal systems, and the availability and nature of children's services will vary widely.[32]

This problem raises practical concerns regarding the provision and collection of information on children and families made subject to child protection proceedings across different countries. Whilst the child may be in one country, potential kinship or secure placements[33] and information regarding previous circumstances, development, health and education may be abroad. Reliable information will be central to good decision-making, but obtaining this

---

27 The Transparency Project, *Hemming, J on Adoption Targets* available at: <http://www.transparencyproject.org.uk/john-hemming-on-adoption-targets-guest-post/>.

28 European Parliament Committee on Petitions, *Petition 1707/2013 on Abolition of Adoption without Parental Confirm (forced adoption).*

29 C. Fenton-Glynn, *Study for the petitions committee of the European parliament 'adoption without consent'* available at: <http://www.europarl.europa.eu/RegData/etudes/STUD/2015/519236/IPOL_STU%282015%29519236_EN.pdf/>.

30 *R and H v United Kingdom*, Application no. 35348/06 (2012) 54 EHRR 2.

31 R. Lamont, 'Care Proceedings with an International Dimension under Brussels II*a*: Jurisdiction, Mutual Trust and the Best Interests of the Child' (2016) 28 *Child and Family Law Quarterly* 67, 83.

32 H. Stalford, *Children and the European Union: Rights, Welfare and Accountability*, Hart Publishing, Oxford 2014, 202.

33 Placement of a child abroad is governed by Schedule 2, para. 19, Children Act 1989 and is subject to the permission of the English court on assessment of the arrangements and whether the placement is in the child's best interests.

information depends heavily on cooperation between social work authorities and courts in each country affected. In England, guidance has been given to social workers[34] on practice in cases where there is an international dimension, but the provision of information may be slow and lacking in detail. If a child is to be placed in another country, a secure legal environment with clear processes for transfer and reception, and responsibility for ongoing legal protection, must be in place.

The controversies and challenges of protecting children in the international context involve the family and the state in litigation, potentially impacting on two different legal jurisdictions. The private international law rules to determine which country has jurisdiction to act to protect the child can be a difficult question. No one would wish to leave a child unprotected, but there are clear political conflicts, as well as legal ones, involved in decision-making in this context. The role and capacities of the child's parents are central to the nature of the dispute itself. How the court perceives and responds to the child's circumstances may be heavily influenced by national practice and legal principles, so the decision on jurisdiction will be key to determining the child's welfare in the long term.

3. EVOLUTION OF JURISDICTION IN PUBLIC LAW PROTECTION OF CHILDREN: WHO SHOULD DECIDE?

Since the turn of the twenty-first century, there has been a clear development in both the law relating to the protection of children in cross-border situations, and in the incidence of such cases. Before the adoption of the Brussels IIA, jurisdictional rules in England and Wales in respect of public law cases were determined by case law, since the Family Law Act 1986, while providing explicit grounds of jurisdiction over private law cases, did not govern jurisdiction over public law.

In *Re M*,[35] a child was made subject to child protection measures in England after the child had moved with his parents from Scotland. Hale J, as she then was, was required to consider the question of whether the English court had jurisdiction over the child, and could place the child with his grandparents.

34 Department for Education, *Working with Foreign Authorities: child protection cases and care orders. Departmental advice for local authorities, social workers, service managers and children's services lawyers*, available at: <www.londoncp.co.uk/files/wking_foreign_auth_cp_court_order.pdf>.

35 *Re M* [1997] Fam 67.

Hale J identified that when drafting the Act, the Law Commission[36] had explicitly excluded public care orders from the scope of the Family Law Act 1986 because orders conferring responsibility on public authorities were regarded as different in kind to private orders.[37] It was suggested that courts should be able to offer substantive protection to children at risk based on their presence in the jurisdiction, without having to consider complicated issues of where the child might be habitually resident at the time.[38] However, the court should also consider whether there is a more appropriate forum for the litigation under the principle of *forum conveniens*. The court observed that, where there is concurrent jurisdiction to protect children, it is to be hoped that the authorities in each country would try to act in harmony, rather than in competition.[39]

In her judgment, Hale J points out that public law proceedings in the international context are distinct from private law ones because the parties before the court will not be the same before each court in public law proceedings, as the public authority will change, whereas they are normally the same in private proceedings.[40] This is an under-appreciated challenge for international family law, which is often predicated on the same parties to the proceedings appearing before both national courts concerned. In this context, not only may the jurisdiction of the litigation change, but also the authority before the court, which may also have a different perspective on the factual issues forming the basis of intervention. The family has little choice over where proceedings are issued, unlike in private law proceedings where the choice is in the hands of the parties to the litigation themselves. The question of the most appropriate forum to determine the application is therefore a central one for the court seised of proceedings in order to protect, to some extent, the interests of family members, including the child.

Whilst *Re M* used presence as the connecting factor founding the English court's jurisdiction, this is potentially too broad for use in substantive child protection proceedings determining the long-term future of the child. It brings within the scope of English child protection law any child who happens to be on the territory. This is appropriate for emergency intervention to protect a child at immediate risk of harm, but only temporary measures should be taken in respect

36 English and Scottish Law Commissions, *Custody of Children – Jurisdiction and Enforcement within the United Kingdom* (1985) (Law Com. No.138).

37 [1997] Fam 67, 70.

38 [1997] Fam 67, 72, relying on *Re R* [1995] 1 FLR 711. See also *Lewisham London Borough Council v D* [2008] 2 FLR 1449, where the inherent jurisdiction of the High Court was invoked under s. 100 Children Act 1989 to try and ensure the return of a child already in the legal care of the public authority to England from Gambia. The court stated that the correct test of jurisdiction was whether the child was habitually resident in England and Wales at the time the care proceedings were issued.

39 [1997] Fam 67, 75.

40 [1997] Fam 67, 72.

of a child who is merely present within the territory and has no other links to the country; otherwise the exercise of jurisdiction risks being exorbitant. The use of *forum conveniens* may be subject to the concern that there may be a preference for the 'known' domestic child protection system, potentially affecting the determination of the appropriate forum.[41] It risks the exorbitant exercise of jurisdiction arising from the (understandable) desire to protect the child.

However, the common law rules of jurisdiction have been superseded by the intervention of the EU and the adoption of the Brussels IIA Regulation. Given the impact of the free movement of persons, and the increased volume of child protection cases involving EU migrants, it has been helpful that the EU has sought to address the difficulties of jurisdiction in this field, and it has clarified the rules in England and Wales given the identified lacunae in the Family Law Act 1986. Article 8, Brussels IIA states that the general ground of jurisdiction for parental responsibility disputes over children is based on the habitual residence of the child. Article 1, Brussels IIA states that it extends to the placement of a child in a foster family or institutional care, but the material scope of the Regulation does not extend to decisions over adoption. It was not immediately clear that Brussels IIA extended its general jurisdiction to cover public law child protection disputes, as well as private litigation. This was clarified in Case C-435/06 *C.*[42] when two children of Finnish nationality were taken into public care and foster placement in Sweden. The Court of Justice of the European Union (CJEU) heard a preliminary reference on the scope of the Brussels IIA Regulation, and stated that, although the decision to take a child into care was not listed under the matters in Article 1, the Regulation governed all decisions on parental responsibility, including child protection,[43] and decisions made under the public law of a Member State.[44]

Brussels IIA therefore provides a general ground of jurisdiction for public law child protection proceedings regarding children who are habitually resident in the jurisdiction. This is the primary ground of jurisdiction and it means that, even if a child is a national of another country, if they are habitually resident, they may be subject to substantive child protection procedure. Even though this means that the child's habitual residence must be assessed as part of an application, it is a more suitable ground of jurisdiction than presence, since it requires some integration between the child and the state taking action over their welfare; it must be the country at the 'centre of their interest'.[45] It provides certainty in the ground of jurisdiction forming the basis of child protection proceedings in England and Wales for a child with connections to another

41 *Spiliada Maritime Corporation v Cansulex Ltd* [1987] AC 460.
42 Case C-435/06 *C*, ECLI:EU:C:2007:714.
43 ECLI:EU:C:2007:714, para. 31.
44 ECLI:EU:C:2007:714, para. 51.
45 Case C-523/07 *A*, ECLI:EU:C:2010:289, para. 40.

country. It has meant that a child who is habitually resident in England, even if they are a national of another country, may be taken into care and adopted. The decisions over care proceedings are governed by the provisions of Brussels IIA. Decisions relating to the adoption of the child, however, fall outside the material scope of the Brussels IIA Regulation.[46]

However, in practice under the Regulation, the possibility of transferring the case to a court is 'better placed' to take the decision over the child under Article 15 Brussels IIA is often explored for foreign national children. This is available to the court where the child has a close connection to another country, for example as a national of that Member State, the foreign court is better placed to hear the case, and the transfer is in the best interests of the child. It has been used to transfer jurisdiction over cases where a child is a national of another Member State. It is restricted to transfers to other Member State courts, and does not apply to transfers to other third country courts. In England and Wales, where an application is made for a care order over a child with links to another Member State, the court should consider whether to make a request to the foreign court to transfer the jurisdiction.[47] This has not always worked smoothly because of the difficulty of ensuring the foreign court is seised, and the question raised above of engaging the public authorities abroad in the proceedings.[48] There have also been examples of difficulty in obtaining evidence regarding whether the foreign court would be 'better placed' to dispose of proceedings and in ensuring cooperation between Central Authorities.[49]

Article 15 Brussels IIA delivers some flexibility to identify the court best placed to hear child protection proceedings and to determine the long-term welfare of the child. It mitigates, to some extent, the problems associated with different forms of disposal in national law, as it permits the system connected to the child and the family to determine the outcome. It means that, in many cases, if the parent(s) have attempted to evade the child protection jurisdiction by travelling abroad, it can be transferred back to the English court.[50] The proposed revisions to the Brussels IIA Regulation would potentially address some of the difficulties that have arisen in interpreting Article 15 in practice.[51]

However, it also raises more clearly the question of differences between national child protection systems, and the impact of the proceedings on the long-term welfare of the child. Article 15 Brussels IIA states that the transfer

---

46 *Re N (Children) (Adoption: Jurisdiction)* [2015] EWCA Civ 1112.

47 *Re E (Brussels II Revised: Vienna Convention: Reporting Restrictions)* [2014] EWHC 6 (Fam), para. 31.

48 *Re HA (A Child) (Care Proceedings: Final Order)* [2015] EWHC 4172 (Fam).

49 *Leicester City Council v S* [2014] EWHC 1575.

50 *In re M (a child) (Foreign Care Proceedings: Transfer)* [2013] Fam 308.

51 European Commission, 'Proposal for a Council Regulation on jurisdiction, the recognition and enforcement of decisions in matrimonial matters and the matters of parental responsibility, and on international child abduction (recast)' COM(2016) 411 final.

must be in the best interests of the child. A full assessment of the child's best interests would suggest considering the child's long-term welfare, including the potential outcomes of any proceedings in each Member State. This provokes consideration of the comparative merits of the different child protection systems of the Member States, which is not normally permitted by EU law because of the principle of mutual trust. Each Member State is required to trust the content and procedure of substantive law provisions of each other Member State without questioning its approach or application. The assessment of best interests has been criticised as not being 'mutual', since other Member States have been vocal in criticising the approach of the English courts to children at risk in the family, and for being used as a rubber stamp merely to confirm a decision on which court is better placed to hear the application.[52]

The UK Supreme Court was asked to consider the interpretation of best interests under Article 15, Brussels IIA in *Re N (Children) (Adoption: Jurisdiction) (AIRE Centre and others intervening).*[53] The Court was asked whether this assessment was limited to questions of forum and whether it was legitimate to consider the eventual outcome of the care proceedings in each jurisdiction as part of the best interests assessment.[54] The Supreme Court held that, whilst determination of the child's best interests in this context was not 'attenuated', it was not legitimate to consider the eventual outcome of the proceedings.[55] The best interests test was interrelated with the test of whether the alternative jurisdiction was best placed to hear the proceedings, but the focus of the enquiry was on the impact of transfer itself in terms of immediate outcome and choices available to the court in determining the application:

> This is not the same as deciding what outcome will be in the child's best interests. It is deciding whether it is in the child's best interest for the court currently seised of the case to retain it or whether it is in the child's best interests for the case to be transferred to the requested court.[56]

By contrast, in Case C-428/15 *Child and Family Agency v JD*[57] the CJEU was asked how the requirements that the court be 'better placed' and the child's best interests were to be interpreted. The transfer must provide some added value, but the assessment of this value cannot include the content of the forum's substantive

52 R. Lamont, 'Care Proceedings with a European Dimension under Brussels II*a*: Jurisdiction, mutual trust and the best interests of the child' (2016) 28 *Child and Family Law Quarterly* 67, 75.

53 *Re N (Children) (Adoption: Jurisdiction) (AIRE Centre and others intervening)* [2016] UKSC 15, [2017] AC 167.

54 [2016] UKSC 15, para. 31.

55 [2016] UKSC 15, para. 44.

56 Ibid.

57 Case C-428/15 *Child and Family Agency v JD*, ECLI:EU:C:2016:819.

family law rules. Rules of procedure and evidence alone may be considered.[58] In determining the child's best interests, the court must assess whether there will be any negative effects of the transfer on the familial, social and emotional attachments of the child or their material situation.[59] The Court stated that:

> the requirement that the transfer must be in the best interests of the child implies that the court having jurisdiction must be satisfied, having regard to the specific circumstances of the case, that the envisaged transfer of the case to a court of another Member State is not liable to be detrimental to the situation of the child concerned.[60]

The interpretation of the requirement of 'best interests' in this context by the CJEU is minimalistic in that it is limited to considering only possible negative outcomes. Whilst both the UK Supreme Court and the CJEU prohibit consideration of the substantive law of the state to which jurisdiction will be transferred and of the potential outcome of proceedings for the child, the CJEU's definition of best interests is restrictive.[61]

Following the UK's notification of the European Council under Article 50 TEU[62] that it intends to withdraw from the European Union, it is necessary to consider the implications for cross-border child protection.[63] The UK Government has suggested that after 'Brexit' it will incorporate EU Regulations into English law in their original form until amended by the UK Parliament by the so-called 'Great Repeal Bill'.[64] However, Brussels IIA relies on reciprocity between Member States in interpreting the rules and recognising judgments. There will exist no obligation on the other Member States to apply the Regulation in return,[65] and the current Regulation is limited in scope to regulating relationships and transfers between Member States – and the UK will no longer fulfil this requirement.

The UK has recently ratified the Hague Children Convention 1996 which will also be in force in all other EU Member States.[66] Article 9 provides for the transfer

58 ECLI:EU:C:2016:819, para. 57.

59 ECLI:EU:C:2016:819, para. 59.

60 ECLI:EU:C:2016:819, para. 58.

61 N. Lowe and H. Setright, 'Transferring the Problem: How Article 15 of the Revised Brussels II Regulation operates in a public law context' [2017] *International Family Law* 13, 18.

62 [2008] OJ C115/13.

63 N. Lowe, 'Some Reflections on the Options for Dealing with International Family Law following Brexit' [2017] *Family Law* 399.

64 Department for Exiting the European Union, *Legislating for the United Kingdom's withdrawal from the European Union*, March 2017.

65 *R (on the application of Miller and another) v Secretary of State for Exiting the European Union* [2017] UKSC 5.

66 Decision 2008/431 authorising certain Member States to ratify, or accede to, in the interest of the European Community, the 1996 Hague Convention on Jurisdiction, Applicable Law, Recognition, Enforcement and Cooperation in Respect of Parental Responsibility and Measures for the Protection of Children [2008] OJ L151/36.

of cases if the court in another contracting state is better placed in a particular case to assess the child's best interests, although it will not necessarily operate on the same basis as Brussels IIA. This means that the English courts could continue to transfer care proceedings where appropriate to other contracting states, including both EU Member States and other signatories to the Hague Child Convention 1996. However, because the Convention is not governed by EU measures, potentially no reciprocal obligation would exist in the same way with other Member States. There is also potential for a national interpretation of the provisions of the 1996 Convention, including terms such as best interests, to be developed, unconstrained by the limitations and approach of the CJEU.

4. CONCLUSION

The field of family law is rapidly adapting to fast-changing social practices and increasingly the international and complex nature of modern family life. The fields of law affected by an international dimension are expanding, requiring closer cooperation and integration of family law rules. The research of Professor Lowe in developing and interrogating this field of law has inspired researchers to engage with the field to challenge the law and encourage more effective legal solutions. An examination of the field of public law child protection demonstrates that this work is necessary to provide a secure legal environment for children at risk that delivers suitable and beneficial outcomes for their future welfare.

NIGEL LOWE AND INTERNATIONAL FAMILY LAW: AN IMMENSE CONTRIBUTION

Mark HENAGHAN and Ruth BALLANTYNE

1. INTRODUCTION

Nigel Lowe is truly the father of international family law. His contribution to the development of international family law has been immense, not only at the doctrinal level, but also as a result of his invaluable statistical analysis, especially in regard to the Hague Convention on the Civil Aspects of International Child Abduction (the 'Hague Convention'). Lowe's contribution is not only important for family law practitioners and academics around the world, it is also essential for the development and improvement of international family law itself.

This chapter will focus on the major themes of Lowe's work on international family law as it applies to children, with a particular emphasis on the need for cooperation and consistency between different countries, for robust administration processes, and for clear empirical data about how international family laws are actually working. The chapter will conclude with an examination of the importance of statistical analysis in determining the gaps that need to be addressed in the future to ensure the efficient and appropriate operation of the Hague Convention.

2. COOPERATION AND CONSISTENCY IN INTERNATIONAL FAMILY LAW

International family law is extremely complex and encompasses both 'the laws governing families with a foreign element' and 'internationally inspired norms governing domestic family law'.[1] To function in any effective manner, international family law requires a great deal of cooperation between judges from different countries and consistent administrative support. To this end, in his writing about international family law, Lowe has long stressed the importance of judicial cooperation across different legal systems and advocated ways in which such cooperation could be enhanced. As Lowe states, international disputes involving children 'need bold and incisive action' to ensure children are not left in jurisdictional limbo.[2]

It can be all too easy for judges to simply deal with the case before them on their reading of the international convention and the papers before them without considering the wider international implications. This creates a number of problems. For example, in cases involving the Hague Convention, courts must trust that children will be safe if they are returned to their countries of habitual residence. This can only be achieved when judges cooperate with each other and understand the thinking processes of judges in other countries. This is a vital aspect of international family law and is particularly important in cases involving children where a myriad of complex and often age-specific factors must be taken into account, and where what is deemed to be in the welfare and best interests of children can differ markedly across countries. Judicial cooperation and understanding can be enhanced in simple ways by, for example, the development of international judicial conferences. As Lowe explains, 'Judicial conferences have been very valuable in bringing judges together to discuss approaches to common problems and to reinforce common understanding.'[3]

Lowe, Mark Everall, and Michael Nicholls also note that bi-lateral agreements may be helpful in terms of enhancing cooperation between different countries, stating that such agreements 'may prove effective in obtaining the return of wrongfully removed or retained children'.[4] However, they accept that the 'exact legal status and effect' of some bi-lateral agreements may indeed be 'unclear'.[5]

Lowe is particularly attuned to the reality that the mere development of legal frameworks, norms, and conventions is not sufficient for international family law

---

1 N. Lowe, 'The Growing Influence of the European Union on International Family Law – A View From the Boundary' (2003) 56 *Current Legal Problems* 439 at 442.

2 N. Lowe, M. Everall and M. Nicholls, *International Movement of Children: Law Practice and Procedure*, Jordan Publishing, Bristol 2004, at viii.

3 Ibid.

4 Ibid. at 527.

5 Ibid. at 529.

to work. Significant administrative support is required to ensure the consistent application of international family law. Whilst litigants and their lawyers like to think that court systems work for them, and judges think they are in control, nothing in the court system would work without robust administrative processes.

Consistent coordination and implementation of international family law is also vital. To this end, Lowe has recommended the creation of a secretariat, or 'high-level inter-departmental Government body, whose remit should be both to develop and to implement overall policy on international family law matters'.[6] This would be a multi-faceted organisation across different departments with 'all international family law under its remit'.[7] Such an inter-departmental body would avoid any possibility of 'silo mentality', which often occurs in modern Western democracies where government departments compete for funding. Avoiding inter-departmental jousting is vital in legal disputes involving children, where children's interests can easily be forgotten by government agencies fighting for funding to survive. Perfectly drafted international family conventions cannot work without robust and comprehensive administrative processes on the ground.

3. STATISTICAL DATA AND INTERNATIONAL FAMILY LAW CONVENTIONS

International family law conventions have been developed to provide a clear framework for determining legal issues involving children in a consistent manner across different countries. However, in reality, such conventions are applied in differing ways depending on the countries involved. As a result, statistical analysis is vital to understanding how international family law conventions are in fact operating.

Lowe has made an invaluable contribution to enhancing understanding of the realities of family law with his ground-breaking empirical work, especially in regard to the Hague Convention. Lowe's research into the operation of the Convention involving applications received by Central Authorities over a 16-year period is an invaluable resource on how the Hague Convention is working on the ground.[8] This section introduces the Hague Convention generally and

---

6 N. Lowe, above n. 1, at 477.

7 Ibid.

8 See N. Lowe, S. Armstrong and A. Mathias, *A Statistical Analysis of Applications Made in 1999 Under the Hague Convention of 25 October 1980 on the Civil Aspects of International Child Abduction*, Hague Conference on Private International Law, The Hague 2001; N. Lowe, E. Atkinson, K. Horosova and S. Patterson, *A Statistical Analysis of Applications Made in 2003 Under the Hague Convention of 25 October 1980 on the Civil Aspects of International Child Abduction*, Hague Conference on Private International Law, The Hague 2006; N. Lowe and V. Stephens, *A Statistical Analysis of Applications Made in 2008 Under the Hague Convention of 25 October 1980 on the Civil Aspects of International Child Abduction*, Hague

then examines a number of general statistical trends about Hague Convention applications and outcomes to provide a greater understanding of how the Convention is actually working.

3.1. THE HAGUE CONVENTION

The Hague Convention was created by the Hague Conference on Private International Law on 25 October 1980 and is currently ratified or acceded to by 98 countries.[9] It has two primary purposes: securing the 'prompt return of children wrongfully removed to or retained in any Contracting State' and ensuring that 'rights of custody and of access under the law of one Contracting State are effectively respected in the other Contracting States'.[10]

The Hague Convention provides a specific remedy for the wrongful removal or retention of children, in that abducted children (under the age of 16) must be promptly returned to the country from which they were wrongfully removed, unless some narrow exceptions are met.[11] The underlying purpose is to 'protect children internationally from the harmful effects of their wrongful removal or retention', together with deterring parents from absconding overseas with their children in breach of the other parent's rights of custody.[12] The Hague Convention does not resolve the custody dispute itself, but rather returns the child so the original country of jurisdiction can address the custody issues between the parents.

3.2. GENERAL STATISTICAL TRENDS

Lowe's figures show clear and important trends about the operation of the Hague Convention. His and Victoria Stephens' statistical analysis of 2015 Hague Convention applications demonstrates that the overall return rates in Hague Convention cases have dropped from 50 per cent of cases in 1999 to

---

Conference on Private International Law, The Hague 2011; and N. Lowe and V. Stephens, *Part I: A Statistical Analysis of Applications Made in 2015 under the Hague Convention of 25 October 1980 on the Civil Aspects of International Child Abduction – Global Report* (Preliminary Document No. 11A. Revised version, February 2018), Permanent Bureau of the Hague Conference, The Hague 2018. Available at: <https://www.hcch.net/en/publications-and-studies/details4/?pid=6545&dtid=57>.

9 See Permanent Bureau of the Hague Conference on Private International Law, *Convention of 25 October 1980 on the Civil Aspects of International Child Abduction: Number of Contracting States to this Convention* (2 August 2017) <www.hcch.net/>.

10 Hague Convention of 25 October 1980 on the Civil Aspects of International Child Abduction (the 'Hague Convention'), Art. 1.

11 Hague Convention, Art. 13.

12 Hague Convention, Preamble.

45 per cent of cases in 2015.[13] This return rate consisted of judicially ordered returns in 28 per cent of applications while 17 per cent involved voluntary returns.[14] Fourteen per cent of Hague Convention applications were withdrawn, 12 per cent ended in a judicial refusal, and six per cent were still pending when the report was finalised.[15] Three per cent of applications concluded with access being agreed or ordered, and Central Authorities rejected a further three per cent of applications.[16] The remaining 16 per cent of applications concluded in a variety of other ways such as by the child reaching 16 years of age, the child going back to the Requesting State, the abductor being arrested, or the death of the applicant.[17] Without such detailed empirical data and the ability to consistently compare those figures across several decades it would be impossible to see how Hague Convention applications have changed over time.

Lowe and Stephens also discovered that the percentage of judicially ordered returns had reduced significantly. For example, in 1999 a total of 74 per cent of Hague Convention court decisions resulted in a return order being made.[18] However, in 2015 65 per cent of court decisions concluded with the creation of a return order.[19] They also determined that the number of judicial refusals had 'decreased significantly, reversing the trend of previous surveys of a steady increase in refusals'.[20]

It is also important to know, not just how many cases involve judicial refusals to return a child, but also the reasons behind such refusals. To that end, the most common grounds (sole and multiple) for judicial refusals to return children in 2015 included the child not being regarded as habitually resident in the Requesting State (in 25 per cent of judicial refusal cases), alongside there being a grave risk (under Article 13(b) of the Hague Convention) that the child's return would expose the child to physical or psychological harm or otherwise place the child in an intolerable situation (in a further 25 per cent of judicial refusal cases).[21] The child having become settled in their new environment (under Article 12 of the Hague Convention) was a reason for refusal in 17 per cent of cases.[22] The child objecting to being returned was the reason for

---

13 N. Lowe and V. Stephens, *Part I: A Statistical Analysis of Applications Made in 2015 under the Hague Convention of 25 October 1980 on the Civil Aspects of International Child Abduction – Global Report* (Preliminary Document No. 11A. Revised version, February 2018), Permanent Bureau of the Hague Conference, The Hague 2018. Available at: <https://www.hcch.net/en/publications-and-studies/details4/?pid=6545&dtid=57>.

14 Ibid.

15 Ibid.

16 Ibid.

17 Ibid. at 12.

18 Ibid. at 3.

19 Ibid.

20 Ibid. at 11.

21 Ibid. at 16.

22 Ibid.

refusal in 15 per cent of judicial refusal cases, and parents seeking return were deemed to have consented (under Article 13(a) of the Hague Convention) to the relocation of the child in 15 per cent of cases.[23] The average age of an 'objecting child' was 11 years old and the children in question ranged in age from four to 15 years old.[24]

The average time taken to resolve applications for return has increased significantly, especially in cases involving judicial refusals to return. The average number of days for an application resulting in a judicial refusal to return in 1999 was 147, as compared with 245 days in 2015.[25] The maximum number of days taken for a judicial refusal to be reached in 2015 was 867.[26] In terms of applications resulting in an order for return, these took on average 107 days in 1999, but increased to 158 in 2015. The maximum number of days taken for a return to be ordered in 2015 was 808.[27] However, some Contracting States resolved applications much more rapidly than others. As Lowe and Stephens note, there were 'significant differences between Contracting States in the time taken to determine applications ... The applications received by some States were resolved significantly quickly, given the number of applications they received'.[28] For example, in 2015 England and Wales resolved 228 applications in an average of 90 days per application;[29] whereas in Peru, it took an average of 321 days per application to resolve the 10 applications to be determined in 2015.[30]

The important statistical work undertaken by Lowe and Stephens clearly demonstrates that not all Hague Convention applications result in the return of a child and that the percentage of returns has decreased over time. It provides vital information as to other ways such applications are being resolved and the reasons behind such outcomes. It also provides clear information about the time taken to resolve Hague Convention applications and notes that the speed of resolution varies between countries. This work has made a substantial long-term contribution to international understandings of the Hague Convention.

3.3. THE CHANGING PROFILE OF THE 'ABDUCTING PARENT'

The original purpose of the Hague Convention was to prevent parents who (for whatever reason) were non-primary caregivers from stealthily removing their children to another jurisdiction in the hope that a different country would

23 Ibid.
24 Ibid. at 17.
25 Ibid. at 21.
26 Ibid. at 20.
27 Ibid.
28 Ibid. at 21.
29 Ibid.
30 Ibid.

award them primary care.[31] The stereotypical target of the Hague Convention was therefore a non-custodial father who had illegitimately relocated his children in an attempt to locate a jurisdiction more sympathetic to his arguments for primary care of his children.[32] Such international 'forum shopping' was often successful because what is deemed to be in the best interests of children varies significantly across cultures, legal systems, and countries.

In more recent times, the majority of Hague Convention cases have involved primary caregivers who remove their children to another jurisdiction. For example, Lowe and Stephens found that 80 per cent of 'abducting parents' in 2015 were the primary caregiver or joint primary caregiver of the children in question.[33] The proportion of parents removing children to a different jurisdiction who are primary caregivers has also been rising steadily. For example, in 2003 a total of 68 per cent of 'abducting parents' were the primary or joint primary carer of the children, which rose to 72 per cent in 2008.[34] These figures are particularly profound considering that the original focus of the Convention was to prevent non-primary caregivers from abducting their children.

The reasons why primary caregivers abduct their children are profoundly different from why non-custodial parents historically removed their children. Many primary caregivers remove their children in an attempt to escape violent and controlling relationships, and/or to return home to their country of origin to access familial support networks.[35] Shared care has also become more common, which is also undoubtedly connected to an increased societal emphasis on both parents being involved in a child's life and a greater acknowledgement that 'both parents retain duties, and responsibilities in relation to their children' after adult relationships have broken down.[36] The increased emphasis on involving both parents makes it more difficult for primary or joint primary caregivers to legitimately relocate, thus more primary or joint primary caregivers unlawfully abduct their children. The Hague Convention was never designed to address this situation, and thus the primary remedy of return may not be in the best interests of these children.[37]

---

31 E. Pérez-Vera, *Explanatory Report on the 1980 Hague Child Abduction Convention*, Permanent Bureau of the Hague Conference on Private International Law, HCCH Publications, The Hague 1982, at para. 13.

32 During the 1970s and early to mid-1980s familial child abductors were much more likely to be male rather than female. See P. Beaumont and P. McEleavy, *The Hague Convention on International Child Abduction*, Oxford University Press, Oxford 1999, at 8–9.

33 N. Lowe and V. Stephens, above n. 13, at 3.

34 Ibid. at 8.

35 Lowe and Stephens found that 58% of Hague Convention applications involved a taking parent or person who was 'going home'. See N. Lowe and V. Stephens, above n. 13, at 9.

36 P. Beaumont and P. McEleavy, above n. 32, at 10.

37 See M. Freeman, 'In the Best Interests of Internationally Abducted Children? – Plural, Singular, Neither or Both?' [2002] *International Family Law* 77 at 82.

Nonetheless, regardless of this changing profile, it is important to note that any abduction will have a significant impact on the children involved. Being taken from a familiar place with established routines, to a foreign country is disruptive to a child's emotional well-being. The negative effects of parental abduction can have long-term consequences. Marilyn Freeman's research into the long-term effects of parental abduction on adults and young people abducted as children found that 'abduction can have extremely serious consequences in many cases'.[38] According to Freeman:[39]

> Interviewees have spoken of it being very 'hard to let people in' and of the terrible loneliness of not being close to both parents; of not being good at intimate relationships but it being safer not having to rely on anyone else; of the constant sense of insecurity; of blocking things out, and turning to drugs or self-harming as distractions for the hurt; of refusing to have children themselves in case history repeats itself; of being numb for much of childhood, and 'just surviving'; of everything being so easily taken away; of relationships completely coloured by fear; of eating disorders, mental health problems, and suicidal depression; of everything being affected, parenting, relationships, career.

However, the reasons behind an abduction can be influential in terms of the impact on the children involved. Children who are removed to a different country by their primary or joint primary caregiver to escape domestic violence are likely to have very different experiences of their abduction than children who are removed overseas by a non-custodial parent seeking primary care.[40] If the abductor is the non-custodial parent then the children will have to adjust to living with a different parent with whom they may not have a fully formed relationship. These children will also have a significantly diminished relationship with the parent who used to be their primary caregiver. Where the abductor is the primary caregiver, the experience may be easier for children because they are more likely to have a strong, established bond with that parent. However, if the children also have a strong emotional connection with the other parent, then the resulting reduction in contact caused by the abduction will be a significant loss to the children.

Lowe and Stephens' statistical analysis of the reality behind Hague Convention applications provides much needed data about significant changes and developing trends since this important international instrument was introduced. It also illuminates areas where the operation of the Hague Convention could be improved.

---

38 M. Freeman, 'International Family Mobility: Relocation and Abduction: Links and Lessons' [2013] *International Family Law* 41 at 46.

39 Ibid.

40 P. Beaumont and P. McEleavy, above n. 32, at 7–8.

4. IMPROVING THE OPERATION OF THE HAGUE CONVENTION

While recognising the importance of the Hague Convention, Lowe emphasises that it is an imperfect instrument for determining international child abduction disputes between parents and guardians. As Lowe states:[41] 'The Child Abduction Convention has so far proved to be an important and successful instrument for dealing with international child abduction … This is not, of course, to say that everything in the Convention world is working perfectly.'

According to Lowe's scholarship, there are several ways in which the operation of the Hague Convention could be improved, including more carefully considering the 'child objection exception' through the development of a universal mechanism by which to better ascertain children's views, alongside greater recognition for those who remove their children from their habitual residence primarily in order to avoid domestic violence.

4.1. THE 'CHILD'S OBJECTION' EXCEPTION

A court can currently refuse to order the return of a child if the child objects to being returned. Article 13 of the Abduction Convention states:

> The judicial or administrative authority may also refuse to order the return of the child if it finds that the child objects to being returned and has attained an age and degree of maturity at which it is appropriate to take account of its views.

Lowe, Everall, and Nicholls note that despite initial reservations about the inclusion of such an exception, 'the fear that it would provide a serious escape mechanism to the obligation to return has largely proved unfounded'.[42] Indeed in 2015 a child's objection to return was only used as the sole reason to refuse to return a child in 10 per cent of Hague Convention applications.[43] This ability to ascertain exactly how the Hague Convention is operating once again demonstrates the importance of careful statistical analysis.

Other problems with this exception, highlighted by Lowe and others, include the fact that the Hague Convention does not currently provide a mechanism for

---

41 N. Lowe, 'The 1980 Hague Convention on the Civil Aspects of International Child Abduction: An English Viewpoint' (2000) 33 *New York University Journal of International Law and Politics* 179 at 205.

42 N. Lowe, M. Everall and M. Nicholls, above n. 2, at 353.

43 N. Lowe and V. Stephens, above n. 13, at 15–16. A child's objection was one or more reason for refusing to return a child in 15% of cases.

ascertaining children's views.[44] This makes it extremely challenging for a court to establish that a child objects to being returned in the first place and does not give children the respect they deserve. There is also no requirement in the Hague Convention to appoint a lawyer to represent the child.[45] This makes it additionally problematic to ascertain what the children's views actually are. To this end, as Lowe states, 'some provision for checking on the child's views ought to be devised'.[46] In Australia, Nicholson CJ held that a court should make its own inquiries about a child's objections, but other courts have not adopted this.[47] In practice it is left to the parent who opposes return to bring the objection to the court's attention. If that parent chooses not to do so, the child's perspective is often ignored.

Greater consistency in dealing with this exception to return is desirable to ensure that all children are properly heard and that any objections they may have are properly considered.

4.2. DOMESTIC VIOLENCE AND THE 'GRAVE RISK' EXCEPTION

Lowe and others recognise that seeking to escape a violent partner is a 'common background to international child abduction'.[48] Although precise figures are unknown, Merle Weiner suggests that primary caregiving mothers who unlawfully remove children to a different jurisdiction are 'often' attempting to escape domestic violence.[49] There are growing concerns that the Hague Convention's primary remedy of return is particularly harsh on such 'abducting parents', especially as the Hague Convention does not specifically address domestic violence.

---

44 See N. Lowe, M. Everall and M. Nicholls, above n. 2, at 352–369; N. Lowe, above n. 41, at 187–191; M. Henaghan, 'Why Judges Need to Know and Understand Childhood Studies' in M. Freeman (ed.), *Law and Childhood Studies*, Oxford University Press, Oxford 2012; and A. Robinson and M. Henaghan, 'Children: Heard But Not Listened To? An Analysis of Children's Views Under s 6 of the Care of Children Act 2004' (2011) 7 *New Zealand Family Law Journal* 39.

45 Some New Zealand courts have approved a lawyer to represent children in Hague cases. See *SMS v NDL* [2012] NZFC 7106; *AHC v CAC* [2011] 2 NZLR 694 (HC); *SE v WMH* (FC Taupo) FAM-2010-069-143, 30 July 2010; and *S v S* (2009) 28 FRNZ 99 (FC).

46 N. Lowe, above n. 41, at 188.

47 See M. Freeman, above n. 37, at 79.

48 N. Lowe, M. Everall and M. Nicholls, above n. 2, at 335. Geoffrey Greif and Rebecca Hegar found violence present in 54% of child abduction cases from a 1993 study of 368 left-behind parents. See G. Greif and R. Hegar, *When Parents Kidnap: The Families Behind the Headlines*, Free Press, New York 1993, at 18–19. See also M. Weiner, 'International Child Abduction and the Escape from Domestic Violence' (2000–2001) 69(2) *Fordham Law Review* 593 at 595.

49 M. Weiner, 'The Potential and Challenges of Transnational Litigation for Feminists Concerned About Domestic Violence Here and Abroad' (2003) 11 *Journal of Gender Social Policy and Law* 749 at 765.

Courts differ as to whether previous domestic violence and the fear of abuse continuing establishes an exception to return because it constitutes a 'grave risk that his or her return would expose the child to physical or psychological harm or otherwise place the child in an intolerable situation' under Article 13(b) of the Hague Convention.[50] The predominant view, as expressed by the Family Court of Australia, is that as long as the country of return has domestic laws that protect spouses, partners, and children from domestic violence then the child is to be returned.[51] The rationale behind this principle is that, as a matter of judicial comity, it is not for the country to which the child has been abducted to tell other countries how to enforce domestic child protection laws, as long as such laws are in place.[52] As Lowe, Everall, and Nicholls state:[53]

> it is important to appreciate that violence *per se* is insufficient to found an Art 13(b) exception, rather, from the court's point of view, the vital consideration is whether the child and abducting parent will have sufficient protection if they return to the State of habitual residence. In assessing this, the court looks at all the circumstances, including the requesting State's ability to give legal protection ... to ensure the protection of the returning parent and child.

However, while most countries have laws protecting family members from violence, the enforcement of these laws varies widely.[54] Most courts will also not accept the grave risk exception to prevent return where there has been no physical violence towards the children involved, even where there has been serious domestic violence between the two parents. As Sharon Nelson explains:[55]

> if there is no evidence that *the child* was harmed, courts will likely find no grave risk. Even in cases where there is clear evidence of spousal abuse, sometimes extremely severe, courts have refused to find grave risk because the child himself was not abused.

---

50 Hague Convention, Art. 13(b). For more detailed examples of how some courts have interpreted domestic violence in relation to the grave risk exception, see B. Lubin, 'International Parental Child Abduction: Conceptualizing New Remedies Through Application of the Hague Convention' (2005) 4 *Washington University Global Studies Law Review* 415 at 428–429.

51 See *Murray and Tam v Director of Family Services (ACT)* (1993) 16 Fam LR 982. For an example of the position in New Zealand see *A v A* [1996] 2 NZLR 517 (CA).

52 On the subject of international judicial comity, see S. Nelson, 'Turning Our Backs on the Children: Implications of Recent Decisions Regarding the Hague Convention on International Child Abduction' (2001) 2 *University of Illinois Law Review* 669 at 691. For more detailed information about 'unrealistic faith' in legal systems to protect women and children from violence, see M. Kaye, 'The Hague Convention and the Flight from Domestic Violence: How Women and Children are Being Returned by Coach and Four' (1999) 13 *International Journal of Law, Policy and the Family* 191 at 198–205.

53 N. Lowe, M. Everall and M. Nicholls, above n. 2, at 335–336.

54 See L. Silberman, 'The Hague Child Abduction Convention Turns Twenty: Gender Politics and Other Issues' (2000) 33 *International Law and Politics* at 239–240.

55 S. Nelson, above n. 52, at 678.

The reality is that once evidence of domestic violence exists, regardless of whether it is directed at an adult partner or a child, that partner and child are at risk. If courts ignore this real and present danger there can be fatal consequences.[56] As Lowe, Everall, and Nicholls rightly note 'courts too readily assume that children will in fact be adequately protected on their return'.[57]

More effective use of this exception provided by the Hague Convention would not damage judicial comity principles; rather it would acknowledge the realities of Hague Convention applications and recognise the fact that even the best domestic violence laws in any country cannot guarantee safety.

5. CONCLUSION

There is no doubt that Lowe has made an immense contribution to the development of international family law and that family law practitioners and academics across the world owe him a significant debt of gratitude. Lowe's formidable doctrinal and statistical scholarship, spanning several decades, provides much needed information about how the Hague Convention operates in practice from a variety of different perspectives, as well as how the Convention could be improved to ensure that it remains fit for purpose well into the future. To this end, Lowe calls for: increased cooperation and consistency in international family law; the ongoing collection and analysis of statistical information about actual Hague Convention applications and outcomes; more satisfactory methods for incorporating children's views, especially in 'child objection' exception cases; and a greater understanding of abducting parents who are fleeing domestic violence.

Ultimately, Lowe is a thoughtful and wise pragmatist, who rightly recognises that, whilst international conventions can never provide perfect answers to international family conflicts, and there is significant room for improvement, we are 'substantially better off with the Convention than without it'.[58]

---

56 See T. Lindhorst and J. Edleson, *Battered Women, Their Children, and International Law: The Unintended Consequences of the Hague Child Abduction Convention*, Northeastern University Press, Boston MA 2012, at 23.

57 N. Lowe, M. Everall and M. Nicholls, above n. 2, at 348.

58 N. Lowe, above n. 41, at 206.

THE SPANISH CONSTITUTIONAL COURT AND PROTRACTED CHILD ABDUCTION PROCEEDINGS: TIME IS OF THE ESSENCE

Cristina González Beilfuss

1. INTRODUCTION

There is no doubt that Nigel Lowe has decisively contributed to an improvement in the implementation of the 1980 Hague Child Abduction Convention.[1] One of the main findings of the statistics he so efficiently elaborates for the Hague Conference on Private International Law, is that time is of the essence.[2] It is well

---

1 Hague Convention of 25 October 1980 on the Civil Aspects of International Child Abduction.

2 In 2017, Nigel Lowe finalised his fourth research study to look into the operation of the Hague Convention of 25 October 1980 on the Civil Aspects of International Child Abduction, the results of which were to be examined at the 7th Meeting of the Special Commission on the Practical Operation of the 1980 Hague Child Abduction Convention and the 1996 Hague Child Protection Convention, held in October 2017. N. Lowe and V. Stephens, *Part I: A Statistical Analysis of Applications Made in 2015 under the Hague Convention of 25 October 1980 on the Civil Aspects of International Child Abduction – Global Report* (Preliminary Document No. 11A. Revised version, February 2018), Permanent Bureau of the Hague Conference, The Hague 2018. Available at: <https://www.hcch.net/en/publications-and-studies/details4/?pid=6545&dtid=57>.

known that the six-week time-limit that the Hague Convention recommends[3] in Article 11, is very often not met and that delayed return orders can be extremely difficult to enforce.[4] Time, it is said, runs in favour of the abductor.

In a decision rendered on 1 February 2016,[5] the Spanish Constitutional Court has apparently gone one step further. It decided that a return order may be in breach of the Spanish Constitution if it is delayed, the child is well-settled in its new environment, and this factor is not taken into account in the return proceedings. Whether the application was initiated swiftly has no relevance.[6] What matters is the impact of time on the child, whose best interests should be paramount.

The present chapter, which is dedicated to Nigel Lowe in admiration and respect, seeks to explain and contextualise the Spanish Constitutional Court's decision. Contrary to what is generally assumed, the decision does not necessarily undermine the Child Abduction Convention, but is a further incentive for accelerating return proceedings and improving Spanish practice.

2. THE FACTS OF THE CASE

Even though it does not seem to play a significant role in the reasoning of the Constitutional Court, it is worth mentioning that in the case at hand, there were allegations of domestic violence. The Spanish mother was spending the summer holidays with the Swiss father in Greece, when there was a violent quarrel between the parents. The Greek police intervened. The mother and the five-year-old daughter then flew with the father's consent from Greece to Spain, to spend

3 The six-week time-limit is, strictly speaking, not binding. If the judicial or administrative authority concerned has not reached a decision within six weeks from the date of commencement of the proceedings, there is, however, a right to request a statement of the reasons for the delay (Art. 11 2nd paragraph).

4 In Preliminary Document No. 10 for the 7th Meeting in October 2017 of the Special Commission on the Practical Operation of the 1980 Hague Child Abduction Convention and the 1996 Hague Child Protection Convention, it is stated that 'Every day counts when it comes to child abduction cases. In fact, each day that the child remains abducted from his/her place of habitual residence has repercussions for the child and contributes to the escalation of the conflict between the parents, the eroding of contact between the child and the left-behind parent (if it has not been severed altogether), and the child's integration into the place to which he/she has been abducted. These factors have a great impact at the time when return is enforced, since the passage of time may cause the child to suffer once again severe emotional instability at the time of return'. Preliminary Document No. 10 is available at: <www.hcch.net>.

5 Sentencia 16/2016, de 1 de febrero de 2016 (BOE núm. 57 de 7 de marzo de 2016).

6 According to Art. 12 of the Convention the fact that the child is settled in its new environment only becomes relevant where the proceedings have been commenced after the expiration of the period of one year.

a few weeks with the maternal grandparents. The child was subsequently not returned to her place of habitual residence in Switzerland but stayed in Spain, where the mother claimed that she had suffered domestic violence throughout her relationship with the father.

In November 2013, three months after the child arrived in Spain, the father initiated return proceedings under the 1980 Hague Child Abduction Convention. On 14 April 2014, the competent Court ordered the non-return of the child to Switzerland, on grounds of the grave risk exception in Article 13(b) of the Convention (physical or psychological harm). On appeal, the order was reversed and, on 31 March 2015, the mother was ordered to return the child to Switzerland. The Court of Appeal in Madrid found that the domestic violence allegations made by the mother were not consistent.[7]

The decision of the Court of Appeal was then brought to the Spanish Constitutional Court under a so-called *recurso de amparo*. This is a constitutional complaint that can be filed against acts or omissions of public bodies that are allegedly in breach of the fundamental rights or freedoms recognised by the Spanish Constitution (Articles 14 to 29 and 30.2 of the Spanish Constitution).

It is important to highlight that the Constitutional Court is not a third instance court. The *amparo* procedure sought to establish whether the right to a fair trial of mother (and daughter) had been breached. The Constitutional Court decided on 1 February 2016, that the return order was not sufficiently reasoned, since it failed to consider the child's best interests. It annulled the return order and sent the case back to the Court of Appeal.

In the meantime, extensive civil and criminal litigation had taken place both in Spain and in Switzerland. The case had attracted media attention and the Constitutional's Court decision was celebrated by some as protecting a victim of domestic violence.

3. THE REASONING OF THE CONSTITUTIONAL COURT

As mentioned previously, the *amparo* procedure is not a third instance appeal. The question examined by the Constitutional Court is therefore not whether the Hague Convention had been correctly applied but whether the Court of Appeal's decision breached Article 24.1 of the Spanish Constitution (right to a fair trial). The Constitutional Court's starting point is therefore its case law on Article 24.1.

---

7 Auto de la Audiencia Provincial de Madrid (Sección 22ª) de 31 marzo 2015 (JUR/2015/117498).

The Court recalled that the right to a fair trial does not imply a right to a correct decision, but to a decision that is sufficiently reasoned. When the decision affects children this requires consideration of the child's best interests, which are a primary consideration according to Article 3.1 of the UN Convention on the Rights of the Child and a paramount concern according to Spanish child protection legislation.[8]

The Court then examined the decision rendered by the Appellate Court and concluded that the Court of Appeal had correctly applied the Convention. It also found, however, that the return mechanism is an urgent procedure that is compatible with the child's best interests only if the child is returned promptly, within a reasonable time-limit. Compliance with the timeline established in the Convention should avoid the child being settled in its new environment at the point when return is ordered.

In this case, however, 20 months had passed between the child's unlawful retention in Spain and the Court of Appeal's decision. The Constitutional Court admitted that this delay was not due to a lack of diligence on the part of the left-behind parent, who initiated proceedings swiftly, three months after the unlawful retention. Rather, it was due to the fact that return proceedings had been delayed. The Court found that whatever the reasons and whoever is responsible for such delay, the best interests of the child require that its present situation be considered by the competent authority, in particular, whether it is settled in its new environment. Failing that, the decision is not sufficiently reasoned and in breach of Article 24 of the Spanish Constitution. As a consequence, the decision was annulled and the case was sent back to the Court of Appeal for a new decision in compliance with constitutional requirements.

4. COMPATIBILITY OF THE REASONING OF THE CONSTITUTIONAL COURT AND THE HAGUE CONVENTION

The Spanish Constitutional Court's decision is a dangerous precedent insofar as it establishes that in cases of delay, the competent authority is bound to examine whether the child is settled in its new environment. This goes beyond what is established in Article 12 Hague Convention, whereby this examination only takes place if return proceedings were initiated more than a year after the unlawful removal or retention. The Constitutional Court reasoned that from the

8 Art. 2.1 Ley Orgánica 1/1996, de 15 de enero, de proteción jurídica del menor (BOE núm. 15, de 17 de enero de 1996).

child's perspective the date at which proceedings are commenced is not the most important factor.

It has been suggested that the Constitutional Court's decision is in breach of the Hague Convention.[9] From the viewpoint of the Spanish legal order it should, however, be recalled that the Spanish Constitution is above an International Convention in the hierarchy of norms. If an International Convention were contrary to the Spanish Constitution it would have to be denounced by Spain. The Spanish Constitutional Court can therefore not be criticised for putting the Constitution first. As will be shown later the Court, in fact, tries to promote an interpretation of the Convention that is compatible with the Constitution.

The special function of the *amparo* procedure should also be considered. The objective of *amparo* is not to evaluate the constitutionality of legal provisions in the abstract, but to review their application in a particular case. In this case the Court of Appeal was found to be in breach of the right to a fair trial, because it had failed to provide an adequate rationale for its decision. What is unconstitutional is not that return was ordered, but that the present situation of the child was not examined. The Court of Appeal could have complied with the Hague Convention and the Spanish Constitution by, for example, making special arrangements for the return of the child together with its mother.

5. THE SPANISH CONSTITUTIONAL COURT AND THE EUROPEAN COURT OF HUMAN RIGHTS

There are evident analogies between the approach of the European Court of Human Rights (ECtHR) and that of the Spanish Constitutional Court. Certain decisions of the ECtHR have been interpreted to impose a requirement on judges to 'assess the best interests' of the child in each individual case.[10] According to the Spanish Constitutional Court the right to a fair trial is breached if the decision does not consider the best interests of the individual child in cases of *protracted* return proceedings.

That there are parallels in the different lines of reasoning is not surprising, since both courts analyse cases from the perspective of the fundamental rights of one particular person, the claimant. By contrast, a private international law

9 C.M. Caamiña Dominguez, 'El interés superior del menor: la integración en un nuevo medio', *Cuadernos de Derecho Transnacional* (Octubre 2016), Vol. 8, N°. 2, p. 86.

10 See L. Walker, 'The impact of the Hague Abduction Convention on the rights of the family in the case-law of the European Court of Human Rights and the UN Human Rights Committee: the danger of *Neulinger*' (2010) 6(3) *Journal of Private International Law* 650.

approach that is based upon an abstract notion of the best interests of children in general, like the one that inspires the Hague Convention, escapes the logic of such a fundamental rights approach.

The Spanish Constitutional Court, however, followed the ECtHR in considering that the Hague Child Abduction Convention can be reconciled with the requirements of the Spanish Constitution. It cited the European Court's finding[11] that:

> a harmonious interpretation of the European Convention and the Hague Convention can be achieved provided that the following two conditions are observed. Firstly, the factors capable of constituting an exception to the child's immediate return in application of Articles 12, 13 and 20 of the said Convention, particularly where they are raised by one of the parties to the proceedings, must genuinely be taken into account by the requested court. That court must then make a decision that is sufficiently reasoned on this point, in order to enable the Court to verify that those questions have been effectively examined.

It also echoed the ECtHR when saying that these factors must be evaluated in the light of the Constitution.

6. TIME MANAGEMENT

It can be argued that the Constitutional Court has created a further incentive for abductors to delay return proceedings, but this is just one side of the coin. This case can also be interpreted as a reminder of the importance of resolving child abduction cases swiftly. The Constitutional Court mentions several times that the circumstances of this case are exceptional, but upon closer examination these exceptional circumstances only partially explain the delays experienced.

Return proceedings were initiated at an ordinary first instance court in Madrid. However, the mother claimed that since the case involved domestic violence, it had to be transferred to a specialised domestic violence court. For the first time since such courts were created, the Court of Appeal in Madrid accepted this line of reasoning.[12]

---

[11] In paragraph 9 of its decision the Constitutional Court cites *Neulinger and Shuruk v Switzerland*, Application no. 41615/07, ECtHR, 6 July 2010, §133, *X v Latvia*, Application no. 27853/09, ECtHR, 26 November 2013, §106, *Blaga v Romania*, Application no. 54443/10, ECtHR, 1 July 2014, §69 and *Ferrari v Romania*, Application no. 1714/10, ECtHR, 28 April 2015, §47.

[12] F.J. Forcada Miranda, 'El nuevo proceso español de restitución o retorno de menores en los supuestos de sustracción internacional.La decidida apuesta por la celeridad y la novedosa Circular de la Fiscalía 6/2015 (Parte II)' *Bitácora Millennium DIPr: Derecho Internacional Privado*, N°. 3, 2016.

This circumstance caused delay but the Special Domestic Violence Court that heard the case at first instance still managed to render its decision within five months from the initiation of the return proceedings. At that time, the child was hardly settled in its new environment.

The main delay occurred on the father's appeal – it took the Court of Appeal in Madrid nearly 12 months to reach a decision. This is in line with the delays typically experienced by the Family Divisions at the Court of Appeal in Madrid, where it takes on average 10–12 months to obtain a decision.[13] Rather ironically the Constitutional Court then took another 11 months to rule on the matter. After 20 plus 11 months[14] it is no surprise that the child was settled in its new environment.

7. NEW PROCEDURAL RULES FOR CHILD ABDUCTION CASES

It is therefore essential to improve Spanish practice to comply with the requirements of the Spanish Constitutional Court. In 2015 new rules of procedure for child abduction cases were enacted.[15] The case under examination might have fared better if they had been in force.

The new rules promote a certain degree of concentration of jurisdiction. Whereas in the past any first instance court corresponding to the whereabouts of the child could hear child abduction cases, only the First Instance Courts corresponding to the capital of the relevant province, Ceuta and Melilla now have jurisdiction.[16] The new rules also require that child abduction cases are heard by first instance courts that normally deal with family cases and seem to exclude the intervention of Domestic Violence Courts.[17]

---

13 See Memoria Anual 2016 de la Audiencia Provincial de Madrid, available at: <http://www.poderjudicial.es>.

14 Since the perspective should be the child's, what matters is not when return proceedings were initiated but when the child arrived in Spain. The child arrived in Spain in August 2013. Three months later the father initiated return proceedings. It took the court at first instance five months to reach a decision which was appealed and then took another 12 months to be decided. The decision by the Constitutional Court subsequently was awaited for another 11 months. The case was thus finally solved more than two-and-a-half years after the child arrived in Spain. The child who had arrived in Spain at the age of five was by then seven and a half. She had spent one third of her life in Spain, where she went to school and lived in a family unit with the mother, her new husband and a sibling.

15 Ley 15/2015, de 2 de julio, de la Jurisdicción Voluntaria, BOE núm. 158, de 03/07/2015.

16 See Art. 778 *quater*. para. 2 LEC.

17 See F.J. Forcada Miranda, above n. 12.

The new rules also establish strict time-limits. According to paragraph 5 of Article 778 *quater* of the law on civil procedure both first instance and appeal proceedings may only take six weeks maximum. Paragraph 11 of Article 778 *quinquies* prescribes that appeals have to be resolved within 20 days.

8. CONCLUSION

Some observers concluded that the Spanish Constitutional Court's decision of 1 February 2016 had driven a coach and horses through the Hague 1980 Child Abduction Convention. This chapter has tried to show that this is not the case. The Constitutional Court is only requiring judges to carefully reason return decisions, particularly in cases of protracted return proceedings, where the child may have settled in its new environment.

If procedures are handled with urgency and a decision is reached swiftly as required by the Convention, there are no constitutional objections to the return mechanism. There is no need to amend the Convention's rules but simply to improve their practical operation along the lines of the 2015 reform of the law of civil procedure in child abduction cases.

NON-RECOGNITION OF CHILD MARRIAGES: SACRIFICING THE GLOBAL FOR THE LOCAL IN THE AFTERMATH OF THE 2015 'REFUGEE CRISIS'

Maarit Jänterä-Jareborg

1. REFUGEE-RELATED CHALLENGES FOR PRIVATE INTERNATIONAL LAW

During just a few months in the second half of 2015 more than a million refugees arrived in Europe, most of them fleeing from the turbulent conditions of countries such as Syria, Afghanistan, Iraq, Somalia or Eritrea; Europeans tend to refer to this period as 'the European refugee crisis'. Two European states chose, initially, a welcoming attitude and became the most popular countries of refuge within the European Union (EU). Germany (with a population of almost 83 million) received approximately 1 million asylum seekers and Sweden (with a population of 10 million) more than 163,000 during this short period. But only a few months later, even they were closing their borders. By then, the lack of political will among the EU Member States to share the burdens of the refugee flows had become evident. We are moving into an era of a 'European refugee break' which includes heated debates on society's ability (or lack of ability) to receive and integrate newcomers from a very different cultural background. A clash of values, with women and children as the constructed victims, has been brought into the limelight.

Due to Nigel Lowe's deep expertise and engagement in international child law, this chapter focuses on the recent developments in both Sweden and Germany to combat *child marriages*, defined as marriages where either party is – or was – under the age of 18 years at the time of the marriage.[1] The traditional position of private international law has been in favour of recognising marriages validly concluded abroad. The explanation lies in the privileged position of marriage as a civil law status with far-reaching legal consequences, and in the importance of recognising legally acquired rights. The rule of recognition has been 'narrowed down' in Sweden, during the last decade, mainly to prevent evasion of Swedish law. Further restrictions are proposed to enter into force on 1 January 2019, with the aim of *protecting* married refugee children from their marriage.[2] Corresponding legal amendments have recently been adopted in Germany.[3] I argue that this current call for *non-recognition*, 'sacrifices the global for the local', in a questionable manner.[4]

---

1 The other categories of marriages, increasingly contested by the states of refuge, consist of forced marriages, polygamous marriages, proxy marriages and non-registered marriages.

2 Terms of reference, for legislation, adopted by the Swedish government, Kommittédirektiv Dir. 2017:25 *Starkare skydd mot barnäktenskap, tvångsäktenskap och brott med hedersmotiv* ['Increased protection against child marriages, forced marriages and honour-driven crimes']. The appointed law committee submitted its report and proposals in December 2017, 'Utvidgat hinder mot erkännande av utländska barnäktenskap' (Increased impediments to recognition of foreign child marriages), SOU 2017:96.

3 Gesetz zur Bekämpfung von Kinderehen, vom 17. Juli 2017.

4 This same trend is also visible on a more regional level, as demonstrated by Resolution No. 1468 (2005) of the Parliamentary Assembly of the Council of Europe, adopted before the 'European refugee crisis' had materialised. In this Resolution, the Parliamentary Assembly of the Council of Europe urges the national parliaments of the Council of Europe Member States to: 'renegotiate, discard or denounce any sections of international agreements and rules of international private law contrary to the fundamental principles of human rights, particularly as regards personal status (para. 14.1); refrain from recognising forced marriages and child marriages contracted abroad except where recognition would be in the victims' best interests with regard to the effects of the marriage, particularly for the purpose of securing rights that they could not claim otherwise' (para. 14.2.4).

2. THE EUROPEAN AVERSION TO CHILD MARRIAGES AND COUNTERMEASURES

Today most Europeans agree that child marriages are morally and socially wrong.[5] A married child is deprived of the right to a full-time childhood and the right to develop his or her full potential, for example, through the loss of educational opportunities. Girl-wives are regarded as particularly vulnerable as they will, in addition, face the strain of pregnancies and childbirths, at the risk of serious and life-long health problems.

To prevent child marriages from taking place, 18 years of age has gradually become established as the minimum for marriage in most European countries. The European front is, however, not uniform. A few European jurisdictions have refrained from reconsidering their old laws and continue to apply a lower statutory marriage age requirement, usually 16 years of age.[6] Others permit a child below 18 years to marry, upon special dispensation by the competent authority. In that case, the child should, usually, be at least 16 years of age. English law, in turn, permits a 16- or 17-year-old child to marry with parental consent. A new European trend is not to permit any exceptions from the minimum marriage age of 18 years. Sweden, Germany and Denmark are examples of European states that recently have abolished the right to obtain dispensation to marry before that age, irrespective of the circumstances of the case, such as the girl's pregnancy or the couple wishing to marry already having children together. Minority group practices or faith-based concerns in favour of an early marriage are, equally, irrelevant.

Problems are compounded on a global level. States have not been able to reach any international agreement on the minimum age for marriage.[7] An ambiguity also exists in relation to who qualifies as a child. The UN Convention on the Rights of the Child (CRC) of 1989 defines a child as a person under

---

5 See G. Lambertz, 'Child Marriages and the Law – With Special Reference to Swedish Developments' in M. Jänterä-Jareborg (ed.), *The Child's Interests in Conflict, The Intersections between Society, Family, Faith and Culture*, Intersentia, Cambridge 2016, pp. 86 f.

6 Scotland, Northern Ireland, Malta and Portugal are mentioned as still valid examples. See, e.g., M. Coester, 'Kinderehen in Deutschland. Stellungnahme der Kinderrechtekommission des Deutschen Familiengerichtstages e.V. [DFGT] v. 29.11.2016' in *Zeitschrift für das gesamte Familienrecht 2017*, p. 79.

7 Numerous international conventions strive, nevertheless, to protect children from marriage. Among the more specific human rights instruments should be mentioned the UN Convention on Consent to Marriage, Minimum Age for Marriage and Registration of Marriages (1962) and the UN Convention on the Elimination of All Forms of Discrimination against Women (CEDAW) (1979). The UN Convention on the Rights of the Child (CRC) is less outspoken on this matter but is interpreted to contain directly connected provisions. Article 24 is usually given as an example, confirming in the context of the child's right to health and to health-services, states' duty to work towards the abolition of harmful traditional practices.

18 years *unless*, under the law applicable to the child, majority is attained earlier (Article 1). The child's marriage is a traditional ground for attaining majority. A European state wishing to refuse recognition of a child marriage, validly concluded abroad, cannot find incontestable support for its position in the CRC.

3. HOW TO REACT TO MARRIAGES AMONG REFUGEE CHILDREN?

In the aftermath of the 2015 European refugee crisis, the media have been eager to report that many of the asylum-seeking children were married upon their arrival in the state of refuge.[8] Many of these married children have been housed together with their spouses in the various accommodation centres. By permitting the spouses to stay together, the state of refuge is, according to the critics, contributing to a continued violation of children's rights and, in fact, 'signalling' its acceptance of child marriage. The picture usually painted, explicitly or implicitly, is that of a teenage girl married off by her family – and against her own will – to an older man. The girl is deprived of any autonomy and made dependent upon her husband. Child marriages are labelled as expressions of so-called honour-driven violence and oppression in family relations, to be combatted by the state of refuge.[9]

In Sweden and Germany, as well as in many other European states, migration authorities and child care authorities quickly adjusted to the criticism by placing underage couples in separate living quarters.[10] However, not all couples were separated and many were permitted to continue to live together. These differences in treatment stem from factors such as the permitted age of sexual intercourse in the state of refuge – usually 16, 15 or 14 years of age – and whether or not the couple have children.

---

8 According to Möller and Yassari, marriages by children have become much more common in Syria since the outbreak of the civil war, and are extensively practiced among Syrians residing in refugee camps in the neighbouring countries. L.-M. Möller and N. Yassari, 'Wenn Jugendliche heiraten. Die Minderjährigenehe aus rechtsvergleichender und international-privatrechtlicher Sicht' in *Kritische Justiz* 50 (2017), 269–285, p. 274.

9 This kind of reasoning is common in, e.g., Swedish, Danish and Norwegian government bills and other preparatory legislative materials, as well as in media reporting.

10 Denmark, in particular, has figured in the international media in this respect. This attention could be explained by Denmark's, from a European perspective, 'hard attitude' to foreign marriages as the basis for family reunification of migrants in Denmark. In the current context, Denmark came to be known for making repeated U-turns, by first placing the asylum-seeking spouses in the same lodgings in Denmark, then separating them, then finding that a forced separation amounted to a violation of Denmark's treaty obligations such as the duty to protect an established family life, and finally by enacting laws which prohibit all marriages involving a person under the age of 18 years as a partner.

In the following, I will focus on how Sweden and Germany have chosen to react to marriages involving a person (allegedly) under the age of 18 years, when the marriage was (allegedly) validly concluded abroad.[11] This focus also requires giving some attention to the closely related issue of the law applicable to the capacity to marry.

4. SWEDEN: A EUROPEAN FORERUNNER

4.1. THE MULTICULTURAL SETTING

Combatting child marriages came onto the Swedish political and legislative agenda in the early 2000s.[12] Foreign-born children were reported to be over-represented among married children in Sweden. In a sense, the then applicable rules of private international law encouraged this, by stipulating that the capacity to marry was subject to the law of the state of nationality. It was claimed to be equally common that children habitually resident in Sweden were married off abroad, during school holidays. In addition, many naturalised Swedish citizens of age married under-age persons abroad, usually in their countries of origin. As a result, Swedish private international law legislation on marriage was thoroughly revised in 2004[13] and additional restrictions to the recognition of foreign marriages were introduced in 2014. According to a recently proposed law amendment, the rules on non-recognition should be extended to cover situations in which, regardless of the parties' ties to Sweden, one of them was under the age of 18 when either of them arrived in Sweden.[14]

4.2. LAW APPLICABLE TO THE CAPACITY TO MARRY

The 2004 law reform restricted all children's right to marry *in Sweden* by requiring the existence of 'special reasons' for granting a dispensation from the legal marriage age of 18 years.[15] To underline the public interest at stake in all

---

11 Caution is necessary, considering that asylum seekers are often not able to produce any reliable documentation of their age or civil status.

12 During the course of only a few decades, Sweden developed into a major country of migration, receiving newcomers from all parts of the world. Since the 1970s, when Swedish industry no longer had an acute need for foreign labour, most of the newcomers have arrived as refugees and on the basis of 'family reunification'.

13 The relevant rules are found in Act (1904:26) on Certain International Relationships, on Marriage and Guardianship ('the 1904 Act'), primarily its Chapter 1 on marriage conclusion.

14 See SOU 2017:96, above n. 2.

15 The Swedish Marriage Code (1987:230), which is a substantive law regulation, was amended to achieve this effect.

marriages solemnised by a Swedish marriage authority, each partner's capacity to marry (including whether any impediments exist to the intended marriage) is to be examined in accordance with Swedish law. Where neither partner to the marriage is connected to Sweden through nationality or habitual residence, which could be the case when they have come to Sweden simply as 'marriage tourists' or are residing in Sweden as asylum seekers, possible obstacles to the intended marriage are to be assessed, *in addition*, in accordance with the foreign law(s) of the parties' citizenship or habitual residence (the selection being made on the basis of each partner's choice).

In the 2014 law reform, the marriage age of 18 years became mandatory[16] and the system of dispensation was abolished. To increase protection against violations of law, special penal law provisions were introduced targeting forced marriages and child marriages, as well as actions leading to such marriages, including formal and informal marriages.[17]

4.3. RESTRICTIONS ON THE RECOGNITION OF FOREIGN MARRIAGES

To prevent circumvention of Swedish law, the 2004 law reform introduced a tailor-made restriction, inspired by Swiss private international law.[18] Any marriage concluded abroad and contrary to a marriage impediment in Swedish (substantive) law was to be refused recognition in Sweden, *if* at least one of the parties at the time of the marriage was a Swedish national or habitually resident in Sweden.[19] Both of these connecting factors have served as the basis for determining the law to which a person is most closely connected, i.e., the personal law. In the case law following the reform, the most commonly violated impediment has been the age requirement of 18 years. This obstacle to recognition resembles the well-established position of English law, laid down in *Pugh v Pugh*,[20] rendering the marriage of a person below 16 years as void in England, if either party was domiciled in England.[21] The comparatively clear

16 See Swedish Marriage Code, Chapter 2, §1.

17 As a consequence of society's increased diversity, what qualifies as a 'marriage' is not self-evident. 'Recognition' may also depend on the context. Whereas purely religious or customary marriages will generally not qualify as marriages for civil law purposes, such marriages may qualify for penalisation or for protective orders, for example when entered into under force or when including an under-age party.

18 Bundesgesetz über das Internationale Privatrecht, vom 18. Dezember 1987, Article 45 para. 2.

19 Chapter 1, §8a para. 1.1 of the 1904 Act.

20 *Pugh v Pugh* [1951] P. 482, [1951] 2 All ER 680 (Divorce Division).

21 The female party to the marriage was 15 years of age at the time of the marriage to a man domiciled in England. The girl's domicile of origin was in Hungary and she was a refugee in

distinction drawn in English conflict of laws between rules applicable to marriage formalities and those governing the capacity to marry (essential validity of the marriage) has developed in the context of preventing evasion of English law by marrying abroad.

4.4. EXCEPTIONAL HARDSHIP MAY STILL RESULT IN RECOGNITION

In Swedish private international law non-recognition of a marriage means that the marriage is null and void, i.e., that it never came into existence, from the point of view of the Swedish legal system. No annulment proceedings are needed – or even available – to establish the marriage's invalidity. Having regard to the harsh consequences of a void marriage in exceptional situations, the 2004 law reform introduced an exception to the rule of non-recognition, based on 'special reasons'.[22] Examples given in the government bill include situations where the link to Sweden at the time of the marriage was of a formal nature only but real and concrete in relation to the jurisdiction where the marriage was celebrated, where a long time has passed and the parties have believed themselves to be married, and situations where regard to the interests of the parties' children strongly favour recognition.[23] It is explicitly stated that the parties reaching the age of 18 should not be a factor in deciding that the original child marriage should be recognised.[24]

Swedish courts have systematically abstained from using this exception in situations where a marriage's validity was at stake, even if the examples given might have raised expectations of some flexibility. In an important precedent, rendered by the Swedish Supreme Administrative Court in 2012,[25] the Court confirmed the decision of the Swedish Population Agency to refuse registration of a marriage validly concluded in Palestine. In the Court's opinion, the female

Austria. The marriage validly took place under the law of Austria where it was concluded and it became valid by Hungarian law after the wife had attained the age of 17 years. A marriage between persons either one of whom is under the age of 16 was, however, forbidden under English law. According to this ruling, English law was intended to affect 'all persons domiciled in the United Kingdom wherever the marriage might be celebrated' and consequently the marriage was invalid, 'since by the law of the husband's domicile it was a marriage into which he could not lawfully enter'. See J.H.C. Morris and P.M. North, *Cases and Materials on Private International Law*, Butterworths, London 1984, p. 246 f., and P. Torremans (ed.), *Cheshire, North & Fawcett: Private International Law*, 15th edn., Oxford University Press, Oxford 2017, p. 916.

22 Chapter 1, §8a para. 2 of the 1904 Act.

23 See Government Bill (proposition) 2003/04:48, pp. 53 f.

24 Government Bill 2003/04:48, p. 32.

25 Swedish Supreme Administrative Court (*Högsta förvaltningsdomstolen*) *HFD 2012 ref. 17.*

partner's pregnancy and the fact that the marriage had been concluded only 10 days prior to her 18th birthday did not qualify as 'special reasons' to recognise the marriage as valid. In this case, the girl was habitually resident in Sweden at the time of the marriage whereas the other partner was from Palestine. The young couple wished to establish their marital home and residence in Sweden.

In the 2014 law reform, the requirement of 'special reasons' for the exception from the rules of non-recognition of a foreign marriage was 'up-graded' to 'exceptional reasons'. Having regard to the exception's limited use in practice, the effect is primarily to further signal society's disapproval of any evasion of Swedish marriage law.

4.5. EVALUATION

Different concerns arise in respect of a marriage yet to be concluded and a marriage already concluded. In the first case, upgrading the minimum age of marriage into an internationally overriding provision is, logically, within a state's autonomy. The state has an interest in deciding who is qualified to enter into marriage and, consequently, to set the mandatory standard applicable to everybody wishing to marry within its territory.

The situation is trickier in respect of a marriage which was validly concluded abroad. Not to recognise it will result in a limping marital status and will risk considerable legal and other confusion, to the detriment of the partners to the marriage. The generally accepted rule renders a marriage validly concluded in the country of celebration as worthy of recognition in other countries.[26] Some states go even further and, in order to render the marriage a legal validity, also recognise it, if it is recognised by the personal laws of each party to the marriage.

The balance struck between the different concerns and approaches found in Sweden's 2004 law reform is based on linking non-recognition to a violation of the marriage impediments under Swedish (domestic) law, but only on condition of at least one party's clear connections to Sweden at the time of the marriage. In this manner, the law amendment provides clear guidance as to the limits of recognition and can *prevent evasion* of the Swedish marriage requirements. Previously, in Sweden, a marriage validly concluded abroad could be refused recognition only under the extremely strict conditions surrounding the use of the public policy (*ordre public*) exception. Case law includes examples where recognition of a marriage validly concluded by a 15-year-old child abroad

[26] This is the position taken in the 1978 Hague Convention on Celebration and Recognition of the Validity of Marriages, Article 9.

was not considered to be contradictory to Swedish public policy, by contrast (at least in some cases) to a marriage concluded by a 14-year-old child.[27] These rulings might be explained by factors such as Swedish law criminalising sexual intercourse with a person under the age of 15 years, in addition to the context where the marriage's validity arose.

4.6. THE CALL FOR FURTHER MEASURES AGAINST CHILD MARRIAGES

An investigation, carried out by the Swedish National Migration Agency (*Migrationsverket*) in 2016, identified among the asylum seekers in Sweden a total of 132 married children, i.e., persons under the age of 18 years, of whom 129 were girls.[28] The actual number of married children is, however, speculated to be much higher. Approximately half of these children had been housed together with their spouses, in the country's various refugee centres. Rules of private international law have come under attack, as the legal basis for the recognition of these marriages, for producing results which contradict basic Swedish societal values. 'Why should society tolerate a refugee child's marriage when it protects its own children from marriage?' became the crucial question. The Swedish government chose, initially, to defend the joint placements by reference to the couple's right to family life, in particular when they had children. Swedish law, furthermore, does not prevent a child who has reached 15 years of age from entering into an intimate de facto union with an adult. On the contrary, Swedish law grants such unions comparatively far-reaching protection.[29]

In the spring of 2017, the Swedish government gave way to the criticism and issued instructions for new legislation. These instructions proposed that a foreign marriage would not be recognised in Sweden, if either party to the marriage was below 18 years of age *at the time of arrival in Sweden*. In such a case, from the point of view of the Swedish legal system, no marriage is deemed to exist. This is an extraordinary solution, having regard to established principles of

---

27 See the case of *MIG 2012:4*, as commented on in the Law Commission report *Stärkt skydd mot tvångsäktenskap och barnäktenskap, SOU 2012:35*. For a comprehensive and highly critical evaluation of the 2012 case, where a child, who had been married off in Iraq at the age of 15 years and without having been consulted, wished now to be reunited with her father now living in Sweden, see S. Mustasaari, 'The married child belongs to no one? Legal recognition of forced marriages and child marriages in the reuniting of families' (2014) 26 *Child and Family Law Quarterly* 261–282.

28 *Migrationsverket, Är du gift? Utredning av handläggning av barn som är gifta när de söker skydd i Sverige*. Report 29 March 2016.

29 Swedish Cohabitation Act (2003:376) (*Sambolagen*). In Swedish law, sexual intercourse with a child under the age of 15 years is prohibited, which explains how the limit for cohabitation is drawn.

private international law. First, it disregards the fact that the marriage could have been validly concluded abroad at a time when the parties had no reason to take Swedish laws into account; accordingly, no evasion of Swedish law is at stake. The refused recognition of the marriage in Sweden means transforming it into a 'limping marriage'. Secondly, it introduces a novel and disputable connecting factor into private international law regulations, namely the age of 'arrival in Sweden', meaning that if either party arrives in Sweden before the age of 18 the marriage will be void, even after both parties reach the age of 18. However, if the partners to a child marriage arrive in Sweden as adults this ground for non-recognition is not applicable. Thirdly, it takes no account of the fact that even an underage person's marriage can result in a family life qualifying for protection. Fourthly, it remains insensitive to any international treaty obligations which could be interpreted to promote recognition, for example, the CRC and the European Convention on Human Rights (ECHR). Fifthly, it leaves unanswered what happens to a married child, once the child reaches the magic age of 18 years. Will this be an independent ground for the right to asylum, if the child protection authorities have separated the child from his/her spouse and there is reason to believe that the family or the country of origin is not willing or able to provide protection against the marriage?

The law committee, set up by the Swedish government to draft the requested legislative amendments, delivered its proposal in December 2017, fully respecting its terms of reference.[30] A generally welcomed government bill has been presented to Parliament, and can be expected to be adopted.[31] The new legislation is proposed to apply as of 1 January 2019.[32]

5. GERMANY: INCREASED PROTECTION AGAINST CHILD MARRIAGES

5.1. THE MULTICULTURAL SETTING

In many respects, the German developments are similar to those in Sweden. According to investigations, 1,475 asylum-seeking minors were registered as

---

30 See SOU 2017:96, above n. 2.

31 The only recent critical account is found in M. Jänterä-Jareborg, 'Att inte svika *gifta* barn är en svår balansgång' in M. Brattström and M. Jänterä-Jareborg (eds.), *För barns bästa, Vänbok till Anna Singer*, Iustus Förlag, Uppsala 2017, pp. 183–204. Previously, however, Mustasaari in particular has drawn attention to 'how the question of recognition of forced marriage or child marriage may be framed in a way that completely excludes human rights aspects from the legal reasoning in these cases'. See S. Mustasaari, ibid., above n. 26, p. 263.

32 Technically, the amendment consists of a new provision inserted as a separate point under Ch. 1 §8a of the 1904 Act.

married, the great majority (1,152) being girls.[33] Approximately one quarter of the married children were married before the age of 14.[34] In June 2017, a law amendment – with the telling heading of 'combatting child marriages' – was adopted and the new law entered into force in July 2017.

5.2. LAW APPLICABLE TO THE CAPACITY TO MARRY

The 2017 law amendment abolished any right to dispensation from German law's minimum age of 18 years for marriage.[35] Until then a minor of at least 16 years of age had been permitted to marry in Germany upon consent given by the family court.[36] And while maintaining the principle of nationality as the main rule – which means that each party's ability to marry is to be assessed in accordance with the law of the state of citizenship[37] – application of the age limit of 18 years became mandatory through the 2017 law reform. That requirement is, thus, elevated into an 'internationally overriding rule' which must always be given effect in Germany, irrespective of the content of the otherwise applicable (foreign) law.

5.3. NON-RECOGNITION OF CHILD MARRIAGES

A marriage where either party was *below the age of 16 years* at the time of the marriage shall, according to the new law, be regarded as null and void in Germany from the date of its conclusion, directly by the force of German law.[38] This applies irrespective of where the marriage was concluded. From the point of view of the German legal system there is no marriage at all (*Nicht-ehe*). Under the previously applicable rules, a marriage concluded by a child below the age of 16 years was voidable, and to be annulled by court decree.

---

33 This number was reported by the German Federal Ministry of Justice. See further, L.-M. Möller and N. Yassari, above n. 8, p. 270.

34 These numbers are confirmed by L.-M. Möller and N. Yassari, above n. 8, p. 270. The authors draw attention to the – unexpected – fact that among the children who had married before the age of 14, the majority were boys (204 compared to 176 girls, the sex of four children remaining uncertain).

35 Gesetz zur Bekämpfung von Kinderehen, vom 17. Juli 2017. This enactment carried out several amendments, inter alia, in the provisions of the German Civil Code concerning marital capacity.

36 The permission was subject to a child's welfare test ('Kindeswohl'), and the other partner was required to be an adult.

37 The Introductory Act to the German Civil Code (EGBGB), Art. 13.1. If a person has an additional citizenship to that of Germany, the German nationality is to be given priority. A person with acknowledged status as a refugee is subject to the law of the domicile/habitual residence ('Wohnsitz').

38 §1303 German Civil Code.

Where either party was *16 or 17 years old* at the time of the marriage, the new law regards the marriage as voidable and to be annulled by German courts.[39] But until its annulment, the marriage exists. Exceptions to the duty to annul the marriage can be made in two cases. First, the marriage may be recognised once both partners have reached adulthood and wish to remain married.[40] This wish must be established before the annulment of the marriage is carried out. Second, if the annulment of the marriage would, due to exceptional circumstances, result in serious hardship to the parties to the marriage, the court may refrain from annulling the marriage (*Härtefallsprüfung*).[41] Examples given in the preparatory works to the reform[42] include terminal illness, risk of the child partner committing suicide, and the restriction of the free movement of a minor EU-citizen.[43] Circumstances *not* qualifying the marriage for exceptional recognition include the girl's pregnancy or that children in common have already been born to the marriage.[44]

The new law has been criticised for going beyond legitimate goals and for ignoring the social, economic and cultural context in which the foreign marriage was concluded.[45] As is the case in Sweden, local values have been extended to cover all marriages, disregarding the mission of private international law to promote justice across national borders.

If, however, either party to a child marriage, validly concluded abroad, arrives in Germany after both partners have reached the age of 18, the grounds of non-recognition are not applicable. This means that even in the future, German private international law leaves scope for the recognition of marriages celebrated abroad when either party was under age. The design here is strikingly similar to that proposed in Sweden.

6. COMPARISONS

Even if the Swedish and German developments are in many ways similar, some important differences can be identified. Sweden emphasises the 18-year

---

39 §1314.1 German Civil Code and Art. 13.3 No. 2 Introductory Act to the German Civil Code. The court is under a duty to annul the marriage, once it is informed about the marriage. See further, L.-M. Möller and N. Yassari, above n. 8, p. 280 and D. Schwab, 'Die verbotene Kinderehe' in *Zeitschrift für das gesamte Familienrecht 2017*, p. 1370.

40 German Civil Code, §1315 Satz 1 Nr. 1 lit. A).

41 Ibid.

42 Begründung, Entwurf eines Gesetzes zur Bekämpfung von Kinderehen, as described by L.-M. Möller and N. Yassari, above n. 8, p. 280.

43 The free movement within the EU would be violated if a marriage validly concluded in another EU Member State by a 16-year-old EU-citizen would be denied recognition in Germany. See M. Coester, above n. 6, p. 79.

44 L.-M. Möller and N. Yassari, above n. 8, p. 280.

45 See, e.g., L.-M. Möller and N. Yassari, above n. 8, pp. 279 ff and D. Coester-Waltjen, 'Kinderehen – Neue Sonderanknüpfungen im EGBGB', *IPRax 2017*, pp. 429 and 436.

minimum age limit for marriages concluded abroad by making them null and void if there is a connection to Sweden.

The German approach is, in comparison, more flexible. It signals the relevance of 16 years as the bottom line for recognition of what was validly constructed abroad. A marriage concluded by a partner who is 16 or 17 years of age is, initially, recognised as a voidable marriage. In this respect, the chosen approach resembles the distinction in English law between a void and voidable marriage.[46] Once the marriage is annulled by a German court, the annulment's effects take place *ex nunc*, as of the annulment decree. The effect is the same when a voidable marriage is annulled by an English court.[47] Under the Swedish approach, no court decree is required to establish the invalidity of the marriage. Different degrees of invalidity simply do not exist. As a 'non-marriage' in the eyes of the Swedish legal system, a foreign child marriage cannot give rise to any marriage-related rights or duties. Under German law, however, this 'simplicity' applies only in respect of a marriage concluded before the 16th birthday of either party.

Both legal systems leave some limited scope for recognising the marriage, contrary to the rule of non-recognition. The German approach appears less rigid, in giving the spouses a choice to be recognised as married once they reach the age of 18. This applies only in the case of voidable marriages which took place after each partner had reached the age of 16. No such option is available in Sweden. On the other hand, the rule of invalidity can, exceptionally, be set aside. This position has not been reconsidered in the recently (December 2017) submitted law proposal, with reference, inter alia, to Sweden's international commitments, such as EU citizens' right to free movement and international conventions.[48] The Swedish model's informality, characterised by the absence of a generally binding court decree confirming the marriage's nullity, lacks the necessary predictability. When the existence of the marriage arises as a preliminary issue in legal proceedings in Sweden, the decision will be taken independently in each case. In a cross-border context, therefore, there is a risk of contradictory legal (and other normative) stances taking place in respect of who is married to whom in the case of a remarriage in Sweden, and who is the legal father of the children born. The number of 'limping marriages' can be expected to increase in both Sweden and Germany.

---

46 See, e.g., J. Hill and M. Ní Shúilleabháin (eds.), *Clarkson & Hill's Conflict of Laws*, 5th edn., Oxford University Press, Oxford 2016, p. 353 ff.

47 *Clarkson & Hill's Conflict of Laws*, above n. 46, p. 355.

48 See SOU 2017:96, above n. 2, English summary, pp. 31 f.

7. THE CHALLENGES POSED TO PRIVATE INTERNATIONAL LAW

Until recently many European states endorsed the idea of 'emancipating' the rules of private international law from national substantive law. They were prepared to transfer the necessary legal competence to EU institutions, enabling the harmonisation of the regulations of private international law on a European, supra-national level. As the above-described Swedish and German developments demonstrate, the laws on what and who qualifies for marriage have, however, remained nationally tainted also within private international law.[49] As exemplified by the Swedish and German developments, the new European trend is to regard the standard of forum law as mandatory and to disregard what applies under the law of the country of celebration or what qualifies as marriage under the parties' personal laws. The personal preferences of the parties to the marriage, their life situation and their right to family life are of little – if any – relevance.

The European Court of Human Rights has been cautious in ruling against the autonomy of any Contracting State to the ECHR in the context of marriage. This caution finds recent expression in the Court's judgment in *ZH and RH v Switzerland* which concerned a young couple's right to family life.[50] In that case, an Afghan asylum-seeking couple in Switzerland had been separated by the Swiss authorities against their will. The male partner had (under the Dublin-rules) been expelled to Italy as the country of arrival, whereas the female partner was permitted to stay in Switzerland. The man returned to Switzerland after only three days and was, de facto, able to remain there. The couple later received asylum in Switzerland and claimed damages with reference to a violation of their right to family life. Switzerland had not initially recognised their marriage, which had been concluded in a religious form in Iran at a time when the female partner was 14 years of age (the man being 18 years). The marriage was not registered in Iran, even though this was required for a valid marriage, and it was

49 Attempts have, however, been made to unify the regulations of private international law, as demonstrated by the Hague Convention of 14 March 1978 on Celebration and Recognition of the Validity of Marriages. This Convention strives to facilitate the celebration of marriages with cross-border links and to improve the recognition of the validity of marriages entered into in other states. In spite of its striking a good balance between the various concerns, only a few states have ratified this Convention. See, e.g., M. Jänterä-Jareborg, 'Combatting child marriages and forced marriages – the prospects of the Hague Marriage Convention in the Scandinavian "multicultural" societies' in T. Einhorn and K. Siehr (eds.), *Intercontinental Cooperation through Private International Law, Essays in Memory of Peter E. Nygh*, T.M.C. Asser Press 2004, pp. 172–175. On criticisms against the Convention, see P. North, *Private International Law Problems in Common Law Jurisdictions*, Martinus Nijhoff Publishers, The Hague 1993, pp. 45 f.

50 *ZH and RH v Switzerland* Application no. 60119/12, ECtHR, 8 December 2017.

concluded contrary to Afghanistan's minimum legal marriage age of 15 years (the couple's personal law). It is therefore surprising that the Swiss authorities chose to recognise the parties' relationship as a marriage after the girl's 17th birthday.[51] As this chapter indicates, differences among the European approaches regarding what qualifies as a marriage and the different degrees of invalidity of marriages are confusing and would be worthy of a separate study.

Returning to the Swedish and German developments, I am of the opinion that, in general, the restrictions posed on the recognition of foreign child marriages merely pay lip-service to the protection of the children concerned. This creates the *impression* that children's rights are taken seriously, while attention is drawn away from the weak prospects of children, once of age, of receiving asylum in the state of refuge. The traditional 'global goals' of private international law are sacrificed for 'local concerns'. What use is an emphasis on the officially promoted right to childhood, if you are deprived of the right to family life with the person you regard as your spouse, as well as a future in your country of refuge?

---

51 This disturbing element in the case is observed in the separate opinion by Judge Nicolaeu. In Nicolaeu's Opinion, importantly, the relationship between the applicants constituted 'family life' within the meaning of Article 8 of the European Convention on Human Rights.

JUVENILE JUSTICE IN BULGARIA: REFORMS AND RESISTANCE

Velina Todorova

There have been several attempts to reform the juvenile justice system in Bulgaria during the last 20 years. The debates produced some legal amendments in 2004 but the overall structure and the ideology of the system remained untouched. Bulgaria regularly receives recommendations to change the system from the UN human rights treaty bodies and mechanisms[1] and also from the Council of Europe.[2] But these have not yet been transformed into the political will to take action.

1 In 1997 'a comprehensive reform of the system of juvenile justice' was recommended (CRC/C/15/Add.66, 1997) – the same in 2008 (CRC/C/BGR/CO/2, 2008), and in 2016 (CRC/C/BGR/CO/3-5, 2016). In 2011 the Human Rights Committee recommended that Bulgaria 'consider, as a matter of priority, the adoption and implementation of the reform of the juvenile justice system in compliance with the rights protected under the Covenant' (CCPR/C/BGR/CO/3, para. 23). See also: A/HRC/16/9; A/HRC/16/L.41.

2 Two Commissioners for Human Rights of the Council of Europe have made similar observations following their visits to Bulgaria: Thomas Hammarberg (2009): 'invites the Bulgarian authorities to reform the juvenile justice system and bring it into line with international and European standards' (at: <https://wcd.coe.int>) and Nils Muižnieks in CommDH (2015)12, para. 61.

This chapter aims to briefly present the latest attempt to reform the juvenile justice system in Bulgaria. The chapter outlines the Draft on Diversion of Underage Offenders from Criminal Proceedings and Implementation of Educational Measures Act ('the Draft Act, 2016'), including the context, the driving forces behind it and the resistance against it.[3]

1. THE CONTEXT IN BRIEF

The main 'pillar' of the Bulgarian juvenile justice system is the Juvenile Delinquency Act (JDA) (in force from 1958, last amended in 2016).[4] This Act was a positive step at the time of its adoption and for some time later, mainly due to its aim to handle juvenile offending within a separate system (based on divergence from the penal justice system enshrined as an option in the Penal Code (1968)). The system created under the JDA cannot be featured under any of the three models currently being conceptualised in the literature – the 'welfare model' (that considers the delinquent behaviour as strongly linked to unfavourable social, economic or family situations), the 'justice model' (the child in conflict with the law is responsible for his/her offence and should be punished, but can always receive treatment) and a 'third path' – restorative justice (it helps to bring the previous two closer to each other but also has its limits).[5] It resembles the 'welfare model' with its declared aim to support the child's social reintegration but it lacks important elements such as interaction with child protection policies and practices. Most importantly, the law does not refer to the best interests of the child as requiring to be assessed and determined within the JDA procedures. The system differs from the 'justice model' mostly on a formal basis. It uses commissions, as an alternative to a court, which can impose so-called 'educational measures' and so act as *quasi* courts. The system holds some elements of the 'restorative justice' model[6] but these measures are not supported by the necessary mechanisms, appropriately trained staff and safeguards for their effective implementation. The most frequent measure applied in the recent past was placement in correctional institutions that provided a ground to define the JDA as a 'specific quasi criminal law'.[7]

---

3 See the Draft, 2016 in Bulgarian at: <http://www.justice.government.bg/117/7446/>.

4 The correct title of this law is: Combatting the Antisocial Acts of Minors and Juveniles Act.

5 J. Zermatten,'Models in Juvenile Justice' in J. Zermatten, P.R. Gapany et al. (eds.), *The Essentials in Juvenile Justice*, Institut international des droits de l'enfant, 2017, pp. 189–205.

6 For example, apology to the victim, compensation by the offender of the damage caused if this is within his/her capacities; community work (Article 13(1) JDA).

7 See: *Gap Analysis of the Bulgarian Juvenile Justice System*, 03.07.2014, produced in the context of the Framework Agreement between the Government of Bulgaria and the Swiss

The JDA's providing for such a 'mixed' system was not questioned until the end of the socialist state in 1989. At the same time, though the JDA has been changed several times to reflect the changing realties, its main concepts have remained the same, for example, with regard to the minimum age of criminal responsibility, case management, the system of educational measures as alternatives to penalties and composition and functions of the local commissions.

The main challenge to the JDA came from the Child Protection Act (CPA) (in force from 2001, last amended in 2016). The CPA introduced the principles and rights enshrined in the Convention on the Rights of the Child (CRC) in a comprehensive manner and stipulated for the creation of: (1) a separate administrative system – central and municipal – for child protection, (2) court-based placement of children in public care, and (3) a mandatory reporting and referral mechanism to provide special protection to children at risk, etc.

The inconsistency between the JDA and CPA resulted in two separate systems working in parallel, which has been widely criticised by both civil society and experts.[8] This criticism has also been recognised by the Government and this motivated the adoption of two policy documents to start the process of reform of juvenile justice: the National Concept on Justice for Children (2011) and a Road Map for the implementation of that Concept in 2013.[9] During 2013–2016 the Ministry of Justice held unprecedented dialogue with the main governmental and non-governmental stakeholders, including the judiciary that resulted in the Draft Act.[10] However, a change in the Government in March 2016 has again stopped the process.

Federal Council concerning the implementation of the Bulgarian–Swiss cooperation programme (<http://swiss-contribution.bg/en/projects/security/strengthening-the-legal-and-institutional-capacity-of-the-judicial-system-in-the-field-of-juvenile-justice>). The analysis is available at: <http://www.childsrights.org/documents/formations/sur-mesure/jj/Final_Gap_Analysis_BulgarianJuvenileJusticeSystem.pdf>, pp. 7–10.

8 Sv. Margaritova, 'Educational Measures for Minor and Juvenile Offenders', Sibi, Sofia 2011, pp. 49–53. See also: National Network for Children, *What is the Average Government Score for Childcare?* 2017, pp. 47–50, at: <http://nmd.bg/wp-content/uploads/2013/12/REPORT-CARD-2017_en-3.pdf>.

9 At: <www.strategy.bg/FileHandler.ashx?fileId=1703> also at: <http://legalworld.bg/47087.mp-podgotvia-otdelen-nov-zakon-za-detskoto-pravosydie.html>. See also V. Micheva, Deputy Minister of Justice, 'Juvenile Justice in Bulgaria' in *Judicial barometer*, 14/2016, pp. 114–116, also available at <http://cli-bg.org/page.php?id=1>.

10 A coalition of non-governmental organisations implemented a public campaign to support the process, see more at: <http://www.capital.bg/politika_i_ikonomika/obshtestvo/vsichko_za_pravata_ni/2015/09/24/2615375_shans_za_spravedlivo_detsko_pravosudie/?>, <http://deca.bg/act-now-item/childhood-with-no-bars/>, <http://nmd.bg/natsionalna-mrezha-za-detsata-izrazi-stanovishte-otnosno-zakon-za-izmenenie-i-dopalnenie-na-nakazatelniya-kodeks/>.

2. MAIN ISSUES IN THE CURRENT DEBATE

2.1. THE MINIMUM AGE OF CRIMINAL RESPONSIBILITY

The minimum age of criminal responsibility as set out by the Penal Code of 1968 is 14 years (Article 31(1)). Children from 14 to 18 years of age ('adolescents' or 'juveniles') are assumed to be criminally responsible only if they have the required maturity in that regard (Article 31(2) Penal Code). Adolescents of 16 years of age can bear not only criminal, but also administrative responsibility.[11] Notwithstanding that criminal majority is fixed at 18 years of age, the Penal Code provides (Article 40(3)) for a category of 'young adults' (from 18 to 21 years of age), who are subject to special care.

The age of criminal responsibility is a legacy of the Socialist state and of its welfare approach to children which has not yet been questioned. However, even during the Socialist period, a category of minor children (from eight to 14 years of age) was created who, though under the minimum age of criminal responsibility, were subject to the provisions of JDA (Article 12(1)) if they commit 'anti-social acts' and in serious cases can be placed in educational (correctional) institutions.[12]

There is one more important outcome of the legislation that has created two categories of minor children: from ages zero to seven, and from ages eight to 14. Before the CPA came into force in 2001, the juvenile justice system was the only system designated to work with children and so the 'categorisation' of children was not discussed. Seventeen years after the new law and child protection system were put in to place, that approach of the legislator has been questioned. The age categorisation of children created confusion between the two systems. As children below the age of 14 are not criminally responsible, in case of behavioural problems, both age groups should be subject to the Child Protection Act. At the same time, those in the second category will also be subject to the JDA. This confusion has been addressed by the unanimous stipulation of the Draft Act, 2016, which states that it should apply to criminally responsible juveniles only, which are the children between 14 and 18 years of age. The stipulation has two aims: first, to end the legislative ambiguity with regard to the minimum age as stipulated by the Penal Code and bring the position into

---

11 For extensive analyses on the subject see: D. Furtunova, 'Country report: Bulgaria' in Sv. Baeva (ed.), *Children Deprived of Liberty in Central and Eastern Europe: Between Legacy and Reform*, Bulgarian Helsinki Committee, Sofia 2014, p. 93 *et seq*. In English at: <http://www.bghelsinki.org/en/media/uploads/documents/reports/special/bhc_(2014)_children_deprived_from_liberty_en.pdf>. Also: *Gap Analysis of the Bulgarian Juvenile Justice System*, above n. 7.

12 The approach to create several categories of children in conflict with the law, with different standards set out in national legislation, has been criticised by the CRC Committee in *General Comment No. 10 (2007) Children's rights in juvenile justice*, para. 30.

line with the jurisprudence of the CRC Committee;[13] secondly, to provide that minor children should be dealt with by the child protection system rather than by the juvenile justice system.

2.2. THE CONCEPTS OF 'ANTI-SOCIAL BEHAVIOUR' AND 'STATUS OFFENCES'

The issue of 'minimum age' is linked to the definition of 'anti-social acts' in the JDA, which permits children to be punished for acts that if committed by adults would not be punishable (so called 'status offences'). The definition is very general and allows for a broad interpretation of the behaviour of children: 'an act that is socially dangerous and illicit or contradicts morals and good manners' (Article 49a of the Supplementary provisions JDA). The regulation of 'status offences' has recently been determined as discriminatory and recommended to be abolished:

> Behaviour such as vagrancy, roaming the streets or runaways should be dealt with through the implementation of child protective measures, including effective support for parents or other caregivers and measures which address the root causes of this behaviour, as established in international standards.[14]

Often, in the Bulgarian context, the regulation of 'status offences' is justified on the basis of the literal interpretation of the UN Standard Minimum Rules for the Administration of Juvenile Justice ('The Beijing Rules'). It has been argued that 'status offences' are acceptable under the UN Rules by reference to rule 3.1 'Extension of the Rules', which states that '[t]he relevant provisions of the Rules shall be applied not only to juvenile offenders but also to juveniles who may be proceeded against for any specific behaviour that would not be punishable if committed by an adult'.[15] However, proper interpretation of rule 3 clarifies that the purpose of the extension is not to promote or validate 'status offences' but only to ensure due process guarantees for the children affected.[16] The proponents also forget to refer to Article 56 of the UN Guidelines for the

13 See Committee on the Rights of the Child, 49th Session, consideration of Reports submitted by States Parties under Article 44 of the Convention: CRC/C/BGR/CO/2 2008, para. 68(c). See also CommDH (2015)12, para. 61.

14 Report by Nils Muižnieks: CommDH (2015)12, para. 61, above n. 2, also in: CRC/C/BGR/CO/2, 2008, para. 69.

15 The most outspoken supporter of this view in Bulgaria is Dr. Sv. Margaritova: *Educational Measures for Minor and Juvenile Offenders*, pp. 27–29.

16 Rule: 3.2 Efforts shall be made to extend the principles embodied in the Rules to all juveniles who are dealt with in welfare and care proceedings. 3.3 Efforts shall also be made to extend the principles embodied in the Rules to young adult offenders.

Prevention of Juvenile Delinquency (Riyadh Guidelines), which reads: 'In order to prevent further stigmatization, victimization and criminalization of young persons, legislation should be enacted to ensure that any conduct not considered an offence or not penalized if committed by an adult is not considered an offence and not penalized if committed by a young person.'[17]

Table 1 below shows the number of children aged 8-17 registered for committing offences and crimes:[18]

Table 1. Children Registered in the Juvenile Justice System

	2013	2014	2015	2016
Total number of children aged 8–17 registered[19] for committing *anti-social acts*[20]	6,439	5,372	6,145	5,754
Children aged 8–13	1,780	1,450	1,793	1,470
Children aged 14–17	4,659	3,916	4,356	4,284
Total number of children aged 8–17 registered for committing *crimes*	6,007	5,402	5,362	4,980
Children aged 8–13	1,457	1,434	1,322	1,168
Children aged 14–17	4,550	3,968	4,040	3,812

The most frequent anti-social acts, as per the National Institute of Statistics, are runaways (from homes, school and institutions), violent and aggressive behaviour, vagrancy and begging, alcohol and drug abuse and prostitution; the most frequent crimes committed by children are theft and crimes correlated to drug abuse. Apparently, a larger share of the anti-social acts that the juvenile

17 UN Guidelines for the Prevention of Juvenile Delinquency (Riyadh Guidelines)/ UN GA Resolution 45/112 of 14 December 1990. See also CRC Committee *General Comment No. 10*, para. 8.

18 Data from the National Institute for Statistics at: <http://www.nsi.bg/en/content/6299/minor-and-juvenile-persons-perpetrators-crimes-sex-age-kinds-crimes-and-statistical>.

19 The registration is a duty of the *Problem Children Offices* (PCO). These are specialised structures taking part in the prevention and combatting of crime and antisocial behaviour of minors and juveniles (as stipulated by Article 27 JDA). PCO are set up at the municipal councils in collaboration with the police and the Minister of the Interior. They are managed and controlled by the National Police as well as by the Central Commission on Juvenile Delinquency. The staff of PCO is composed of inspectors with higher pedagogical education (that is, a teacher's qualification). Their total number in the country is around 250 persons. To hold this post, they undergo a special selection procedure and a compulsory specialised training in the Police Academy to the Ministry of the Interior. They are most often the people who propose the implementation of an educative measure under JDA.

20 The child population in Bulgaria is constantly decreasing. By the end of 2015 it was approximately – 1,100,000 children which amounted to 15% of the total population (7,153,784 people). National Institute for Statistics, at: <http://www.nsi.bg/sites/default/files/files/pressreleases/Population2015_CV8W6X5.pdf>.

justice system deals with are 'status offences', not crimes. The abolition of 'status offences' has been proposed in the recent policy documents of the Government but this proposal has been questioned in the current debate.[21]

3. WHEN THE CHILD IS AT 'RISK' OR IS IN CONFLICT WITH THE LAW

The proposals to exclude children aged 8–14 from the justice system and to abolish the notion of 'status offences' has given rise to heated discussion. The main opposition came from the Ministry of Interior, Ministry of Labour and Social Policy (MLSP) and the Central and local commissions to combat juvenile delinquency. They rejected the proposals based on 'public safety' concerns, as well as concerns that the child protection system is not designed to work with children with behavioural problems. Those children, MLSP argues, should remain under the juvenile justice system in order to be addressed by the special measures that are different from the common approach of social work and social services.

The formal legal ground for the opposition coming from the child protection system (CPA) criticises the confusing terminology and concepts of the two statutory regimes with regard to child in need of protection. The CPA introduced the concept of 'child at risk', mainly due to the need to establish clear grounds and mechanisms by which to provide public care for children without parental care, but also to initiate policies for child protection.[22] A 'child at risk' is defined (by (§1(11), Additional provisions CPA) as a child:

a) who has no parents or has been left without their care for a long period of time;
b) who is a victim of abuse, violence, exploitation or any other non-humane or humiliating treatment or punishment within or outside his family;
c) for whom there is a danger of impeding his physical, mental, moral, intellectual or social development;
d) who suffers mental or physical disability as well as from chronic diseases;
e) who is at risk of dropping out of school or who has dropped out of school.

---

21 For the current critique against the regulation of 'status offences' in Bulgaria see: <https://www.unicef.bg/assets/PDFs/2016/UNICEF_Statement_Diversion_and_Educational_Measures_Act_BG_final.pdf> and <http://nmd.bg/en/national-network-for-children-supports-the-extension-of-the-concept-of-a-child-at-risk-in-the-draft-roadmap-to-implement-state-policy-for-children-and-juvenile-justice/>.

22 The major issue in Bulgaria in 1998–2000 was institutional care, and the Act contributed to the start of a process of deinstitutionalisation of child care and development of family-based care. Therefore the lack of parental care on various occasions was considered the main 'risk' factor for the child. Concerns that the concept of 'child at risk' could often be discriminatory and stigmatising have been expressed several times but have not been addressed yet.

Alongside this the JDA refers to children that can be considered at risk, when: 'a) their permanent or current address cannot be established; b) they are arrested for vagrancy, begging, prostitution, alcohol abuse, distribution or use of drugs or other intoxicating substances ...' (Article 35(1) JDA). The Act also provides a definition of the 'uncontrolled child' as 'a person under the age of 18 who has been left without parental care or the care of the persons substituting for the parents' (Article 49a(3), Supplementary provisions JDA).

It is obvious that a child could be simultaneously considered in need of care under the CPA and an offender under the JDA. The punishment of children for their misbehaviour has been a constant topic of concern for human rights NGOs in Bulgaria.[23] There is a widely-shared opinion that the status offences signal problems with child care and this is supported by several analyses of the risk factors, produced by the State Agency for Child Protection (2009, 2013). These clearly demonstrate that children who behave anti-socially are children at risk, within the meaning of the law, although this is not explicitly set out in the definition of the CPA.[24] Even when the behaviour of a child under 14 escalates to acts defined as crimes under the Penal Code, the reasons for that conduct and the specifics of the child's age place the child in the category 'child at risk' and therefore such children should be dealt with by the child protection system.[25]

It is true that the child protection system in Bulgaria is still developing, even after 17 years since its establishment under the CPA. The problem with the child protection system is not so much related to its immaturity but to the lack of political will to strengthen it. The system constantly experiences shortcomings in terms of numbers and training of personnel, lack of adequate resources

---

23 This debate has been brought to the attention of the European Court on Human Rights. The Court, however, in *A. and Others v Bulgaria*, Application no. 51776/08, ECtHR, 29 November 2011, paras. 61–62, (in French and in Bulgarian only) found that the term 'anti-social behaviour' was indeed unclearly defined in the legislation but had been sufficiently clarified in the jurisprudence. That allowed the Court to decide that placement in a correctional boarding school is not in breach of Article 5 of the European Convention on Human Rights and does not constitute 'unlawful detention'. See more in: *Children Deprived of Liberty in Central and Eastern Europe: Between Legacy and Reform*, above n. 11, pp. 50–55 and 107–114. In 2016, the CRC Committee urged Bulgaria to: 'Ensure that children placed in specialized educational facilities have access to protection measures under the Child Protection Act' (CRC/C/BGR/CO/3-5, 2016, para. 61(a)). See also: N. Petrova-Dimitrova, *Children in Conflict with the Law*, UNICEF, UNDP – Bulgaria, Sofia 2000, pp. 15–16.

24 See the Bulgarian CPA in English at: <http://www.refworld.org/docid/44ad32014.html> See also: *Report of the State Agency for Child Protection on the situation of the Educational Boarding Schools and Socio Pedagogic Boarding Schools in 2013*, at: <http://sacp.government.bg/media/filer_public/2016/01/12/dazd-proverka-spi-vui-2013.pdf> and the Road Map (2013).

25 See also CRC Committee, *General Comment No. 10*, above n. 12, para. 9.

(salaries, working conditions, budget for services, etc.) and recognition.[26] The decline became obvious after 2011 when all the declared reforms were halted and the system started to defend itself against any attempts to enlarge the scope of its beneficiaries to include, for example, children affected by international migration, children with 'difficult' behaviour, children addicted to drugs and other substances, dropouts from school, etc. Similar attitudes are expressed in the education system. Despite its long-term existence, there are also problems in the juvenile justice system, which is understaffed and underfinanced, with members of the local commissions working on a voluntary basis without professional training. So, the underdevelopment of key systems as well as the lack of meaningful coordination between them are huge obstacles for the reform of the juvenile justice system.

4. ACTS AND 'ACTORS'

4.1. DIVERSION

The Draft Act, 2016 attempts to introduce comprehensive principles and measures of restorative justice, as well as to expand the ways in which cases can be 'diverted' and treated outside the justice system. Opportunities for diversion exist under the current system too as the prosecutor (at the pre-trial stage) or the judge has a discretionary power to divert the child from the penal proceedings or to cancel the case and refer it to the local commissions that could impose educational measures (Article 61 Penal Code in conjunction with Article 13 of the JDA).

The Draft Act maintains the same approach but also seeks to introduce a complete diversion procedure to be used by specialised police officers, public prosecutors or the court (Article 4(1), (4)). The decision to include the police among the authorities mandated to decide on diversion was not unanimous. Similarly, lengthy discussions were held with regard to the criteria for diversion. Reasonable reservations were expressed concerning diversion by the police, based on 'capacity' and 'integrity' concerns and the majority was inclined to leave the decision entirely to the prosecutor and the judge. The final Draft Act attempts to balance the two views and, more importantly, the concern that diversion should be based on a clear legal ground rather than on discretion. The rule proposed is that diversion should take place where the relevant authority believes that educational measures will be appropriate to encourage the lawful behaviour

[26] For six consecutive years the National Network for Children, the main umbrella NGO in Bulgaria, has produced an evaluation of the state policies and legislation in the sectors relevant to child rights protection. Usually the child protection system receives low scores: <http://nmd.bg/wp-content/uploads/2017/05/REPORT-CARD-2017_en.pdf>.

of the juvenile and to support his/her personality development (Article 4(5)). Furthermore, diversion may be carried out for any offence, except for crimes that are punishable by 10 or more years of imprisonment (Article 4(6)).

Diversion can only take place if the child has given consent after he/she has been informed in an appropriate way of the nature of the proceedings and the contents and effects of the educational measures. Where the juvenile has not given his/her consent, criminal judicial proceedings shall follow in accordance with the general rules (Article 4(2)). The proposed rules governing diversion have not raised any objection so far on the part of prosecution and judiciary.

4.2. SPECIALISATION

The Draft Act stipulates that the whole range of professionals would be involved in its implementation, all of whom should have specialised knowledge of the rights of the child and the rules governing children in conflict with the law (Article 7). Such a stipulation is unique in Bulgarian legislation. It particularly applies to judges, public prosecutors, investigating authorities and specialised police officers, but also to lawyers representing the child, officials involved in the implementation of the Act, and the persons participating in the implementation of the educational measures or providing the relevant services. The Draft Act also requires appropriate standards to be adopted for the different professions by the relevant bodies.

There are no specialised courts in Bulgaria for children in conflict with the law but there have been specialised investigation and prosecution offices[27] and there is now a requirement for such specialised investigations.[28] The debate on specialisation is long-standing and can be found in the policy documents[29] as well as in numerous recommendations by the CRC Committee.[30] However the reforms have been put on hold for so many years that the substantive debates have lost their impetus. These in fact never attracted much attention from the judiciary but rather from civil society organisations and some academics.[31]

---

27 Since 2012, by virtue of Order of the General Prosecutor, some specialisation started in the public prosecutors for juvenile cases but it does not have a clear basis in the law.

28 Although Article 385 of the Penal Procedure Code requires special training for the investigation officers dealing with children in conflict with the law, the provision remains unclear since corresponding rules are missing in the special statutes for police and investigation service.

29 National Concept on Justice for Children (2011) and a Road Map for the implementation of that Concept in 2013, above n. 9.

30 See CRC/C/15/Add.66,1997, para. 34, and the CRC/C/BGR/CO/2 23, 2008, para. 68(d).

31 See more in: V. Todorova, 'Family Justice in Bulgaria: The Old System and the New Demands' in M. Maclean and J. Eekelaar et al. (eds.), *Delivering Family Justice in 21st Century*, Hart Publishing, Oxford 2015. pp. 107–121.

4.3. THE SYSTEM

The current juvenile justice system in Bulgaria consists of (1) the regular court and prosecution system dealing with children aged 14–18 in conflict with the law, and (2) the administrative system (local commissions) particularly designed to deal with prevention and the imposition of measures concerning 8–18 year olds. The local commissions are set up at municipality-level, but are guided by the Central Commission.[32] The commissions do not have permanent staff, apart from a secretary that also fulfils other tasks in the municipality. Representatives of the municipal administration in charge of education, health care and social welfare, of the police, and also NGOs, psychologists, pedagogues, lawyers, medical doctors and public figures are members under the JDA that function on a sessional basis. The members are not specifically trained, nor are there standards for the profession.

Despite their scarce human and financial resources the JDA attributes important functions to the local commissions, e.g. policy development, case management (imposition of educational/disciplinary measures and their implementation), coordination, after care, etc.[33] The wide-ranging nature of these functions means that local commissions cannot be qualified as independent and impartial bodies, since they carry out proceedings and exercise both prosecution and adjudicatory functions, which violates the principle of division of powers. In order to align the *quasi jurisdictional* function[34] of the commissions with human rights standards the JDA was amended in 2004 to secure (some) due process rights for the child.[35]

The above mentioned concerns debated during the last 20 years in Bulgaria resulted in a loss of credibility of the current juvenile justice system. This is despite the fact that it is formally in accordance with Article 40(3) of CRC which encourages States Parties to seek to promote measures for dealing with children alleged as, accused of, or recognised as having infringed the penal law without resorting to judicial proceedings, whenever appropriate and desirable. This is the reason the Draft Act proposes abolishing the JDA and closing down the commissions at central and local levels. The idea is that the functions dealing with children in conflict with the law will be concentrated within a system of specialised police, prosecution and courts. The judicial system would be granted

32 Article 8, para. 2 of the JDA. Aproximately 280 local commissions are functioning in the country; more at: <http://www.ckbppmn.government.bg/localComission/>.

33 Article 10 JDA.

34 See *A and others v Bulgaria*, Application no. 51776/08, ECtHR, 29 November 2011, para. 107.

35 Still, the procedure is inquisitorial and offers weak guarantees for fair trial and for the respect of the right of the child to be heard and for his/her best interests to be taken as the primary consideration.

extensive power to divert the child to a network of services of a different nature – educational, social, therapeutic and others.

4.4. THE MEASURES

The question of measures has also attracted extensive debate. The JDA sets out a list of measures that reflect the concept of non-punitive intervention and, to a certain extent, of restorative justice (Article 13(1)). Two types of measures can be imposed in cases involving children aged 8–18 years, namely, non-custodial measures (imposed by the local commissions and executed in the community/family environment) and custodial measures (placement of the child in a correctional institution). Placement in institutions used to be at the discretion of the local commissions until 2004 when it was transferred to the court. The weakest point of the measures is the lack of the necessary structures, trained professionals and budget allocations for their implementation. The most debatable are the custodial measures.[36] In 2016, a total of 189 children were placed in the two Socio-Pedagogical Boarding Schools[37] (63 children out of 189) and in the four Correctional Boarding Schools[38] (126 children out of 189).[39]

The Government is clear about the shortcomings of these measures but no action has been taken so far. In its reply to the Report of the Commissioner for Human Rights of the Council of Europe (2015) the Government states that: 'In the last two years in the SPBS and in the CBS a number of checks were made by

[36] Placement in Socio-Educational Boarding Schools or in Correctional Boarding Schools (Article 13, para. 1, points 11–13 JDA).

[37] Socio-Pedagogical Boarding Schools (SPBS) are established under Arts. 2, 28–33 of the JDA and the related regulations Schools of the Ministry of Education and Science of 1999. They are institutions for corrective or *preventive* placement for children above the age of eight on the ground of: (1) committed anti-social act; or (2) living in an environment conducive to anti-social behaviour. The measure allows for 'preventive' deprivation of liberty of children from socially disadvantaged families, although education is provided at the institutions. The main reason for keeping SPBS is the need to fill the gap of missing services for children and families from certain communities.

[38] Correctional Boarding Schools (CBS) are established under arts. 2, 28–33 of the JDA and accommodate children above the age of eight, having committed anti-social acts and adolescent offenders for whom the non-custodial disciplinary measures have proven insufficient and no appropriate social environment exists for their normal development. The fact that the majority of children come from family environments, indicates the need for new measures and services that include extensive work with the family.

[39] Due to the constant criticism of these institutions, the Ministry of Education and Science closed down most of them and the number of placements decreased dramatically. The general public shares the concern for their serious contribution to the criminalising of the children placed there. Experts focus on their role of protecting the social order rather than preventing re-offending and supporting the social reintegration of the child. For a systematic and exhaustive critique see: *Children Deprived of Liberty in Central and Eastern Europe: Between Legacy and Reform*, above n. 11, pp. 294–298.

the Ministry of Education and Science, the State Agency for Child Protection, the Supreme Administrative Prosecutor's Office and the Regional Inspectorates on Education. The concrete findings confirm the necessity of *urgent amendments in the respective legislation*. Infringements and omissions have been found out in the activity and the functioning of boarding schools, related not only to the level of the educational process, but also to the insufficient capacity of the staff for unspecific social functions. A change in the model of the activity of these institutions from educational to social is needed, for example by *creating centres near the place of residence of the children*.'[40]

The Draft Act proposes the following system of measures ranked by the intensity of the intervention: cautions; restorative measures; prohibitions; obligations; special supervision; and placement in a centre for educational supervision (Article 9(1)). These measures can be imposed only on criminally liable children aged 14–18 years. The measures are alternatives to penal sanctions[41] and combine punishment with educational and social support to the child who has broken the law.

A great novelty of the Draft Act is the proposal to introduce mediation and a family council (family group conference) to implement the restorative measures. The court may refer the case to mediation with the mutual consent of the victim and the offender in order to reach an agreement between them to eliminate the harm caused. This could take many forms, including through an apology, work or compensation (Article 36 (1)–(2)). Unlike in the civil law justice system, mediation is not part of the Bulgarian penal justice system.[42] NGOs with experience of providing social services within the child protection system have proposed the idea of the family council (family group conference). The family council is tasked with preparing an individual plan for the juvenile in accordance with his/her needs, capabilities and wishes, as well as considering the opinion of the victim.

---

40 See the *Comments of the Bulgarian Government to the Report of the Commissioner for Human Rights following his visit to Bulgaria on 9–11 February 2015* (2015), at: <https://wcd.coe.int/com.instranet.InstraServlet?command=com.instranet.CmdBlobGet&InstranetImage=2779693&SecMode=1&DocId=2289852&Usage=2>. And more at: <http://www.socialplatform.org/blog/civil-dialogue-in-bulgaria-two-versions-of-the-same-story/>.

41 Article 62 of the Penal Code provides for the following penalties to be applied to juveniles: deprivation of liberty; probation; public censure; deprivation of the right to practice a certain profession or activity. The *maximum duration of imprisonment*, which can be imposed on juveniles is up to ten years for children aged between 14 and 16 and up to 12 years for young persons between 16 and 18. Persons under 16 years of age may also be punished with an administrative punishment – detention at the units of the Ministry of the Interior for a term of 15 days or a fine for minor hooliganism. Punishments for juveniles can be replaced, or *reduced* with respect to length and severity. A *life imprisonment* cannot be imposed on children under the age of 18.

42 More on the Bulgarian law and practices on mediation in: V. Todorova, 'Family Justice in Bulgaria: The Old System and the New Demands', above n. 31, pp. 116–118.

Special supervision measures may also be imposed that entail the assignment of a person or family to supervise and support the lawful behaviour and the effective reintegration of the child in the community. This could be carried out by a parent/guardian, teacher, other relatives or foster family. The measure of supervision may be imposed in conjunction with a referral to social, health and educational support programmes and services in the community (Article 19). The only custodial measure is a placement by the court in a Centre for Educational Supervision as a last resort measure (Article 20).

The system of measures is interrelated with the established system of social services in Bulgaria.[43] The idea is that measures should be implemented in a multidisciplinary manner in order to achieve prevention of reoffending and the social reintegration of the child. Thus, the Draft Act aims to create a system that builds on the practices of social services and new services for educational support.[44] The Draft Act also proposes administrative structures be created under the Ministry of Justice that will be responsible for the implementation of the measures in closed cooperation with the social and educational systems.

5. CONCLUSION

The current attempt to reform juvenile justice in Bulgaria reached this exceptional stage due to the strong leadership of experts that worked for the Government in 2009–2013. Following the departure of these experts, the reforms have slowed down to reach the current level of uncertainty. The Ministry of Justice has a Draft Act that could be submitted to Parliament but it lacks confidence and expertise, and the nationalist and populist parties that have entered Parliament could also be an obstacle. On the other hand, there is a strong civil society and community of social service providers who continue to demand reforms and work to counter resistance to them. This is the only bright spot in the gloomy picture of Bulgaria's current policies with regard to the rights of the child.

---

43 The development of the social services sector should be attributed to the Child Protection Act, 2000 and the Social Assistance Act (SAA) 1999. Social services can be provided in the community or in specialised institutions after exhaustion of all other opportunities. Providers of state-funded social services may be NGOs, trade companies, the state and the municipalities, which must be registered or licensed where their services are provided to children. The regulation supported the development of various services, standards and trained providers as well as the demand for services. See more at: <http://bcnl.org/en/analyses/quality-of-the-social-services-in-bulgaria-2008.html>.

44 Created by the new Act on Pre-school and School Education, 2015.

OVERRIDING MANDATORY PROVISIONS IN EU FAMILY LAW REGULATIONS

Dieter Martiny

1. INTRODUCTION

This contribution on overriding mandatory provisions in EU family law is dedicated to my highly esteemed colleague Nigel Lowe. For nearly two decades we have worked together in the Commission on European Family Law (CEFL), to develop common principles in different fields of family law and bridge the differences between civil and common law approaches. Throughout this time I have respected Nigel Lowe's openness to foreign law and his exceptional competence. He has also made outstanding contributions to the Council of Europe[1] and the Hague Conference, in particular on child abduction and child protection.[2] He also recognised the impact of European Union law on family law at an early stage.[3] Today, as we are confronted with a whole range of European Regulations in the field of international family law, we face some challenges as old problems are brought into a new light.

2. THE PROBLEM OF MANDATORY AND OVERRIDING MANDATORY PROVISIONS

Mandatory law (*ius cogens*) means rules that cannot be derogated from by contractual agreement.[4] Such rules are not a new phenomenon in family law. Quite to the contrary, in many fields of family law there was no party autonomy in either domestic or international cases. However, today there is a growing 'contractualisation' in domestic family law.[5] There is also a growing, if limited, recognition of party autonomy in international family law. As a result, the issue of placing limits on this autonomy and the protection of the weaker party has gained importance.[6]

In European private international law the applicable law is determined by uniform conflict-of-laws rules. These provisions generally distinguish between

1 N. Lowe, 'The Impact of the Council of Europe on European Family Law' in J.M. Scherpe (ed.), *European Family Law* vol. I, Edward Elgar, Cheltenham 2016, pp. 95–123.

2 See N. Lowe and M. Nicholls, *International Movement of Children*, 2nd edn., LexisNexis, Bristol 2016.

3 N. Lowe, 'The Growing Influence of the European Union on International Family Law' (2003) 56 *Current Legal Problems* 439–480.

4 See in more detail H.C. Grigoleit, 'Mandatory Law: Fundamental Principles' in J. Basedow, K. Hopt and R. Zimmermann (eds.), *Max Planck Encyclopedia of European Private Law* vol. II, Oxford University Press, Oxford 2012, p. 1126 *et seq.*

5 F. Swennen, 'Private Ordering in Family Law: A Global Perspective' in F. Swennen (ed.), *Contractualisation of Family Law – Global Perspectives*, Springer, Heidelberg 2015, p. 1 *et seq.*

6 See P. Wautelet, 'Party Autonomy in International Family Relationships' in C. Cauffman and J. Smits (eds.), *The Citizen in European Private Law*, Intersentia, Cambridge 2016, pp. 23, 35 *et seq.*

different categories of national mandatory rules. 'Simple' mandatory rules form a part of the applicable law, the *lex causae*.[7] If they are of foreign origin, they will be applied together with the foreign law. This means that in fields where there is party autonomy a choice of a law by the parties is also a choice of the mandatory rules of that law. There is, however, also another category of mandatory provisions. Such rules of fundamental importance are 'internationally mandatory' or 'overriding mandatory' rules.[8] Domestic rules of this kind will be enforced directly also against a chosen foreign law. In this context, many questions have to be answered: should all overriding mandatory provisions be treated alike or are there some provisions which have to be protected at any price? And how is one to handle mandatory provisions of third countries?

3. DIFFERENT TECHNIQUES FOR MANDATORY RULES

3.1. DIFFERENT TECHNIQUES

Overriding mandatory provisions may be applied or taken into account in different ways. In private international law, each subject generally has a defined scope of applicable law and, traditionally, this applicable law also includes mandatory provisions for each jurisdiction. The application of such provisions is therefore subject to the general conflict-of-laws rules. However, in some instances these general rules will not be appropriate because the different aims pursued mean that another law, predominantly the *lex fori*, should be applied. This is particularly the case where party autonomy is involved. There are several mechanisms which are used for establishing a more differentiated connection.

3.2. SPECIAL CONNECTIONS

3.2.1. Establishing Special Connections

One approach for applying a provision in departure from the general conflict-of-laws rules is to formulate a unilateral or even a multilateral rule which is connected to a certain aspect of the issue (a 'special connection'). Such rules, based on appropriate points of connection, can then take into account the

---

7 Other expressions are 'internal' or 'internally' mandatory provisions, see M. McParland, *The Rome I Regulation on the Law Applicable to Contractual Obligations*, Oxford University Press, Oxford 2015, para. 9.156.

8 M. Wilderspin, 'Overriding mandatory provisions' in J. Basedow, G. Rühl, F. Ferrari and P. de Miguel Asensio (eds.), *Encyclopedia of Private International Law* vol. II, Edward Elgar, Cheltenham 2017, p. 1330 *et seq*.

protective purpose of the substantive law provisions and guarantee the application of domestic or foreign law under certain, more or less narrowly defined, circumstances. There are many examples of this approach in international, European and national regulations.

3.2.2. Hague Conventions

A special connection to the habitual residence of the maintenance creditor determines the applicable law for the waiver of maintenance (Article 8(4) Hague Maintenance Protocol 2007).[9] Special mandatory rules are also employed in the Hague conventions. Under the Hague Maintenance Protocol 2007 (the Maintenance Protocol), overriding mandatory provisions are applied in cases where the question of whether the creditor can renounce his or her right to maintenance is otherwise determined by the law of the state of the habitual residence of the creditor. Article 14 of the Maintenance Protocol states that even if the applicable law provides otherwise, the needs of the creditor and the resources of the debtor of maintenance payments shall be taken into account in determining the amount of maintenance. This is a substantive conflict-of-laws rule that is binding on the Contracting States, regardless of the manner in which the law applicable to the maintenance obligation is treated.[10]

3.2.3. National Private International Law

Often there exist more or less differentiated specific conflict-of-laws rules regarding the personal effects of marriage, such as for the liability for obligations regarding household costs[11] or for the need for consent of the other spouse.[12] Another example is the right to use the marital home and the household goods: under German conflict-of-laws rules, the use of the marital home and household goods that are located in Germany is governed by domestic law.[13] The purpose of this rule is to enforce the law of the place of location and the application of the *lex fori*.

---

9 Protocol of 23 November 2007 on the Law Applicable to Maintenance Obligations [2009] OJ L331/19.

10 A. Bonomi, *Explanatory Report on the Hague Protocol of 23 November 2007 on the Law Applicable to Maintenance Obligations*, The Hague 2013, para. 179.

11 For example, in the Netherlands see: Art. 10:39 New Dutch Civil Code. English translation by M.H. ten Wolde et al., (2011) 13 *Yearbook of Private International Law* 657 *et seq*.

12 Art. 10:40 New Dutch CC.

13 Art. 17a German Introductory Act to the Civil Code (IACC), which, however, covers also protective orders against domestic violence. See, for an equivalent multilateral conflict-of-laws rule, Art. 48(3) Belgian Code of Private International Law. Cf. A. Panet, 'Le statut personnel en droit international privé européen : les lois de police comme contrepoids à l'autonomie de la volonté?' *Revue critique de droit international privé* (*Rev. crit. d. i. p.*) 104 (2015), 837, 852.

Matrimonial property is of interest not only to spouses but also for third parties and the general public. Often there is also a special rule for the protection of third parties. This exists in Dutch law[14] and also in the German codification of private international law, where there is a special rule on the protection of third parties. Pursuant to Article 16(1) of the German Introductory Act to the Civil Code (IACC), if the matrimonial regime is governed by foreign law and one of the spouses has his or her habitual residence within Germany or carries on a trade therein, then the effect in relation to third parties applies *mutatis mutandis* and the foreign matrimonial regime is considered as that mutually agreed upon.[15] Objections to a legal transaction can only be made if the marriage contract has been entered in the marriage property register or was known to the third party.[16]

Additionally, under Article 16(2) IACC, where they are more advantageous to a bona fide third party than the foreign law would be, §§1431 and 1456 of the German CC apply *mutatis mutandis* in respect of legal transactions relating to the provision of the necessities of life procured within Germany, and to the presumption as to personal property located in Germany.[17] By contrast, the situation is different in England and Wales due to the lack of matrimonial property law restrictions and the application of the *lex fori* on the consequences of divorce.[18]

3.3. OVERRIDING MANDATORY PROVISIONS

Rules on overriding mandatory provisions are not common in international conventions (for European conflict-of-laws rules see section 4.1). However, the concept of overriding mandatory provisions has developed in the interpretation of private international law in national courts or in legal literature. For example, under French law the '*régime primaire*' applies in matrimonial law.[19] In France there was also a tendency to regard the '*contribution aux charges du mariage*' as directly applicable (or *loi d'application immédiate*),[20] but this is now covered

---

14 See Art. 10:46 New Dutch CC.

15 Art. 16(1) IACC, §1412 German CC.

16 §1412(1) German CC.

17 See §§1357 and 1362 German CC.

18 Cf. N. Lowe and G. Douglas, *Bromley's Family Law*, 11th edn., Oxford University Press, Oxford 2015, pp. 830–832, 920–925.

19 Art. 212 *et seq.* Code civil [CC]. See Cass. civ. 20 octobre 1987, *Rev. crit. d. i. p.* 77 (1988), 540 note Y. Lequette; I. Barrière Brousse, 'Le patrimoine des couples internationaux dans l'espace judiciaire européen' *Journal du droit international (Clunet)* 144 (2017), 485, 489–492; K. Kroll-Ludwigs, *Die Rolle der Parteiautonomie im europäischen Kollisionsrecht*, Mohr Siebeck, Tübingen 2013, pp. 552–553.

20 Art. 214 CC. See Cass. civ. 20 octobre 1987, *Rev. crit. d. i. p.* 77 (1988), 540 note Y. Lequette.

by the Hague Maintenance Protocol. The principle of overriding mandatory provisions has also been codified in several Member States, e.g. in Belgium[21] and the Netherlands.[22] It is, however, not easy to determine under what circumstances these rules find application in family law. Furthermore, foreign overriding mandatory provisions pose special problems.

3.4. PUBLIC POLICY

Public policy had traditionally been used as an exception to certain rules to allow domestic courts to protect what they consider to be fundamental values. Such a clause is used in the Hague Conventions, for example, in the fields of maintenance obligations[23] and matrimonial property.[24] Under the Matrimonial Property Regulations the application of a foreign law may be refused if such application is manifestly incompatible with national public policy.[25] This approach corresponds with the provisions of other Regulations.[26]

There are also many examples of the use of public policy in the interpretation of private international law by the national courts. One such instance relates to discriminatory foreign law rules. Here, public policy is generally invoked in its negative function – to resist the use of an offending foreign law. However, public policy may also be used in the opposite way, i.e. to justify making domestic

---

21 Art. 20 Belgian Code of PIL of 16 July 2004. English translation *Rabels Zeitschrift für ausländisches und internationales Privatrecht* 70 (2006) 235 *et seq.*

22 Art. 10:7 New Dutch CC.

23 Art. 13 Hague Maintenance Protocol 2007.

24 Art. 14 Hague Convention of 14 March 1978 on the Law Applicable to Matrimonial Property Regimes (1977) 16 ILM 14.

25 Art. 31 Council Regulation (EU) 2016/1103 of 24 June 2016 implementing enhanced cooperation in the area of jurisdiction, applicable law and the recognition and enforcement of decisions in matters of matrimonial property regimes [2016] OJ L183/1 ('Matr. Prop. Reg.'); Art. 31 Council Regulation (EU) 2016/1104 of 24 June 2016 implementing enhanced cooperation in the area of jurisdiction, applicable law and the recognition and enforcement of decisions in matters of the property consequences of registered partnerships [2016] OJ L183/30 ('Part. Reg.').

26 Art. 21 Regulation (EC) No. 593/2008 of 17 June 2008 on the law applicable to contractual obligations ('Rome I Reg.') [2008] OJ L177/6; Art. 26 Regulation (EC) No. 864/2007 of 11 July 2007 on the law applicable to non-contractual obligations ('Rome II Reg.') [2007] OJ L199/40; Art. 12 Council Regulation (EU) No. 1259/2010 of 20 December 2010 implementing enhanced cooperation in the area of the law applicable to divorce and legal separation ('Rome III Reg.') [2010] OJ L343/10; Art. 35 Regulation (EU) No. 650/2012 of 4 July 2012 on jurisdiction, applicable law, recognition and enforcement of decisions and acceptance and enforcement of authentic instruments in matters of succession and on the creation of a European Certificate of Succession [2012] OJ L201/107 ('Succession Reg.'). Cf. K. Kroll-Ludwigs, above n. 19, pp. 557–559.

provisions directly applicable. Today this approach is increasingly superseded by rules on overriding mandatory provisions.[27]

4. EUROPEAN CONFLICT-OF-LAWS RULES ON OVERRIDING MANDATORY PROVISIONS

4.1. DIFFERENT CATEGORIES OF OVERRIDING MANDATORY PROVISIONS

4.1.1. European Approach

Apart from where the *lex fori* applies, European international family law mainly follows the traditional continental approach where the applicable law is determined by employing objective connecting factors and to a certain extent also by party autonomy. Also, in principle, the applicable law encompasses (simple) mandatory rules. This approach can pose difficulties as it must first be determined what is covered by the applicable law. Generally there is a provision listing the different issues covered by the Regulation.[28]

4.1.2. Definition of Overriding Mandatory Provisions

In European private international law, the overriding mandatory provisions of the *lex fori* are generally enforced by way of an exception. According to Article 9(1) Rome I on contractual obligations, overriding mandatory provisions are provisions to be used by Member States in order to safeguard their public interests, such as political, social or economic interests, irrespective of the law otherwise applicable to the contract. Article 16 Rome II on non-contractual obligations follows the same approach. This so-called *Arblade* formula was developed in the case law of the European Court of Justice.[29] This definition is aimed mainly at economic laws and was not originally developed in the context of private international law but rather in relation to the fundamental rights of Union law.

---

27 See D. Martiny, 'Public Policy' in J. Basedow, K. Hopt and R. Zimmermann (eds.), *Max Planck Encyclopedia of European Private Law* vol. II, Oxford University Press, Oxford 2012, p. 1395 *et seq*.

28 See the scope of the applicable law in Art. 27 Matr. Prop. Reg./Part. Reg., Art. 12 Rome I Reg., Art. 15 Rome II Reg., Art. 23 Succession Reg.

29 Joined Cases C-369/96 and C-376/96, *Criminal proceedings against J.-C. Arblade and Arblade & Fils SARL* (C-369/96) *and B. Leloup, S. Leloup and Sofrage SARL* (C-376/96), ECLI:EU:C:1999:575. See M. Wilderspin, above n. 8, pp. 1330, 1331–1334.

Though overriding mandatory provisions are the exceptions, the dividing line between them and simple mandatory provisions can be difficult to draw.[30] There has always been a tendency to declare simple mandatory rules as overriding provisions and it is also unclear whether provisions can be overriding mandatory provisions while at the same time being provisions generally setting forth the applicable law.[31] This issue is often very relevant in contractual relationships where only the general conflict-of-laws rules apply (for example, commercial agents),[32] as some contractual relationships contain special provisions (e.g. consumer contracts, individual labour contracts, insurance).[33]

The European Succession Regulation relates to national special rules imposing restrictions concerning or affecting succession with regard to certain assets, namely certain immovable property or enterprises located in states which, for economic, family or social considerations, restrict succession in relation to such assets. The European Succession Regulation states that the rules of the state in which the property is located should apply to the succession in so far as, under the law of that state, they are applicable irrespective of the law applicable to the succession.[34] For example, national domestic or foreign overriding mandatory provisions still apply with regard to farmland[35] and a proposal to introduce general overriding mandatory provisions was unsuccessful.[36]

4.1.3. Overriding Mandatory Provisions of the Lex Fori

Under Article 9(2) Rome I, nothing in the Regulation shall restrict the application of overriding mandatory provisions of the *lex fori* on contracts. Likewise, pursuant to Article 16 Rome II Regulation, overriding mandatory provisions of the *lex fori* are to be applied.

A special case is Article 10 Rome III on the application of the law of the forum. This states that the *lex fori* shall apply where the applicable law makes no provision for divorce or denies one of the spouses equal access to divorce or legal separation on the grounds of their sex. Since the introduction of divorce in Malta, there are only a few jurisdictions which do not have legal provisions for divorce, e.g. the Philippines. An extensive debate has developed on the second

30 H. J. Sonnenberger, 'Overriding mandatory provisions' in S. Leible (ed.), *General principles of European private international law*, Wolters Kluwer, Alphen aan den Rijn 2016, pp. 117, 121–123; M. Wilderspin, above n. 8, pp. 1330, 1331.

31 See M. Wilderspin in R. Plender and M. Wilderspin, *The European private international law of obligations*, 4th edn., Sweet & Maxwell, London 2015, para. 12-046.

32 See Arts. 3 and 4 Rome I Reg.

33 See the *leges speciales* Arts. 6, 7 and 8 Rome I Reg.

34 Art. 30 Succession Reg.

35 K. Kroll-Ludwigs, above n. 19, pp. 554–557; P. Wautelet in A. Bonomi and P. Wautelet (eds.), *Le droit européen des successions*, 2nd edn., Bruylant, Brussels 2016, Article 30 paras. 1, 5. P. Wautelet, ibid. Article 30 para. 19.

36 See P. Wautelet, above n. 35, Article 30 para. 3.

scenario regarding unequal access to divorce. One interpretation is similar to a public policy clause and looks for intolerable effects in the individual case.[37] The other approach is more abstract, in the sense of a domestic overriding mandatory provision,[38] for example, Islamic law would already lead to an exclusion of this law – which seems to be an unnecessarily harsh response. One consequence would be that for example a divorce by *talaq* could, per se, not be recognised.[39]

4.1.4. Foreign Overriding Mandatory Provisions

Foreign overriding mandatory provisions were initially given special treatment under Article 7(1) Rome Convention.[40] This states that, when applying national law, effect may be given to the mandatory rules of the law of another state with which the situation has a close connection. In considering whether to give effect to these mandatory rules, regard shall be had to their nature and purpose and to the consequences of their application or non-application. This rule was highly controversial and some countries, such as Germany and the United Kingdom, made use of an opt-out reservation. There was an extensive debate over the circumstances in which the provision should apply and what 'taking into account' means.[41] There is always a dilemma between favouring a party under factual pressure to obey the foreign rule and the need for setting clear boundaries as to when contractual obligations may be displaced.

The successor provision of Article 9(3) Rome I contains a much more restrictive rule.[42] This states that effect may only be given to the overriding mandatory provisions of the law of the country where the obligations arising out of the contract have to be or have been performed, in so far as those provisions render the performance of the contract unlawful. For example, Greek

---

37 Cf. H. Duintjer Tebbens, 'Divorce – A Fundamental Right?' in Permanent Bureau of the Hague Conference on Private International Law (ed.), *A Commitment to Private International Law – Essays in Honour of Hans van Loon*, Intersentia, Antwerp 2013, pp. 123, 129–130.

38 P. Winkler von Mohrenfels, 'Art. 10 Rome III-VO: Kollisionsrechtliche Eingriffsnorm oder Spezialfall des ordre public?' in N. Witzleb, R. Ellger, P. Mankowski, H. Merkt and O. Remien (eds.), *Festschrift für Dieter Martiny*, Mohr Siebeck, Tübingen 2014, pp. 595 *et seq*; A. Sahner, 'Europeanization and doctrines of Private International Law: New Developments in International Family Law' in B. Heiderhoff and I. Queirolo (eds.), *European and international cross-border private and economic relationships and individual rights*, Aracne editrice, Ariccia 2016, pp. 159, 215–217.

39 This approach has been proposed, however, in the conclusions presented on 14 September 2017 by the Advocate-General of the European Court of Justice Saugmandsgaard Øe in Case C-372/16 *Soha Sahyouni v Raja Mamisch*, ECLI:EU:C:2017:686, para. 90–104.

40 Rome Convention on the law applicable to contractual obligations of 19 June 1980 [1980] OJ L1.

41 See M. Wilderspin, above n. 31, para. 12.038.

42 See H. J. Sonnenberger, above n. 30, 123–127. For the legislative history see M. McParland, *The Rome I Regulation on the Law Applicable to Contractual Obligations*, Oxford University Press, Oxford 2015, paras. 15.57–15.90.

emergency measures to reduce the public wage bill are only given effect abroad as overriding mandatory provisions of the place of performance. This is not the case for a Greek teacher teaching in Germany under an employment contract subject to German law. However, overriding mandatory laws of a third state (in this case Greece) may nevertheless be taken into account as a matter of fact if the applicable German law so allows.[43] Not all European Regulations contain rules on foreign overriding mandatory provisions. Such provisions are not dealt with in Article 16 Rome II. There is a debate as to whether this is a deliberate exclusion[44] or simply a gap which could be filled by an extensive interpretation or in combination with national conflict-of-laws rules.[45]

4.2. MATRIMONIAL PROPERTY REGIMES

4.2.1. *Broad Approach Toward Matrimonial Property Consequences*

The Matrimonial Property Regulations use a broad concept of matrimonial property law and matrimonial property consequences,[46] for which an autonomous European characterisation is necessary.[47] The scope of the Regulations is defined by the provisions on the scope of the applicable law in Article 27, which contains a list of issues.[48] All rules concerning the property relationships – and not only object-related matrimonial property rules – are within their scope.[49] This includes both the matrimonial property regime in the narrow sense and also all property-related conditions arising between the spouses and in connection with third-party relations when such conditions result directly from the matrimonial relationship or its dissolution.[50] Therefore, general or personal effects of marriage

---

43 See Case C-135/15, *Republik Griechenland v Grigorios Nikiforidis*, ECLI:EU:C:2016:774.

44 A. Dickinson, *The Rome II Regulation*, Oxford University Press, Oxford 2008, para. 15.25; D. Jakob and P. Picht in T. Rauscher (ed.), *Europäisches Zivilprozess- und Kollisionsrecht EuZPR/EuIPR* III, 4th edn., Otto Schmidt, Köln 2016, Art. 16 Rom II-VO para. 9; M. Wilderspin, above n. 31, para. 27-007.

45 For a consideration of foreign mandatory rules as so-called moral data, J. von Hein in G.-P. Calliess (ed.), *Rome Regulations*, 2nd edn., Kluwer Law International, Alphen aan den Rijn 2015, Art. 16 Rome II para. 21.

46 Art. 1(1), Art. 3(1)(a) Matr. Prop. Reg., Art. 1(1), Art. 3(1)(b) Part. Reg.

47 Recital 18 Matr. Prop. Reg./Part. Reg.

48 See Art. 27 Matr. Prop. Reg./Part. Reg.

49 Recital 18 Matr. Prop. Reg.

50 The *Document de travail des Services de la Commission* lists in Annexe 1 the contributions of the spouses to the expenses of the marriage, responsibility for household debts, protection of the family home, free exercise of a profession, right to a personal deposit account and a securities account, right to representation and protection against acts endangering the interests of the family. See *Annexe au Livre Vert sur le règlement des conflits de lois en matière de régime matrimonial, traitant notamment de la question de la compétence judiciaire et de la reconnaissance mutuelle*, COM(2006) 400 final.

are also within the scope of the Regulation, for example restrictions on disposal (Article 27(d)). This is of particular importance in France, where the '*régime primaire*' – rules for all marriages – is distinguished from the matrimonial property regime.[51] The French approach observes the principles of equality and solidarity between spouses and, to a certain extent, this approach has also been followed by the CEFL Principles on matrimonial property.[52] The '*régime primaire*' covers personal effects but also the spouses' mutual maintenance obligation and other rules on patrimonial matters of French law. Despite some doubts, the patrimonial effects are, in principle, included in the Regulation.[53]

The relationship with third parties, particularly creditors, is also protected by general mandatory provisions.[54]

One difficulty here is that issues of matrimonial property often overlap with other questions, which raises problems of characterisation and it is often not totally clear what is covered by the Regulations and what is not. On the whole, immutability of the matrimonial property regime (Article 26), unity of the applicable law (Article 21) and the exclusion of *renvoi* (Article 32) provoke possible contradictions with the law of property and the law of the place where the couple actually lives.

4.2.2. *Overriding Mandatory Provisions*

4.2.2.1. Respecting Overriding Mandatory Provisions

As with other European Regulations, the Matrimonial Property Regulations adopt the concept of overriding mandatory provisions. The ordinary connection does not affect the application of overriding mandatory provisions of the law of the forum.[55] Article 30(2) of the Matrimonial Property Regulations repeats the classical *Arblade*-formula: that respect for overriding mandatory provisions is regarded by a Member State as crucial for safeguarding its public interests, such as its political, social or economic organisation.[56] It must be assumed that the

51 See H. Péroz, 'Les lois applicables au régime primaire', *Clunet* 144 (2017), 813 *et seq.*

52 See general rights and duties in Principles 4:1–4:9; K. Boele-Woelki, F. Ferrand, C. González Beilfuss, M. Jänterä-Jareborg, N. Lowe, D. Martiny and W. Pintens, *Principles of European Family Law regarding Property Relations between Spouses*, Intersentia, Cambridge 2013.

53 L. Perreau-Saussine, 'Le nouveau Règlement européen "Régimes matrimoniaux"' *Semaine Juridique (JCP)* 2016, 1926, 1928–1929. – I. Barrière Brousse, *Clunet* 144 (2017), 485, 490–491 argues, however, that this would be an encroachment in the personal effects of marriage.

54 *Document de travail*, above n. 50, para. 3.

55 Art. 30(1) Matr. Prop. Reg. Critical, A. Panet, *Rev. crit. d. i. p.* 104 (2015), 837, 853 ff.; K. Kroll-Ludwigs, above n. 19, pp. 564–567.

56 Recital 53 Matr. Prop. Reg./Part. Reg.; Art. 30(1) Matr. Prop. Reg./Part. Reg.

protection of private interests alone is not sufficient for a characterisation as an overriding mandatory provision and it is necessary that

> public order legislation applies to national provisions compliance with which has been deemed to be so crucial for the protection of the political, social or economic order in the Member State concerned as to require compliance therewith by all persons present on the national territory of that Member State and all legal relationships within that State.[57]

Nevertheless, it cannot be ignored that the *Arblade*-formula is not particularly well suited to the field of matrimonial property.[58] To a certain extent, the concept of overriding mandatory provisions transforms the problem into one regarding the reach of national substantive law, and in so doing it leaves open a considerable margin of appreciation.

4.2.2.2. Categories of Overriding Mandatory Provisions

It is uncertain what kind of overriding mandatory provisions of the *lex fori* are covered by the Matrimonial Property Regulations. The Recitals explain that overriding mandatory provisions cover rules of an imperative nature, such as rules for the protection of the family home.[59] However, this is the only example given. Recital 53 states that the exception has to be interpreted strictly in order to remain compatible with the general objective of the Regulations.[60] However, it is arguable that a special connection providing for the protection of the family home according to the *lex fori* would have been a better solution.[61]

Under the existing law it is left open which other aspects could be characterised as overriding mandatory provisions. There can be no uniform answer but it is particularly doubtful whether the broad French approach is reflected. One issue is joint liability for household debts.[62] Others are the right to representation and protection against acts endangering the interests of the family.[63] There are also doubts as to the need for consent of the other spouse concerning donations or the giving of guarantees.[64]

---

57 Case C-184/12, *United Antwerp Maritime Agencies (Unamar) NV v Navigation Maritime Bulgare*, ECLI:EU:C:2013:663 n. 47.

58 See in more detail K. Kroll-Ludwigs, above n. 19, pp. 551–557.

59 Recital 53 Matr. Prop. Reg. See, for example, Art. 215(3) French CC. Agreeing H. Péroz *Clunet* 144 (2017), 813, 823/824, 828; L. Perreau-Saussine *JCP* 2016, 1926, 1928–1929. Contra I. Barrière Brousse *Clunet* 144 (2017), 485, 491–492.

60 Recital 53 Matr. Prop. Reg.

61 A. Panet, *Rev. crit. d. i. p.* 104 (2015), 837, 854 *et seq.*

62 Art. 220 French CC. Contra H. Péroz *Clunet* 144 (2017), 813, 828.

63 Arts. 217, 218, 220-1 French CC.

64 M.H. ten Wolde, 'Voortvarend Nederlands voorzitterschap! De Verordening huwelijksvermogensstelsels 2016' *Nederlands Internationaal Privaatrecht (NIPR)* 2016, 248, 257.

As to the fate of the special connections contained in national private international law, several questions arise. A special connection can be upheld only if its content is not covered by the Regulation. Because there are no pertinent special connections in the Regulations, the general applicable law can lead to conflicts. There is, therefore, a certain pressure to replace special connections of national law with the search for overriding mandatory provisions.

This has consequences, for example, regarding liability for obligations in connection with household costs.[65] It is not clear whether the German conflict-of-law rule on the contractual liability of the spouses vis-à-vis third parties in Article 16(2) IACC will be affected by the Regulation.[66] It has also been argued that the German conflict-of-law rule in Article 17(a) IACC on the use of the matrimonial home and household goods is superseded by the Regulation, but that as an overriding mandatory provision it will not ultimately be impacted by the Regulation.[67] The same result was proposed for the similar §82(2) Austrian Civil Code.[68]

4.2.2.3. Foreign Overriding Mandatory Provisions

In contrast to Rome I but in line with Rome II, neither the Matrimonial Property Regulation nor the Partnership Regulation has a provision on overriding mandatory provisions of third countries. It has been argued that foreign provisions are not covered[69] but it is doubtful that there are situations of a significant importance where there is a similar factual need to follow such foreign rules.[70] Registration rules remain outside the scope of the Regulation (Article 1(h)).

4.3. CONFLICT WITH THIRD-PARTY PROTECTION

The effects of the matrimonial property regime on a legal relationship between a spouse and a third party also fall within the scope of the Regulation.[71] Thus, the

65 Art. 27(c) Matr. Prop. Reg.

66 Superseded according to B. Heiderhoff, 'Vorschläge zur Durchführung der EU-Güterrechts-Verordnungen' *Praxis des Internationalen Privat- und Verfahrensrechts (IPRax)* 2017, 231, 235. Undecided, D. Henrich, 'Zur EU-Güterrechtsverordnung' *Zeitschrift für Europarecht, internationales Privatrecht und Rechtsvergleichung (ZfRV)* 2016, 171, 174.

67 D. Henrich *ZfRV* 2016, 171, 173.

68 Ibid.

69 M.H. ten Wolde *NIPR* 2016, 248, 257; K. Dengel, *Die europäische Vereinheitlichung des internationalen Ehegüterrechts und des internationalen Güterrechts für eingetragene Partnerschaften*, Mohr Siebeck, Tübingen 2014, p. 347.

70 K. Kroll-Ludwigs, above n. 19, pp. 555–556.

71 Art. 27(f).

Regulation covers, for example, not only restrictions on the sale of the property as a whole[72] but also rules on the liability of the other spouse for contracts for the purchase of necessities.[73] However, there is a special provision in Article 28 which deals with the effects in respect of third parties. Notwithstanding Article 27(f), the law applicable to the matrimonial property regime may not be invoked under certain conditions. A spouse cannot rely on it against a third party unless the third party knew or, in the exercise of due diligence, should have known of that law (Article 28(1)). Article 28(2)(a) contains a detailed list of contexts where the third party's knowledge of the law is deemed to exist. These include (1) the law applicable to the transaction, (2) the law of the parties' habitual residence and (3) the law of the *lex rei sitae*. The observance of the rules on publicity is also deemed equivalent to knowledge (Article 28(2)(b)). If the protective rule cannot be invoked, the effects of the matrimonial property shall be governed, inter alia, by the law of the state in which the property is situated or in which the assets or rights are registered (Article 28(3)).

There is, however, no provision clarifying the relationship between overriding mandatory provisions and the protection of third parties.[74] This becomes relevant, for example, if there is a restriction such as Article 215(3) French Civil Code. One could argue that such provisions remain unaffected by the good faith provisions of Article 28 due to the wording of the Regulation, their nature and their protective propose.[75] The mandatory application cannot be ousted by the subjective knowledge of a third party. Article 28 would make the overriding mandatory provision at least partially ineffective. Another approach, more favourable for business transactions, is that the protection of third parties follows a balanced approach, which is also in this context applicable.[76] It can be assumed that the question is unlikely to find a definite answer without a decision of the ECJ.

5. CONCLUSION

The concept of overriding mandatory provisions, in the past applied mainly in the law of international obligations, is now also being used in matrimonial

72 For example, see §1368 German CC and D. Henrich, *ZfRV* 2016, 171, 174.

73 For example see §1357 German CC and D. Henrich, *ZfRV* 2016, 171, 174. Questionable according to B. Heiderhoff, *IPRax* 2017, 231, 232, 235.

74 See for the draft D. Martiny, 'The Effects of Marital Property Agreements in respect of Third Parties' in A.-L. Verbeke, J.M. Scherpe and C. Declerck (eds.), *Confronting the Frontiers of Family and Succession Law – Liber amicorum Walter Pintens* vol. I, Intersentia, Antwerp 2012, p. 903.

75 A. Dutta, 'Das neue internationale Güterrecht der Europäischen Union' *Zeitschrift für das gesamte Familienrecht* 2016, 1973, 1983.

76 J. Weber, 'Die Europäischen Güterrechtsverordnungen' *Deutsche Notar-Zeitschrift* 2016, 659, 688.

property law. Through this approach fundamental mandatory provisions may be enforced. This also means, however, that difficulties already known from the law of obligations now have to be resolved in international family law as well. The original concept, with its emphasis on the tensions between contractual freedom and economic law regulation, has to be adapted to matrimonial property, which, with the focus on the protection of family interests, may be understood as a case of 'social or economic order'.

The application of overriding mandatory provisions restricts the broad scope of the applicable matrimonial property law, and the impact of this rather rigid technique is not yet totally clear. One of the effects of the Matrimonial Property Regulations is that some national connections (particularly special connections) and the correspondingly applicable national law will not be given effect in the forum state. Consequently, there may be a temptation to replace certain, previously applicable, national connections through the application of overriding mandatory provisions; this, in turn, may result in the substantive law of the forum state being too readily characterised as having an overriding mandatory nature. The overriding mandatory provisions approach inherently risks giving national (i.e. forum state) protective provisions too much weight. It would perhaps have been a more appropriate and more flexible solution if the Regulations had prescribed a special connection for sensitive issues. In any event, it will be necessary to narrowly interpret the application of overriding mandatory provisions.

Another field of uncertainty is the unsolved relationship between overriding mandatory provisions and the protection of third parties. These difficulties are another example of the limits of a European unification which is restricted only to private international law.

PART III

THE FUTURE FOR FAMILY AND CHILD LAW

THE HAGUE CHILD ABDUCTION CONVENTION IN A CHANGING WORLD

Rhona SCHUZ

1. INTRODUCTION

The world has changed in many different ways over the four decades which have passed since the Permanent Bureau of the Hague Conference on Private International Law started researching the subject of international child abduction in 1977. This research led to the drawing up of the 1980 Convention on the Civil Aspects of International Child Abduction ('Abduction Convention'), the express aim of which is to protect children from the harmful effects of international abductions. Many of the changes which have taken place have had a significant impact on the phenomenon of international child abduction and the implementation of the mandatory return mechanism adopted in the Convention. These changes include: new social norms and trends which have resulted in changes in the characteristics of abductors; new legal norms, especially increased recognition of the human rights of children and their parents relevant to family disputes; and new psychological and other research which provides insights, inter alia, in relation to the developing capacities of children and the impact on them of separation from primary caregivers and exposure to domestic violence. In addition, regional and global political developments have, on the one hand, resulted in the European Union adopting its own distinct model for intra-EU cases and, on the other hand, led to a continuing worldwide expansion of the Abduction Convention, including accession by a wider variety of states (including Japan, Iraq, Russia and Pakistan) whose legal systems, political climate and culture are quite different from the liberal, secular Western democracies of most veteran Contracting States. The objective of this chapter is to consider some of the challenges which the Abduction Convention now faces in the light of the various developments mentioned above and to suggest courses of action which might help to promote uniform, child-centred and effective implementation of the Convention. I will divide these challenges into three: interpretation and application (section 2); child participation (section 3); and compliance (section 4).

A chapter on the continuing challenges faced in implementing the Abduction Convention is particularly appropriate for a volume in honour of Nigel Lowe, in light of the remarkable contribution which Nigel has made to the literature on this Convention over the past two decades. In addition to his major book with Michael Nicholls, *International Movement of Children*,[1] which includes a comprehensive treatment of the Convention and many academic articles dealing with particular aspects of the Convention, Nigel also co-authored a series of country reports, which provided highly useful information on the way in which the Convention was applied in different Member States. Perhaps Nigel's most unique contribution has been his empirical research, published as four statistical surveys, providing data in relation to the implementation of the Convention worldwide in 1999, 2003, 2008 and 2015.[2] These surveys are absolutely invaluable in enabling us to understand the working of the Convention globally, regionally and nationally and to detect changing trends over the years. The recently published 2015 Survey shows a relatively modest increase in Convention applications worldwide,[3] no real change in the global return rate[4] and an improvement in the average time taken to process applications.[5] I will be referring to specific findings of this survey in the course of the chapter.

---

1 N. Lowe and M. Nicholls, *International Movement of Children: Law Practice and Procedure*, 2nd edn., Jordans, Bristol 2016.

2 N. Lowe and V. Stephens, *Part I: A Statistical Analysis of Applications Made in 2015 under the Hague Convention of 25 October 1980 on the Civil Aspects of International Child Abduction – Global Report* (Preliminary Document No. 11A. Revised version, February 2018), Permanent Bureau of the Hague Conference, The Hague 2018. Available at: <https://www.hcch.net/en/publications-and-studies/details4/?pid=6545&dtid=57>. Published to inform the 7th Meeting of the Special Commission on the Practical Operation of the 1980 Hague Child Abduction Convention and the 1996 Hague Child Protection Convention (October 2017).

3 2,270 return applications made to 72 central authorities (does not include applications made directly to the courts of the requested state), ibid. at 6.

4 45% (this figure is based on 2,002 applications). This is slightly lower than in 2008 (46%) and considerably lower than in 2003 (51%) and 1999 (50%). However, it should be noted that there is a reduction in the number of cases withdrawn (14% as opposed to 18%) and pending (6% as opposed to 8%) and a large increase in 'other outcomes' (16% as opposed to 4%), ibid. at 11.

5 164 days compared to 188 days in 2008, ibid. at 20.

2. INTERPRETATION AND APPLICATION

Whilst the number of Contracting States, currently 98[6] and the continually increasing number of applications are clearly a considerable achievement, the true test of success is implementation of the Convention in a way which promotes its objectives. This in turn requires uniform interpretation and application of the Convention. However, in fact, perusal of the case law reveals considerable disparities in interpreting and applying some of the concepts in the Convention in different jurisdictions and sometimes even within jurisdictions.[7] In this section, I will discuss briefly two of these concepts and analyse the impact of recent case law and other developments.

2.1. HABITUAL RESIDENCE

One of the most difficult concepts in the Convention, apparently not anticipated by the drafters of the Convention, has proved to be that of habitual residence. Over time, it became clear that different approaches[8] were being used in the critical determination of where the child was habitually resident immediately before the wrongful removal or retention.[9] Some judges treat the intention of the parent(s) who had the right to decide where the child lived as determinative, whilst others take a more child-centric approach, looking at the objective facts relevant to the degree of integration of the child in the environment in question. In recent years, a number of jurisdictions, including significantly the EU,[10] have adopted a hybrid approach, similar to that advocated by the current

---

6 Status Table (as of 21.08.2017) <https://www.hcch.net/en/instruments/conventions/status-table/?cid=24>.

7 R. Schuz, 'Disparity and the Quest for Uniformity in Implementing the Hague Child Abduction Convention' (2014) 9 *Journal of Comparative Law* 3.

8 R. Schuz, 'Habitual Residence of Children under the Hague Child Abduction Convention – Theory and Practice' (2001) 13 *Family and Child Law Quarterly* 1.

9 Habitual residence in a Contracting State other than the requested State is one of the conditions for triggering the mandatory return mechanism. For detailed discussion of the role of concept of habitual residence in the Abduction Convention, see R. Schuz, *The Hague Child Abduction Convention – A Critical Analysis*, Hart Publishing, Oxford 2013, 180–185.

10 See Case C-523/07 *In Proceedings brought by A*, [2009] ECR I-2805 [38] and Case C-497/10 PU *Mercredi v Chaffe* [2011] 1 FLR 1293. For discussion of adoption of this approach by the UK Supreme Court, see R. Schuz, 'Habitual Residence of the Child Revisited: A Trilogy of Cases in the UK Supreme Court' (2014) 26 *Child and Family Law Quarterly* 342 (Schuz, 'Trilogy'). It should be noted that not all judges in the EC appear to have internalised the child-centric approach. See, e.g. the judgment of Ryan J in the Irish Court of Appeal in *KW v PW* [2016] IECA 364, where the emphasis was on the whether the mother had consented to the move from Australia to Ireland, and compare with the judgment of Hogan J who looked at the short period in Ireland from the children's point of view.

author in 2001,[11] which, whilst taking a factual approach, treats the intention of the parents as a relevant factor.[12] Some of the implications of the hybrid approach have been clarified in recent cases. Thus, for example, the CJEU has held that a child cannot be habitually resident in a place where he has never been physically present.[13] Similarly, the UK Supreme Court has held that there is now no rule that one parent cannot unilaterally change the child's habitual residence,[14] and that when a child moves lawfully from one country to another, the fact that his parent(s) intend(s) to abandon the former habitual residence will not, per se, result in the child losing his habitual residence prior to acquiring a habitual residence in the new country.[15]

However, the parental intention approach is still applied by most Circuits in the US[16] and, until very recently, in Canada.[17] Moreover, greater consensus in relation to the test to be applied in determining habitual residence will not, per se, resolve all problems. In particular, it is still far from clear what will be the impact of the temporary or potentially temporary nature of the stay in the new country.[18] Take, for example, the case of *AR v RN (Scotland)*,[19] in which it was undisputed that the parents had intended the mother and children to stay in Scotland for a year during her maternity leave. The UK Supreme Court upheld the decision of the Inner House of the Court of Session that the children's

---

11 R. Schuz, 'Habitual Residence' above n. 8, 16.

12 See R. Schuz, *The Hague Child Abduction Convention*, above n. 9, 192–195.

13 CJEU in Case C-111/17 PPU *OL v PQ*, ECLI:EU:C:2017:436. This accords with the view of the majority of the UK Supreme Court in *A v A and Another (Children: Habitual Residence) (Reunite International Child Abduction Centre and Others Intervening)* [2013] UKSC 60, discussed in R. Schuz, 'A Trilogy', above n. 10, 352–355.

14 *AR v RN (Scotland)* [2015] UKSC 35, [17]. One consequence of this change, together with the focus on the integration of the child, is in that in cases of unlawful retention following an agreed stay for an extended period, the child's habitual residence may change at some point before the date planned for return and so at the date of retention, the Convention will no longer apply. This can be seen from the recent case of *Re C (Children)* [2018] UKSC 8, in which the UK Supreme Court held that repudiatory retention can occur before the planned date of return, where the travelling parent's intention not to return is manifested by some objectively identified act or statement, ibid. at [51].

15 *Re B (A Child)* [2016] UKSC 4 (holding that the relevant question was whether at the relevant time, there had been 'a requisite degree of disengagement' from the environment in the country where the child had been habitually resident before the move).

16 The US Supreme Court has twice refused applications for certiorari based on the need to resolve the circuit split (*Stern v Stern* 132 S Ct 1540 (2012) and *Cahue v Martinez* (Order List for 20.03.17, <http://caselaw.findlaw.com/us-supreme-court/032017zor.html>).

17 On 20 April 2018, the majority of the Supreme Court of Canada adopted the hybrid approach in *Office of Children's Lawyer v Balev* 2018 SCC 16, overturning the ruling in *Balev v Baggott* 2016 ONCA 680, (2016) 405 D.L.R. (4th) 98.

18 There was also uncertainty in relation to this question under the 'settled purpose' parental intention approach previously applied in the UK, see R. Schuz, *The Hague Child Abduction Convention*, above n. 9, 198–200.

19 [2015] UKSC 35.

habitual residence had already changed after four months in Scotland, on the basis that the children had come to live in Scotland and their life there had the necessary quality of stability,[20] even if the stay was of limited duration. With respect, this reasoning doesn't seem to give any weight at all to the parental intentions or the nature of the stay in Scotland, and one would have expected to find a more careful balancing of the factors pointing in each direction. It is true that where small children are concerned, it is more difficult to assess their degree of connection with their new environment independently of that of their caregiver, but this might be considered to be a reason to give *more* weight to joint parental intention,[21] rather than less. In addition, in cases concerning the increasing number of families with a transnational lifestyle, any determination of habitual residence is likely to be arbitrary and will not necessarily lead to fulfilment of the objectives of the Convention.[22]

Whilst the fact-intensive nature of the enquiry and the infinite number of possible factual matrices make it difficult to provide clear-cut guidance, there are a number of steps which might be taken in order to promote uniformity and provide greater certainty, which should reduce the number of cases in which the issue of habitual residence is litigated.[23] First, since courts are likely to be influenced by policy considerations in borderline situations in which either of two countries could reasonably be held to be the child's habitual residence,[24] express reference to these considerations will ensure transparency and provide a basis for more uniform jurisprudence. Secondly, in accordance with the policy considerations of not discouraging beneficial foreign travel and of honouring

---

20 Ibid. at [23].

21 This was the view expressed by the Israeli District Court in FamA 666-06-16 *Plonit v Ploni* (Nevo, 13.07.16) (holding that a two-year-old child who had spent five months in Israel with her parents, while they were looking into the possibility of emigrating from the US, had not acquired a habitual residence in Israel (confirmed by the Supreme Court in RFamA 5726/16 (Nevo, 24.07.16)).

22 See D. Bozin-Odhiambo, 'Re-examining habitual residence as the sole connecting factor in Hague Child Abduction Convention Cases' (2012) 3 *Family Law Review* 4.

23 In 2015, 22% of judicial refusals were based on a finding that child was not habitually resident in the requesting state (this is an increase from the earlier figures of 18% (2008); 15% (2003) and 12% (1999)), N. Lowe and V. Stephens, 2015 Survey, above n. 2 at 19. A recent Lexis search (carried out on 27.07.17) of Abduction Convention decisions by US federal appeal courts within the previous 12 months revealed that out of 14 cases, in eight the only or main issue was habitual residence. It should also be noted that that during the past three years, the issue of habitual residence has been brought before the UK Supreme Court on six occasions (four of them involving Hague applications).

24 See R. Schuz, 'Policy Considerations in Determining the Habitual Residence of a Child and the Relevance of Context' (2001) 11 *Journal of Transnational Law and Policy* 101. (Relevant policy considerations include not leaving a child unprotected from abduction; not allowing an abductor to be rewarded; ensuring adjudication of the substantive dispute in the *forum conveniens*; not discouraging beneficial foreign travel; and honouring agreements and court orders).

agreements, express agreements in writing by parents to preserve their child's habitual residence during a relatively short foreign stay should be upheld, unless the factual situation is inconsistent with such a finding.[25] Thirdly, consideration should be given to the preparation of a Guide to Good Practice on determining habitual residence, recommending adoption of the combined approach, providing guidance as to the various factors and policy considerations to be taken into account, and giving examples of common situations.

2.2. GRAVE RISK OF HARM

Article 13(b) provides that a request for return of a child may be refused where the taking parent shows that there exists 'a grave risk that return would expose the child to physical or psychological harm or otherwise place him in an intolerable situation.' This is one of the most commonly pleaded exceptions[26] and that most commonly relied upon by courts.[27] The main reason for this seems to be, as demonstrated by all the Statistical Surveys, that 'the paradigm has shifted.'[28] The drafters of the Convention had in mind abductions carried out by non-custodial parents, in which cases the chance of return to the custodial parent causing harm to the child was minimal. However, in practice the latest figures show that 80 per cent of taking parents are sole or joint primary carers[29] and 73 per cent are mothers.[30] In such cases, the risk of return causing harm is much more likely, especially where there is a background of domestic violence or the abducting parent is not prepared to return with the child. Thus, it is hardly surprising that there are significant disparities between the way in which the exception is applied by different courts[31] and that there has been considerable academic criticism of the overly restrictive approach taken by most courts.[32]

---

25 P. McEleavy, 'A protocol for the 1980 Hague Convention' (2010) 1 *International Family Law* 59 suggests that agreements should be binding where the stay is for up to 18 months.

26 Draft Good Practice Guide to Art. 13(1)(b), available at <https://assets.hcch.net/docs/0a0532b7-d580-4e53-8c25-7edab2a94284.pdf>, para. 2.

27 In 2015, 17% (sole reason) and 21% (one of a number of reasons), compared with 2008 figures of 21% and 27% respectively, N. Lowe and V. Stephens, 2015 Survey, above n. 2 at 15.

28 Lady Hale in 'Foreword' to R. Schuz, *Hague Child Abduction Convention*, above n. 9, xi.

29 Compared to 72% in 2008 and 68% in 2003, N. Lowe and V. Stephens, 2015 Survey, above n. 2 at 8.

30 Compared to 69% in 2008 and 68% in 2003, N. Lowe and V. Stephens, 2015 Survey, ibid. at 7.

31 R. Schuz, 'Disparity' above n. 7, 13–20.

32 See e.g. R. Schuz, *The Hague Child Abduction Convention*, above n. 9, 315–316, M.H. Weiner, 'Intolerable Situations and Counsel for Children: Following Switzerland's Example In Hague Abduction Cases' (2008) 58 *American University Law Review* 335; M. Weiner, 'International Child Abduction and the Escape from Domestic Violence' (2000) 69 *Fordham Law Review* 593; C. Bruch, 'The Unmet Needs of Domestic Violence Victims and their Children in Hague Child Abduction Convention Cases' (2004) 38 *Family Law Quarterly* 529; C. Kubitschek, 'Failure of the Hague Abduction Convention to Address Domestic Violence and its Consequences' (2014) 9 *Journal of Comparative Law* 111.

With the aim of promoting greater uniformity, a draft Guide to Good Practice on Article 13(1)(b), developed by a working group of experts,[33] has been published[34] and was discussed at the Seventh Special Commission Meeting in October 2017. Most of the comprehensive and pragmatic draft Guide is devoted to recommending practices which will ensure that children will not be returned where they cannot be adequately protected, whilst minimising the delay in dealing with applications, in accordance with the fundamental objective of the Convention. Helpfully, the Guide urges competent authorities to avoid pre-judging situations, but rather to consider the specific facts of each case. Thus, for example, where return of a young child will mean separation from his primary carer, courts are to examine all the facts of the case, including the ability of the left-behind parent to care for the child and the reasons for the abductor's refusal to return, rather than to dismiss outright the claim that the grave risk exception applies, as is currently the practice of many courts.[35]

The draft Guide conveys two particularly important messages which should be internalised by judges and other actors who deal with return applications under the Abduction Convention. The first message is the need to ensure that protective measures, designed to protect the child after return, are actually enforceable and effective in the requesting state. This is now more important than ever, in view of the expansion of the Convention to states which have very different legal and social norms. The draft Guide discusses various means by which enforceability might be checked, primarily via the network of Hague Judges or Central Authorities.[36] However, the benefits of using judges in this context are overstated, since general information can be provided equally well by Central Authority legal officers.[37] More significantly, the fact that measures are enforceable legally does not necessarily mean that they will

---

33 Set up in accordance with 'Conclusions and Recommendations of the Sixth Special Commission', <www.hcch.net/upload/wop/abduct2012concl_e.pdf>, para. 82.

34 Above n. 26.

35 R. Schuz, *The Hague Child Abduction Convention*, above n. 9, 280–281, but cf. the Russian case of *Thompson v Thompson* (unreported, 12.12.16), in which the St. Petersburg Municipal Court dismissed an appeal against a decision refusing to return a four-year-old girl to Spain, on the basis of the grave risk exception, because her mother did not intend to return to Spain, even though there was no evidence that the father was not capable of looking after the child and no objective reasons were given to justify the mother's stance. The court relied on Principle 6 of the Declaration of the Rights of the Child from 1959, which states that a child should not be separated from his mother other than in exceptional circumstances, ignoring the fact that his has been overtaken by the UN Convention on the Rights of the Child and that the mother was *causing* the separation.

36 See Mathew Thorpe, 'Judicial Activism: A 20-Year Evolution' in this volume.

37 R. Schuz, *The Hague Child Abduction Convention*, above n. 9, 296-8. Indeed, a document circulated by the Permanent Bureau (Working Doc. 2 E) to provide information on judicial communications expressly states (fn. 7) that much of the information provided by judges might be available via the Central Authority.

be effective *in practice* and judicial or other legal personnel may not actually have information as to the situation on the ground. Thus, in order to ensure more realistic assessment of the effectiveness of protective measures, it may well be necessary to also obtain information from additional sources, such as social work agencies and relevant voluntary organisations in the requesting state.[38]

The second important message is that as a result of research studies, helpfully summarised in Annex 3 of the draft Guide, we now know far more about the dynamics and impact of domestic violence,[39] and this knowledge is highly relevant to those abduction cases in which there is a background of such violence. In particular, it has been shown that there is a correlation between spousal violence and child abuse and that long-term harm may be caused to children who are exposed to violence between their parents, even where there has not been any violence or threat thereof against *them*. Moreover, there is evidence that violence may increase following separation.[40] Nonetheless, in my view, the draft Guide does not clarify sufficiently the implications of this research for decision-making in relation to Article 13(1)(b). On the one hand, it is made clear that, in contrast to the view taken by some courts,[41] the grave risk exception can be established in cases where the left-behind parent has abused the taking parent, without the need to prove that the child in question is liable to suffer from some specific psychological disorder.[42] On the other hand, however, the draft Guide states that there is no automatic presumption that the grave risk exception will be established in cases of partner violence and that the impact of such violence on the children should be considered on a case-by-case basis in the light of the expert evidence.[43] It is not clear what questions the expert is to address. Is he or she supposed to refer to the likelihood of harm to the *particular* child, in the light of the severity of the violence and his or her psychological make-up, or rather to the validity or significance of the various research studies? In either case, it seems that such evidence will be highly speculative and likely to depend on the views of the particular expert, which will lead to non-uniform application. Similarly, the draft Guide is vague about the burden of proof in relation to the adequacy of protective measures. In the text it states that in general the burden should not fall entirely on the left-behind parent,[44] but a

---

38 In some cases, there will be evidence brought by the taking parent that he/she was not afforded protection in the past, as in *Borisovs v Kubiles* [2013] O.J. No. 863, Supreme Court of Canada.

39 For a definition, see Draft Good Practice Guide, above n. 26, Annex 3 at 11.

40 Ibid. at 12.

41 See R. Schuz, *The Hague Child Abduction Convention*, above n. 9, 283.

42 As in the case of *Blondin v Dubois* 238 F3d 153 (2d Cir. 2001), in which return was only refused on the basis of the medical evidence that the children would suffer from post-traumatic stress syndrome if they were returned to France, where they had been exposed to violence by their father against their mother.

43 Draft Good Practice Guide above n. 26, 83–84.

44 Ibid. at 36.

footnote adds that account should be taken of the gravity of the behaviour of the left-behind parent.[45]

In my view, it is necessary to take a more definitive stance in relation to the burden of proof, which better reflects the weakness and vulnerability of domestic violence victims and their children.[46] Thus, I would suggest that in cases where serious spousal abuse has been shown, it should be presumed that the grave risk exception is established. This presumption can be rebutted where the left-behind parent can prove that, in the light of the particular circumstances, there is no real risk of harm to the child[47] or that there are enforceable protective measures which can be taken which will effectively protect the child from harm.

3. CHILD PARTICIPATION

Perhaps the most tangible result of the doctrine of children's rights in general and the UN Convention on the Rights of the Child in particular has been the recognition that children have a right to have a say in processes affecting their lives. Thus, although the impact of recognition that children are independent rights-holders for Abduction Convention cases is wider than giving effect to their specific rights,[48] in practice ensuring that children's participation rights are protected in the Abduction Convention process is likely to be the most important step towards adoption of a child-centric approach.

Whilst the child objection exception in Article 13[49] clearly provides a means to give some effect to the child's participation rights, the extent to which this potential will be realised depends on the extent to which practices are adopted which ensure that children are given the opportunity to be heard and the extent to which due weight is given to their views. Moreover, the child's right to participate is not limited to cases where he objects to returning.[50] The available research

---

45 Ibid. at fn. 155.

46 This is even more essential in the US where a higher standard of proof applies in relation to the Art. 13(1)(b) exception ('clear and convincing evidence'), International Child Abduction Remedies Act s. 4(e)(2)(A).

47 If, for example, the child was not a witness to the violence and the left-behind parent has a record of good, non-violent parenting. Where the child is old enough, his/her attitude to the left-behind parent and his/her desire to return will be weighty factors.

48 See R. Schuz, 'Thirty Years Of The Hague Abduction Convention: A Children's Rights Perspective' in A. Diduck, H. Reece and N. Peleg (eds.), *Law in Society: Reflections on Children, Family, Culture and Philosophy, Essays in Honour of Michael Freeman Law and Michael Freeman*, Brill-Nijhoff, Leiden 2015, 607–616.

49 Which provides, 'The judicial or administrative authority may also refuse to order the return of the child if it finds that the child objects to being returned and has attained an age and degree of maturity at which it is appropriate to take account of its views.'

50 C. Fenton-Glynn, 'Participation and Natural Justice: Children's Rights and Interests in Hague Abduction Proceedings' (2014) 9 *Journal of Comparative Law* 129, 134.

suggests that there are considerable disparities in relation to the treatment all of these issues between and within jurisdictions.[51]

For example, whilst the requirement of Article 11(2) of Brussels IIA Regulation that children be given the opportunity to be heard when applying Articles 12 and 13 of the Abduction Convention[52] appears to be pioneering, there is evidence that in practice it is not always implemented.[53] Moreover, whilst there is a welcome move in some legal systems towards direct hearing of children by judges,[54] restrictions on the use made of these meetings might in fact limit the extent to which they give effect to the child's participation rights. The official view in England and Wales is that a meeting with the judge is intended 'to enable the child to gain some understanding of what is going on, and to be reassured that the judge has understood him/her', and not to gather evidence.[55] Thus, it seems that the judge should not rely on what the child said to him or her or the judge's own impressions, but must instead rely on the CAFCASS report in determining what weight to give to the child's views.[56] With respect, this approach seems to undermine the very purpose of giving the child the right to be heard by the ultimate decision-maker. On the other hand, the case of *Re KP*[57] illustrates how a child can be prejudiced by a meeting in which he was expected to make submissions and justify his views without prior preparation.[58] This case surely demonstrates the need to ensure that where a child objects to his or her return, an independent legal representative is appointed who can put forward the child's position and defend it in judicial examination.[59]

Similarly, literature surveying the case law in a variety of jurisdictions[60] reveals that whilst some courts are now taking a more liberal approach, recognising that the child objection exception reflects the autonomy interests of children, many others still adopt a restrictive stance, taking a paternalistic approach to the maturity of children and to the independence and validity of their objections, and exercising their discretion to order return even where the exception is established.[61] Moreover, the fact that there has been no increase

---

51 R. Schuz, 'Disparity' above n. 7, 21–24.

52 Unless this is inappropriate having regard to his or her age or degree of maturity.

53 C. Fenton-Glynn above n. 50, 135–138; Proposal for Council Regulation on jurisdiction, recognition and enforcement of judgments in matrimonial matters and matters of parental responsibility and on international child abduction (recast), COM(2016) 411, 4.

54 R. Schuz, *Hague Child Abduction Convention*, above n. 9, 376–380.

55 2010 Guidelines on Meeting Judges, quoted in *Re KP (a child)* [2014] EWCA Civ 554, [36].

56 *Re KP*, ibid. at [59].

57 Ibid.

58 So, the Court of Appeal was right to order a re-hearing before a different judge.

59 For a detailed discussion of the arguments for and against separate representation in abduction cases, see R. Schuz, *Hague Child Abduction Convention*, above n. 9, 396–403.

60 Ibid. at 323–342; K. Trimmings, *Child Abduction Within the European Union*, Hart Publishing, Oxford 2013, 196–236; R. Schuz, 'Thirty Years of the Child Abduction Convention' above n. 48, 619–621.

61 For a recent example see *Re F (children)* [2016] EWCA Civ 546.

in the percentage of refusals based on child objections tends to suggest a prevailing restrictive approach.[62] Accordingly, if we are to ensure that children's participation rights are more widely realised, further steps are required. Indeed, this has been recognised by the European Commission, which, in its proposal to recast the Brussels IIA Regulation, has recommended upgrading the current requirement to hear the child, including providing that due weight should be given to the views of the child.[63]

At a global level, the draft Guide on Article 13(1)(b)[64] is extremely helpful in promoting child participation. Throughout the draft Guide, reference is made to the need to involve children in the proceedings, and the Children's Rights Committee's General Comment No. 12 on the Right of the Child to be Heard is annexed to the draft Guide.[65] However, in my view, there is a need for a separate Guide to Good Practice on the subject of Child Participation in Abduction Convention cases. Such a Guide would, inter alia, expressly address: the apparent tensions between the objectives of the Abduction Convention; current research in relation to the determination of maturity and the capacity of children to understand and form independent views; the implications of the different ways in which children might be heard; and the value of separate representation for children. The Guide would not be restricted to the child objection exception but would also refer to and give examples of the relevance of children's views and perspectives in relation to other issues, such as determination of habitual residence, whether there has been settlement, the grave risk exception, and the exercise of discretion where one of the exceptions is established.

4. COMPLIANCE

It is clear that there are problems of compliance with the Convention by some Contracting States, although it is difficult to ascertain the extent of the problems. Whilst the Statistical Survey provides us with data for each Contracting State in relation to outcomes and time taken to process applications,[66] return rates have to be treated with some caution, especially in relation to states which only receive a few return applications, inter alia, because non-return does not per se

---

62 In 2015, 10% (sole reason) and 13% (one of a number of reasons) compared to 10% and 17% respectively in 2008, N. Lowe and V. Stephens 2015 Survey above n. 2 at 15–16. The average age of children abducted increased slightly from 6.4 in 2008 to 6.8, ibid at 10.

63 Proposal for Council Regulation, above n. 53, 42 (new art. 20).

64 Above n. 26.

65 Ibid. Annex 4.

66 In 2015, some states took much longer than the average time to process applications, e.g. Peru (321 days), Ukraine (300 days) and Brazil (297 days), N. Lowe and V. Stephens 2015 Survey, above n. 2 at 21.

indicate non-compliance[67] and because the figures do not indicate whether return orders were actually enforced. The US State Department's annual reports give a better indication of compliance because they provide specific assessment of the operation of the Convention in individual states and label as 'non-compliant' those who do not resolve cases in accordance with the Convention in a timely manner.[68] However, these reports only provide a partial picture, because they are based entirely on the State Department's experience in outgoing cases.

Accordingly, the first step to ensuring greater compliance is to increase the transparency of the operation of the Convention in each Contracting State, including publication of a representative sample of judicial decisions from all Contracting States. At the Seventh Special Commission in October 2017, the Permanent Bureau launched a modernised version of INCADAT and announced plans to ensure much wider coverage of cases and timely reporting via national correspondents.[69] These developments are most welcome, but since it is likely that some states will not report cases, I would make two practical suggestions to increase transparency, although they both have resource implications. The first is for more Contracting States, particularly those who have a considerable number of outgoing cases, to prepare reports similar to those published by the US State Department. Secondly, the Central Authorities of *requesting* states should forward to the Permanent Bureau judicial decisions sent to them in outgoing cases from states who do not themselves provide reports of their cases.[70] These decisions and summaries of them would be published on INCADAT, taking into account confidentiality protections in the requested state.

The second stage, in my view, is to analyse more carefully the reasons for non-compliance, so that counter-measures can be taken. To the extent that the problem is incorrect interpretation and application of the Convention, more judicial training is required. However, it is likely that often non-compliance stems from inadequate funding,[71] organisational difficulties or lack of political will.[72] These problems are not easily overcome ex post facto, after the new state's

---

67 Although a pattern of more judicial refusals than returns in states with a reasonable number of applications does suggest incorrect application by the courts, e.g. in Poland 35% judicial refusals (17 cases) as opposed to 15% judicial returns (7) and 17% voluntary returns (8) out of 48 applications, N. Lowe and V. Stephens 2015 Survey, above n. 2, at Annex 4.

68 For 2017 Report, see <https://travel.state.gov/content/dam/childabduction/complianceReports/2017%20ICAPRA%20Report%20-%20Final.pdf>.

69 At present, INCADAT, the database set up by the Permanent Bureau of Hague Conference, contains summaries of cases from less than half of the Contracting States and is often not up-to-date as it depends on voluntary submissions, Draft Good Practice Guide, above n. 26, 19.

70 Where the decision has been translated into one of the official languages, the Central Authority should send this and if not, the Permanent Bureau will have to organise translation.

71 E.g. *Guide to Good Practice*, Part I on 'Central Authority Practice', available at <http://www.hcch.net/upload/abdguide_e.pdf>, para. 1.1.

72 L. Wardle, 'The Merit of Modesty: Abduction, Relocation and the Hague Abduction Convention' (2014) 9 *Journal of Comparative Law* 89, 106. In relation to Eastern European states, see K. Trimmings, above n. 60, 177–180.

accession has been accepted by other Member States.[73] However, lessons might be learned for future policy in relation to acceptance of newly acceding states. A mechanism should be set up for centralised examination of whether such states are able and prepared to put in place the legal[74] and administrative framework necessary for proper operation of the Convention. In addition, I would suggest that newly acceding states be obliged to send judicial and administrative personnel for training organised via the Permanent Bureau and to agree to take account of the Good Practice Guides and available leading case law from other Contracting States.[75] Of course, all this may involve considerable costs, including for translation, but we cannot hope to achieve uniform implementation of the Convention without taking concrete steps to promote a global jurisprudence.[76]

5. CONCLUSION

Whilst it might be tempting to rest on our laurels, in light of the apparent success of the Abduction Convention, we need to continue to take steps to ensure that the Convention is interpreted and applied uniformly in a way which fulfils the objective of protecting children from the harmful effects of international abduction. Guides to Good Practice seem to be the best available mechanism for furthering this goal[77] and so, as indicated above, I would suggest preparation of Guides in relation to habitual residence and child participation.

The expansion of the Convention provides the potential for protecting more children. However, this potential will only be realised if the new Contracting States actually comply with the Convention.[78] Some may take the view that it is better to accept acceding states even if they are not sufficiently committed to the Convention, in the hope that they will, over time, become compliant. However, this approach may be overly optimistic and ignores the difficulties which might be faced in ensuring protection of children who are returned to states with very different social and legal norms from those in the majority of

---

73 For a discussion of the possibility of sanctions, see R. Schuz, 'Disparity', above n. 7, 46–48.

74 Including their readiness to implement concentration of jurisdiction, see e.g. Draft Good Practice Guide, above n. 26, 93.

75 In the case of *Thompson v Thompson*, above n. 35, the Russian appeal court refused to take into account foreign case-law provided by the appellant, on the basis that Russia is not a precedent system (personal communication from father's lawyer).

76 L. Silberman, 'United States Supreme Court Hague Abduction Decisions: Developing a Global Jurisprudence' (2014) 9 *Journal of Comparative Law* 49, 49–51.

77 Many states have reported that these have been of assistance (in answer to question 11 of the 2010 questionnaire: <www.hcch.net/index_en.php?act=publications.details&pid=5291&dtid=33>), although there is no concrete proof of their effectiveness.

78 It should be borne in mind that the 2015 Statistics do not include States who only acceded recently, such as Russia, Pakistan and Iraq.

Contracting States. Indeed, analysis of acceptances of accessions suggests that states are influenced by these concerns.[79] A centralised mechanism, as suggested above, for assessing the readiness of newly acceding states to implement the Convention, including their commitment to global jurisprudence, would both assist existing Contracting States in deciding whether to accept accessions and transmit a clearer message to acceding states of what is expected of them.

Finally, and perhaps most importantly, the only way to test whether the Convention is successfully protecting children is to undertake empirical research on the long-term outcomes for children following return under the Convention. The limited research to date[80] provides cause for concern that in some cases forced return is causing harm to children and that returning families are not receiving the protection and support which they need in order to minimise the negative impact on the children of the return. It is now widely acknowledged that there is a need for much larger-scale surveys[81] and it is to be hoped that such research will be conducted in the near future.

---

79 A. Efrat and A.L. Newman, 'Deciding to Defer: the Importance of Fairness in Resolving Transnational Jurisdictional Conflicts' (2016) 70 *International Organization* 409 (showing, inter alia, that legal and political affinity are positively associated with acceptance of accessions and that a gap between the accepting and acceding country in relation to law and order, and a Muslim majority in the acceding state, are both negatively associated with acceptance of accessions).

80 M. Freeman for Reunite Research Unit, 'Outcomes for Children Following an Abduction', <www.reunite.org/edit/files/Library%20-%20reunite%20Publications/Outcomes%20Report.pdf>, 35; D. Bozin-Odhiambo, 'Constructing the "best interest of the child" standard: Hague Child Abduction Convention return proceedings and beyond' (2014) 8 *New Zealand Family Law Journal* 26.

81 See Report of Experts Meeting on Domestic Violence and the 1980 Convention (London, 13.06.2017), available at <https://assets.hcch.net/docs/3dff779b-53dd-4228-903e-fe777e79b4f1.pdf> and para. 81 of the Conclusions and Recommendations of Seventh Special Commission Meeting, available at <https://assets.hcch.net/docs/edce6628-3a76-4be8-a092-437837a49bef.pdf>.

USING RESEARCH TO IMPROVE OUTCOMES FOR ABDUCTED CHILDREN

Nicola Taylor and Marilyn Freeman

1. INTRODUCTION

In August 2009 the Right Honourable Lord Justice Thorpe, then Head of International Family Justice for England and Wales, hosted the International Family Justice Judicial Conference for Common Law and Commonwealth Jurisdictions at Cumberland Lodge, Windsor, England. This included an afternoon session devoted to international relocation, which had become one of the most controversial and difficult issues in family law internationally – and of increasing concern due to the rise in cross-border relationships and international mobility. At that time, empirical studies on relocation disputes following parental separation had been undertaken in Australia,[1]

[1] P. Parkinson, J. Cashmore and J. Single, 'The Need for Reality Testing in Relocation Cases' (2010) 44 *Family Law Quarterly* 1.

New Zealand[2] and England and Wales,[3] and members of each research team were invited to present their respective research findings at the Conference to help inform the discussion. This was the first time we (Nicola and Marilyn) met in person; our previous exchanges having been undertaken via email. So it was with some excitement, and a great many thanks to Professor Nigel Lowe – a leading figure at the Conference – that our individual efforts on relocation were recognised and a new working relationship forged between us. Professor Lowe and Dr. William Duncan, then First Secretary of the Permanent Bureau at The Hague, invited us to collaborate on a joint presentation and written paper reviewing the international research evidence on relocation for the forthcoming International Judicial Conference on Cross-Border Family Relocation. This Conference, attended by 50 judges and experts, was held in Washington DC, in March 2010.[4] Our paper was one of the few reviews at the time of the empirical evidence on mobility and relocation and underpinned the Washington Declaration on International Family Relocation that resulted from the Conference. Our paper was subsequently published in the *Family Law Quarterly*.[5]

Professor Lowe's kick-starting of our collaborative work on relocation – the lawful means by which separated parents seek to relocate with their children – inevitably led onto our consideration of international child abduction; the unlawful means by which some separated parents choose to 'relocate' with their children. As flipsides of the same coin, it has been important to us to consider the nexus between relocation and abduction. This includes, of course, the fact that the return of an abducted child, ordered by a court under The Hague Convention on the Civil Aspects of International Child Abduction 1980, can be followed by relocation proceedings in the state of habitual residence. However, the quest for consistency of legal principles has proven to be challenging in relocation disputes internationally,[6] but has been less problematic in the international child abduction field because of the existence of the 1980 Hague Convention and the role of Central Authorities, the Hague Network of Judges and the Hague Permanent Bureau. This agreed international approach, and the infrastructure supporting it, provide a degree of co-ordination and coherence that is, as yet, absent from the relocation field.

2 N.J. Taylor, M. Gollop and M. Henaghan, *Relocation Following Parental Separation: The Welfare and Best Interests of Children*, University of Otago, Dunedin, New Zealand, 2010.

3 M. Freeman, *Relocation: The reunite Research*, Research Report. Research Unit of the Reunite International Child Abduction Centre, London 2009.

4 The Conference was co-hosted by the Hague Conference on Private International Law, the International Centre for Missing and Exploited Children and the US Department of State.

5 N.J. Taylor and M. Freeman, 'International Research Evidence on Relocation: Past, Present and Future' (2010) 44(3) *Family Law Quarterly* 317–339.

6 Thorpe LJ, 'Relocation – The Search for Common Principles' (2010) 1(1) *Journal of Family Law and Practice* 35–39.

This chapter focuses on how research can be used to improve outcomes for abducted children. Few empirical research studies have been undertaken in the international child abduction field, although a plethora of books, case law analyses and legal/judicial commentaries have been published.[7] The empirical studies that do exist primarily involve statistical surveys into the operation of the 1980 Hague Convention, clinical case studies, case-file analyses, parental questionnaires, telephone surveys, and interviews with family members and professionals regarding their experiences of international child abduction and, where relevant, Hague Convention proceedings. We review the most notable of these types of studies and give consideration to what their findings contribute to our understanding of international child abduction. Our response to the call for a more rigorous evidence base on legal and welfare outcomes concludes the chapter.

2. RESEARCH CONTRIBUTIONS ON INTERNATIONAL CHILD ABDUCTION

2.1. STATISTICAL SURVEYS

While the 1980 Hague Convention provides an internationally agreed mechanism amongst its 98 State Parties for dealing with child abduction, its interpretation and implementation are matters for each individual State Party since there is no supra-national body controlling its application. Although autonomous interpretation would be desirable, the way in which abductions are approached, and how they are resolved, can differ in practice between states.[8] To track these trends over time, and to provide reliable data to inform discussions at the 4th (2001), 5th (2006), 6th (2011) and 7th (2017) Special Commissions on the

---

7 See, for example, M. Bailey, 'Canada's Conflicted Approach to International Child Abduction' in W. Atkin (ed.), *International Survey of Family Law*, Jordan Publishing, Bristol 2016, 81; P. Beaumont and P. McEleavy, *The Hague Convention on International Child Abduction*, Oxford University Press, Oxford 1999; R. Lamont, 'Mainstreaming Gender into European Family Law? The Case of International Child Abduction and Brussels II Revised' (2011) 17(3) *European Law Journal* 366–384; N. Lowe and M. Nicholls, *International Movement of Children: Law, Practice and Procedure*, 2nd edn, Jordan Publishing, Bristol 2016; P. McEleavy, 'The European Court of Human Rights and the Hague Child Abduction Convention: Prioritising Return or Reflection?' (2015) 62(3) *Netherlands International Law Review* 365–405; R. Schuz, *The Hague Child Abduction Convention: A Critical Analysis*, Hart Publishing, Oxford and Portland OR 2013; L.J. Silberman, 'Interpreting the Hague Abduction Convention: In Search of a Global Jurisprudence', *New York University Public Law and Legal Theory Working Papers* (Paper 18, 2006): <http://lsr.nellco.org/nyu_plltwp/18>.

8 L.J. Silberman, above n. 7, p. 9: 'Thus, the effectiveness of the Convention is left in the hands of the respective Central Authorities and the national courts that implement and interpret the Convention.'

Practical Operation of the 1980 Hague Convention, Professor Lowe undertook surveys of all the applications received by Central Authorities in the years 1999,[9] 2003,[10] 2008[11] and 2015.[12] The statistical trends over this 16-year period are set out in the most recent Global Report,[13] co-authored with Victoria Stephens, and include the number of applications each Central Authority received; the 'taking persons' in return applications; the children involved; the outcomes of the applications; and the length of time it took to reach a final outcome.[14] A Regional Report[15] has also been published, traversing the outcomes of applications in 2015 to which the Brussels IIA Regulation[16] applied. The great value of this longitudinal comparative research is that it provides, across time, an overview of the general operation of the Convention, a profile of abducting family characteristics, and global insight into the statistical trends apparent in the workings of Central Authorities and the courts in 1980 Hague Convention proceedings. The number of incoming applications and the number of states have steadily increased over the period this statistical data has been collected, with some consistent trends evident.

2.1.1. The Taking Person

In 2015, 73 per cent of taking persons were the mothers of the children involved in the application; a figure that has increased when compared with the 69 per cent

9 N. Lowe, S. Armstrong and A. Mathias, *A Statistical Analysis of Applications Made in 1999 under the Hague Convention of 25 October 1980 on the Civil Aspects of International Child Abduction – Project Report*: Permanent Bureau of the Hague Conference, The Hague 2001.

10 N. Lowe, *A Statistical Analysis of Applications Made in 2003 under the Hague Convention of 25 October 1980 on the Civil Aspects of International Child Adoption (2007 Update)*, Hague Conference on Private International Law, 2008; N. Lowe, 'The 2003 statistical study' (2006) XI *The Judges' Newsletter on International Child Protection* pp. 77–79.

11 N. Lowe and V. Stephens, *A Statistical Analysis of Applications Made in 2008 under the Hague Convention of 25 October 1980 on the Civil Aspects of International Child Abduction*, Preliminary Document Nos. 8A–8C (2011). Permanent Bureau of the Hague Conference, The Hague 2011.

12 N. Lowe and V. Stephens, *Part I: A Statistical Analysis of Applications Made in 2015 under the Hague Convention of 25 October 1980 on the Civil Aspects of International Child Abduction – Global Report* (Preliminary Document No. 11A. Revised version, February 2018), Permanent Bureau of the Hague Conference, The Hague 2018. Available at: <https://www.hcch.net/en/publications-and-studies/details4/?pid=6545&dtid=57>. Published to inform the 7th Meeting of the Special Commission on the Practical Operation of the 1980 Hague Child Abduction Convention and the 1996 Hague Child Protection Convention (October 2017).

13 Ibid.

14 Ibid. at para. 6.

15 N. Lowe and V. Stephens, *Part II: A Statistical Analysis of Applications Made in 2015 under the Hague Convention of 25 October 1980 on the Civil Aspects of International Child Abduction – Regional Report* (Preliminary Document No. 11A of September 2017).

16 Council Regulation (EC) No. 2201/2003 of 27 November 2003 concerning jurisdiction and the recognition and enforcement of judgments in matrimonial matters and the matters of parental responsibility, repealing Regulation (EC) No. 1347/2000. In force since 1 March 2005.

recorded in 1999 and 2008, and the 68 per cent in 2003. Fathers accounted for 24 per cent of the taking persons in 2015; a slight decrease from the previous two surveys. The growth in joint parenting has emerged as one of the stand-out trends in 2015 with 20 per cent of the taking persons being the child's primary carer, 60 per cent a joint-primary carer and 20 per cent a non-primary carer. Overall, 80 per cent of taking persons in 2015 were the primary or joint-primary carer of the children involved (compared with 72 per cent in 2008 and 68 per cent in 2003). The trend towards a majority of taking persons 'going home' to the state in which they were brought up, or in which they have family ties, was confirmed again in 2015 in 58 per cent of applications, compared with 60 per cent in 2008, 55 per cent in 2003 and 52 per cent in 1999.

2.1.2. *The Children*

The average number of children involved in the applications ranged from 1.5 in 1999 to 1.3 in 2015. The majority of the applications involving a single child has gradually increased from 63 per cent in 1999 to 70 per cent in 2015. There has always been a fairly equal gender split between the numbers of boys and girls, with 53 per cent of children being male and 47 per cent female in both 1999 and 2015. The average age of a child involved in a return application has climbed slightly from 6.3 years in 2003 to 6.8 years in 2015. Of the 2,997 children involved in the 2,270 return applications in 2015, the greatest proportion were aged three to seven years. The young age of the abducted child cohort has particular implications for the ascertainment of children's views and the 'child's objections' exception in child abduction proceedings.

2.1.3. *Outcomes*

The overall return rate in 2015 was 45 per cent, slightly lower than the 46 per cent in 2008, but markedly lower than the rates in 2003 (51 per cent) and 1999 (50 per cent). The number of judicial refusals and withdrawn applications also decreased significantly in 2015, reversing the previous trend of a steady increase in refusals. These 2015 decreases seem to be explained by the significant proportion of applications (16 per cent, 318) that ended in other outcomes, including voluntary agreements (84 applications), the applicant's inaction (84), and a diverse range of other less frequent outcomes (such as the arrest of the abductor, death of the applicant, inability to trace the child, the child having returned to the Requesting State or having turned 16).[17] Of the 2015 applications decided in court, 65 per cent ended in a return

[17] N. Lowe and V. Stephens, above n. 12, para. 58.

(compared with 61 per cent in 2008, 66 per cent in 2003 and 74 per cent in 1999), 28 per cent in a judicial refusal and six per cent in orders for access or another voluntary agreement. Some jurisdictions had a notably high proportion of returns compared with the global average 45 per cent return rate, for example, New Zealand (83 per cent, 25 applications), Scotland (64 per cent, 16 applications), Turkey (60 per cent, 26 applications) and Australia (58 per cent, 24 applications). In contrast, a low proportion of applications ended in return in Austria (five per cent, one application) and Sweden (24 per cent, six applications), though many applications received by these Central Authorities remained pending.

2.1.4. *Refusals*

There was a sharp increase in the number of applications judicially refused in 2015 (25 per cent) because the child was found not to be habitually resident in the Requesting State.[18] There was also an increase in applications refused based on Article 13(a) due to the consent (nine per cent) or acquiescence (15 per cent) of the left-behind parent. While the most common combined (sole and multiple) reason for refusal remained Article 13(b) (25 per cent), the proportion of refusals in which it was relied upon was lower than in 2008. Similarly, there was a decrease in applications refused because the applicant had no rights of custody (seven per cent) or was not exercising their right of custody (six per cent) or based on the child's objections (15 per cent).

2.1.5. *Timing*

Voluntary returns, judicial returns and judicial refusals were generally all resolved more quickly in 2015 than in 2008, but more slowly than in 2003 and 1999. As in previous surveys, voluntary returns were resolved most quickly, followed by judicial returns and then judicial refusals.

2.1.6. *Workload*

The workload varied considerably between Central Authorities, with the US handling the greatest number of incoming and outgoing applications (597), followed by England and Wales (578), Germany (457), Mexico (306) and France (294). Conversely, 13 Central Authorities (six of which were in Canada) handled no applications at all.

---

[18] Ibid. at para. 87.

2.2. EARLY EMPIRICAL RESEARCH ON CHILD ABDUCTION

2.2.1. 1980s and 1990s

Empirical research on child abduction commenced in the US during the 1980s and aimed to provide evidence of its effects on children. These studies primarily involved domestic 'child snatchings' (rather than international abductions), were small-scale in nature, and drew on case reports or case-file analyses from clinical, therapeutic and criminal justice contexts.[19] For example, psychiatrist Lenore Terr treated 18 abducted children over a six-year period and reported on their symptomatology in 1983.[20] Demonstrable emotional effects from their abduction experiences were exhibited by 16 of the children, of whom 11 suffered from post-traumatic stress syndrome. Other reactions related to mental indoctrination, grief and rage, and rejection of the abducting parent. While all the children made progress with therapy, most still showed effects of the abduction experience at termination or follow-up. Other case reports of abduction effects noted 'anniversary reactions' and severe sleep disturbances.[21] Much less child psychopathology was found in a study of 37 abducted children in divorce/access cases due to the short duration of the abductions (65 per cent lasted less than one week), which mostly involved siblings being abducted together.[22]

Agopian's study involved interviews with five abducted children, aged six to 11 years who had been missing for periods ranging from six to 42 months, and with their custodial parents.[23] While the parents all reported some psychological trauma to the children, reactions varied greatly and this was linked to such factors as the child's age at the time of their abduction, the length of time they were missing, the treatment they received, their lifestyle and experiences while missing, and the type of therapy and support provided upon recovery. Other early American research analysed the records of missing children's organisations,[24]

---

19 M. Freeman, 'The Effects and Consequences of International Child Abduction' (1998) 32(3) *Family Law Quarterly* 603–621.

20 L.C. Terr, 'Child Snatching: A New Epidemic of an Ancient Malady' (1983) 103 *Journal of Pediatrics* 151–156.

21 D.H. Schetky and L.H. Haller, 'Parental Kidnapping' (1983) 22 *Journal of the American Academy of Child Psychiatry* 279–285; N. Senior, T. Gladstone and B. Nurcombe, 'Child Snatching: A Case Report' (1982) 21 *Journal of the American Academy of Child Psychiatry* 579–583.

22 W.A. Cole and J.M. Bradford, 'Abduction During Custody and Access Disputes' (1992) 37 *Canadian Journal of Psychiatry* 265.

23 M.W. Agopian, 'The Impact on Children of Abduction by Parents' (1984) 63 *Child Welfare* 511–519.

24 R. Forehand, N. Long, C. Zogg and E. Parrish, 'Child Abduction: Parent and Child Functioning Following Return' (1989) 28 *Clinical Pediatrics* 311–316; R.F. Janvier, K. McCormick and R. Donaldson, 'Parental Kidnapping: A Survey of Left-behind Parents' (1990) 41 *Juvenile and Family Court Journal* 1–8.

and calls to a hotline aimed at preventing child abduction.[25] A national household telephone survey of 10,544 randomly selected households identified 142 children in 104 households who had experienced parental abduction within the United States, with a higher proportion than other studies of brief abductions lasting only a few days following, for example, short-term violations of custody arrangements.[26] Interviews with counsellors and an analysis of court files in a Los Angeles county found that some abductors acted for purposes of revenge, while others were psychologically enmeshed with the child or perceived the child to be at risk.[27] Some of these children suffered severe psychological trauma, including from the lies they were told and the manipulation of their identities while on the run.

2.2.2. *Longitudinal Research*

To move beyond the small-scale studies that had characterised much of the early research on child abduction, Hegar and Greif initiated a study in 1989 that ultimately enabled longitudinal data to be collected on parents' perspectives of their children's well-being over time.[28] Their more substantial sample was built by contacting missing children organisations in each of the States listed in a publication of the National Center for Missing and Exploited Children.[29] Fourteen child-find organisations in 16 American States and in Canada agreed to co-operate with the study and mailed an eight-page, 95-item, questionnaire to parents who had requested their assistance following an abduction, whether their child(ren) had been recovered or not. Of the 2,666 questionnaires distributed to parents, 371 usable responses from searching parents were returned in 1989. Fifty-five per cent of the respondents (the searching parents) were mothers, and 45 per cent were fathers. Thus the abducting parent was the father in 55 per cent of the cases and the mother in 45 per cent. The children were almost evenly split between boys (55 per cent) and girls (45 per cent), with a modal age at abduction of two years. Three-quarters of the children were six years old or younger. Most of the abductions had occurred within the past three years and usually when the child was in the care of the abductor (64 per cent). In half of the

25 R. Forehand, N. Long and C. Zogg, 'Preventing Parental Child Abduction: Analysis of a National Project' (1991) 30 *Clinical Pediatrics* 549–554.

26 D. Finkelhor, G. Hotaling and A. Sedlak, 'Children Abducted by Family Members: A National Household Survey of Incidence and Episode Characteristics' (1991) 53 *Journal of Marriage and the Family* 805–817. No more than 12% of the children were taken out of State.

27 I.J. Sagatun and L. Barrett, 'Parental Child Abduction: The Law, Family Dynamics, and Legal System Responses' (1990) 18 *Journal of Criminal Justice* 433–442.

28 R.L. Hegar and G.L. Greif, 'Parental Kidnapping Across International Borders' (1991) 34 *International Social Work* 353–363.

29 R.L. Hegar and G.L. Greif, 'How Parentally Abducted Children Fare: An Interim Report on Families Who Recover Their Children' (1993) 21 *The Journal of Psychiatry and Law* 373–384.

cases the abduction occurred during court-ordered visitation. Only one child was abducted in two-thirds of the cases. Domestic violence was a feature in one out of every eight cases. The respondents reported that the primary reason for the abduction was the abductor's desire to hurt the respondent (77 per cent), followed by the abductor's anger over their break-up (23 per cent).[30] A smaller proportion regarded the abduction as motivated by a desire to be with the child, to protect the child or to have more contact with them.

The 371 cases concerned abductions originating in the United States. Only 77 (11 per cent), involving 118 children, crossed international borders to 27 different countries. A number of key variables distinguished the international from the domestic abductions.[31] The children abducted internationally tended to be older and more likely to be part of a larger sibling group. The international abductors were also older and had higher educational levels than their domestic counterparts. Foreign-born abductors fled to their country of origin in 71 per cent of the international cases, and also fled to non-Hague Convention countries more often than American-born international child abductors. Only 39 per cent of the international abductions involving non-Hague Convention countries resulted in recovery of the child, whereas the child was returned in 84 per cent of those abductions to Hague Convention countries – highlighting the efficiency of 1980 Hague Convention proceedings in international child abduction cases.

The researchers subsequently used their 371 survey participants to undertake a variety of follow-up studies including semi-structured telephone interviews with 173 participants (47 per cent of the original sample) in 1991,[32] with the characteristics of 69 of these families being subsequently examined in greater detail.[33] To obtain longitudinal data, the parents who completed the original 1989 survey and the 1991 follow-up were recontacted by telephone in 1993, and again in 1995, and asked about their own, and their children's lives.[34] Of the 39 parents who participated in the 1995 follow-up, 21 were mothers and 18 were fathers. Nearly half (48 per cent) of the 39 parents remained worried about another abduction and two-thirds (64 per cent) reported that their recovered children had received mental health services by 1995. The children were found to be progressing well over time, but psychological scores revealed they were less well-adjusted than a normative group.[35] The characteristics of

---

30 R.L. Hegar and G.L. Greif, 'Abduction of Children by Their Parents: A Survey of the Problem' (1991) 36(5) *Social Work* 421–426.

31 R.L. Hegar and G.L. Greif, above n. 28.

32 R.L. Hegar and G.L. Greif, above n. 29, p. 377.

33 R.L. Hegar and G.L. Greif, above n. 29.

34 G.L. Greif, 'The Long-term Impact of Parental Abduction on Children: Implications for Treatment' (1998) 26 *The Journal of Psychiatry and Law* 45–60.

35 Ibid. at 53.

five cases in which the children's scores had worsened between 1993 and 1995 were examined more closely.[36] Despite the very small sample, these findings were consistent with earlier studies 'suggesting that the length of time missing, experiences while missing, and the length of time since reunion can combine to affect a child's adaptation.'[37] The impact of an abduction can also be mediated by children's receipt of mental health services. Greif and Hegar also interviewed 17 parents regarding their motivations for abducting their children and going into hiding[38] and used a multiple regression model to explore parental assessment of the post-return adjustment of school-aged children.[39] This found that children's adjustment following their return was best explained by characteristics of the child and family before the abduction occurred. Greif has also published case studies detailing the long-term aftermath of child abduction and its implications for family therapy,[40] and reported on the reunification experiences of eight (now adult) abductees, four left-behind parents and one abductor.[41]

2.3. FREEMAN: QUALITATIVE RESEARCH

In 2003, Freeman undertook research on the outcomes for abducted children returned to a jurisdiction in Europe.[42] The 30 interviews related to 22 cases, as both parents were interviewed in eight families (36.36 per cent) and 33 children. Fourteen (63 per cent) of the 22 cases involved an abduction by the mother. The report concluded that an abduction situation could not be resolved without fallout, against which it is impossible to fully protect the returning parent and child. The Hague Convention was operating more as a problem-mover, than a problem-solver, as the familial problems leading to the abduction still needed to be resolved on return. The giving, mirroring and honouring of undertakings were also considered.

Three years later Freeman interviewed 25 of the original 30 participants from the 2003 study, and five additional participants, to explore the effects of

36 Ibid. at 53.

37 Ibid. at 56.

38 G.L. Greif and R.L. Hegar, 'Parents Who Abduct: A Qualitative Study with Implications for Practice' (1994) 43 *Family Relations* 283–288.

39 R.L. Hegar and G.L. Greif, 'Parental Assessment of the Adjustment of Children Following Abduction by the Other Parent' (1993) 2(2) *Journal of Child and Family Studies* 143–157.

40 G.L. Greif, 'The Long-term Aftermath of Child Abduction: Two Case Studies and Implications for Family Therapy' (2009) 37(4) *The American Journal of Family Therapy* 273–286.

41 G.L. Greif, *Family Reunification After a Lengthy Abduction*, National Center for Missing and Exploited Children, Virginia 2010, 1–40.

42 M. Freeman, *The Outcomes for Children Returned Following an Abduction* (Research Report for the reunite Research Unit), Reunite International Child Abduction Centre, Leicester 2003.

international child abduction.[43] This again made a total of 30 interviews relating to 22 cases and 33 children. Both parents were interviewed in approximately one-third of the cases. Left-behind and abducting parents provided their perceptions about the effects of the abduction on their children, noting that some of these effects were on-going several years after the abduction and return; 72 per cent believed their children had been adversely affected by the abduction experience. However, they also described how the children 'shut it all away' and chose not to discuss it. The left-behind and taking parents also spoke of the effects of the abduction on themselves, and their wider families, some of which were shared in common – particularly depression and their lack of security and absence of trust following the abduction. The findings highlighted the length of time it took them to really understand what the experience had done to them. Lack of post-return support was also a recurrent theme.

Unusually, this 2006 project also included interviews with a sample of abducted children, undertaken by members of Cafcass. Hearing from the children directly, and independently of their parents, greatly enhanced understanding of the effects on children of international child abduction. Ten children, aged 10 to 18 years, were interviewed from seven of the families participating in the study. At the time of the abduction, 40 per cent were aged four years and under, 50 per cent were aged between five and nine years, and 10 per cent were over 14 years of age. The time the children spent away ranged from six weeks to 14 months, but one child never returned to live in his country of habitual residence. In two cases (30 per cent) the children were abducted by their fathers, who they did not consider to be their primary carer. Seventy per cent of the children were abducted by their mother, who they described as their primary carer, and whom they did not appear to experience as an abducting parent. All 10 children were found to be adversely affected by the abduction in different ways, including feelings of dislocation and stress. The event remained vivid and very real for some considerable time, as the abductions had occurred five years or more prior to their interview. The findings highlighted children's need for protection from conflict, parental burdens and pressures. The children wanted to be listened to and to have a say in decisions affecting their lives.

In 2014, Freeman turned to specifically investigate the long-term effects of abduction.[44] While on a small-scale, this research offered insights into the experiences of previously abducted children, both at the time of their abduction and on into their adult lives. This echoed a number of key findings from Freeman's earlier studies, in particular, the continuing use in later life of the strategies learned in childhood for dealing with the abduction, including 'blanking out', as well as

---

43 M. Freeman, *International Child Abduction: The Effects* (Research Report for the reunite Research Unit), Reunite International Child Abduction Centre, Leicester 2006.

44 M. Freeman, *Parental Child Abduction: The Long-term Effects*, International Centre for Family Law, Policy and Practice, London 2014.

the enduring nature of the effects reported in the immediate aftermath of the abduction. This relates especially to the lack of trust pervading abductees' ability to form and maintain friendships and intimate relationships, which can prevent them from having satisfying, mutually responsive and connective alliances in their lives. The challenges of return/reintegration into the left-behind family, at whatever stage that might occur, were often major obstacles for all members of the abducted child's family, and the psychological barriers created by the abduction were sometimes impossible to repair. The lack of support, and feeling alone and isolated once they had been returned, often emerged in the research participants' accounts. The tensions they experienced, and often handled on their own, while trying to understand the way they actually felt, as opposed to the way they thought they were supposed to feel, led on many occasions to mental health issues requiring treatment in adult life. Those not returned experienced difficulties that included an enhanced sense of unworthiness linked to a feeling of not being good enough to be found by the left-behind parent, by whom they felt abandoned and unprotected.

2.4. OTHER MORE RECENT RESEARCH

Kruger analysed 667 files from Child Focus (297), the Ministry of Foreign Affairs (71) and the Central Authority (443) open during 2007[45] and 2008[46] that mainly involved children abducted from or to Belgium.[47] The 886 children were aged 0–17 years, with a mean age of six years. The mother was the abductor in 65.2 per cent of the cases, and the father in 33.4 per cent of cases. In 1.3 per cent of the cases the child was abducted by a relative. Over half of the abductions (52 per cent) occurred during holiday time. Sixteen cases in which the child had been abducted to Belgium involved the Hague Convention, and 73 where the child had been abducted from Belgium. Kruger also conducted interviews with 20 professionals and 25 parents (15 fathers and 10 mothers), 23 of whom were left-behind parents and two were abducting parents.

Recently, the EWell project was undertaken in Europe on the psychological effects of international child abduction on the well-being of abducted children.[48] Another study, funded by the British Academy, on the

---

45 164 cases of international child abduction that occurred in 2007 involving 225 children.

46 133 cases of international child abduction that occurred in 2008 involving 188 children. The remaining 370 files concerned abductions occurring before 2007 that had not been resolved by 1 January 2008.

47 T. Kruger, *International Child Abduction: The Inadequacies of the Law*, Hart Publishing, Oxford 2011.

48 The results of this study by Child Focus, Center IKO, CFPE – Enfants Disparus, Missing Children Europe and the French Central Authority were represented at a conference in Antwerp, 22–23 November 2017.

child's objections exception in the 1980 Hague Convention, was also recently completed by Freeman and Taylor.

International child abduction in the context of domestic abuse and family violence has become of increasing concern due to the tensions created between discouraging child abduction and protecting victims.[49] Greif and Hegar reported that not all abductions are traumatic, particularly when the child is now living in a stable environment with a parent with whom they have a secure bond.[50] This can include situations where the abducting parent is a victim of domestic violence and is fleeing, with the child, from the abusive relationship. Some commentators argue that an overriding concern not to undermine the 1980 Hague Convention 'imposes unnecessary hardships on domestic violence victims and their children'[51] and this can lead to an unrealistic faith in the ability of the legal system to protect them from violence.[52] Recommendations to increase the likelihood of safe outcomes include greater awareness about the impact of violence and abuse on familial relationships, targeted research, training[53] and a willingness to interpret the Convention's provisions to provide more protection for domestic violence victims and their children within Article 13(b).[54] A 2017 Experts' Meeting on Issues of Domestic/Family Violence and the 1980 Hague Convention reported that:

> The challenge of striking the correct balance between resolving and properly investigating cases involving domestic and family violence (to the extent required by the grave risk exception under the Convention) and maintaining the expedition necessary to return children without undue delay was emphasised. It is important to recall also the legitimate needs and expectations of the left-behind parent.[55]

---

49 B. Quillen, 'The New Face of International Child Abduction: Domestic-Violence Victims and Their Treatment Under the Hague Convention on the Civil Aspects of International Child Abduction' (2014) 49(3) *Texas International Law Journal* 621–643.

50 G.L. Greif and R.L. Hegar, 'Impact on Children of Abduction by a Parent: A Review of the Literature' (1992) 62(4) *American Journal of Orthopsychiatry* 599–604.

51 C.S. Bruch, 'The Unmet Needs of Domestic Violence Victims and Their Children in Hague Child Abduction Convention Cases' (2004) 38 *Family Law Quarterly* 529–545, at 529.

52 M. Kaye, 'The Hague Convention and the Flight from Domestic Violence: How Women and Children are Being Returned by Coach and Four' (1999) 12(2) *International Journal of Law, Policy and the Family* 191–212.

53 S. Shetty and J.L. Edleson, 'Adult Domestic Violence in Cases of International Parental Child Abduction' (2005) 11(1) *Violence Against Women* 115–138.

54 M.R. Weiner, 'International Child Abduction and the Escape from Domestic Violence' (2000) 69(2) *Fordham Law Review* 593–706.

55 University of Westminster and The Hague Conference on Private International Law, *Report on the Experts' Meeting on Issues of Domestic/Family Violence and the 1980 Hague Child Abduction Convention*, London (Information Document No. 6). 7th Special Commission on the Practical Operation of the 1980 Hague Child Abduction Convention and the 1996 Hague Child Protection Convention, The Hague 2017, at para. 25.

The Permanent Bureau of the Hague Conference on Private International Law has drafted a *Guide to Good Practice on Article 13(1)(b)* with the objective of promoting greater consistency in the application and interpretation of this article in accordance with the terms and objectives of the 1980 Convention.[56]

3. USING RESEARCH TO IMPROVE OUTCOMES FOR ABDUCTED CHILDREN

Very little research actually exists on international child abduction. That which is available has been helpful in raising awareness of the intra-familial dynamics and effects where abduction has occurred, and the tensions existing within the legal machinery underpinning the 1980 Hague Convention. The statistical surveys and other research findings have provided much-needed insight into the operation and effect of the Convention and have the potential to build momentum for changes in practice and policy that can address the challenges in honouring the integrity of the Convention while properly protecting abducted children from further harm. The methodological and sample recruitment challenges of conducting research in this field go some way towards explaining the limitations and gaps in the existing evidence base. The 7th Special Commission on the Practical Operation of the 1980 Hague Child Abduction Convention and the 1996 Hague Child Protection Convention recently approved a Conclusion and Recommendation on the desirability of further research addressing:

a) the short-term and long-term outcomes for children and relevant family members, including taking and left-behind parents; and
b) the impact and effectiveness of protective measures, other judicial and legal processes, support services, and/or arrangements to apply post-return.[57]

This strong international consensus on the need for interdisciplinary research offers enormous potential for new collaborative efforts to extend the current evidence base. However, to truly improve the outcomes for abducted children, their families and the family justice system any new wave of research needs to overcome the rigorous methodological challenges inherent in recruiting a representative sample in a global abduction context and longitudinally investigating the well-being of these children over time.

---

56 Permanent Bureau, *Draft Guide to Good Practice on Article 13(1)(b) of the Hague Convention of 25 October 1980 on the Civil Aspects of International Child Abduction* (Preliminary Document No. 3). 7th Special Commission on the Practical Operation of the 1980 Hague Child Abduction Convention and the 1996 Hague Child Protection Convention, The Hague 2017.

57 Conclusion and Recommendation no. 81, p. 11, 17 October 2017, The Hague.

BREAKING THE EXISTING PARADIGMS OF PARENT–CHILD RELATIONSHIPS[1]

Jens M. SCHERPE

It is a great honour and great pleasure to contribute to this *Festschrift* for Nigel Lowe. To the family law community of the United Kingdom he has long been known as one of the outstanding family lawyers of his generation and co-author of the most comprehensive family law textbook, *Bromley's Family Law*. But what many family lawyers from these isles may not know is that on the Continent,

[1] This chapter is based on a plenary lecture given at the International Society of Family Law's 2017 World Conference in Amsterdam in July 2017, and on elements of previous work, particularly J.M. SCHERPE, *The Present and Future of European Family Law*, Edward Elgar, Cheltenham 2016.

he is *the* English family lawyer.[2] Through his comparative and international work, particularly for the Council of Europe and the Commission on European Family Law, he was (and still is) representing the family law of England and Wales in Europe – and beyond. His importance in this cannot be overstated. Anyone working on comparative or international family law with an interest in English family law knows Nigel or at least knows of Nigel, and certainly has read his work. Therefore, I am delighted to contribute this chapter to this volume in honour of England and Wales' 'Mr. Family Law'.

1. IN THE BEGINNING THERE WERE TWO, AND THEY WERE MARRIED – AND NOW?

Family law for a long time was only centred on one particular family unit: a man and a woman, united in (indissoluble) marriage. Marriage was the proper framework for having children, and therefore this was where proper parent–child relationships were created, meaning that each child legally had one mother and one father.[3]

But we now live in the twenty-first century. Today we live in a world where marriages often end in divorce; where an increasing number of children grow up in families that do not conform to the 'traditional' view of what a family is; where categories of gender are not as fixed as they used to be; where persons legally classified as men can give birth to children; where some persons are not legally classified as male or female; where children are not necessarily genetically related to (all) their legal parents and indeed may have three genetic parents, and even more social parents. The law has been too slow to react to societal changes (on which see section 2 below) and medical advances (on which see section 3 below), and these issues need to be dealt with as a matter of urgency. For this, suggestions are made in this chapter on how to structurally change the way we deal with parental relationships by splitting them up and going beyond the two-parent-paradigm (below at section 4).

2. SOCIETAL CHALLENGES TO THE TWO-PARENT PARADIGM

The lived realities of families have changed fundamentally since the 1950s. Marriage may still be a corner-stone or bedrock for families and family law, but it

2 What even fewer will know is that Nigel was kind enough to act as examiner for my Cambridge PhD in comparative family law. I am very grateful to him that he took on this task, allowed me to pass and did not scare me too much.

3 Of course, some did not, for example if the child was born out of wedlock or if one of the parents had died, but this certainly was the ideal.

can no longer claim to be the only family form recognised, and certainly not the only family form that generates children. Arguably, family law is moving from being marriage-centric to being child-centric.[4] In any event, societal changes have put the existing family law structures under considerable pressure. These will now be looked at briefly with regard to the topic of this chapter, namely parent–child relationships.

2.1. DIVORCE/RELATIONSHIP BREAK-UP

Divorce is now possible in almost all jurisdictions.[5] This has raised the question of what the legal parent–child relationship should be after divorce. While there are no universal answers to this, in Western jurisdictions the trend certainly is towards giving spouses equal status with regard to the children, at least nominally – and the same often applies when non-marital relationships with children break up.[6] This in itself, and also the exercise of parental responsibility and the issues arising from it, can be problematic. But add to this a new relationship and/or marriage of one of the spouses. If that spouse takes an active parenting role, their new partner/spouse may well want to do that too. But since the law in most jurisdictions (but see section 4.5 for some exceptions) works on the basis of an unalterable two-parent paradigm, this means either that the new partner can only obtain a minor form of parental responsibility[7] or that the previous spouse has to lose their legal position if the new partner is to acquire it. But from the child's perspective there may well be three (or more) fully active parents, one of which just happens not to be the (biological) parent. The law arguably ought to accommodate the child's view on who is acting in a parental function, and

---

4 For an overview of the developments see e.g. the national reports in J.M. Scherpe (ed.), *European Family Law Volume II – The Changing Concept of 'Family' and Challenges for Domestic Family Law*, Edward Elgar, Cheltenham 2016.

5 The Vatican being the only jurisdiction in Europe that does not permit divorce, as is the Philippines in Asia.

6 Although often the laws on parental responsibility privilege the mother of the children over the father, see J.M. Scherpe, 'Establishing and Ending Parental Responsibility – A Comparative View' in R. Probert, S. Gilmore and J. Herring (eds.), *Responsible Parents and Parental Responsibility*, Hart Publishing, Oxford 2009, pp. 43–62; J.M. Scherpe, 'Nichteheliche Kinder, elterliche Sorge und die Europäische Menschenrechtskonvention', *Rabels Zeitschrift für ausländisches und internationales Privatrecht (RabelsZ)* 73 (2009) 935–961; J. Ferrer-Riba, 'Parental Responsibility in a European Perspective' in J.M. Scherpe, *European Family Law Volume III – Family Law in a European Perspective*, Edward Elgar, Cheltenham 2016, pp. 284–310; and the national reports in K. Boele-Woelki, B. Braat and I. Curry-Sumner (eds.), *European Family Law in Action, Volume III: Parental Responsibilities*, Intersentia, Antwerp 2005.

7 E.g. the 'kleines Sorgerecht' in Germany, on which see J.M. Scherpe, 'Establishing and Ending Parental Responsibility', above n. 6.

enable those whom it perceives as parental figures not only socially but also legally to act as such in some way.

2.2. ADOPTION

Adoption of course is older than all legal rules in place today. There may be many reasons why children are put up for adoption, but irrespective of that, the fact remains that the child will normally then have biological parents (the birth parents) and legal parents (the adoptive parents). Adoption in most jurisdictions creates full legal relations between the child and the adoptive parents, and extinguishes most or all legal ties with the birth parents. But increasingly not only do children want to know who their birth parents are, and potentially establish contact and social relations with them, but also birth parents increasingly seem to want to know about 'their child'.[8] Many jurisdictions therefore have established various forms of post-adoption contact as well as adoption registers, etc. It appears, therefore, that there may be a need for the recognition of all parents, birth and adoptive, in some form.

2.3. SAME-SEX, INTERSEX AND TRANS PARENTS, AND 'RAINBOW' FAMILIES

The paradigm of 'a child has one father and one mother' in many jurisdictions simply no longer holds true. In the age of recognition of same-sex relationships (either as marriage or as some form of registered partnership)[9] not only are these horizontal relationships recognised, but also their vertical relationships,[10] i.e. the relationship between adults and children. More and more jurisdictions allow adoption by same-sex couples,[11] and increasingly same-sex couples are given access to artificial reproductive techniques and surrogacy[12] – and thus

---

8 See e.g. B. SLOAN, 'Post-Adoption Contact Reform: Compounding State-Ordered Termination of Parenthood?' (2014) 73 *Cambridge Law Journal* 378.

9 K. BOELE-WOLEKI and A. FUCHS (eds.), *Same-Sex Relationships and Beyond: Gender Matters in the EU*, Intersentia, Cambridge 2017; I. CURRY-SUMNER, 'Same-sex relationships in a European perspective' in J.M. SCHERPE (ed.), *European Family Law Volume III – Family Law in a European Perspective*, Edward Elgar, Cheltenham 2016, pp. 116–145; J.M. SCHERPE and A. HAYWARD (eds.), *The Future of Registered Partnerships*, Intersentia, Cambridge 2017.

10 On that distinction see J.M. SCHERPE, above n 1.

11 See e.g. C. FENTON-GLYNN, 'Adoption in a European perspective' in J.M. SCHERPE (ed.), *European Family Law Volume III* – Family Law in a European Perspective, Edward Elgar, Cheltenham 2016, pp. 311–340, esp 328–331.

12 On this see J.M. SCHERPE, C. FENTON-GLYNN and T. KAAN (eds.), *Eastern and Western Perspectives on Surrogacy*, Intersentia, Cambridge forthcoming 2018.

become parents (more on medial challenges to family law in section 3 below). But many children have been growing up with parents of the same-sex, either because they were conceived in a previous relationship, or adopted by an individual who then happened to live in a same-sex relationship, or they were conceived by 'DIY fertilisation'.

In addition, there are many reported cases, and sadly many reported court cases, where a male couple and a female couple decided to have children together (with one of the men providing the sperm and one of the women carrying the child), or a female couple asked a friend to provide donor sperm privately.[13] At least at the beginning the intention often was for all of them to act as parents of the child – even though the law would only allow two of them to be legal parents (in most jurisdictions, but see section 4.4 below). In many cases this led to acrimonious disputes when the relationships between the adults broke down or other disagreements arose. Since the law for the most part was unable to recognise the parental involvement of all 'parents', the outcomes often were (and still are) very unsatisfactory and detrimental to the child.

In any event, today a child may indeed be born and not have a legal mother and a legal father, as they may well have two parents with the same legal gender. Furthermore, in an increasing number of jurisdictions it is now possible to legally change one's gender without having to submit to physical changes to one's body.[14] Hence persons that are legally male can give birth to a child, and persons that are legally female can 'father' a child. Also, a small but growing number of jurisdictions now allow persons not to be legally registered as either male or female.[15] This seriously challenges the traditional notions of 'mother' and 'father' and may be yet another reason[16] to abolish these legal categories and simply replace them with 'parent'[17] (on this see also section 4.3 below).

---

13 On this see L. Smith, 'Tangling the web of legal parenthood: legal responses to the use of known donors in lesbian parenting arrangements' (2013) 33 *Legal Studies* 355–381, with further references.

14 There thankfully seems to be a growing consensus on the de-medicalisation and de-pathologisation of legal gender transition, and an increasing awareness that requiring physical alterations of the body and/or sterilisation are a severe human rights violation. Cf. on this European Court of Human Rights, *AP, Garçon and Nicot v France*, Application nos. 79855/12, 52471/13 and 52596/13, (06.04.2017), [2017] ECHR 338; for Germany: Bundesverfassungsgericht 11.01.2011, *Bundesverfassungsgerichtsentscheidungen (BverfGE)* 128, 109; for Italy: Supreme Court, Decision no. 15138 of 20.07.2015. For a comparative overview see J.M. Scherpe and P. Dunne, 'The Legal Status of Transsexual and Transgender Persons – Comparative Analysis and Recommendations' in J.M. Scherpe (ed.), *The Legal Status of Transsexual and Transgender Persons*, Intersentia, Cambridge 2015, esp. pp. 639 ff., and the national reports in that volume.

15 For example in Germany, India and Nepal. On this see J.M. Scherpe, A. Dutta and T. Helms (eds.), *The Legal Status of Intersex Persons*, Intersentia, Cambridge forthcoming 2018.

16 The others being gender equality/equal parenting and, of course, same-sex parents.

17 As Malta has done when same-sex marriage was introduced (Marriage Act and other Laws (Amendment) 2017), and Ontario when the law of parentage was modernised in 2016

3. MEDICAL CHALLENGES TO THE TWO-PARENT PARADIGM

In addition to those societal challenges (and often intertwined with them), advances in medicine have created additional, and arguably even more fundamental, challenges to family law.

3.1. DNA TESTING

The old adage '*pater est quem nuptiae demonstrant*' was the presumption that was used in order to give children a father in an age where children were only supposed to be born in wedlock. But the advent of first blood-testing and then genetic testing today means we can establish who is the actual genetic father. Jurisdictions have reacted very differently to these challenges, with some giving priority to 'the truth' and being very permissive with regard to testing,[18] and others giving priority to the established social parental relationship and only allowing such tests under limited circumstances.[19] But whatever the approach taken, the legal question arises as to which status the 'other father' should have.[20]

3.2. ARTIFICIAL REPRODUCTIVE TECHNIQUES, GAMETE AND MITOCHONDRIA DONATION

Since it is now medically possible to use donor gametes and/or donate embryos, and a large number of jurisdictions now allow access to artificial reproductive techniques,[21] an increasing number of children are born to parents who are

(cf. All Families Are Equal Act (Parentage and Related Registrations Statute Amendment) 2016, SO 2016, c.28). On abolishing the legal categories of 'mother' and 'father' and replacing them with 'parent', see also J.M. Scherpe, above n. 1, esp. p. 131.

18 For example England and Wales, see e.g. *Re H and A (Children) (Paternity: Blood Test)* [2002] EWCA Civ 383; see also A. Bainham, 'Truth Will Out: Paternity in Europe' (2007) 66 *Cambridge Law Journal* 278.

19 For example Germany; on this see §1600 Bürgerliches Gesetzbuch (BGB, German Civil Code) and its application and interpretation by the courts, e.g. Bundesverfassungsgericht, BVerfgE 108, 82. On this see also European Court of Human Rights, *Kautzor v Germany*, Application no. 23338/09, [2012] ECHR 516 and *Ahrens v Germany*, Application no. 45071/09, [2012] ECHR 515.

20 See e.g. *Anayo v Germany*, Application no. 20578/07, [2010] ECHR 2083.

21 Although there seems to be a rather different approach to male and female fertility issues, cf. J.M. Scherpe, above n. 1, 89 ff. and esp. 98 ff.

not genetically related to them. At the same time, many jurisdictions struggle with the notion of the right to know one's (genetic) origin, and indeed some jurisdictions have removed donor anonymity for that very reason.[22]

Furthermore, as medical sciences undoubtedly will continue to advance, there may well be very important medical reasons for wanting to know more about the gametes used for procreation/the identity of the donor (for example 'Is there a history of breast or bowel cancer in your family?'); it may well be the case that the information required is not restricted to the 'genetic profile' in the narrower sense. In any event, there appears to be the need to establish some form of legal link to the 'genetic parents'.

In addition, some jurisdictions now also allow not only egg or sperm donation but also mitochondria donation in cases where this is medically warranted to avoid hereditary diseases.[23] This undoubtedly is a great boon to the individuals concerned. But it also creates the question of what status (if any) the donor of the mitochondria should have, given that – strictly speaking – the child in question has three genetic parents.

3.3. SURROGACY

The fact of birth used to be enough to establish motherhood without any doubt ('*mater semper certa est*'). But with surrogacy not only being possible but having developed into a (largely unregulated) global market,[24] in a number of jurisdictions this is simply no longer true. Here it may be legally certain who the parent is; though it is not necessarily the woman who gave birth but can also be the commissioning parents – who may well be two men, so that the child legally has no mother. Therefore, jurisdictions are faced with the question of what legal status, if any, the surrogate should have with regard to the child.

A surrogate is not just a 'womb for hire'. She contributes much more to the creation of the child, by sharing her body and indeed her antibodies with the child. Her contribution may not be a genetic one (unless the surrogacy is a so-called 'traditional' one),[25] but it certainly is biological and as such may deserve, or even require, recognition. Moreover, the children concerned may well want to know (of) the woman who carried them for nine months and gave birth to them.

---

22 As, for example, Sweden and the United Kingdom.

23 See e.g. in the United Kingdom the Human Fertilisation and Embryology (Mitochondrial Donation) Regulations 2015.

24 On this see J.M. Scherpe, C. Fenton-Glynn and T. Kaan, above n. 12.

25 The most famous cases being documented in Genesis 16:1–16.

4. 'SPLITTING A PARENT', OR DIFFERENT LEVELS OF PARENTAL LINKS: PARENTAGE, PARENTHOOD, PARENTAL RESPONSIBILITY

As has been shown above, family law, and particularly the law concerning children, is facing considerable challenges through societal changes and scientific and medical advances. The traditional, gendered allocation of parental positions is outdated, as is the limitation to two persons holding said parental positions. To accommodate all existing family forms, the parental position therefore could be (and indeed should be), as Andrew Bainham has suggested,[26] split into three levels: parentage; parenthood; and parental responsibility.[27] In the following, this chapter builds on this terminology and the distinctions Bainham has drawn, and develops them further.

While differentiations between different levels of parental involvement exist in many jurisdictions, what is lacking is a coherent, structured approach that can accommodate the full range of modern family forms. It also needs to be pointed out at the outset that none of these legal positions by necessity needs to be limited to two persons, and indeed this chapter suggests that they should not be.[28] The exact legal consequences deriving from the allocation of parentage, parenthood and parental responsibility of course may well be different from jurisdiction to jurisdiction because of societal and cultural differences. However, as it is argued here, breaking up the parental position into these three levels would actually enable legal systems to deal adequately with modern family relationships and family structures, as a 'means of recognising the distinctive interests which children have in establishing and sustaining links' with persons involved in their lives.[29]

4.1. BRIEF EXPLANATION OF THE TERMS

Parentage in this chapter is meant to be the legal position allocated to those who have a biological relation to the child. As already mentioned above (at sections 3.2 and 3.3), this can (and arguably should) not only include

---

26 A. Bainham, 'Parentage, Parenthood and Parental Responsibility: Subtle, Elusive Yet Important Distinctions' in A. Bainham, S. Day Sclater and M. Richards (eds.), *What is a Parent? A Socio-Legal Analysis*, Hart Publishing, Oxford 1999, pp. 25–46, esp. 26 f.

27 It needs to be acknowledged that while this terminology works in the English language, it is much more difficult to replicate in/translate into other languages.

28 Indeed, several jurisdictions, including California, British Columbia and Ontario allow for multiple parenthood already (on this see section 4.3 below), and England and Wales and Finland permit multiple holders of full parental responsibility (on which see section 4.5 below).

29 A. Bainham, above n. 26, pp. 26 f.

those who have made a genetic contribution (which would include donors of mitochondria) but also other physical biological contributions, such as those made by surrogates.[30]

Parenthood denotes persons who are by law declared to be the parents of a child and with whom kinship is established. This would, for example, be the couple who conceived a child through artificial reproductive techniques, or the adoptive parents.

Parental responsibility is the term used for a person who legally is permitted to exercise some, many or all of the functions traditionally associated with being a parent, i.e. take decisions on behalf of the child, etc. Other terms used by statutes in some jurisdictions are 'guardianship' or 'custody'.[31] Holders of parental responsibility are permitted, and even expected, to do (some of) the parenting (though not necessarily living with the child). Hence parental responsibility could be allocated to any person having a significant parental function with regard to the child.

4.2. THE 'NORMAL' AND THE 'ALSO NORMAL' BUT LESS COMMON

It needs to be pointed out that for the majority of cases (which may be deemed to be the traditional, 'normal' ones), parentage, parenthood and parental responsibility will be vested in the same person(s). But distinguishing between different levels of what may be called 'parental connections' or 'links' to the child can be an extremely useful tool where distinctions between persons need to be made. These cases, as outlined above, may be less common than the 'normal' ones, but certainly are not completely extraordinary, and in any event are likely to become more common in the decades to come.

But even in 'normal' cases the distinction can be very useful and help to clarify the social and legal relations between adults and children. For example, in adoption the adopters will obtain parenthood and parental responsibility for the child, but the birth parents retain parentage. Or in the case of the remarriage of the resident parent, the new spouse in many jurisdictions can obtain some form

---

30 Unlike Bainham (cf. A. Bainham, above n. 26) I would therefore suggest that persons who are not genetically related to the child could have parentage as well. On the term 'biological' parents, see also M. Johnson, 'A Biomedical Perspective on Parenthood' in A. Bainham, S. Day Sclater and M. Richards (eds.), *What is a Parent? A Socio-Legal Analysis*, Hart Publishing, Oxford 1999, pp. 47–71.

31 For an explanation why the term parental responsibility is to be preferred see J.M. Scherpe, 'Establishing and Ending Parental Responsibility', above n. 6. The Commission on European Family Law (CEFL) advocates using the plural, i.e. parental responsibilities, cf. K. Boele-Woelki et al., *Principles of European Family Law Regarding Parental Responsibilities*, Intersentia, Antwerp 2007, pp. 30 f.

of parental responsibility while the former spouse and genetic parent of the child retains parentage and parenthood, and often also parental responsibility.

However, the problem is that in in many jurisdictions what is proposed here to be split into three levels is inextricably linked by a limited understanding of being a parent and parenting – and the two-parent paradigm. While parentage is rarely recognised as a specific legal category (and is usually subsumed into/restricted to determining parenthood), distinctions between parenthood and parental responsibility are more common. That said, in most jurisdictions having parenthood is a necessary requirement for *full* parental responsibility. But merely declaring one person legally a parent and then letting all consequences flow from that disregards the links a child might have to other persons. It might also not reflect the lived reality of the child or the other persons involved. Children themselves just call persons whom they socially perceive to be their parents 'mummy' or 'daddy'. Children are not lawyers – they just express their feelings, their love for a person by using these terms. These feelings are not necessarily restricted to two persons, but the law very often restricts parental positions to two. However, there is no logical necessity for the different parental positions, once recognised as such, to be restricted to two persons on each level. On the contrary, the whole point of splitting the parental position is that different lived realities can be accommodated. Crucially, each jurisdiction could, based on the distinctions made, decide which legal consequences – if any – are to flow from holding parentage, parenthood and parental responsibility.

4.3. MULTIPLE PARENTAGE

Parentage reflects the biological link between a person and the child. Hence, donors of gametes and mitochondria but also surrogates could (and should) fall into this category. Therefore, more than two persons can have parentage. Take, for example, a female couple where one of them donates an egg; this egg is fertilised with donor sperm and then implanted in the other woman who carries the child to term. Here the two women and the donor would have parentage. This expressly recognises the genetic and gestational contributions of the persons concerned, and also allows the child to fully know about their biological origins.

It is worth noting that other than being registered as having parentage, no immediate legal consequences need to flow from this. In other words, whether or not those having parentage have specific rights and duties is a different matter. Moreover, whichever (if any) rights and duties are allocated, they may well differ depending on the type and nature of the biological contribution. By detaching parentage from parenthood (and parental responsibility) it is possible to establish a hierarchy among those with parental links, and parenthood and parental responsibility ought to take priority regarding the child, as they entail a different and more intense social commitment.

But in addition to providing mere information, having parentage could become legally relevant. For example, if the person holding parentage dies and leaves no living heirs, the child could, for policy reasons, be legally entitled to inherit rather than the estate falling to the state. Parentage might also be relevant when considering prohibited degrees of relationships because of consanguinity. Another, perhaps more controversial example would be the case where the only persons with parenthood or parental responsibility die. The person having parentage then could, if appropriate under the circumstances, be among the group of people (which presumably would include other next of kin, if any) to be considered for a more active role in the life of the child and potentially acquire parenthood or parental responsibility if this were in the best interest of the child. Furthermore, the persons holding parentage could, similarly to adoptive parents, be given the right to receive regular updates (e.g. annual) on the child. In the right circumstances contact akin to post-adoption contact may also be regulated. However, as the child needs to be at the centre of these policies, any decisions on this, be they statutory or in individual cases, must be subject to promoting the best interest of the child.

4.4. MULTIPLE PARENTHOOD

Parenthood should be allocated to those persons with whom the child has the closest social links and consequently the closest legal link. Importantly, parenthood also establishes kinship. As is already the case, for example, in adoption, but also in case of artificial reproductive techniques and surrogacy, allocation of parenthood can be independent of any biological link between parent and child. Therefore, parenthood does not have to be tied to the two-parent paradigm and does not necessarily have to be restricted to two persons. Indeed, there are some international examples of the recognition of multiple parenthood.

In California, section 7612(c) of the California Family Code allows courts to recognise multiple parents if the recognition of only two parents would be detrimental to the child. It is then stated in the provision that

> [i]n determining detriment to the child, the court shall consider all relevant factors, including, but not limited to, the harm of removing the child from a stable placement with a parent who has fulfilled the child's physical needs and the child's psychological needs for care and affection, and who has assumed that role for a substantial period of time.

On this, the explanatory notes to the Bill state:

> Most children have two parents, but in rare cases, children have more than two people who are that child's parent *in every way* ... It is the intent of the Legislature that this

bill will only apply in the rare case where a child truly has more than two parents (emphasis added).[32]

Hence, in California multiple parenthood is possible by court order, based on actually assuming a parental role, being an active part of the child's life, i.e. by 'parenting-by-doing'. A genetic link, however, is not required.

By contrast, in British Columbia multiple parenting can be regulated by the potential parents themselves, but only in cases of artificial reproduction. Section 30 of the Family Law Act of British Columbia[33] permits agreements between potential parents on parenthood in these cases. No specific genetic or other ties are required, but the agreement needs to be made in writing before the birth, and the birth mother must be one of the designated parents. Thus, in British Columbia multiple parenthood can arise in the context of artificial reproductive techniques as a result of the intention of the parents embodied in a written agreement. Again, no genetic link to the child is required, nor do there seem to be any considerations regarding the best interest of the child.

In 2016 Ontario introduced the All Families Are Equal Act,[34] which has been called the 'most progressive parentage legislation in the world'.[35] The legislation takes an intention-based approach to defining the child/parent relationship that better reflects the diversity of families and does not discriminate on the basis of gender, marital status, sexual orientation, gender identity, or use of assisted reproduction.[36] Consequently, Ontario legislation now avoids the usage of the terms 'mother' and 'father' and merely refers to 'parent', with the term 'birth parent' being used for the person giving birth.[37]

The new legislation, in force since 1 January 2017, goes beyond the context of assisted reproduction and, quite uniquely, also permits intention-based parentage

---

32 Section 1, California Senate Bill No. 274, Chapter 564, An Act to amend Sections 3040, 4057, 7601, 7612, and 8617 of, and to add Section 4052.5 to, the Family Code, relating to family law, available at <http://leginfo.legislature.ca.gov/faces/billNavClient.xhtml?bill_id=201320140SB274>. It is further stated expressly that the 'purpose of this bill is to abrogate *In re MC* (2011) 195 Cal. App. 4th 197 insofar as it held that where there are more than two people who have a claim to parentage under the Uniform Parentage Act, courts are prohibited from recognizing more than two of these people as the parents of a child, regardless of the circumstances'.

33 Family Law Act [SBC 2011] Chapter 25.

34 All Families Are Equal Act (Parentage and Related Registrations Statute Law Amendment), 2016.

35 J. Radbord and K. Jordan, 'The Law of Parentage Catches up with LGBTQ and Assisted Reproduction', 11th Annual Family Law Summit, Law Society of Upper Canada, 7 March 2017.

36 However, Joanna Radbord (ibid.) maintains that some provisions remain discriminatory.

37 As defined in section 1(1) Children's Law Reform Act. The birth parent always is the parent of the child, unless the parentage has been relinquished by the surrogate, cf. sections 6(2), 10 and 11 Children's Law Reform Act, or the child was adopted.

(or indeed the right not to be a parent) in certain cases where conception has happened through sexual intercourse. According to section 7(4) Children's Law Reform Act, the presumption of parentage does not apply if the person and the intended birth parent agree in writing[38] that the person does not intend to be a parent of the child – thus effectively allowing 'natural' sperm donation through intercourse.[39]

Ontario now also allows a child to have multiple parents, provided there is a pre-conception parentage agreement (of no more than four parties) and the further conditions are met.[40] Any person having an interest may apply for a court declaration of parentage (or non-parentage, as the case may be).[41] Such declarations will only be made if in the best interest of the child in cases where the declaration would lead: (1) to the child having more than two parents, or (2) to the child having one other parent, in addition to his or her birth parent, if that person is not a parent of the child under sections 7 (presumptions), 8 (artificial reproductive techniques) or 9 (pre-conception parentage agreements).[42]

The key advantage of allowing multiple parents is that this enables the law to accommodate the lived realities of children and parents and the multitude of modern family constellations, including children in same-sex relationships, divorce and remarriage as well as the issues raised by artificial reproductive techniques, for example in the case of known gamete donors who are intending to play an active role in the life of the child. However, the acquisition of multiple additional parenthood should always be contingent upon it being in the best interest of the child.

Allowing multiple parents can be used to recognise both genetic and social connections to the child, and also, in the interest of the child, can increase the pool of persons with legal responsibilities towards the child – for example with regard to maintenance and succession law.

A disadvantage of allowing multiple parents might be the need to distinguish between different holders of parenthood and to establish a hierarchy, for example

---

38 But if the agreement not to be a parent, i.e. the sperm donation through intercourse, can conclusively be proven, then this may apply even in the absence of a written agreement, cf. the decision by the Ontario Superior Court of Justice (Family Court) in *MRR v JM*, 2017 ONSC 2655 (28.04.2017).

39 Section 7 is entitled 'Other biological parent, if sexual intercourse', and establishes presumptions of parentage. But subsection 7(4), entitled 'Non-application, insemination by a sperm donor' allows for sperm donation through sexual intercourse without legal parenthood being assigned to the donor. In the latter case, the legislation even provides for the spouse of the birth parent to be recognised as the parent, provided there was consent (cf. section 8(2) and (3) Children's Law Reform Act).

40 Section 9 Children's Law Reform Act. This also applies in cases of surrogacy, cf. sections 10 and 11.

41 Section 13(1) Children's Law Reform Act.

42 Section 13(4) and (5) Children's Law Reform Act.

giving those with whom the child resides greater rights and duties. Inevitably, there will be conflicts between holders of parenthood, and these will have to be resolved. However, conflicts between parents certainly are not unknown to the law (on this see also section 4.5 below). They have been dealt with for decades in cases of divorce and other family disputes already, so this issue presumably could be overcome.

As already advocated above (at section 2.3) and elsewhere,[43] multiple parents inevitably (as the Ontario example shows) mean that the legal categories of 'mother' and 'father' should become social categories, and that the designation as 'parent' should establish the legal parent–child relationship.

4.5. MULTIPLE PARENTAL RESPONSIBILITY

The third and final level is that of parental responsibility. Parental responsibility allows for active participation in the life of a child, but does not establish kinship.[44] Crucially, unlike parentage and parenthood, parental responsibility will come to an end when the child in question comes of age.

In most jurisdictions, England and Wales and Finland being notable exceptions (on which see below), full parental responsibility can only be held by two persons. This is, in many ways, the worst effect of the two-parent paradigm, as parental responsibility is meant to be about parenting, not being a parent. Yet the limitation to two persons persists, despite the fact that the term is parental, not parent responsibility.

Social realities have in many jurisdictions led to the introduction of at least some 'minor' form of parental responsibility which can be held by additional persons.[45] But full parental responsibility can only be held by two persons – usually those designated as parents by law (or in the terms of this chapter, having parenthood). Therefore, for example, if a step-parent wants to acquire full parental responsibility, this means that one of the existing holders or parental responsibility must lose it. Furthermore, the legal construct of parental responsibility is usually such that it is held jointly by the two persons (or solely by one person). If held jointly, then certain decisions need to be taken jointly. This can put a great burden on the person who is the primary carer.

But why does this have to be the case? Why can there not be three (or more) holders of parental responsibility? This would not make them parents (i.e. give them parenthood), but legally acknowledge their social function in the life of

43 See references in n. 17 above.

44 Or, as Andrew Bainham has put it, 'parental responsibility does not include the wider legal effects of parenthood', cf. A. Bainham, above n. 26, p. 33.

45 E.g. in Germany, Switzerland and Scotland, see the references in n. 7 above.

the child, and allow for rights and duties to be attached. As mentioned, England and Wales (and Finland) have broken away from the two-person paradigm for parental responsibility and allow other persons to acquire parental responsibility in addition to those who hold it already. The Commission on European Family Law (CEFL), in its Principles of European Family Law Regarding Parental Responsibilities, recommends the same.[46] The underlying concept is that of individual, rather than joint parental responsibility. This means that each holder of parental responsibility can act alone, unless one of the stipulated exceptions applies. This arguably empowers those who are the primary carers, as it reverses the burden: where the parental responsibility is joint, the primary carer wanting to act will have to go to court if the other holder of parental responsibility refuses their legally required consent; where parental responsibility is individual, the primary carer can act without such consent, and it is the other holders of parental responsibility who will have to get a court order to prevent a specific act from happening.[47]

Allowing more than two persons full parental responsibility can be enormously useful in family conflict situations. For example, if a spouse remarries and wants their new spouse to be 'a real parent' this will often create some tension. If only two persons can have full parental responsibility, that means that either the old spouse ('first you steal my wife, now you steal my child!') or the new spouse will lose out, so that inevitably adversarial positions will be taken. A 'minor' form of parental responsibility here creates a hierarchy and may well lead to the feeling of only having an 'inferior link' to the child – or perhaps, by extension, even for the child to have an inferior link to the new parental figure. This type of conflict undoubtedly can be detrimental to the child. It could be avoided and the issue easily resolved by giving the new spouse parental responsibility *in addition* to those who already have it, so without extinguishing any of the existing parental responsibilities.

An argument against this could be that this may increase the – often very acrimonious – number of disputes between holders of parental responsibility, as there would now be more parental responsibility holders. However, this actually is not true, for two reasons: first, the conception of individual rather than joint parental responsibility reduces the burden of the primary carer (as just explained above), and mere 'nuisance refusals' of consent, often used primarily to annoy the other parent/former partner rather than to act in the best interest of the

---

46 K. Boele-Woelki et al., above n. 31, esp. pp. 66 ff.

47 For a discussion of this in greater detail see J.M. Scherpe, above n. 1, esp. pp. 110 ff. See also J.M. Scherpe, 'Establishing and Ending Parental Responsibility', above n. 6, and J.M. Scherpe, 'Elterliche Sorge von nicht miteinander verheirateten Eltern in England und Wales' in D. Coester-Waltjen, V. Lipp, E. Schumann and B. Veit (eds.), *Alles zum Wohle des Kindes? Aktuelle Probleme des Kindschaftsrechts*, Universitätsverlag Göttingen, Göttingen 2012, pp. 71–84.

child, are less likely to occur. But secondly, and more importantly, the substance over which such disputes arise does not change, and thus the 'opportunities' for conflict do not increase merely because there now are more holders of parental responsibility. As I have written elsewhere,[48]

> [t]here generally are only two answers to questions on which a decision concerning the child has to be taken. Should the child receive a religious upbringing or not? Should it be vaccinated against a disease or not? Should the name of the child be changed or not? The number of options does not increase with the number of holders or parental responsibility, and presumably if a conflict arises, the holders of parental responsibility will generally be in 'camps' of which there will normally only be two. In the examples given above, the 'normal' grouping in this kind of conflict therefore would be the mother and her new husband on the one side and the father and his new wife on the other.

The number of potential conflicts does not change, and the fact that there may now be more participants is unlikely to increase the number of disagreements. These can be resolved with the same mechanisms already in existence in jurisdictions still operating with the limitation of two full holders of parental responsibility.

The approach focusing on the allocation of parental responsibility of course is not limited to cases of partnering/re-parenting. It could also be applied to other situations, particularly those created by artificial reproductive techniques. It allows persons to assume a parental position without legally becoming a parent – i.e. without also having parentage or parenthood. Parental responsibility arguably is what matters most in everyday life, as it enables the persons without parenthood to take an active role in the life of the child (for example foster carers, new partners of the birth parents, grandparents). Thus, jurisdictions unwilling to accept multiple parenthood could, at least to a certain extent, accommodate modern family forms by allowing multiple holders of parental responsibility.

5. A FAMILY LAW FOR ALL FAMILIES

The traditional laws governing parent–child relations, based on the assumption that each child has two parents, are increasingly coming under pressure through societal changes and advances in medicine. Arguably, in many jurisdictions the point has been reached where the law is no longer able to reflect the lived realities of families and therefore is no longer fit for purpose. This results in acrimonious social and legal disputes, often to the detriment not only of the adults but particularly the children.

---

48 J.M. Scherpe, above n. 1, p. 110.

Instead of merely trying to amend the existing laws, which in many jurisdictions continue to be based on the two-parent paradigm, this chapter suggests that the law of parent–child relations should be reconceptualised, in order to adequately reflect the biological origin and the social relations of the child. This can be done by 'splitting' the current parental position into three different levels: parentage, parenthood and parental responsibility. None of these logically needs to be, and arguably should not be, restricted to two persons in the twenty-first century.

Having these different levels would allow each jurisdiction to attach the legal consequences to each parental level it deems appropriate and in the best interest of the child. Needless to say, there are no universal answers to what these legal consequences should be, as this depends on the individual traditional, societal and legal context.

It is important to reiterate that for the majority of children the proposed legal 'split' would make no difference, and parentage, parenthood and parental responsibility would be vested with the same two persons. But in other cases, this structure might help to accommodate the right of a child to know their biological origin, reflect the child's lived realities and allow more than two persons to be their parents or at least have legally recognised parental functions.

www.ingramcontent.com/pod-product-compliance
Ingram Content Group UK Ltd.
Pitfield, Milton Keynes, MK11 3LW, UK
UKHW051846100926
8556IPUK00005B/481

9 781780 686417